Scientific Management,
Socialist Discipline,
and Soviet Power

Russian Research Center Studies, 84

. . . . . .

Scientific Management, Socialist Discipline, and Soviet Power

. . . . . .

Mark R. Beissinger

Harvard University Press

Cambridge, Massachusetts

1988

This book is printed on acid-free paper, and its binding materials
have been chosen for strength and durability.

Library of Congress Cataloging-in-Publication Data

Beissinger, Mark R.
   Scientific management, socialist discipline, and Soviet power
Mark R. Beissinger.
   p.   cm. — (Russian Research Center studies ; 84)
   Bibliography: p.
   Includes index.
   1. Industrial management—Soviet Union   2. Central planning—
Soviet Union.   I. Title.   II. Series.
HD70.S63B4 1988
338.947—dc 19   87-30887
   ISBN 0-674-79490-7 (alk. paper)   CIP

To Margaret

Acknowledgments

This book could not have been written without the advice and support of a wide range of scholars and institutions. Above all, I wish to thank Harvard University's Russian Research Center, which provided a most hospitable and stimulating intellectual environment for me throughout the entire length of this project. I am especially grateful to its director, Adam Ulam, who continues to inspire me with his great insight and wit. Among those who were influential in the conception and implementation of this study or who commented on draft chapters were Donald Aufenkampf, Jack Austin, Abram Bergson, Joseph Berliner, Jorge Dominguez, Marshall Goldman, Loren Graham, Thane Gustafson, Jerry Hough, John Lubin, Joel Migdal, Jack Montgomery, Aleksandr Nekrich, David Powell, Robert Putnam, Boris Rumer, Zena Sochor, and Raymond Vernon. I owe a special debt to Yuri Gastev, who was kind enough to allow me to examine his father's notes and manuscripts. A number of students and research assistants helped in tracking down materials, including Alex Bass, Roy Sinai, and Susan Zayer.

Fieldwork for this project was carried out in part during the 1979–80 academic year under the auspices of International Research and Exchanges Board (IREX) and Fulbright-Hays grants. My Soviet colleagues not only were gracious hosts but also provided me with a unique learning experience in the true spirit of cultural exchange. For their critical help I thank in particular Vitalii Ozira, Gavril Popov, Igor Skorobogatov, and Aleksei Sobrovin, as well as the entire instructional staffs of the Faculty of Organizers at the Plekhanov Institute of the National Economy and of the Economics Faculty of Moscow State University.

Finally, to my parents and especially to Margaret, my wife, who encouraged me through many a sleepless night due to this book and whose support and help went far beyond the call of matrimonial duty, I express my gratitude and love.

Contents

Introduction   1

Part I   The First Cycle

1. From Revolution to Rationalization   19

     Early Encounters
     Adults and Children
     First Steps
     How Not to Work
     A Cheka for Organization
     The Agitator and the Stopwatch

2. Scientific Management at the Helm   59

     The Politics of Technocracy
     Education or Training
     The Commissariat of Organization
     The Bureaucratic Economy

3. Stalinism as Antibureaucracy   91

     Wreckers and Rationalizers
     Cultural Revolutions
     A Fatal Reform
     From Rationalization to Coercion

4. The Triumph of Violence   127

     The Revolt against Rationality
     "Cadres Decide Everything"
     The School of Life

Part II The Second Cycle

5. The Rebirth of Managerialism   159

    "Harebrained Schemes" and Administrative Secularization
    The "Idealists" and the "Practical Men"
    Complex Approaches

6. The Science of Victory   187

    The Politics of Executive Training
    Pink and Not Quite Expert
    The Case Study and the Business Game
    Professionalization from Above

7. The Irrational Rationalizers   221

    The Classroom and the Factory
    Clients and Experts
    The Wheel of the Treadmill
    The Abacus and the Computer

8. Discipline and Reform   261

    The Indulgency Pattern
    Rationalization and Responsibility
    Discipline or Decentralization

Conclusion   285

Notes   301

Index   349

Scientific Management, Socialist Discipline, and Soviet Power

The multiplicity of forms for transliterating Russian into English presents special problems. Throughout this book I have followed the Library of Congress system of transliteration with one exception: names and places which are customarily used in English have retained their English spelling. Thus, Trotskii is rendered Trotsky; Gor'kii, Gorki; Khar'kov, Kharkov; and so forth. All translations, unless otherwise indicated, are my own.

Introduction

Central planning has been and remains a core feature of modern-day socialism. Indeed, in any socialist society it would be difficult to avoid assigning the central role in coordinating production to the state, since socialism aspires to escape the political, social, and economic anarchy of markets by vesting ownership and control over production in the hands of the community. In the absence of markets, the state is the only institution capable of organizing such an endeavor. Except for a few isolated experiments, socialism the world over has been accompanied by central planning, and central planning has in turn been accompanied by massive bureaucratization. Particularly within Soviet-style systems, bureaucratization has been carried to an extreme as a result of the attempt to subject entire societies to central planning. Unlike West European and other varieties of socialism, communist systems have not confined planning to a small number of strategic industries or to the regulation of markets, but have instead established central planning as the basic principle of social organization within society.

This book analyzes the political implications of one aspect of central planning: overbureaucratization.[1] How has the excessive and uncontrollable bureaucratization that central planning begets affected the evolution of national politics in Soviet-style systems?

What strategies have been available to communist leaders for asserting control over the far-flung activities of a bureaucratic society? How effective have these strategies been, how have they evolved over time, and what have been their consequences for communist politics?

The central problem that bureaucracy raises the world over is accountability.[2] All organizational leaders require strategies for overcoming manifestations of rigidity within their organizations and for accomplishing goals in the face of pervasive organizational resistance. This is particularly so within large organizations because of the problems of coordination and control that size raises. Anthony Downs identified a tendency toward rigidity in large government bureaus. The larger and more complex a bureaucratic organization grows, he asserted, the more "its top officials suffer from an increasing leakage of authority." Downs mentioned a number of strategies by which leaders can counteract the effects of ossification, among them: the establishment of separate monitoring bureaus, greater specialization and professionalization, and increasing centralization of decision-making. But rather than alleviating the situation, these strategies only intensify rigidity. The bureau "becomes a gigantic machine that slowly and inflexibly grinds along in the direction in which it was initially aimed. It still produces outputs, perhaps in truly impressive quantity and quality. But the speed and flexibility of its operations steadily diminish." Eventually "top-level officials are unable to accomplish certain high-priority tasks through the normal bureaucratic structure," leading to a crisis of effectiveness. Downs suggested several additional remedies to which leaders might resort: the establishment of specialized organizations outside normal bureaucratic channels, mobilizational campaigns against bureaucratic distortions, and periodic "shake-ups" of the middle levels of the organization. Although these measures may give temporary relief from ossification, "eventually the new forms of organization become just as unmanageable as the old ones were," and "the leaders' frustrations will gradually rise until they are stimulated to undertake another reorganization."[3]

Not all large organizations experience the kind of rigidity described by Downs. Organizations with imprecise or multiple goals in conflict with one another, such as exist in centrally planned economies, are known to have more difficulties performing tasks than organizations with clear objectives. Successful organizations not only demonstrate an ability to adapt to changing environmental conditions, but also frequently shape their environments in order to prevent rigidity. Some organizations are more tolerant of rigidity than others. As James March and Herbert Simon observed, organizations that satisfice, such as public bureaucracies, engage less frequently in an active search for problems than do organizations that optimize, such as market organizations.[4] Downs argued that in most cases when a bureau starts experiencing rigidity "its sovereign will soon begin hearing loud feedbacks from clients, suppliers, regulatees, rivals, and allies." Organizations under constant pressure from such feedbacks are least likely to become rigid. He proposed that rigidity is especially likely in communist bureaucracies because of their large size and their weak feedback from clientele.[5] Market organizations, by contrast, with their overriding organizational objective of profits, their strong and regular feedback from clientele, and their survival resting on overcoming manifestations of rigidity, are subject to a spontaneous and diffuse discipline that makes rigidity less likely.

Governments in market systems also grapple with problems of bureaucratic responsibility. But because government in market systems is limited in scope, bureaucratic rigidity does not directly influence basic structures of power or national socioeconomic goals to the same extent as in a centrally planned society. Under central planning, bureaucratic organization is all-encompassing; the overall vitality of the economy, long-range programs of social modernization, and the power of dominant groups depend directly on the effectiveness of bureaucratic authority. Communist government is not simply bureaucratic government; it is *unlimited* bureaucratic government. The inability of communist leaders to exercise effective control over their bureaucracies not only undermines key policy goals, but also threatens the vitality of the system of authority upon which the entire social order rests.

Bureaucratic rigidity in communist systems can be destabilizing, for it fosters widely shared perceptions of a crisis of political authority and gives rise to a perceived need for a transformation in basic political structures, processes, and roles. Claude Ake has noted that political stability ensues when the "dysfunctional processes generated by the system and the environment are neutralized to the extent of keeping them from altering . . . the structure of the political system."[6] Bureaucratic rigidity can give rise to a crisis of legitimacy; but it does not necessarily pose a direct threat to the survival of communist regimes. Nor is the instability in policies and political processes that rigidity fosters necessarily dysfunctional. A certain level of change is necessary for the vitality of any political system, for in the absence of change, stagnation and decline are likely. But as Samuel Huntington and Jorge Dominguez observed, "to be stable a political system has to provide regularized and accepted means for changing its participants, leaders, and policies in an orderly (i.e., relatively peaceful) manner."[7] A political system that is incapable of engaging in change or which changes only through extraordinary and irregular means cannot be considered fully stable.

The capacity of communist systems to exercise control over their societies, their centralized authority structures, and their satisficing economic behavior allow them to be more tolerant of bureaucratic rigidity than market organizations, and perhaps even more tolerant than other types of political systems. But the price paid for this tolerance is the periodic rise of national crises of institutional effectiveness, manifested in a growing gap between administrative performance and administrative aspirations and loss of public morale and legitimacy.

This book examines successive strategies by which Soviet leaders have responded to the problem of organizational rigidity. By administrative strategy, I mean a consistent set of policies aimed at overcoming manifestations of rigidity, restoring responsiveness to bureaucracy, and providing the coherence that is essential to any healthy organization. In particular this book focuses on the relationship between two instruments to which Soviet leaders have repeatedly resorted in their quest to establish organizational cohesion in an administered society: Scientific Management and disciplinary coercion.

Scientific Management can be defined as an intellectually complex set of techniques for coordinating human behavior in organizations or for providing organizational members with the skills and knowledge to do so. During the course of the twentieth century Scientific Management and its intellectual descendant, management science, have expanded to encompass a broad array of methodologies, techniques, and institutions aimed at accomplishing these goals. Among the organizational tasks they have performed have been establishing standards and norms governing performance; training personnel; creating systems for documentation, accounting, and information handling; automation; the design of methods for evaluating, recruiting, and selecting personnel; establishing organizational structures and distributing rights and responsibilities within organizations; scheduling, planning, and coordination of operations; and aiding decision-making.

Throughout much of the twentieth century there has been a mutual attraction between Bolshevism and Scientific Management. So strong at times has this affinity been that Stalin himself once defined "the essence of Leninism" as "the combination of Russian revolutionary sweep with American efficiency."[8] To many Bolsheviks Scientific Management has symbolized the aims and goals of the revolution itself: the creation of a new type of industrial society, infinitely more productive than capitalism, but devoid of the class discord and conflict of the marketplace—the realization of Engels' dream of transcending class relationships by replacing "the management of people" with "the management of things and the regulation of the production process."[9] Others too have been attracted to Scientific Management as a means for increasing productivity and control over organizational activities. As Max Weber recognized, the lure of modern organizational techniques has been their potential for transforming an organization into "a precision instrument which can put itself at the disposal of quite varied—purely political as well as economic, or any sort of—interests in domination." To Weber, Scientific Management was the essence of modern bureaucracy, which he defined as "the exercise of control on the basis of knowledge." As Weber observed, "in this respect, it makes no difference whether the economic system is organized on a capitalistic or socialistic basis." Complex organizational techniques would be even more necessary under socialism as a substitute for the organizing effects of prices.[10]

Bureaucratic discipline lies at the core of communist conceptions of political authority. It was over the issue of discipline that Lenin founded the Bolshevik party, and it was by means of discipline that communist movements have been able to coordinate the efforts of their professional revolutionaries to seize and to maintain power. But discipline has been called upon to play a role in communist societies far greater than simply providing for the unity of party command. In the absence of markets, bureaucratic discipline, in the sense of the obedient fulfillment of tasks, plans, and programs on the basis of hierarchical authority, is the cornerstone upon which a centrally planned society is built.[11] Central planning has often been likened to a form of military organization and has been conceptualized by Western experts as a "command economy," whose operations rest upon organizational obedience rather than upon market exchange.[12]

Both expertise and discipline were seen by Weber as defining features of bureaucratic organization. Later studies, however, suggested that professional expertise and bureaucratic discipline are frequently at odds with each other. Blau and Scott, for instance, argued that bureaucratic discipline and organizational expertise should be viewed as "alternative methods of coping with areas of uncertainty" in organizations. "Discipline does so by reducing the scope of uncertainty; expertness, by providing the knowledge and social support that enable individuals to cope with uncertainty and thus to assume more responsibility." A discipline that is too rigid "stifles professional judgments," while conversely, "hierarchical authority is weakened by increasing technological complexity in an organization with its resulting emphasis on technical expertness for all personnel, including those on the lowest operating levels."[13]

The arguments of this book can be distilled into four propositions. First, excessive bureaucratization has imparted a significant degree of instability to Soviet political and administrative processes due to the repeated rise of organizational rigidity and crises of effectiveness. In Soviet-style systems administrative strategies have been characterized by periodic swings, at times bearing the features of deep social and political emergencies. Rather than a smooth evolution, one observes significant discontinuity and oscillation in administrative strategies over the course of Soviet history—the consequence of the intractability of the problems of an excessively bureaucratized social system. Soviet-style systems experience a continual series of crises of effectiveness due to their rejection of markets for providing coherence within organizations. They must engage in a constant search for ways of restoring organizational coherence and vitality or must suffer the consequences of rigidity and a loss of morale.

Second, in trying to deal with overbureaucratization, the Soviets tend to engage in cycling behavior. Not only has each administrative strategy triggered its own series of bureaucratic vicious circles, but similar organizational problems and similar administrative solutions to these problems have reappeared over time, even in different historical contexts. This is not to say that significant change has not taken place in Soviet politics and administration, nor that enormous industrial progress has not been made. The goals of the Soviet political system have shifted from revolutionary transformation to social management; the structure of power within the Soviet leadership has altered; Soviet society is more complex that it was fifty years ago; and arbitrary mass terror is no longer practiced. But in spite of these changes, the need for responsive organization remains the central political and administrative problem facing the Soviet leadership. The evolution of Soviet politics has taken place within a broader institutional framework which over time continually reproduces certain patterns of behavior among organizational actors. As a result, broadly similar issues and broadly similar solutions to these issues tend to reappear over extended periods of time.

As March and Simon point out, cycling behavior in organizations is a sign of "ineffectual search," a "neurotic" organizational reaction which is indicative of profound misperceptions of the sources of organizational problems.[14] Cycling behavior within Soviet-style systems has been caused by the refusal of communist leaderships to recognize the inherent limits of large-scale bureaucratic organization, which periodically requires extraordinary intervention in order to overcome manifestations of rigidity. Indeed, the constant need for such intervention from above provides communist leaderships with a major source for their authority and dominance within the political structure. The power of communist leaderships is not based solely upon the discipline of hierarchy, as totalitarian models of communist politics suggest; nor are communist leaders simply helpless in their struggle to hold administrators accountable, as some versions of the pluralist approach imply. The repeated need to restore organizational discipline in the face of rampant bureaucratic mismanagement and stagnation furnishes communist political leaders with innumerable occasions for exercising legitimated authority.

Third, the instability of Soviet administrative strategies has resulted in a corresponding instability in the influence of specialist elites. The totalitarian model places great emphasis on the functional and subordinate roles experts play in providing communist leaders with effective methods of political control based on rational technique. Zbigniew Brzezinski and Samuel Huntington maintained that in communist systems technological and scientific advances are "harnessed to the purposes of control and manipulation," while in liberal democracies these same forces are "harnessed to the purposes of stimulation and persuasion." New techniques of economic management and coordination "may make possible for the first time *both* further economic development and the retention of the ideological-political structure" of domination in communist systems.[15] The industrial convergence model, by contrast, maintains that experts assume a dominant position in decision-making because of the superiority of technique over other means for providing social cohesion. A growing appreciation of the need for expertise in communist systems has led to a diffusion of power to specialists and professional administrators.[16]

Neither of these models is concerned with the conditions that allow for effective utilization of expertise. But within a centrally planned society the organizational discipline that lies at the heart of the political and administrative process inevitably conflicts with the independence experts require to apply their knowledge and techniques effectively. On the one hand, the discipline of hierarchy undermines the legitimacy of expertise by undermining its effectiveness. On the other hand, the conditions necessary for experts to apply their knowledge undermine the hierarchical discipline upon which the obedient fulfillment of economic plans rests. As a result, rather than unlinear and unidirectional trends toward more effective political control over bureaucracy or toward technocratic domination, the effectiveness of technique and the influence of expert groups are inherently unstable.

Finally, I argue that excessive bureaucratization has fostered the rise of radical administrative strategies for dealing with the diseases of bureaucracy. Unlimited government is government that is unmanageable by ordinary means. Because it is unmanageable, it encourages the pursuit of extremist solutions to organizational problems. Radical administrative strategies include such phenomena as the penetration of utopian technocratic ideologies into government, mass mobilization against bureaucratic distortions, and the use of governmental coercion to root out organizational resistance. One can find instances of such strategies in other organizational contexts. Rarely does one find them at the societal level, as part of consciously pursued government policies that embrace the entire social and political order. These phenomena have emerged time and again within Soviet politics and within communist politics more generally. Like ambitious and utopian ideologies, bureaucracy, when it is instituted on an all-embracing and universal scale, generates radical political responses to its deep-seated problems.

In this book I treat the Soviet political system from a holistic point of view, as a single organizational entity, a "USSR Incorporated" that is subject to organizational analysis like any other organization; Soviet history is viewed as the continuing and unbroken evolution of this bureaucracy-writ-large rather than a series of discrete and unconnected eras.[17] This approach has several advantages. It draws on a body of theory on organizations to explain Soviet political evolution and to compare organizational situations in the USSR with those that have arisen elsewhere. Second, it focuses on the politics of systemic change rather than looking solely at the process of politics or at the functioning of institutions alone. Third, it focuses on the deeper structure of recurring patterns of behavior that take place within a fairly continuous organizational context—that is, a context of overbureaucratization. Finally, the core feature of central planning is the attempt to treat society in precisely this fashion—as a single organizational entity, and there is good reason to believe that Soviet leaders view their own system in this way.

Soviet leaders have pursued at least six broad administrative strategies to overcome bureaucratic rigidity within the institutional framework of central planning: (1) limited decentralization, delegating decision-making authority to middle managers while employing a mixture of administrative controls and economic incentives to coordinate managerial behavior; (2) the use of managerial techniques and managerial professionalism to improve productivity, predictability, and coordination; (3) mass mobilization to bring pressure upon administrators or workers to perform in a more responsive and effective manner; (4) the propagation of social norms aimed at raising productivity through persuasion and peer pressure; (5) greater centralization; and (6) the imposition of sanctions and the use of coercion to restore declining levels of discipline. These delegative, managerial, mobilizational, normative, centralist, and disciplinary strategies seek to substitute for the diffuse and spontaneous discipline of market competition. Each has appealed to specific constituencies and has been associated with particular sets of elites and values. And each has contained its own dysfunctions, which have eventually set in motion a search for new policies and strategies.

The larger, more complex, and more centralized organizations grow, the more they experience a need to delegate authority. In their study of employment security agencies, Peter Blau and Richard Schoenherr found that "the administrative pressures engendered by a large volume of managerial duties and a complex structure exert constraints to decentralize decisions, whether top executives will it or not." But decentralization requires trust, since it threatens basic organizational purposes and power structures and increases the variability of decisions by middle management.[18] A lack of trust among hierarchical levels and between organizations, the threat of a reapportionment of authority that undermines central goals, greater variability in the behavior of economic units and individuals, and greater social differentiation have made the risks of market reform in industry rather high to communist leaderships. Though a number of communist systems have braved these risks (not without difficulties), communist leaderships more often have imposed limits on the extent to which they are willing to decentralize authority.

The pursuit of a delegative strategy of limited decentralization contains fewer of the risks associated with full-fledged market reforms. Since many of the operational controls designed to ensure conformity with central priorities remain in place, the freedom of management is still constrained. Managers find themselves torn between the requirements of hierarchical conformity and the use of discretion. Moreover, even a modest delegation of authority to middle management (enterprise directors) complicates the task of control and coordination by higher management (politicians, ministers, and planners). As a result, limited decentralization is frequently followed by a gradual recentralization of authority.[19]

One way organizational leaderships attempt to overcome problems of coordination and discipline when engaging in decentralization is to establish indirect mechanisms of control that place operations on a more reliable footing and reduce variability in the decisions of middle management. Standardization, documentation systems, formalized recruitment practices, increased qualifications of employees, and automation are associated with successful efforts at decentralization.[20] A managerial strategy based on the use of Scientific Management to improve productivity, predictability, and coordination falls into this category.

In any organization there is an inherent ambiguity in the roles played by rationalizers. By establishing indirect mechanisms of control, management experts reduce the scope of discretion for middle-level managers and encourage the recentralization of authority. Yet professionalization, which makes managerial discretion predictable, assumes that managers are provided with the decision-making power to exercise independent judgment. Rationalizers themselves are frequently pulled between their disparate tasks of serving top management through automation, standardization, and documentation, and serving middle management by providing the discretion, skills, and professional outlooks that would allow them to exercise independent judgment. Rationalization through technique and rationalization through professionalism represent alternative forms of technocratic influence, each with its own constituencies and consequences.

A persistent theme in the literature on bureaucracy is the limits which politics impose on the effectiveness of technique and the professionalization of administration. Francis Rourke has written of "the difficulties that confront all efforts to apply the magic of managerial science to public administration." In his words, "political considerations, in the sense of both value conflicts and the play of conflicting forces within the community, continue to have a major influence upon administrative decisions even in a setting of managerial science."[21] The same factors which engender dysfunctional bureaucratic behavior on the part of administrators in the absence of management science continue to do so in its presence. Within a nonmarket environment, the managerial revolution is a self-limiting revolution.

A mobilizational strategy based on the attempt to drown bureaucracy through participation has had deep roots in communist ideology and its protest against capitalist industrialism. A mobilizational strategy has appealed to ideologically oriented elites and to segments of the working class as a means for making administration more responsive to citizens' demands and for overcoming the inequalities in power, status, and rewards inherent in bureaucratic hierarchies. At times these protests have been harnessed by communist regimes to root out bureaucratic inertia, corruption, and opposition. Mobilizational movements have also been directed against rationalizers, who have been viewed by the ideologically orthodox, as well as by some workers, as imposing an alien industrial discipline upon the working class.

Scientific Management is a fundamentally capitalist doctrine; it first emerged from the marketplace in societies whose basic political and economic tenets have been rejected by communist elites. Rationalizers have occupied the precarious position of a bridgehead for capitalist work culture in a system publicly committed to the abolition of capitalism. Moreover, rationalizers have tended to import technocratic ideologies of social engineering and administrative professionalism along with the techniques they have borrowed. Many have instinctively opposed mass participation in management as leading to dilettantism in administration. Proponents of mobilizational strategies have frequently charged management experts with distrust of the masses, with seeking to elevate management into a separate caste within society, and with representing the interests of alien classes and powers. Mobilizational strategies complicate the task of administration, distract administrators from fundamental tasks, and are difficult to control and to sustain over a long period of time. For these reasons, communist regimes have frequently attempted to bureaucratize participation in administration, thereby undermining its effectiveness as a means for holding administrators accountable to popular concerns.

A normative strategy aimed at raising the production consciousness of organizational members through propaganda and social norms has likewise been proposed by ideologically orthodox elites as a substitute for markets and for organizational techniques. The purpose of a normative strategy has been to create a new organizational man through persuasion rather than through economic incentives, training, or force. It usually involves efforts at mass mobilization and may be combined with assaults upon administrators, but is not necessarily directly against the established bureaucratic order. Hannah Arendt pointed to the important organizing effects of propaganda.[22] But were the sources of bureaucratic behavior only a matter of culture or consciousness-raising, the problems posed by bureaucracy would have disappeared long ago. As effective as propaganda has been in convincing people to do what they ordinarily would not do, when propaganda is in conflict with incentive structures and the requirements of organizational roles, it is usually self-interest that wins out.

The causes of a centralist strategy involving the concentration of administrative decision-making in the hands of organizational leaders and top management lie in a lack of trust in middle management, in a perceived danger to an organization's survival, or in a perceived threat to the achievement of goals which leaders hold in high priority. A lack of trust in middle management may be objective or subjective on the part of top-level decision-makers; indeed, the untrustworthiness of middle management has frequently been used by leaders to justify the preservation and extension of their decision-making power. Centralization may also be conditioned by other factors: culture, ideology, leadership style and personality, the clarity of an organization's goals, or the openness of its decision-making processes. Of course, nothing breeds trust more than success, or distrust more than failure; organizational leaderships who, rightly or wrongly, perceive their core goals or their survival to be threatened tend to assume centralized decision-making patterns.[23]

Perhaps the major instrument that communist systems have employed in pursuing a centralist strategy has been the use of the party apparatus (or at times some other bureaucracy) as a monitoring organization and as a surrogate manager, identifying organizational problems as they arise, enforcing discipline, and providing the coordination which is typically lacking within the state bureaucracy.[24] But in its roles in industrial decision-making, the party has constantly been pulled between its duties as an enforcer of bureaucratic discipline and as a surrogate manager. At times the values and outlooks of management have penetrated into the apparatus (and in some cases into the party leadership), undermining its role as enforcer of discipline and turning party officials into supply agents of management. In other cases attempts to impose more effective discipline and control upon the managerial elite have been accompanied by calls for the party apparatus to withdraw from its coordinating and managerial activities in industry. Because of these ambiguities, the party itself naturally becomes an arena for conflict over administrative strategy.

The main advantage of a centralist strategy is its capacity to carry out a limited number of high-priority tasks quickly.[25] But the complexity of managerial structures and operations, the excessive volume and poor reliability of information, the difficulty of controlling more than a limited number of priority tasks, and the lack of incentive for middle management to engage in risk exert strong pressures for a delegation of authority. Efforts to promote rational organization are usually conducted simultaneously with a centralist strategy, and a portion of the intelligentsia is engaged in enhancing central control over administrators. But a centralist strategy usually drives a wedge between middle managers and rationalizers due to the conflicting administrative pressures it generates.

In his study of industrial management, Alvin Gouldner identified what he called "punishment-centered bureaucracy," under which disciplinary actions were invoked by management in response to a perceived decline in obedience.[26] Those who run a command economy naturally tend to view administrative problems as matters of law enforcement and of compliance with the bureaucratic orders and rules that they themselves have established. A disciplinary strategy can be coupled with purges and massive replacements of personnel. Sanctions against worker absenteeism, drunkenness, and poor performance are usually enacted, and efforts are made to uncover mismanagement and corruption. Disciplinary strategies have also been accompanied in communist systems by criticisms of "wage leveling" and calls for the introduction of differentiated wage scales—attempts to institutionalize bureaucratic obedience through rewards and sanctions.

Disciplinary strategies are attractive during periods of attempted innovation, since organizational resistance is a likely response to change. But as effective as sanctions often are in shaping behavior, as a long-term strategy for ensuring compliance they suffer from a number of problems. Administrative experience worldwide suggests that efforts to crack down on violations of bureaucratic rules usually prove temporary because of the high cost of enforcement and the organizational tensions they generate.[27] Campaigns for discipline in communist administration have usually been of short duration. If they are to be sustained over a long period of time, new and more severe measures of coercion must be enacted, leading to the further isolation of leaders, pervasive resistance, and eventually a mounting spiral of coercion. Terror can be understood as an extreme form of discipline based upon the utopian misconception that organizational inertia can be eradicated by liquidating those perceived, rightly or wrongly, as holding back change and by intimidating those who remain. This type of managerial psychosis has been described in the following terms:

> If an organizational change could be accompanied by a complete replacement of all the personnel immediately and indirectly affected, resistance to change would cease to be a significant problem, simply because the newcomers would have no pre-set standards or reference points against which to evaluate the changes. Indeed, for them no change has taken place, since they were not aware of and did not experience the organizational environment prior to the change.[28]

Terror must be understood within the organizational context which calls it into being and against which, in part, it is directed.

The chapters which follow trace the rise and decline of administrative strategies over Soviet history. Part One is devoted to an examination of the first broad cycle of Soviet administration, encompassing the period from the revolution to the late thirties. Within a bureaucratic economy, Soviet leaders were instinctively drawn toward technocratic, coercive, and mobilizational approaches to their vexing organizational problems. In the aftermath of the revolution Lenin embraced the technocratic ideologies of Scientific Management as his major means for dealing with bureaucratic disorders. But this strategy failed to provide the organizational cohesion for which Bolshevik leaders yearned and instead fostered considerable tension throughout the industrial hierarchy. Stalin exploited these tensions to discredit his rivals and to legitimize efforts to impose discipline upon the bureaucracy and upon society. Within a bureaucratic context the line between legitimate rationalization and premeditated sabotage is often difficult to distinguish—a confusion which provided Stalin with a pretext for mobilizing attacks upon the intelligentsia and the bureaucracy. Frustration with the growth of bureaucratic disorders and with the unsatisfactory pace of economic development led to still more forceful strategies of restoring discipline. Eventually coercion substituted entirely for technique as a means of providing organizational cohesion.

Part Two examines a second broad cycle in Soviet administrative strategies, encompassing the period from Stalin's death to the mid-1980s. Its implicit argument is that a number of significant analogies can be drawn between the evolution of administrative strategies in the 1920s and 1930s and in the post-Stalin period as a result of continuities within the organizational environment of administration in these two periods. Similar forms of behavior, similar administrative problems, and similar approaches to these problems appeared, giving rise to a cycling syndrome. As in the past, Soviet leaders were drawn to imported theories of management science and to grandiose technocratic schemes as surrogates for market mechanisms. When these proved inadequate to control the growth of bureaucratic disorders, coercive and mobilizational strategies were embraced. In the concluding chapter these patterns are compared with analogous phenomena in other communist contexts.

PART
ONE

. . . . . .

The First Cycle

1

. . . . . .

From Revolution to Rationalization

*The old bureaucratism has been smashed, but bureaucrats
still remain.*

—*Joseph Stalin, April 1919*

Upon attaining power the Bolsheviks faced vexing dilemmas of
industrial authority. The strains of war and the crumbling of the old
order were keenly felt at the industrial enterprise. The Bolshevik
seizure of power at first only amplified this disintegration. Simply
from February 1917 to May 1918, labor productivity fell by 80 percent.[1] Taking Bolshevik slogans about self-management seriously,
workers spontaneously nationalized industries and set up workers'
councils for administering production. Managers and specialists
from the old regime found themselves under attack or arrest.

The civil war and continued hostilities with Germany neces-
sitated that the Bolsheviks restore industry, especially defense-
related industry, to normal levels of operation quickly. In this
situation worker indiscipline and bureaucratic mismanagement
represented mortal dangers to the very survival of the revolution.
During these years disciplinary, centralist, normative, mobilizational, and managerial strategies all found reflection in Bolshevik
policies. The early years of Soviet power can largely be understood
as a struggle between these disparate administrative strategies and

the political forces that stood behind them. An underlying tension between the proponents of each remained beneath the surface of Bolshevik politics throughout the 1920s. But by the early twenties the regime had come to embrace techniques of Scientific Management borrowed from the capitalist West as its primary approach for restoring discipline to a decaying industrial order.

Early Encounters

From the moment Taylorist experiments were first conducted in Tsarist Russia in the years following the 1905 revolution, Scientific Management sparked unusual interest within the nascent Russian Social Democratic Labor Party. This interest also generated schisms that would plague the Bolsheviks for several decades. The stakes involved were the soul of the Russian revolution. The basic appeal of Bolshevism in societies undergoing the birth pangs of the industrial revolution has been its unique combination of industrial and anti-industrial messages: its simultaneous condemnation of the enslavement of the worker to his machine and its glorification of the organizational and technical achievements of the machine age.[2] This duality was reflected in Bolshevik attitudes toward the organizational revolution which capitalism was experiencing in the beginning of the twentieth century.

The Scientific Management movement had provoked vocal and at times violent worker protest in Western Europe and America. Many socialists believed that Taylorism would crush worker solidarity, beget unemployment, impose an onerous work burden on laborers, and lead to deleterious effects upon their health.[3] As Taylorism was imported onto Russian soil on the eve of the war, opposition to Scientific Management was imported onto Russian soil as well. In 1913, when attempts to apply Taylorist techniques at the Renault automobile plant in Billancourt, France, touched off a strike of four thousand workers, the event was prominently reported in the Russian liberal press. Press commentary condemned the Taylor system for "excluding any kind of initiative, thinking, or manifestation of personality, turning the worker into a mechanism whose slightest movements are perfected . . . under the observation of the 'chronometer.'"[4] Reports such as this, along with the growing propaganda activities of Russian Taylorists, sparked a debate within the intelligentsia over the morality of the new science of organization. The Populist V. P. Vorontsov accused Taylorists of creating "a system for the scientific exploitation of the work force," "squeezing not only sweat, but also the life juices of the worker" and "turning him into an automaton." "The rapid application of this system," Vorontsov argued, "will burst forth into levels of unemployment and oversaturation of the market with goods, bearing the character of a true catastrophe."[5]

Like its foreign brothers, the Russian working class was deeply distrustful of the Taylor system. The Soviet Taylorist Aleksei Gastev once observed that those employers in St. Petersburg who attempted to apply Taylorism before the war "already took into account the scandalous experience of the West and approached the matter much more gently by focusing on the purely technical side" of the method. All the same, "the working masses and worker organizations behaved sharply negatively towards the system." In the years immediately preceding the war, St. Petersburg's metal-working plants were plagued by a wave of industrial unrest that in many cases centered around the tensions generated by the introduction of Taylorist techniques. At the Aivaz plant, considered a showplace of Taylorism in prerevolutionary Russia, a massive strike erupted in spring 1913 in protest against conditions created by plant rationalization. A young student from the St. Petersburg Polytechnical Institute who had demonstrated considerable arbitrariness in his use of chronometry was carted out of the plant on a wheelbarrow to the jeers of workers. According to Gastev, during the war, when applications of Taylorism grew more frequent in defense industry, "a sharper mood against the system" developed. But cases of open protest against Taylorism during these years were rare due to the patriotic fervor that engulfed the country.[6]

Given the level of working-class antagonism to Taylorism, the ambivalence it met within the Russian intelligentsia, and the condemnations it provoked from trade unionists and socialists abroad, the unusually warm reception, and at times open enthusiasm, with which Taylorism was received within the nascent Russian Social Democratic Labor Party seems strangely out of place. In the years immediately following the First World War, "technocratic or engineering models of social management appealed to the newer, more syncretic, and sometimes more extreme currents of European politics."[7] Like Marxism, Scientific Management preached the dream of a perfectly ordered industrial world free of strife and class conflict. As one Russian Taylorist expressed it, through the application of science and rationality in organizational affairs "harmony between the interests of employers and workers" could be achieved.[8]

Writing in November 1913, the Menshevik N. N. Sukhanov criticized the alarmist views on Scientific Management held by Vorontsov and others among the liberal intelligentsia. Rather than seeing Taylorism as "the evil of the day," Sukhanov differentiated the harmful aspects of the conditions and forms of applications of Taylorism under capitalism from the progressive "rational-technical elements" inherent in the method; he called the latter "completely correct, necessary, and potentially very fruitful." The effects of Taylorism on workers were not very different from those of production automation under capitalism. Just as Marx had noted that it was not against the machine, an objective and inevitable part of the production process, but rather against the uses to which the machine was put that the proletariat should direct its animosity, Taylorism was an objective factor of production against which it was fruitless to rebel. Since Taylorism multiplied productivity several times over, its widespread application could provide socialist parties with new arguments for shortening the working day and for wage concessions. Most important, "full mechanization and full Taylorization" would be as relevant for a socialist economy as for a capitalist one. In fact, the principles of Taylorism would "develop and be personified to their logical ends" only under socialism, where they would not be limited by capitalist economics in the scope of their use, but would be stripped of their harmful aspects and harnessed for preserving the health and energy of the worker.[9]

These arguments foreshadowed Lenin's first reactions to the Taylor system, which he developed in a short article in *Pravda* in March 1913. Lenin recognized Taylorism as part of "the progress of technology and science" under capitalism, a new technique capable of "working out the most economical and the most productive approaches to labor." The gist of the article, however, was a polemical attack upon Taylorism as a "'scientific' system for squeezing sweat" out of the worker, a capitalist trick endangering the worker's health, subjecting him to inhuman work pressures, and favoring the young and strong over the old and weak.[10] But if in March 1913 Lenin showed ambivalence toward Taylorism, by March 1914 he had become an open admirer. A second article published at that time waxed enthusiastic over the enormous successes of the Taylor system in raising productivity. Taylorism under capitalism, Lenin wrote, "is directed against the worker, leading to greater pressure and oppression upon him, and limited, moreover, to the rational, intelligent distribution of labor *within the factory.*" If only Taylorism were applied to society as a whole and were not limited by the laws of capitalist competition! "Taylor's system," he wrote, "without the knowledge and against the will of its authors, is preparing that time when the proletariat will seize all social production into its hands and will assign its own workers' commissions for the proper distribution and regulation of all social labor." If Taylorism could be "redeemed from its enslavement to capital," it would "give thousands of opportunities to cut the work time of the organized workers by a quarter, providing them with four times as much well-being as now."[11]

Whereas Sukhanov had been most impressed by the possibilities of Taylorism for easing the burden of work, Lenin was absorbed by the Taylor system's potential for achieving greater levels of productivity and production, for ushering in the period of material abundance and prosperity promised by Marxism. Almost by definition Lenin and his Bolsheviks were obsessed with the power of effective organization as a weapon in the achievement of political goals. Ironically, the Bolsheviks were prominently represented among the leaders of the strike at Aivaz in the spring and summer of 1913, having used the issue of Taylorism to wrest control over the metalworkers union from their Menshevik rivals.[12] Yet, less than six months later Lenin was jubilant over the enormous contribution Taylorism would make in paving the way for communist society.

Not all in the Russian socialist movement were so capable as Lenin of reconciling the egalitarian goals of Marxism with the methods and aspirations of Scientific Management. Taylor's system relied on piece-rate wages for stimulating labor, with wage norms set through supposedly objective observation. Marx had argued that piece-rate payment "is the form of wages most in harmony with the capitalist mode of production," because it allows the bourgeoisie to "increase the efficacy of the working-day by intensifying labor" rather than by increasing work hours. Piece-rates, Marx wrote, were "the most fruitful source of reductions of wages and capitalist cheating." They laid the foundation for "a hierarchically organized system of exploitation and oppression" of the worker. They facilitated "the interposition of parasites between the capitalist and the wage-laborer" and caused the worker to "strain his labor-power as intensely as possible."[13]

Although Marx and Engels recognized that technological and organizational complexity would require that management remain as a function under socialism, they argued that management as an exclusive category of people administering production would eventually cease to exist when, under communism, the division of labor had been overcome. A populist strand within Marxism looked to Scientific Management as a means for effecting a cultural revolution in class relationships and for making every man a manager through education and the simplification of the managerial process. These sentiments were echoed by Lenin on the eve of the revolution in his work *State and Revolution*. In a propagandistic appeal to the anarchist elements then so powerful within the Bolshevik movement, Lenin claimed that workers would easily learn to manage industry starting with the less complex functions of management, which had been "simplified by capitalism to an extreme, to the unusually simple operations of observation and record keeping, knowledge of the four arithmetical operations, and issuing the corresponding vouchers, and are accessible to any literate person."[14]

Others within the Russian social democratic movement believed the populist view to be an idyllic and naive understanding of the organizational revolution capitalism was experiencing. In 1913 A. A. Bogdanov, Lenin's chief rival within the Bolshevik party and his former lieutenant, warned that Taylorism not only created a worker aristocracy, favoring some groups of workers over others, but it would also lead to a dulling of the senses of workers through constant repetition of muscular movements, making it more difficult for workers to develop the intellect necessary to run industry. Rather than breaking down class barriers to the managerial suite, Scientific Management would bring about the rise of a new caste of professional industrial supervisors and efficiency experts who would impose their rationality upon the working class rather than act in the interest of workers.[15]

Only two years after Bogdanov's warning against the technocratic dangers of Taylorism, a group of political exiles in the remote Siberian village of Narym began a series of philosophical discussions on the use of Taylorism as a means for transforming human culture under socialism. Among the participants were a number of revolutionaries who would later rise to important positions in the Soviet regime: Aleksei Rykov, future member of the Politburo and leader of the Right Opposition in the late twenties; Vladimir Kosarev, chairman of the Tomsk Provincial Executive Committee and high party official in the 1920s; Abram Gol'tsman, a leader in the Soviet trade union movement; and Aleksei Gastev, soon to become the father of Soviet Taylorism. It was during these discussions, which Gastev later described as one of the more important "laboratories" for his work, that he developed the idea of a science of "social engineering" based on Taylorism, a science for adjusting man to the requirements of machine.[16]

Born in 1882 in the town of Suzdal, Aleksei Gastev had followed a path not unlike that followed by a whole generation of Russian revolutionaries. His father, who died when Gastev was two, was, like Lenin's father, a provincial schoolteacher; after his death, Gastev's mother supported him as a dressmaker. After studying at a gymnasium and a local technical school, Gastev entered the Moscow Teacher's Training Institute. In 1900 he was expelled for political activities and fled to Switzerland and France, where he joined the Russian Social Democratic Labor Party in exile in 1901, later becoming an active member of its Bolshevik faction. In 1908, however, Gastev decided to put an end to his career as a professional revolutionary, not unlike many of the young intellectuals attracted to the Bolshevik fold who, in the conservative atmosphere following the 1905 revolution, left the party to pursue their own interests.[17] After 1905 serious splits plagued the Bolsheviks, and esoteric creeds penetrated their ranks. In a period when Lunacharskii and Bogdanov were drawn to the philosophies of Ernst Mach and Richard Avenarius, Gastev was attracted to the ideas of Taylor.

From 1908 to 1910 Gastev found employment as a metalworker at the Vasileostrovskii Trolley Depot. The head of the depot, an admirer of Taylor, initiated a study of the depot's production operations. None other than Gastev, the fugitive revolutionary disguised as worker, was chosen to make the rounds of the workshops to register the wear on belts and sprockets and to analyze the repair of trolley cars. This project sparked in him the idea of developing "a science for the social construction of enterprises."[18] In 1910 Gastev was arrested and sentenced to exile in Siberia. He made his way instead to Paris, where he worked in plants owned by Citroën and Clément-Bayard. At Clément-Bayard, he later wrote, "I became acquainted with the organization of quality-inspection work conducted with unusual thoroughness directly in plant conditions, in the shop." At Citroën—whose owner, André Citroën, had been influenced by the example of Ford during a visit to the United States in 1912, the very year Gastev worked for the company—Gastev witnessed the first applications of assembly line production in France. While there he also became acquainted with technical handbooks published by the French metalworkers union. These served as models for norm handbooks that Gastev would later compile in Soviet Russia.[19]

In 1913 Gastev returned illegally to St. Petersburg and found employment as a metalworker at the Aivaz plant. At the very time when the workers of Aivaz, led by Bolshevik organizers, were rising in protest against the Taylor system, the young Gastev found the experiments at the plant "the most sensational and the most influential" of his work experiences. At Aivaz, Gastev later wrote, "one could see that technical and organizational revolution which the unseen organizer, penetrating all the pores of the factory like a bandit at night, was carrying out." Here Gastev "discovered the horrifying difference between the self-mastery of the West European proletariat and the production anarchism in the behavior of the Russian proletariat." From that time on "the idea of the norm came to be seen [by me] as a definite social factor, as a definite social phenomenon."[20]

Gastev's experiences at Aivaz were interrupted in 1914 by his arrest and exile to Siberia. In Narym he used his forced rest "to engage in a philosophical interpretation of all that empirical material I had gathered in my earlier work at plants both in Russia and abroad."[21] After the February Revolution he returned to Petrograd and was elected general secretary of the metalworkers union. At the time owners of a number of Petrograd enterprises were negotiating with the metalworkers over the introduction of piece-rates. Although the union rank and file instinctively opposed this move, in early 1917 an agreement was reached permitting piece-rate payment in enterprises where, in the opinion of management, it was necessary for the normal functioning of the plant. Gastev joined the leadership of the metalworkers union after this agreement had been hammered out. But he and his comrade from Narym, Abram Gol'tsman, formed what Gastev called "a friendly group" within the union that pushed for the introduction of piece-rates and production norms on a more systematic basis. As a result of these efforts, the first piece-rate tariff tables in Russian industry were published in 1917.[22] At a time when the Kerensky government was mismanaging the country, Gastev and his technocratic followers were steadily gaining influence within the union.

Adults and Children

Within weeks of the revolution Gastev and his "friendly group" initiated a campaign to adopt piece-rates as the major form of wage payment and to establish norm-setting bureaus to regulate wage rates by means of time-and-motion analysis. In January 1918, at the founding congress of the metalworkers union, Gastev and his supporters pushed through a resolution advocating the adoption of piece-rates in those metalworking plants where it was considered "technically feasible." Nevertheless, opposition to Taylorism within the Russian working class was strong. Already in December 1917 the printworkers union, then under Menshevik influence, had come out firmly against piece-rates, which, it was argued, "harmed the health of workers, dulling their mental abilities and lowering their real wages." In January 1918 the railroad workers union adopted a similar resolution that condemned piece-rates for leading to "the physical exhaustion and a decline in the intensity and productivity of labor . . . and to an increase in unemployment." Gastev later wrote that interest in the Taylor system at the time "turned out to be more solid among managers" than among trade unionists and workers, and that the position of most trade union officials "was settled by the consumer mood of the masses."[23]

The propaganda campaign unleashed by Gastev aroused stormy arguments. The occasion for these controversies was a series of meetings between trade union and governmental officials at the end of March 1918 on the disorganization of Russian industry. Representatives of the metalworkers union put forth their "Platform on Worker Industrialism," which criticized "elective administration based upon pure democracy and not upon industrial order." It envisaged the application of a broad system of "social norm-setting" throughout the country. Not only were norms, in the form of Taylorism and piece-rate payment, necessary for reestablishing labor discipline in the economy, but social norm-setting would eventually be necessary for regulating the entire life of the workers' state, including "foreign trade, the participation of national and foreign capital, and finally a certain international industrial orientation."[24] Opponents of piece-rates viewed this as nothing less than a restoration of capitalism. Trade union chairman V. V. Shmidt aimed at a compromise; he called for the establishment of a minimum production quota for workers, as well as a halt to the decline in living standards that accompanied the revolution and which, in his view, was the chief cause of lower productivity.[25]

The growing importance of the labor discipline issue led Lenin to intervene. He summoned Shmidt and G. D. Veinberg, a representative of the metalworkers union, to a meeting of the Presidium of the Supreme Council of the National Economy (VSNKh) to discuss the problem. Lenin was hardly a neutral arbiter of the dispute; at a time of growing industrial disorder and under the influence of the metalworkers' example, the onetime prerevolutionary admirer of Taylorism had become a convinced and open supporter. He came down firmly on the side of the metalworkers and spurred on Shmidt to produce a strong resolution on the labor discipline issue. In a draft version of his pamphlet *Important Tasks of Soviet Power,* Lenin added a long passage extolling the benefits that the universal application of Taylorism under socialism would bring. "We should introduce the Taylor system and American scientific methods for increasing labor productivity throughout all of Russia, combining this system with a shortening of work time and with the use of new approaches to production and to the organization of labor without any harm to the work capacities of the toiling population." In a bow toward the populist vision presented in *State and Revolution,* Lenin claimed that the widespread application of Taylorism would allow each citizen to spend only six hours a day on physical labor and to devote four hours a day to managing the state.

Lenin fully expected that the road to communism via Taylorism would bring "many difficulties," for though "the most advanced elements of the working class" would comprehend these dialectical twists and turns, "certain strata" among the workers would greet Taylorism with "bewilderment and possibly even opposition." He had entrusted Shmidt and Veinberg with the task of drafting a resolution on labor discipline. But at a meeting of the All-Union Central Council of Trade Unions (VTsSPS) shortly afterwards, opposition to piece-rates and Taylorism was firm. Angered by the way in which VTsSPS had been watering down the resolution, Lenin ordered that it be strengthened to include not only the unconditional application of piece-rates and Taylorism throughout Soviet industry, but also the imprisonment of workers who blatantly violated labor discipline.[26]

When VTsSPS met again, it adopted a resolution on labor discipline that, contrary to Lenin's urgings, bore the mark of a compromise. Without mentioning Taylorism directly, the resolution touched on piece-rates as "one measure, within the general system of measures" that might be considered by trade unions in strengthening labor discipline provided such measures did not "exhaust the employee." The document advised unions to create norm-setting bureaus, but it left the determination of the activities of these bureaus in the hands of the unions themselves. And rather than approving penal discipline against unruly workers, the resolution proposed that unions establish their own disciplinary measures, which in extreme cases might include expulsion from the union.[27]

Ideological opponents of Taylorism found powerful supporters within the Bolshevik left wing as well as among the Mensheviks, then prominently represented in the trade union movement. Biting critiques of Taylorism, the piece-rate system, and punitive measures against workers poured forth from Bolshevik and Menshevik publications in Bukharin's home base of Moscow. At the end of April Lenin was forced to defend his advocacy of Taylorism and disciplinary coercion before the left communists at a meeting of the Central Executive Committee of Soviets (TsIK), where he accused Bukharin of "throwing sand in the eyes of the workers." He attacked Bukharin and Osinskii for their stands on Brest-Litovsk, piece-rates, Taylorism, and the use of specialists from the old regime, and linked their views with the positions of the Menshevik opponent. "Only those who can comprehend that it is impossible to create or introduce socialism without learning from the organizers of [capitalist] trusts," Lenin asserted, "are worthy of being called communists . . . we must learn from them if we are to be communists and not children with infantile notions."[28]

Opponents of Taylorism, however, continued to hold sway within the trade union movement. In the middle of May, piece-rates were condemned as "an old, outdated form of the speed-up system" by the All-Russian Conference of Construction Workers, which, in a bow to Lenin, allowed the possibility of introducing them only where "workers are insufficiently disciplined."[29] The issue provoked a major confrontation at the First All-Russian Congress of Councils of the National Economy (Sovnarkhozy) in late May. Gastev, who addressed the congress, hinted that economic sabotage was being carried out not only by remnants of the capitalist class but by the proletariat as well, which was putting up "enormous opposition" to piece-rate payment and norm-setting. The widespread application of Taylorism in Russia, he said, was "inevitable . . . no matter who would be in power—Lenin, Pal'-chinskii, or Skoropadskii." He called for training a generation of "social engineers" from among skilled workers. In response, opponents of Taylorism ridiculed Gastev as a "poet of capitalism." Taylorism, they said, "can bring us nothing but Russian Orientalism." A resolution condemning the Taylor system failed to gain a majority. But the opposition was strong enough to cause the trade union leadership to conclude that for the time being widespread application of Taylorism was politically impossible.[30] Only in January 1919, at the Second All-Russian Congress of Trade Unions, was trade union approval forthcoming on these issues. Even this resolution encountered serious opposition from those who accused the trade union leadership, then firmly in Bolshevik hands, of "caving in and even taking the initiative" in promoting "that most refined form of exploitation of hired labor."[31]

In spite of resistance, the use of piece-rates spread rapidly during these years. In July 1918 21 percent of the labor force worked under the piece-rate system; by September 1918 that figure had climbed to 31 percent. As might be expected, the establishment of piece-rates remained a haphazard affair. Where norm-setting bureaus were set up, they lacked the guidance and expertise to perform their functions properly. Gastev later wrote that by the end of 1918 "it was clear that it would be impossible to get along without the creation of special institutions that would . . . create a methodology of organization."[32] From that moment on, he devoted his energies to the realization of this project. At the end of 1918 Gastev became head of the department of the arts in the Ukrainian Commissariat of Enlightenment. At a meeting of the commissariat's collegium in early 1919 he put forth his most ambitious project yet: the creation of a "school for the social-engineering sciences." Gastev claimed that the proposal was "very positively received" and was blocked only by the incursions of Denikin and the intensification of civil war in the south.[33] Thoughts of a similar project were contemplated simultaneously by Lenin, who in late 1918 and early 1919 suggested that an "Institute for Taylorism," devoted to "the study and practical realization of the principles of the scientific organization of labor," be created. The project met serious objections from left communists on the grounds that Taylorism was nothing less than a "sweat-shop system."[34]

By the onset of 1919, arguments over hiring prerevolutionary specialists in managerial posts overshadowed the issue of borrowing capitalist organizational techniques. In May 1918 at the First All-Russian Congress of Sovnarkhozy Lenin had successfully sponsored a resolution calling for the employment of specialists from the old regime. The rapid influx of bourgeois specialists into administrative bodies aroused protest within the trade unions and from the approximately 5500 former workers, known as red directors, who occupied the remaining posts in industry. In 1919, as Lenin noted, there was hardly a week when, in one form or another, the issue of the relationship between the red directors and the bourgeois specialists was not debated in the Council of People's Commissars (Sovnarkom). The party program approved by the Eighth Party Congress in March 1919 declared that workers would have to learn the art of management from bourgeois specialists "for a considerable period of time," while expressing the hope that, by "rubbing shoulders with the rank and file of the workers and also with the most advanced among the class-conscious communists," specialists could be won over to the Bolshevik cause.[35]

But as the civil war entered its most intense, final phase, the

economic situation continued to deteriorate. By 1920 gross industrial production in the largest of Russia's industries slumped to only
18 percent of prewar levels, and gross production per worker to
only 26 percent.[36] This economic collapse was due in large measure
to the disruptions of war. But in many cases it was traceable to the
rampant red tape and poor organization induced by the excessive
centralization of War Communism and to what the regime routinely
referred to as a "lack of discipline" on the part of the working
class. Almost by instinct, the Bolsheviks reached for centralist solutions to problems which, at least in part, had been caused by
excessive centralization. This paradox was cited by critics of the
regime, who turned their attention to the growing cancer of "bureaucratism" afflicting all sectors of political and industrial life.
When the civil war drew to a close and the economic situation did
not improve, the issue of authority relations in industry became a
source of acrimony.

The major function of industry under War Communism was to
supply the Red Army with needed supplies. It was only natural,
therefore, that Trotsky, as People's Commissar for Military Affairs,
should come forth with his own solution to the problems of industrial management. Obsessed with his successful experience as com-
mander-in-chief, he proposed a program for the "militarization of
labor" that envisaged the imposition of strict military discipline
upon industrial relations, the total subordination of the trade unions
to managerial authority, and the creation of labor armies. Among
Trotsky's allies in his quest to militarize labor were the proponents
of Taylorism within the ranks of the Bolsheviks.

A. Z. Gol'tsman, Gastev's friend from their years of exile in
Narym and a member of Gastev's group within the metalworkers
union, had a major influence on Trotsky's program. Gol'tsman had
argued for the creation of a new "officer corps" for industry, a
"worker aristocracy" of managers recruited from the working class
and trained in the new science of organization.[37] Gol'tsman's idea,
which for a brief time enjoyed Lenin's support, was an outgrowth
of Gastev's school for social engineers. At the very time when
Gol'tsman was advancing the idea of training a worker aristocracy,
Gastev was calling for a cultural revolution in the Russian working
class, through the universal application of Taylorism, in *Proletarskaia kul'tura,* the mouthpiece of the Proletkult movement. Gastev

shocked the progressive intellectual readership of the journal by defending Taylorism as the logical means for creating the new communist man. "Machines," Gastev asserted, "would be transformed from the managed into the managers," and social norms would penetrate all aspects of proletarian life: "strikes, sabotage, social creativity, food consumption, apartments, and finally, even the intimate life of the proletariat, right down to its aesthetic, mental, and sexual needs." The article elicited a storm of protest, not least from the founder of the Proletkult movement, Bogdanov, who called Gastev's scheme nothing less than "monstrous Arakcheevism"—a charge soon to be leveled against Trotsky.[38]

Under the influence of Gol'tsman and Gastev, Trotsky incorporated portions of the Taylorists' program into his own platform. In January 1920 he identified the militarization of labor directly with the goals and aims of the Taylorists.

> A whole number of features of militarism . . . blend with what we call Taylorism . . . If you take militarism, then you'll see that in some ways it was always close to Taylorism. Compare the movements of a crowd and of a military unit, one marching in ranks, the other in a disorderly way, and you'll see the advantage of an organized military formation . . . And so the positive, creative forces of Taylorism should be used and applied.[39]

The current economic situation, Trotsky concluded, under which "80 percent of human energy is wasted on trying to get groceries," is "the negation of Taylorism."

In March 1920 three political groupings emerged at the Ninth Party Congress over the issue of labor discipline. In their three platforms were the outlines of the major administrative strategies pursued by the Bolsheviks in the years to come. Trotsky argued for stripping trade unions of their managerial functions and imposing discipline upon the proletariat by force—by blacklists, penal battalions, and concentration camps. The force of disciplinary and coercive measures, he argued, "will reach its highest degree of intensity in the organization of labor in the period of transition" from capitalism to socialism.[40]

In addition to Trotsky and his Taylorist allies, a new faction emerged within the party's left wing, the Democratic Centralists, who criticized the growing bureaucratization of party and industrial life and defended worker participation in managerial decision-making. Among the sympathizers of the Democratic Centralists were a large number of red directors and trade union officials who viewed Trotsky's program as a reactionary and draconian effort to repress workers and to exclude them from the managerial suite. These officials were particularly critical of Gol'tsman's plan for training a worker aristocracy, which, they argued, sought to replace *kollegial'nost'* (collective decision-making) with *genial'nost'* (rule by the technically gifted). The Democratic Centralists defended the sanctity of the industrial collegium, calling it "a special kind of laboratory in which workers were to be taught the art of management," "a necessary upper class of a management school, giving final training and a much broader outlook" to proletarian administrators.[41]

Lenin at first was attracted to the spirit of Trotsky's theses, but found it necessary to distance himself from the political furor surrounding them. Whereas Trotsky tied Taylorism to a program of labor coercion, Lenin differentiated the use of force from the use of technique for fostering organizational efficiency, drawing a line between disciplinary and managerial strategies. On the eve of the congress he emphasized the special character of managerial work. "One might be an excellent revolutionary and agitator, but be completely unsuitable as an administrator." Rather, "in order to manage, one must be competent, one must know all the conditions of production fully and in detail, one must know the technology of this production at its contemporary level, and one must have a certain scientific education." Kollegial'nost', he declared at the party congress, should be abolished because it generated red tape and bureaucratic impediments. Ridiculing the view that the collegium represented a form of management school for workers, Lenin sarcastically called it "a preparatory class for school." Drawing applause from the floor, he added: "We are now adults, and we will be held back in all fields if we behave like school children."[42]

First Steps

The birth of the Soviet Scientific Management movement can be dated to 1920. In that year, in the wake of the abolition of collective management and while Trotsky was propounding his program of labor militarization, the Soviet government took its first steps to support managerial research. Though the civil war was virtually over, the first institutions in Soviet Russia for the promotion of Scientific Management were organized not in the civilian sector but in military industry. Before the revolution there had been considerable interest in applying Taylorism to Russia's defense plants. Due to Trotsky's policy of employing specialists from the old regime, many who had participated in these prerevolutionary experiments continued to work in the post-1917 military establishment. Trotsky's personal interest in promoting Taylorism led to the creation of an Initiative Commission for the Scientific Organization of Production under VSNKh's Council for Military Industry (Promvoensovet) in April 1920.[43]

Gastev and his supporters were also taking steps of their own to organize systematic research on Taylorism. In July 1920 Gol'tsman, a member of the Presidium of VTsSPS and head of its tariff department, raised the issue of creating an institute for labor research jointly under VTsSPS and the People's Commissariat of Labor (Narkomtrud). Some within the Presidium received the idea skeptically, reacting to it, in the words of one witness, "in a most critical manner." Nevertheless, the proposal was approved, and Gastev was asked to head the new institute. In September 1920, "in the interest of the development of proper tariff and norm-setting procedures," VTsSPS formally decreed the establishment of an Institute of Labor. When Narkomtrud approved the merger of its own Institute for the Experimental Study of Live Labor with Gastev's institute one year later, the new unit was renamed the Central Institute of Labor, or TsIT.[44]

It was on the railroads, however, that the movement for the scientific organization of labor—or as it was then already known, NOT (*nauchnaia organizatsiia truda*)—assumed significant proportions. Due to declining rates of productivity and the strains of war, in 1920 the railroad arteries of Soviet Russia were in crisis. Compared with 1913, when 17 percent of all engines were out of commission, in 1920 more than half of all engines were in need of repair. Freight traffic stood still, even though the overall volume of railroad traffic had declined considerably and the number of personnel employed had increased from 815,000 in 1913 to more than 1.3 million by 1921.[45] Using this crisis to his advantage, Trotsky persuaded Lenin to assign him to head the troubled People's Commissariat of Railroads. Once there, Trotsky began to implement his program of labor militarization. To overcome opposition within trade union circles, in August 1920 Trotsky established a separate trade union committee, Tsektran, which became the focus of sharp controversy within the party and a lightning rod for discontent over Bolshevik labor policies.

Throughout 1920 Trotsky relied upon Taylorist forces inside and outside the commissariat to ward off attacks on his program of labor militarization. During the summer a conference sponsored by pro-Taylor forces within the union (Gol'tsman was among the twenty-five members of Tsektran's ruling committee) was held to discuss how Taylorism might be used to repair locomotives. This was not a new subject for Russia; Taylorism had been applied with some success on Tsarist railroad lines in the years preceding the revolution. Two positions collided at the conference. Some participants, mainly Tsektran officials, argued for quick efforts to implement Taylorist techniques. Another group, composed primarily of engineers and specialists, some familiar with prerevolutionary experiments in this area, objected that applications of Taylorism were inconceivable, given the shortages of metal that plagued repair shops and the backwardness of railroad equipment. Over the heads of the specialists, the conference approved resolutions calling for the introduction of piece-rates and the establishment of norm-setting bureaus.[46]

By early fall Zinoviev had joined the opponents of Tsektran and issued a call for its dissolution. In November 1920, in large measure to force through his policies within the transportation unions in the face of mounting protest, Trotsky resolved to convene a conference to discuss rationalization on the railroads. He assigned an "organizational troika" to make arrangements for the meeting. The troika subsequently expanded the conference to include all branches of the economy. Its aim was to pose the issue of Taylorism in a broader context, since "the principles of the scientific organization of labor are generalizable for all aspects of economic life."[47] Undoubtedly this decision met with the approval of Trotsky, who hoped the publicity of an expanded conference would aid him in subduing his trade union rivals. But the strategy backfired, since it provided Trotsky's opponents with an opportunity to bring in reinforcements from outside.

The First All-Russian Conference on NOT that convened in Moscow in January 1920 was transformed into a national event, a show-trial on the proper role of Taylorism in the Soviet republic. It was attended by more than four hundred delegates and received extensive coverage in the press.[48] Its organizational presidium was chaired by V. M. Bekhtirev, a prominent Russian physiologist with Bolshevik sympathies. As the founder of the State Institute for the Study of the Brain in Petrograd in 1918, Bekhtirev had long been interested in labor hygienics. But his scholarly interests and ideological leanings gave the conference a different outlook from that intended by its organizers. Although more than half of the delegates were transportation workers, less than a third of the proceedings were actually devoted to rationalization on the railroads.[49] Instead, the major polemics revolved around the potential harm and benefits of the Taylor system—with Taylorists, whose views were defended primarily by Gastev, clashing sharply with anti-Taylorists, whose chief spokesman was O. A. Yermanskii.

Yermanskii had become involved in the revolutionary movement in the 1880s and was a member of the Menshevik faction. From 1918 to 1921 he served on the Menshevik Central Committee and was the leader of the party's left wing. But in the words of one of his Menshevik contemporaries, "this small man had colossal ambitions and an inflated opinion of himself, and even had pretensions toward 'replacing' Martov in the Central Committee." In April 1921, shortly after the First All-Russian Conference on NOT, Yermanskii decided to "leave temporarily" the ranks of the Mensheviks, feebly promising his comrades that he would rejoin when the political situation improved. To many Mensheviks, Yermanskii's betrayal was seen as an effort to save his own skin at a time when the Mensheviks were experiencing severe repression at the hands of the regime.[50] It was a pattern that was to repeat itself in Yermanskii's behavior several times over the following twenty years.

In 1918, when Lenin publicly endorsed the universal application of Taylorism throughout Russia, Yermanskii published an impassioned critique condemning Soviet interest in Scientific Management. Under his adopted identity as the engineer A. O. Gushko, Yermanskii had been employed by the Russian Technical Society before the revolution, where he was exposed to the Taylorist ideas then so popular among St. Petersburg's technical circles. In particular, the work of one German specialist, physiologist Edgar Atzler, attracted his attention. Atzler and his colleagues conducted experiments estimating the expenditure of energy required for various tasks. They concluded that the demands of the Taylor system were excessively fatiguing to the worker and threatened his health.[51] These findings neatly paralleled objections to the Taylor system raised by the labor movement. Among Yermanskii's allies at the First All-Russian Conference on NOT were, in the words of one analysis, "representatives of medical science who considered it necessary to keep in mind, above all, the potential preservation of the strength and health of workers in deciding issues of the organization of labor." Yermanskii saw his role as "defending the Marxist position" on the Taylor issue, arguing that Taylorism led to an "intensification" of labor rather than an increase in productivity and brought about the physical exhaustion of the labor force.[52]

The visible presence of prerevolutionary Taylorists at the First NOT Conference was a sore in the eyes of the ideologically orthodox and a source of considerable friction. As one communist participant described the atmosphere of the meeting, "A number of skirmishes took place between the communists and former Cadets; the forms of address of 'citizen' and 'comrade' alternated one after another, as might be expected at a time of quarrels concerning the methods of organizing labor."[53] The primary defender of the specialists and the methods they represented was Gastev, who by this time was already employing prerevolutionary Taylorists at his new institute, TsIT. In the words of one old communist who knew him well in 1919, Gastev was "totally consumed" and "passionately infatuated" with the idea of NOT. To him Taylorism represented a way of refashioning man in the image of machine, of achieving a perfectly ordered industrial society by means of the slide rule and the stop watch. "Engineering," Gastev once wrote, "is the very highest expression of work," and its creative application, "not only to organizational design, but also to remaking man, is the very highest scientific and artistic wisdom."[54] At the First NOT Conference Gastev unveiled his latest work, entitled "How One Should Work" (*Kak nado rabotat'*), which consisted of sixteen commandments for a new work culture. "We spend the better part of our lives at work," Gastev argued, "and we need to learn to work so that it grows easier and becomes a constant, vital school."[55] Gastev's rules were made into a series of popular posters, one of which hung in the reception room to Lenin's office.

The resolutions of the conference were a patchwork of compromises between these two factions; indeed, later Gastev and Yermanskii would each claim that the document supported his position.[56] Not only was much effort spent, with little success, trying to define "the scientific organization of labor," but the final resolutions called for yet another, this time broader, meeting to mull over these unresolvable issues once again. The only common resolution recognized the achievements of Taylor but warned against too close an identification of Taylorism with Scientific Management, since Taylorism also contained "unscientific elements leading mainly to an excessive increase in the intensity of labor." Serious disagreements undermined measures aimed at further coordination of the movement. In one working section Gastev pushed through a resolution recognizing TsIT as the central coordinating organ of the NOT movement. But when this same resolution was brought up for the approval of the entire gathering, it was narrowly defeated. The conference favored a central organization, but it "does not believe that it has the right, at the present moment, to select an authoritative organ to act in the name of Scientific Management with all the necessary authority," because of "the uncertainty of the attitudes of executives of economic *narkomaty* and the trade unions towards this issue." The resolutions drew the approval of at least one powerful supporter; within a few days of the conference Lenin commanded his aides to "order literature from America, Germany, and England on Taylorization and the scientific organization of labor."[57]

On January 25, 1921, while the First NOT Conference was still in session, the Workers' Opposition published its famous theses on restoring workers' control to industry. Although the issue of Taylorism was not among the explicit concerns of the faction, it drew its primary support from those unions where Taylorist techniques had been applied most vigorously—the transportation and metalworking industries. The Workers' Opposition arose as a protest movement against the growing bureaucratization of industrial and party life and against the disappearance of any semblance of worker participation. Beneath this protest lay a deep apprehension of the increasingly visible presence of Tsarist specialists in key managerial posts and of the methods of management they brought with them. Although the platform of the Workers' Opposition was soundly defeated at the Tenth Party Congress, the sailors of Kronstadt revolted while the congress was in session. The political tensions surrounding Taylorism and labor militarization played a key role in provoking the mutiny. In February a wave of industrial unrest paralyzed Petrograd; it was led primarily by transport workers protesting Trotsky's antilabor policies, including the application of Taylorist methods. The Kronstadt revolt was first sparked when sailors from the Kronstadt fortress made contact with these striking workers.[58] A month after the suppression of the uprising, a government document on rationalization spoke of "the instinctive mistrust of workers toward all kinds of experiments directed at extracting greater productivity from them." Such mistrust, it said, had placed "a number of strong obstacles" before the Taylorists and had demonstrated the need for "observing extreme caution and deliberation" in introducing NOT, lest overzealousness lead to further disturbances.[59]

How Not to Work

The proclamation of the New Economic Policy (NEP) in 1921 marked a major shift in Bolshevik administrative policies. Under the new system, private market activity was permitted in the trade network, and some small industry was privatized. Large-scale industry, however, remained firmly under the control of the state, subject to a confusing variety of arrangements. Trusts were placed on independent economic accounting (*khozrashchet*), with the right to finance the purchase of materials and labor at their plants. But significant control over the activities of trusts remained in the hands of VSNKh through financial and pricing policies, the appointment and dismissal of officials, inspection, the administrative transfer of material resources from one unit to another, and, at times, simply direct order. In some branches the work of trusts was planned from above in a manner closely resembling the classic model of a command economy.[60]

With its emphasis upon economic efficiency, NEP opened new possibilities for state support of rationalization activity. Indeed, by the end of 1921 Gastev could write that "we are now experiencing a kind of 'epidemic' of labor studies," with thousands drawn into the field for the first time.[61] But controversy continued to plague the new science of organization. The First All-Russian NOT Conference had revealed significant ideological and methodological differences within the ranks of management experts and had done nothing to resolve the problem of leadership in the movement. Moreover, the austere economic and financial conditions of NEP would place limits on the extent to which the Scientific Management movement could rely upon state support. From 1921 to 1923, when work on Scientific Management was expanding, ideological and methodological differences within the NOT movement widened as a result of a new competition to secure control over limited state resources.

Nowhere was this more clearly exhibited than in the struggle over the control and financing of NOT institutes. In September 1920 Gastev had been allotted 1.2 million rubles from VTsSPS for organizing TsIT. The money, however, was not there to be given. For the first year of its existence the employees of TsIT were paid in kind, not in cash. At the end of October 1920 Gastev sent an urgent plea to the VTsSPS Presidium for financial and organizational support. He had gathered together a staff for the institute "despite very unfavorable conditions." But he was compelled to release "the most valuable employees," since "I am not in a position to guarantee them housing or even a minimal supply of shoes." "I have one employee," he wrote, "who is conducting most valuable work, but who goes around literally without any soles on his shoes, and not one of my employees has a room."[62] In November VTsSPS decreed material aid for TsIT, but the money promised by the trade union leadership never materialized.

In desperation Gastev appealed to Lenin, who in June 1921 wrote to the People's Commissariat of Finance requesting aid for TsIT. Lenin inquired whether it would be possible to obtain the funds "by selling some of the Romanovs' possessions in Germany." But no money was ever received by TsIT; instead, Gastev's request for half a million gold rubles was gradually cut from half a million to 100,000, from 100,000 to 20,000, and from 20,000 to 8,000. Even this last amount was never received in full by TsIT, which, by this time, had learned "to rely on self-sufficiency while waiting for foreign blessings." As Gastev noted, "We began to collect any equipment we could get by chance and created our own apparatus on the spot; in the absence of metal, we began to make things out of wood." In November 1922 Gastev submitted a proposal to VTsSPS to alleviate TsIT's financial difficulties by attracting the patronage of West European and American capitalists, who would be drawn into an international aid society for TsIT. The proposal was rejected by the trade union leadership. Only in June 1923 was the financing of TsIT's activities resolved; the Council for Labor and Defense (STO) then decreed that TsIT should be officially included in the state budget. By then TsIT had already found ways of financing itself through its consulting and training activities.[63]

Obtaining suitable premises for the institute was a matter of enormous red tape and bureaucratic struggle. In September 1920, when TsIT was first created, it was situated in a small room in Moscow's "Elite" Hotel. Its only equipment consisted of a table, two chairs, writing implements, and a hand-written sign on the door. Attempts by VTsSPS to find new quarters for the institute proved unsuccessful until February 1921, when VTsSPS appealed to the Moscow Soviet for help. TsIT was given temporary quarters in an old mansion, replete with "piles of garbage, drafts, a leaky roof, a flooded basement, and a gaping emptiness." Gastev found holding on to the building more difficult than repairing it, as Narkomtrud undertook a serious effort to snatch the premises. At one point it apeared that the institute would be homeless. But persistent protests by VTsSPS to the national government caused Narkomtrud to retreat.[64]

The explosion of interest in Scientific Management that followed the First NOT Conference and the difficult financial condition of the country created a keen competition among rival NOT groups for funds, fanning discord between them. At the end of 1920 twenty Scientific Management groups and institutes existed in Soviet Russia. Two and a half years later, though the number had grown to fifty-eight, a large proportion of the original twenty no longer existed.[65] Frictions were particularly evident between TsIT, chosen by STO in August 1921 as the central coordinating center for NOT institutions, and NOT groups in the provinces.

In March 1921 a recently returned delegate from the First NOT Conference, I. M. Burdianskii, and a group of military commissars convened a conference on Scientific Management in Kazan. The conference attracted more than two hundred people and elected a seven-member bureau charged with organizing Scientific Management research in the town. There is a grisly twist to the early work of the Kazan NOT Bureau: while millions of peasants were starving to death in the surrounding countryside during the famine of 1921, the bureau investigated the organization of bread baking and the distribution of food rations in Kazan city. Given the famine and the propensity of the NOT Bureau to poke its nose into controversial issues, it is little wonder that local officials did not take the bureau very seriously. The entire support it received during its first year of existence consisted of a room with a table and two chairs. As Burdianskii later noted, the attitude of local officials toward the bureau was "sarcastic, as if [we were] an extravagance suited for America, but not for the RSFSR."[66]

In December 1921 Gastev summoned a conference of representatives of Scientific Management organizations to confirm TsIT's coordinating role for the NOT movement. The conference upset representatives of provincial organizations because of the arrogant attitude of TsIT employees. The meeting established a Secretariat of Institutions Studying Labor (SUIT), under the chairmanship of TsIT, to act as a national coordinating center. Burdianskii requested that SUIT submit a request for ten thousand rubles to VTsSPS for his financially troubled Kazan Bureau. Since TsIT was experiencing its own monetary difficulties, Gastev decided not to act on the proposal and returned the request to Kazan. In January 1922 Burdianskii attempted once again to goad Gastev into raising the issue of financing with VTsSPS, but without success. As a result, the bureau was left entirely without funds. In desperation, Burdianskii appealed to SUIT, which, against the objections of TsIT, voted to approach the trade union leadership.[67]

By this time the rift between Burdianskii, who accused TsIT of failing to live up to its obligations, and Gastev, who feared that the financial requests of the young upstart from Kazan would jeopardize his own, had become irreparable. Gastev, however, prevailed within the trade union bureaucracy; a meeting of the VTsSPS Secretariat not only left in Gastev's hands the final decision on whether the Kazan NOT Bureau should be subsidized, but it also decreed "the organization of institutes of labor under local trade union bureaus" to be "undesirable." In the aftermath of this decision, Burdianskii transferred his bureau to the jurisdiction of Narkomtrud, where he received "great moral and to some degree even material support." Even so, the Kazan Institute for NOT, as it was then renamed, received only three thousand rubles during its first three years of existence, and by the end of 1923 the financial position of the institute was still "very serious."[68]

Burdianskii's experience was typical of most provincial NOT institutes. The Taganrog Institute for the Scientific Organization of Production traced its roots to a school for training workers organized in February 1920 by a group of Bolshevik engineers led by P. M. Esmanskii. Esmanskii's school barely functioned in its first year. But in early 1921 several representatives from the school returned from the First NOT Conference with the idea of converting it into a research institute on Scientific Management. Esmanskii's institute was an orphan from the beginning. It received no state subsidies, and most of its funds were obtained from private contributions and from the profits of three experimental flour-milling plants, which the institute exploited for commercial purposes.[69]

By the spring of 1922 one could detect the formation of a group consciousness, forged out of their common misfortune, among provincial *NOTisty*. Divisions within SUIT over the funding of provincial NOT institutes were so acute that SUIT was no longer capable of functioning; it ceased to meet and slipped into inactivity. In November 1922 Esmanskii wrote to Burdianskii suggesting joint lobbying efforts "before the central organs of the republic . . . for more solid material and moral support." Several weeks later they wrote to G. M. Krzhizhanovskii, chairman of Gosplan, decrying their "beggarly existence without sufficient support from central and local state organs." They requested that Krzhizhanovskii organize a special section under Gosplan to provide NOT institutes with funding, as well as with enterprises where experiments could be conducted. Burdianskii and Esmanskii met with Krzhizhanovskii in December, and their proposal received a positive response.[70] But by early 1923 the Scientific Management movement had become embroiled in a bitter political struggle that would soon overshadow these conflicts.

A Cheka for Organization

In May 1922 Lenin suffered the first of a series of paralyzing strokes that would gradually remove him from the conduct of public affairs. In his intermittent periods of activity from August 1922 to March

1923 he turned his attention to what he considered the most vexing legacy of his revolution: bureaucracy. No shortage of words existed for describing the administrative morass into which the revolution had sunk: "bureaucratism," "bureaucratic deviation," "bureaucratic degeneration," "petty bureaucratic tutelage," "agency narrow-mindedness," and "red tape" were ubiquitous terms in the vocabulary of party debates. As Lenin declared at the Tenth Party Congress, "Bureaucratism in our state apparatus has the significance of such a sore that it is even spoken about in our party program."[71] In moments of quiet reflection during his convalescence, he contemplated the cure for the administrative diseases that he, as chief bureaucrat of the Soviet state, had helped to create.

In fairness to Lenin, even before his physical incapacitation he had demanded, with Bolshevik severity, a decisive struggle against red tape "according to all the rules of the military arts." In September 1921 he had ordered the People's Commissariat of Justice to bring to trial "without fail four to six cases of Moscow red tape . . . making a political trial out of each case."[72] On Lenin's insistence and continual prodding the assignment was carried out; in January 1922 several officials of VSNKh were convicted of causing unnecessary delays in the production of spark plugs, even though shortages of fuel, raw materials, and labor plagued the industry. But Lenin found that the methods of the Chekist were not easily transferred to problems of bureaucratic organization. High officials in VSNKh protested these police tactics, and Lenin was forced to instruct the court (even before the case came to trial) that the guilty should receive no punishment. A later attempt by Lenin in March 1922 to try officials from VSNKh for red tape and mismanagement was dismissed by the courts. The decision sent Lenin into a rage; he ordered that the judge be given "a strict reprimand" for his "formal bureaucratic attitude toward the case." The leader of the revolution spared no efforts during these months to bully minor officials and administrators, whom he threatened with prison terms and arrest.[73]

By the spring of 1922, however, Lenin began to ponder other approaches to the problem. At the Eleventh Party Congress at the end of March, he raised the issue of the incapacity of red directors to manage industry; red directors, he said, were not leading but being led by bourgeois specialists. In order to manage, "one must study, but in our country no one studies; in our country orders and decrees are waved right and left, but the result is entirely not what is wanted." In April he authored a decree calling on TsIT to translate and publish the best foreign literature on Scientific Management,[74] and in May he asked one of his deputies to fetch a long list of literature on Scientific Management from the libraries of TsIT, the Socialist Academy, and STO. According to his aide, Lenin "obviously intended to write a work on the scientific organization of labor," but was prevented from doing so by the stroke he soon suffered.[75] When Lenin began to recover in August, he turned his attention once again to Scientific Management. Writing a review of Yermanskii's recently republished work on Taylorism, he praised the book as "fully suitable . . . as an obligatory textbook for all trade union and secondary schools" but for "the author's verbosity." In November 1922 Lenin argued that the replacement of bourgeois specialists by red directors was proceeding too fast: "we should work over the course of many years to improve our apparatus, to change it, and to attract new forces," but "in a short period of time, nothing can be accomplished."[76] For Lenin, however, time was running out; in the middle of December he experienced yet another stroke that left the right side of his body paralyzed.

As his health gradually improved, Lenin turned his attention to the reorganization of the People's Commissariat of Worker and Peasant Inspections (NKRKI). Less than a month after the Bolshevik seizure of power, a special Collegium for State Control had been established for "eradicating bureaucratism and red tape." The continual reorganizations this collegium experienced were indicative of broad-based dissatisfaction with its work. In May 1918 it was transformed into the People's Commissariat of State Control. In April 1919 it was reorganized under Stalin's command and instructed to inspect the work of all state organizations and to prepare proposals "for simplifying the apparatus of Soviet power, eliminating parallelism in work, and reorganizing the system of management in one or another field of state life." In early 1920 it was renamed the People's Commissariat of Worker-Peasant Inspections, and cells for assistance were created in factories, military units, and villages for mobilizing the population to combat corruption and bureaucratic disorders. But as a report on the NKRKI at the end of 1920 pointed out, the control organs suffered from "a lack of understanding of their tasks or an inability to put them into practice, an excessively formal approach, and a limiting of their activity to a picayune, formal control over only the financial and material side of things."[77] In 1922 the NKRKI diversified in a new direction, called "normalization" (*normalizatsiia*), whose goal was to improve accounting systems, the flow of paperwork, warehouse and storage facilities, and administrative structures. A special Department for Normalization was created in the NKRKI bureaucracy.

Criticism of the NKRKI throughout these years was rampant. Twice Trotsky appealed to Lenin to disband the organization; in each case, Lenin refused. In August 1922, while recovering from his first stroke, Lenin announced his intention to revamp the entire organization. NKRKI activities were to be directed away from mass mobilization, control, and inspection and toward improving the managerial apparatus through Scientific Management.[78] Lenin returned to this theme in January and March 1923, on the eve of his final stroke, in two articles published in *Pravda:* "How We Should Reorganize Rabkrin" and "Better Fewer but Better." He called for transforming the NKRKI into "a weapon for improving our apparatus, a truly model institution." Rabkrin, as the NKRKI was known, was to become the central coordinating agency for the NOT movement in Russia; it was to act as an organ for introducing rationalization measures throughout the bureaucracy and as a scientific center for the development of management theory. Rabkrin, Lenin declared, should announce a competition for the best textbooks on Scientific Management, dispatch its employees to Germany, England, America, and Canada to study these issues, and train all its employees in the new science of organization. The NKRKI staff should be slashed from its then current level of 1300 to only 300 or 400 employees, all of whom should be subjected to tests, composed by a special commission, on their knowledge of administration and Scientific Management. And Rabkrin should be merged with the Central Control Commission (TsKK) of the party, which, according to Lenin's plan, was to be enlarged and to direct the work of the commissariat. In the words of one management specialist of the time, Lenin was calling for nothing less than "a Cheka for the liquidation of organizational illiteracy."[79]

Lenin fully expected that the bureaucrats from the NKRKI, and in particular the so-called *praktiki* (officials lacking education), would "announce that these demands are incapable of being fulfilled or will laugh at them scornfully." In August 1922, when he had first presented his ideas to the collegium of NKRKI, they had been flatly rejected. The reaction of NKRKI officials six months later was not very different.[80] A majority of the Politburo, with the single exception of Trotsky, voted to suppress the publication of Lenin's project. Kuibyshev even wanted to trick the old man by ordering the printing of a single issue of *Pravda* carrying Lenin's articles that would be shown to the dying leader only. But on Krupskaia's and Lenin's insistence, the articles appeared.[81]

The situation changed considerably on March 6, when Lenin suffered his final stroke, a blow that left him permanently incapacitated. Sympathy for the dying leader then transformed what would have been a hotly contested struggle into a symbolic test of loyalty to the party in a time of national crisis. Opposition to Lenin's plan narrowed to two circles: Osinskii and his followers, who expressed doubts about its practicality and called for more far-reaching reforms;[82] and the red directors, some fearing extensive party interference in management, and others (the praktiki) fearing that Lenin's proposals might threaten their jobs. In the early 1920s the red directors were growing increasingly conscious of their common group identity. In a concession to them, the resolutions of the Eleventh Party Congress in April 1922 had encouraged the creation of an association for Bolshevik administrators. In March 1923, five days after Lenin's stroke, a Club for Red Directors, with 120 members, sprang into existence in Moscow under the organizational guidance of G. L. Piatikov, then a close ally of Trotsky in intraparty struggles. Over the next year membership in the club would more than double, and twenty-seven similar associations would arise in other cities, transforming the clubs into a major political force.[83]

Differences emerged at the Twelfth Party Congress over approaches to economic administration. Leonid Krasin, representing the more educated Bolshevik managers, made an impassioned plea against party interference in industrial management. Krasin's critique of Lenin's proposals was a logical sequel to Lenin's ideas. If, as Lenin had argued, the party was in need of professional management, then shouldn't it confine itself to propaganda and agitation and keep its nose out of industrial affairs? And if the party was unwilling to narrow the scope of its activities, then shouldn't it transform itself into a body of professional managers in order to do the job properly? The ruling oligarchs of the party hardly appreciated Krasin's frankness in pointing out the inconsistencies of their policies. Delegate after delegate poured scorn on the Bolshevik manager. No, Zinoviev replied, Krasin is making "a very, very big mistake"; "the party should direct literally every field of the economy." Zinoviev accused Krasin of slipping over to the Menshevik enemy. Bukharin likewise lashed out at Krasin for representing a "purely managerial" (*chisto-proizvodstvennaia*) outlook, which, he said, was rampant in some corners of the state apparatus—"a special engineering point of view that is totally indifferent whether it be capitalism or not capitalism, the proletariat or not, but cares only that production increases and grows with every passing day, that technology is repaired, and so on."[84]

The less-educated red directors were concerned over how Lenin's proposals might affect their careers. Politician after politician sought to reassure these managers that the professionalization of management envisioned by Lenin would not threaten their positions and that a new generation would not be trained to take their places. Zinoviev even announced that the task of recruiting managers for Soviet industry was "in essence completed."[85] Although the resolutions of the congress called for training new managerial employees on a "systematic" basis, they also emphasized that "the diminishing number of worker-communists in some economic organs is a dangerous phenomenon for the party." They urged red directors "who have not managed to acquire the necessary knowledge . . . to fill some of the existing gaps in their knowledge" through special instructional programs.[86]

Three days after the end of the congress V. V. Kuibyshev was chosen to head the NKRKI, now combined with the party's Central Control Commission (TsKK). Not until September did the new organ emerge from the ordeal of reorganization. Financial control over managerial activities was transferred to Narkomfin, and divisions related to the commissariat's new duties as the national coordinating center for the Scientific Management movement appeared. An Office for the Improvement of the State Apparatus was created to administer rationalization in the state bureaucracy, and a national Council for the Scientific Organization of Labor (SOVNOT), under the chairmanship of Kuibyshev, was organized to take the place of the moribund SUIT. For the first time funding began to flow freely to money-starved NOT institutes. But the NKRKI soon found itself at the center of a heated battle for control over the Scientific Management movement. The outcome of this battle depended upon which NOTisty were better able to influence the thinking of the NKRKI.

The Agitator and the Stopwatch

In early 1923, encouraged by Lenin's interest in Scientific Management and his plan for reorganizing Rabkrin, the ideological and methodological divisions of the Scientific Management movement broke into a full-scale war that shaped the development of Soviet rationalization policies for more than a decade. The seeds of this conflict had been sown in part by the intense competition among research institutes for funding. In the fall of 1922 disgruntled leaders of provincial NOT institutes joined forces to search for support in Moscow. There they found willing confederates among the ideological opponents of TsIT. In early 1922 the communist cell of TsIT clashed with Gastev over the institute's technocratic orientation. Three members of the cell (I. N. Shpil'rein, G. G. Torbek, and M. P. Rudakov) left in protest. Several months later the conflict resurfaced when an inspector from the NKRKI appeared at TsIT's doorstep to investigate charges of embezzlement leveled against Gastev by the vanquished communists.[87]

In their quest to remove him from the leadership of TsIT, Gastev's enemies were supported by the NKRKI, Gosplan, Narkomtrud, and the Moscow city party organization. In September 1922 the Moscow city party committee convened a conference of communists engaged in NOT research. The conference came under the influence of two groups highly critical of TsIT: Yermanskii and his student following, and former members of the communist cell of TsIT. Disapproving remarks were leveled at TsIT for its indiscriminate borrowing of capitalist organizational methods. A temporary bureau (including Torbek, Shpil'rein, S. Kaplun, and Ia. M. Shatunovskii) was elected to prepare a declaration. Soon Burdianskii and Esmanskii made contact with the bureau, and with its help the two approached Gosplan, where Shatunovskii was employed, for material support. At a meeting of SUIT in December the two groups joined forces to push through a resolution calling for a second national conference on NOT to be convened in March 1923 for "eliminating the lack of coordination and consensus" among NOT institutes.[88]

The ideological opponents of TsIT were irked by government support for Gastev's technocratic approach to the study of labor. Among the greatest scandals on their list was TsIT's Laboratory No. 7, known as the social-engineering laboratory. Here, Gastev had undertaken the design of a "social-engineering machine," an apparatus intended, as Gastev later wrote, "to constantly force the creation of the productive instincts of man."[89] Laboratory No. 7 was the embodiment of Gastev's dream of a science of social engineering, as was evidenced in the guiding slogan of TsIT: "Mankind learned how to process things; the time has come to thoroughly process man." The social-engineering machine attracted powerful supporters within the Soviet hierarchy. In March 1923 the ruling council of TsIT, then chaired by trade union leader Mikhail Tomskii, declared the machine to be "the basis for constructing the human and machine mass necessary for the victorious mastery of the forces of nature." V. A. Avanesov, deputy head of the NKRKI, called it "an idea . . . of enormous significance . . . which should give very tangible results."[90]

A second objection of TsIT's opponents centered on its methodology for improving labor operations, known as *rubka zubilom,* or chisel-cutting. TsIT had borrowed Frank Gilbreth's "cyclographic" technique of photographing separate elements of labor gestures in order to analyze, in painstaking depth, the most minute worker operations, such as cutting with a chisel (whence the name came).[91] Some of TsIT's opponents found this empirical approach too similar to Taylorism as practiced in the West; the individual worker was the object of empirical observation by efficiency experts, whose aim was to intensify rather than ease the burden of labor. Others believed the goal of NOT should be to develop a set of general management principles rather than to study worker motions. The opponents of TsIT also objected to its philosophy of a "narrow base." This idea, related to Gol'tsman's advocacy of a worker aristocracy, posited that a small nucleus of workers who had thoroughly mastered a narrow set of operations could serve as models of efficiency for the rest of the proletariat. These worker-technicians, called instructors, would be trained within the confines of the institute, sent abroad for exposure to Scientific Management as practiced in the West, and then dispatched throughout Soviet industry to train their fellow workers. To TsIT's critics, "the principle of a narrow base" smacked of the same elitism the party had condemned in the trade union debates of 1920 and 1921.[92]

In January 1923 a coalition of TsIT opponents calling itself the "communist fraction" in NOT published a manifesto entitled "Our Platform," which lashed out at TsIT's social-engineering approach to NOT and its lack of support for provincial NOT institutes.[93] The biting tone of the theses evoked a wave of concern in VTsSPS, which called a special meeting of its Presidium to discuss the situation. It was addressed by Gastev and Kaplun, a signer of the platform and a member of the collegium of Narkomtrud. Gastev called his critics "fantasizers and romantics" who were brandishing slogans while eschewing practical work. Kaplun retorted by accusing TsIT of "striving to turn man into a soulless machine" and of making no distinction between Taylorism as practiced under capitalism and NOT as it should be practiced under socialism. VTsSPS backed Gastev on all major points and called for "protecting" TsIT from "all attempts to thwart" its work.[94]

Soon afterward the Moscow city party committee convened its "communist fraction" in the Club of Narkomtrud. It condemned Gastev's "ideology" as "reactionary" and decided to speed up efforts at agitation in favor of the "Marxist" line in Scientific Management. Attempts were made to enlist the sickly Lenin in the struggle against Gastev's social engineering, but without success.[95] TsIT, too, engaged in efforts to mold opinion. In January a press bureau was established there, and a series of articles on the institute were initiated in *Pravda*. TsIT also convened a conference on the numerous NOT study groups that were surfacing at higher educational institutes (*vuzy*) around the capital. But the meeting turned into a tense confrontation when student opponents of Gastev invited Yermanskii to address the gathering. According to press reports, "a lively debate, bearing a sharply polemical character," followed.[96]

During the summer of 1923 a dramatic change occurred in the NOT movement that significantly strengthened TsIT's opponents.

In May there were no more than fifty-eight institutes, bureaus, and study circles engaged in NOT work in the entire country, and nearly a third of these were concentrated in Moscow.[97] By the end of the summer, NOT had been transformed into a mass movement involving tens of thousands—a transformation due largely to the efforts of one man, Pavel Kerzhentsev.

Kerzhentsev belonged to the intellectual wing of the Bolshevik underground, an archetypal representative of those who called themselves "agitators." As a young professional revolutionary he had participated in the publication of the party's underground newspapers in Russia. After his arrest in 1912, he emigrated to London and then Paris, where he was a correspondent for the party press. When Kerzhentsev returned to Russia at the end of 1917, he worked as deputy editor of *Izvestiia* and as director of the Russian Telegraph Agency (ROST), the forerunner of TASS. He also became deeply involved in the activities of Proletkult. But when Proletkult came under fire from Lenin for its independent cultural views, Kerzhentsev was dispatched to Sweden as Soviet ambassador. There he turned his attention to a new interest: Scientific Management. In 1922, while still abroad, he published a book entitled *Principles of Organization*. Though highly critical of Taylor, it argued for a carefully selected borrowing of Western theories and their use to effect a cultural revolution through the creation of a society of "organized men." In March 1923 the book was praised by Lenin as a model management textbook.[98]

Kerzhentsev returned to Russia in the spring of 1923 to become a member of the editorial board of *Pravda*. Soon thereafter he was drawn into the ideological conflicts over Scientific Management and sided with the critics of TsIT. In mid-July he published an article in *Pravda* decrying wasted hours spent at endless meetings and conferences. Within ten days, "in view of the extraordinary number of articles, inquiries, and telephone calls" the piece evoked, he convened a public meeting at the offices of *Pravda* to found a voluntary society, the Time League, devoted to rooting out waste in public institutions. When four hundred people arrived at the meeting, quarters had to be rented from the neighboring Printers' Club at the last minute.[99] Kerzhentsev enjoyed powerful support for his project; the nine-member presidium elected at the meeting included not only Gastev and Shpil'rein (from opposing sides in the debates over

NOT), but also Evgenii Preobrazhenskii (Trotsky's ally and a proponent of rapid industrialization), Vsevolod Meierkhol'd (the avant-garde master of experimental theater), and Aleksandr Kosarev (secretary of the Bauman district Komsomol organization in Moscow and destined to lead the Soviet youth movement under Stalin). Indicative of the presence of a large number of his supporters, Trotsky (along with the crippled Lenin) was chosen honorary chairman of the league.[100]

Through skillful public relations worthy of Madison Avenue, Kerzhentsev successfully mobilized tens of thousands into the cells of the Time League. Only one month after the founding of the league, forty-four cells with nearly a thousand members had sprung up in Moscow alone. By the end of 1923 the Moscow membership had quadrupled to more than four thousand, 62 percent of whom were party members. By that time the organization had made its appearance in more than seventy-five cities and towns. The rapid growth of the league became a cause of contention within its ruling presidium. Gastev wanted to confine membership growth; the resolution of this issue in favor of Kerzhentsev and the dominance of TsIT opponents in the presidium led Gastev to quit its ranks. Two groups were particularly well represented in the Moscow organization: soldiers and students. The first cells of the league were organized in the military, and Kerzhentsev himself observed that army cells "were the most active and solid in Moscow." And by October 1923 more than a third of all cells in Moscow were located at vuzy.[101]

The Time League's main task as spelled out in its charter was to struggle for "the correct and efficient use of time in all walks of social and private life."[102] The ultimate goal of the league was nothing less than full-scale cultural revolution. As Kerzhentsev expressed it, "The struggle for time is a daring struggle to make a new man worthy of our transition to the epoch of communism. Our human material, spoiled by the epoch of Tsarism but sprinkled with the holy water of revolution, should adapt to new conditions of work. Down with foolishness, with Oblomovism, with slovenliness, and with lack of discipline!" In addition to wearing the league's membership button, members were sworn to observe strict punctuality in attending meetings, to fulfill their work duties precisely, and to root out waste and mismanagement at work. Each cell had the right to impose fines on its members for disorderliness or tardiness, and blatant violators were subjected to agitation sessions on the importance of accuracy in their lives. Attacks were made on excessive paperwork, long lines, and indolent bureaucrats. Student members kept track of the wasted minutes of their professors on special charts distributed by the league. In the spirit of Gilbreth, time cards were circulated to all members for the purpose of measuring every minute of their daily routine. In addition to the league's journal, *Time,* hundreds of newspapers, bulletins, and posters were published; Meierkhol'd arranged propaganda plays, called "living newspapers," to spread the new gospel. In the course of one year seventy-seven thousand man-hours were spent by the members of the league in their fight against bureaucratism—approximately the same amount of time wasted in a single year in a Soviet commissariat at meetings and conferences.[103]

To Kerzhentsev the Time League was more than a successful experiment in mass mobilization; it was a conscious model demonstrating how the principles of Scientific Management should be realized in a socialist state, a counterexample to Gastev's social engineering. Kerzhentsev criticized Soviet Taylorists for wanting "to conduct work on NOT in Saratov and Perm as if it were taking place in Massachusetts or Pennsylvania." TsIT, he said, wanted to "leave the working masses on the sidelines"; it had elevated the principle of a narrow base into a "rude fetish," and it took "a purely laboratory approach" to NOT.[104] By contrast, Gastev accused Kerzhentsev and his followers of taking a "literary agitational" approach to Scientific Management, of being dilettantes who dreamed of creating a "communist" NOT.[105] In the fall of 1923 the gap between Kerzhentsev, who by then was the leader of the "communist fraction," and Gastev had become an irreparable breach.

The focus of these squabbles shifted to the Second All-Union Conference on NOT, which had been postponed several times because of failure to agree on its format. In late 1923 responsibility for organizing the conference was transferred from TsIT to the NKRKI. At a meeting of SOVNOT in December, Kuibyshev, its chairman, attempted to reconcile the two camps by appealing for "less theorizing" and "more realism" on both sides.[106] Instead, in the early months of 1924 a torrent of platforms appeared in the press. First came the platform of TsIT, signed by Gastev and Gol'tsman, among others. They expressed concern that Kerzhentsev and his ally Radus-Zenkovich, head of the Section for Labor and Production of the NKRKI, had been chosen by Kuibyshev to make the organizational arrangements for the conference.[107] Next came the platform of the Sverdlovites, Yermanskii's radical-student following in the Communist Academy, who accused Gastev of propagating "vulgar-bourgeois 'Taylorism'" and complained that the NKRKI had not yet taken measures to ensure proper communist leadership over the NOT movement.[108] Finally, there was the so-called Platform of the Seventeen, a series of theses written by Kerzhentsev and approved by a motley alliance including the "communist fraction," the Sverdlovites, representatives of provincial NOT institutes, and members of the Moscow Club for Red Directors. The document directed its main fire against TsIT's "petty-bourgeois perversion of Taylorism," but reserved some bile for other "deviations" in the NOT movement, such as Bogdanov's "idealistic" theorizing on organizational science, the Soviet followers of Fayol, and the theories of Yermanskii, whose Menshevik past made him more of a liability than an asset.[109] A series of recriminations and charges filled the press up to the opening session of the conference. As Kuibyshev wrote, "the passions of the polemics were the equivalent of those we had during party debates."[110]

The issue was now in the hands of Kuibyshev, who, as head of the NKRKI, had a strong interest in ending the scuffle. When he convened a small meeting of nine of the individuals involved, "it led to nothing"; "relations grew more strained among them," some claiming "to represent the proletarian position in NOT, as opposed to the others, who reflected the bourgeois line." In a second effort at reconciliation he called a meeting of seventy people, at which he proposed a commission for working out a common platform. But this suggestion was met with "indignation from both sides." As Kuibyshev later observed, "They called me an opportunist, a compromiser, and said that I did not understand the class differences between their positions."[111]

In frustration Kuibyshev resolved to end the conflict by writing his own platform on NOT and forcing it on the warring factions. When the document had been prepared, he invited "representatives of the extreme points of view," Gol'tsman and Kerzhentsev, to a conference. Gol'tsman immediately agreed with the platform, but Kerzhentsev was reluctant to give a straight answer. Kuibyshev had come down squarely on the side of TsIT. Bogdanov's "harmful theorizing" about the existence of a general science of organization was rejected as "unmarxist," and the importance of "the spontaneous organization of workers for improving a specific enterprise" (the Time League) was recognized. At the same time, Kuibyshev took to task "a number of comrades" for harboring "dangerous illusions" and for underestimating the achievements of the West in Scientific Management. Kerzhentsev, in particular, was singled out for committing this "cardinal, principal mistake." By contrast, the value of TsIT's approach and of the "active participation of the trade unions" in NOT work was implicitly recognized.[112]

After a year of postponements the Second All-Union Conference on the Scientific Organization of Labor opened in March 1924 at the Polytechnical Museum in Moscow. The elitist profile of the gathering was conspicuous: of the 383 delegates, 87 percent were classified as intelligentsia, 72 percent had a higher education, 70 percent were from Moscow, and roughly two-thirds did not belong to the party.[113] In spite of Kerzhentsev's attempts to bring NOT to the masses, the Scientific Management movement in Soviet Russia, as elsewhere, was to remain the prerogative of the specialist. The conference opened with a speech by Kuibyshev. The NKRKI, he said, stood for "the practical point of view"; it regarded the recent polemics over NOT as "pointless." In the war against bureaucracy all available means should be utilized. The time had come to get down to "practical" and "businesslike" work to improve the state apparatus.[114] When Kuibyshev sat down, his deputy and close friend, N. M. Shvernik (later to become Stalin's trade union boss), handed him a note: "Well done, Valerian! . . . You stated the essence of the work at hand in a very popular way, and not in stiff language as the NOTisty usually do."[115]

The speech was followed by declarations from Kerzhentsev and Gol'tsman pledging support for Kuibyshev's platform. A resolution was adopted, with only one negative vote, endorsing TsIT's methodology of labor training.[116] It was the final act of a political drama that had lasted for more than two years. Through Kuibyshev's intervention, open state support was bestowed upon the advocates of radical technocratic approaches to administrative rationalization. But although the opponents of TsIT had been overcome, they had not been entirely routed; within five years Gastev's enemies would reemerge to launch a new assault on the institute. In the meantime, as a result of the decisions of the Second NOT Conference, Soviet Scientific Management was to experience a golden age of experimentation and expansion.

2

• • • • • •

Scientific Management at the Helm

Does the average German work better than the average Russian?
Of course he works better.
Does the average German know what the Scientific Organization of Labor is?
Of course he doesn't know. He's never even heard of it.
And has the average Muscovite heard of the Scientific Organization of Labor?
Of course he has. He even thought up an abbreviation for it—"NOT."
Well, if that's so, then why not take the German?

—Aleksei Gastev, November 1923

By the mid-twenties Soviet Russia had created one of the strongest bases in the world, outside of America and Germany, for Scientific Management research. Approximately 108 organizations were conducting work on NOT, and a bibliography of NOT literature published in 1924 noted the existence of more than 2400 titles in the Russian language. Far-ranging contacts were established with Scientific Management enthusiasts in the United States and Western Europe. A number of Soviet NOT institutes maintained permanent representatives abroad to keep the motherland abreast of the latest research and scientific trends. Frequent sorties were made by management experts to collect foreign literature, buy Western equipment, and exchange information. By the end of 1924 these trips had grown so costly that SOVNOT resolved to confine foreign sojourns to "special expeditions" with a "strictly defined object" of research.[1] Perhaps in no other country at that time did enthusiasts of Scientific Management enjoy such close contact with and pervasive influence over ruling politicians. The Twelfth Party Congress had proclaimed Scientific Management the basis of Bolshevik administrative policy. The refashioning of the NKRKI into a national center for the NOT movement laid the organizational foundation for realizing Lenin's dream of applying Scientific Management throughout Russia. The monetary support that poured into NOT research alleviated the financial famine which many institutes had experienced in their first years of existence. And a number of decision-making channels had opened through which NOTisty could participate in the formulation of national administrative policies.

But if the mid-1920s constituted a golden age for Soviet Scientific Management, by the end of the decade much of the glitter had faded. The basic task of the NOT movement in the second half of the twenties was to translate abstract theories into a real improvement in the operation of the Soviet bureaucracy. Thanks to the support of influential patrons in the party, far-reaching technocratic schemes were adopted as official policy. Nevertheless, throughout these years powerful forces thwarted efforts to improve administration. If rationalization had been merely a matter of summing up discrete improvements in individual subunits and measuring their savings in ruble value, the overall balance sheet might have favored the practitioners of Scientific Management. Soviet NOTisty did succeed in eliminating instances of red tape, training a skilled work force, creating improved systems of accounting and paperwork, trimming the fat from bloated staffs, and organizing less cumbersome bureaucratic structures. But as so often happened, either the benefits of these measures proved transient, swallowed by an entrenched culture of bureaucracy, or new bureaucratic disorders arose where none had been observed before. Considerable friction became apparent between rationalizers and the entire industrial hierarchy. When new goals of rapid industrialization were adopted in 1928, it was clear that the Soviet bureaucracy was no more rational and no more efficient than it had been in 1924.

The Politics of Technocracy

No bureaucracy, no matter how well ordered, is immune from the encroachments of politics. This is especially true when efforts are being made to enact profound organizational changes. Rationalizers require the protection and extraordinary authority of political leaders, for efforts to enact change affect the relative power of elites and citizens and inevitably cause conflict over power and policy. The Soviet Scientific Management movement flourished in the mid-twenties precisely because of its ability to find and retain political patrons who both protected rationalizers against fallout from their controversial measures and provided an institutional base from which to implement their technocratic schemes. Throughout this period, rationalizers continued to come under attack from their political opponents, and their hold over specific institutional bases waxed and waned. Nevertheless, the backing they received from powerful figures within the party and government enabled them to exercise a consistent influence over policy.

Less than a month after defeating Kerzhentsev at the Second NOT Conference, his opponents consolidated their control over the NKRKI by forcing him to resign from SOVNOT and attacking his hold over the Time League. In late 1923 and early 1924 considerable consternation had already arisen within the trade unions, the party, and the NKRKI over the implications of a nongovernmental mass association organized on a territorial basis whose aim was to attack bureaucratism in the state bureaucracy. Some within the party apparatus viewed the league as a competitor. Though Kerzhentsev vehemently denied these accusations, he used the league to lobby local party organizations for stiffer laws against bureaucratic mismanagement and work-place indiscipline. In May 1924 VTsSPS and the NKRKI circulated a joint letter calling on the cells of the Time League to merge with local trade union organizations.[2] Two months later the association was renamed "The NOT League"—indicative of a shift away from mass mobilization against indolent officials and toward cooperation with the state apparatus.

Despite attacks, the league continued to flourish; its membership actually grew by five thousand in late 1924 and early 1925. But soon afterwards Kerzhentsev was dispatched abroad again, this time as Soviet ambassador to Italy, and the chairmanship of the league passed to Elena Rozmirovich, a close ally of Gastev and one of Kerzhentsev's most bitter foes. In early November SOVNOT ordered the league "decentralized," its Presidium disbanded, and its journal transferred to the trade unions. Several months later the league was formally "liquidated" and its cells merged with trade union enterprise commissions.[3]

As policy increasingly shifted toward an engineering approach to administrative problems, control over the Scientific Management movement passed to Gastev and his allies. In September 1924 Gastev sent Kuibyshev a memorandum on "establishing the priority of the engineer over the literary writer" in NOT work. He put forth a broad-ranging plan for reorganizing SOVNOT by "totally excluding those people who are known to have only a general competence . . . in NOT and who are entirely unnecessary for the work of SOVNOT, as they are for the work of a business institution." According to the plan, SOVNOT would be transformed from a representative organ of the NOT movement into a consulting organ for the NKRKI. Gastev's proposals received Kuibyshev's support, and in November the composition of SOVNOT was altered. Gastev was made deputy chairman, and direction over the council was placed in the hands of a three-member bureau, consisting of Gastev, Kuibyshev, and Rozmirovich.[4]

Having captured SOVNOT, Gastev and his allies used their new regulatory powers to shape the direction of NOT research throughout the country. A circular letter from the NKRKI at the end of 1924 directed local officials to replace "old methods of research based primarily on questionnaires and a familiarity with documents and materials" with "truly scientific (i.e., precise) methods of direct observation of all processes in nature." Political priorities were imposed on research agendas; broadly theoretical work unconnected with practical efforts at rationalization was to be eliminated, and research was to be channeled toward rationalizing the trade network, then the object of the regime's concern due to the "scissors crisis." In conformity with Gastev's interest in promoting industrial norms, a Central Bureau for Standardization was formed under SOVNOT in July 1924. In 1925 the bureau was upgraded to a

Committee for Standardization under STO, chaired consecutively by Kuibyshev and Gastev.[5]

The new emphasis on applied work was reaffirmed at the end of 1925 when, on the initiative of VSNKh chairman Dzerzhinskii, an All-Union Conference on Rationalization convened in Moscow. Like Kuibyshev, Dzerzhinskii played the role of patron to the Scientific Management movement, particularly after the Twelfth Party Congress. But his close ties with management practitioners colored his perspective. By 1925 Kuibyshev had become a proponent of rapid industrialization; as he described his views in a letter to the Sovnarkom, "the system of management at present should be subordinated to a significant degree to the interests of developing industry." Dzerzhinskii, Kuibyshev wrote, was by contrast "worried about the 'system of management.' " As leader of VSNKh, Dzerzhinskii had become painfully aware of the mountains of paperwork and red tape that inhibited his subordinates from properly fulfilling their duties. In his impatience to battle bureaucracy, the former Cheka chief proposed to the Politburo in 1925 that he be made "dictator for economic policy," an ambition that Kuibyshev opposed.[6] Dzerzhinskii's conference on rationalization aimed at furthering these aspirations. The dominance of practitioners over theoreticians (80 percent of the delegates were managers) was reflected in the nuts-and-bolts orientation of the meeting. The ideological disputes that had plagued the NOT movement in the preceding years were hardly mentioned. When they were, the delegates came down firmly against "abstract principles" and "a shock-work approach" to NOT. The main goal of the meeting was to invigorate rationalization efforts by working through plant management rather than imposing measures from outside, particularly from Kuibyshev's NKRKI.[7]

The influence of Gastev and his allies over the NOT movement lay precariously in the hands of politicians. In the early twenties he had found a powerful patron in Trotsky, but by 1924, when Trotsky's authority was under attack, Kuibyshev, with his enthusiasm for rapid industrialization and his control over the NKRKI bureaucracy, was a safer bet. Kuibyshev and Gastev developed a close friendship during these years; Gastev would often visit the Kuibyshev home for meetings that dragged on late into the night. Even Kuibyshev's role, as head of the NKRKI, in purging Gastev's erstwhile allies in the Left Opposition did not mar the relationship. At a meeting of the NKRKI, Gastev passed a note to his patron requesting that a "certain Comrade Rozhitsyn," a Left Opposition supporter known to Kuibyshev for his "serious theoretical deviations," be transferred from Kharkov to Moscow for work at TsIT. Kuibyshev thought the move might be "useful," since, as he told Gastev, in Moscow "he will be more quickly straightened out."[8] For Gastev, developing a sense for the direction of political winds was necessary for maintaining his influence in the corridors of power.

In 1926 these winds shifted again. Within the NKRKI a tension had always existed between those who believed the commissariat's main task was rationalization and those who believed it should focus primarily on enforcing discipline by weeding out corruption and mismanagement. In June 1925 Kuibyshev, reflecting his patronage over the NOT movement, reaffirmed that although the NKRKI's control functions would always be necessary, emphasis should be placed on rationalization. In accordance with his vision, the volume of rationalization work increased to 50 percent of the NKRKI workload (up from 12.5 percent the year before), and the volume of control and inspection work decreased from 82 percent to 28 percent.[9] But in the spring of 1926, with the struggle against the Left Opposition in full swing, Stalin resolved to reinvigorate the NKRKI as a political and disciplinary weapon. In April the issue was debated at a plenum of the TsKK. There, in a turnabout, Kuibyshev noted the existence of "a false conception among some employees that controlling and checking work should gradually die out . . . and that what is needed is that all attention be paid to rationalization." Many NKRKI employees, he noted, "have come to repudiate a whole series of types of investigation, saying that no matter what kind of disorder is occurring in one or another district, this is not our work, but rather the work of legal organs; if there is a crime there, let them study the matter, but our work is mainly rationalization, and we will engage in it and confine ourselves to the limits of those tasks which we have been given."

Kuibyshev announced a plan intended to enhance central direction over the NOT movement. The entire rationalization effort of the NKRKI was to be concentrated in the hands of a Rationalization Sector, whose purpose would be to coordinate a new drive for efficiency. Soon afterwards, Stalin and Kuibyshev circulated a letter to all party organizations announcing the inauguration of a campaign for a "strict regime of economy" to root out inefficiency, corruption, and mismanagement in the state apparatus. If the Soviet state were to be successful in industrializing the country, the document said, savings would have to be accumulated by squeezing the fat out of the bureaucracy. The NKRKI was called upon to lead this struggle, through both the rationalization measures it sponsored and its inspection activities; this second direction of work, the letter said, was to be given greater attention.[10]

When Dzerzhinskii died in July 1926 and Kuibyshev was chosen to replace him as VSNKh chairman, Gastev's hold over NKRKI policies began to falter. At Gastev's urging, in December 1925 Kuibyshev had obtained the approval of the Fourteenth Party Congress for a Third All-Union Conference on NOT, whose purpose would be to unite the Soviet rationalization movement around a common methodology. According to the resolutions of the congress, the NOT movement was to be purged of "agency organs of rationalization working without a well-rounded, competent study of the process of work and on clearly unscientific foundations, as well as pseudoscientific research institutes"; a "collective audit" of rationalization organs was to be conducted, selecting the "healthiest" among them. In February 1926 SOVNOT set September as the date of the conference. From February through July extensive preparations proceeded under Gastev's direction. But the conference was suddenly canceled shortly after Kuibyshev's departure for VSNKh.[11] Apparently the proponents of the conference lost their base of support after Kuibyshev's transfer. Gastev was chosen to replace Kuibyshev as chairman of SOVNOT; but without his patron to back him his promotion proved to be ephemeral. At the end of 1926, as one of Gastev's opponents described it, SOVNOT "quietly died without an obituary."[12] Although his influence over rationalization policies survived, Gastev's institutional base shifted from the NKRKI to Kuibyshev's VSNKh and Tomskii's trade unions.

These fluctuations in Gastev's fortunes were closely connected with the selection of Stalin's personal friend, Sergo Ordzhonikidze, to replace Kuibyshev in November 1926 as head of the NKRKI. Ordzhonikidze wanted the NKRKI to concentrate on weeding out corruption and mismanagement and act as a sharper political weapon against Stalin's opponents. Upon assuming his new duties, he reversed Kuibyshev's recent reorganization of the rationalization movement; instead, he began to criticize "an inclination toward a certain academicism" in the work of the commissariat.[13]

Ordzhonikidze's transfer to the NKRKI had repercussions for other NOTisty as well. Kuibyshev and Esmanskii had not been particularly close. But Kuibyshev had defended Esmanskii and his institute against local party officials in Taganrog and the Northern Caucasus who were displeased with the institute's practice of renting local flour mills for its experiments and using the proceeds to support the institute. Constant complaints had been raised that the institute was improperly paying the employees of the mills and was overpaying peasants for their grain. The continual friction between the institute and the Northern Caucasus regional committee, including a number of attempts to prosecute the institute for its practices, had absorbed the energies of Esmanskii's staff. Twice Kuibyshev had come to the institute's rescue: once with a special decree reaffirming his support for Esmanskii, and a second time by assigning a deputy director to the institute whose sole responsibility was to improve communications with local party officials.[14] But Kuibyshev's efforts to save the institute came to naught, for his replacement, Ordzhonikidze, was none other than the former First Secretary of the Northern Caucasus party committee. Ordzhonikidze's revenge on Esmanskii was achieved in March 1927, when the Taganrog Institute was liquidated by order of the NKRKI—a harbinger of what would come when darker political clouds descended upon the NOT movement.

Education or Training

One of the main areas in which the political and ideological conflicts surrounding rationalization were manifested in the 1920s was educational policy. The Bolsheviks came to power claiming they would create a new type of industrial society; education was universally seen as the instrument for realizing this transformation. But the issue of who should receive what kind of training immediately became the object of controversy due to the extreme shortage of skilled industrial personnel and the uncertainty of the Marxist solution to the problem of education.[15] Selecting the type of training to be offered industrial personnel involved deeply held ideological values of equality and social justice. The ideologically orthodox viewed education as a means for the cultural uplift of the working class; it was to foster well-rounded and cultured individuals capable of acting as masters of a new civilization. Those interested in restoring the country's tattered economy, by contrast, viewed education as a means of forging skilled cadres capable of manning the industrial hierarchy. The Scientific Management movement's interest in educational policy was grounded in a similar faith in the power of education to foster a rational industrial order. At the center of Taylor's innovations lay the training of workers in the most efficient approach to labor operations, the adjustment of the motions of man to the requirements of factory organization. Like their foreign associates, Soviet NOTisty viewed industrial leadership as an independent profession that could be taught.

In the West, and particularly in the United States, training programs for teaching managers the new science of organization appeared with increasing frequency during these years. By contrast, despite efforts by Soviet NOTisty to create similar programs, the training of Soviet managers in management theory and techniques hardly occurred during this period, partly because of the influence of poorly educated red directors and partly because of resistance within the educational bureaucracy. In December 1922 a survey of industrial personnel indicated that of those plant directors who were party members, 81 percent had no education beyond elementary school, and some had had no schooling whatever.[16] Given their background and their competitive relationship with their specialist rivals, these managers had a personal interest in keeping educational requirements for managerial positions at a minimum.

Scientific Management enthusiasts who sought to create special training programs for managers at the college and midcareer levels soon discovered that it was impossible to attract interest in managerial training when the vast majority of managers were barely capable of reading and subtracting, let alone comprehending chronometry or Gantt charts. At the Kazan Institute, where four-month evening courses for training industrial administrators in NOT were organized, only seven of the twenty-five managers enrolled finished the program. Students lacked the proper background to understand the subject, and regular attendance was hindered by their daily administrative load.[17] Proposals for introducing NOT into higher-education curricula and for creating special management schools surfaced frequently. At the Second All-Union Conference in March 1924, one farsighted delegate even outlined a plan for a network of management schools whose trainees possessed "nature-given talents," had passed an entrance examination, and were trained by means of case-study and situational learning techniques not unlike those used in American business schools today. These schemes were openly opposed by red directors, who argued instead for more general educational courses aimed at bringing their knowledge up to the level of bourgeois specialists.[18]

A series of measures adopted by the NKRKI in the second half of 1923 and patterned after ideas raised in Lenin's last articles closely mirrored the training proposals of the NOTisty. Beginning in July 1923, eight examination commissions for selecting personnel were established in the commissariat. In addition, a new training program in NOT was organized at the law faculty of the Sverdlov Communist University, but it was capable of accommodating only thirty NKRKI trainees per six-month session.[19] In 1923 and 1924 the NKRKI made a concerted effort to introduce instruction in Scientific Management into higher education. In January 1924 the Scientific Council of Narkompros resolved to initiate NOT instruction in "at least two *vuzy* in Moscow and Petrograd" on an experimental basis. But the idea of creating special faculties for NOT was rejected by the Narkompros bureaucracy, which preferred to keep the new subject under the control of existing disciplines and departments. In October 1924 a conference of *vuz* rectors agreed to establish an introductory course on NOT for first-year students and an advanced course for older students in several vuzy, but educational administrators insisted that both courses be conducted within existing vuz specializations.[20]

Nothing could have been more disturbing to red directors than proposals such as these, which, in their view, aimed at training a new generation of administrative personnel capable of pushing them out of the managerial suite. Well-organized and conscious of their interests, the red directors put forth their own notions about the country's management development needs at meetings of SOV-NOT, NKRKI departments, and VSNKh. In 1925, with Dzerzhinskii's blessing, one of the Moscow-based clubs for red directors began offering instructional courses for its membership. The aim of these courses for red directors was "to increase the general educational level of trainees," to enhance their qualifications relative to their specialist rivals. By the end of 1927 similar programs had appeared in Moscow, Leningrad, Kharkov, Sverdlovsk, and elsewhere, and more than a thousand executives had been trained. Most of the trainees were former workers in their thirties who had only recently joined the party and who lacked the proper training and experience necessary for the important industrial posts they held. Of the first class, 40 percent had joined the party between 1918 and 1924, and another 40 percent had only joined in the previous year. More than half were plant directors; yet the overwhelming majority had attended only two or three years of elementary school, and many had to be taught basic arithmetical operations.[21]

At first the courses included a 45-hour lecture series on Taylorism, as well as lectures on various managerial functions. But much of this material was beyond the comprehension of the red directors. Forty-two percent of the trainees in the 1926–27 session failed the program's course in bookkeeping, since they lacked basic mathematical skills. It was quickly found that more time had to be devoted to general education, particularly mathematics, and accordingly the time allotted for management-related subjects was cut back. As the final report on the first year of operation stressed, lectures on management, though in theory necessary for managers, had to be eliminated because "they defy systematization on the scale and level required by the trainees."[22]

A great many trainees found it difficult to balance the dual burden of work and study. By June 1925, three months after the courses began, absenteeism had grown to 25 percent. When the first class graduated in July 1926, only 55 percent of the original 143 were still in the program. A survey of those who had dropped out indicated that more than a third had done so because of "work overload." The next graduating class had a better record: 81 percent of the original 119 finished the program. But reports indicated that exhaustion from daily work routines had seriously undermined attentiveness in the classroom.[23]

With the onset of industrialization the red directors obtained still other training programs. In March 1927 the Central Committee decreed that an "Academy for Upgrading the Qualifications of the Administrative-Command Staff of Industry" be created under VSNKh. Some Western scholars have interpreted the Industrial Academy as part of Stalin's subsequent efforts to create a new Bolshevik technical and administrative elite.[24] Although the academy programs eventually evolved in this direction, their original purpose was not the training of a new elite, but rather the retraining of red directors. The facilities of the All-Union Industrial Academy were located at a Moscow-based club for red directors, and the decision to create it preceded the Shakhty affair and the July 1928 Central Committee Plenum—the key landmarks in Stalin's new managerial recruitment policies—by a year and a year and a half respectively. Stalin argued at the time for short-term courses for Bolshevik administrators. By contrast, the Industrial Academy was originally a three-year full-time program whose trainees were recruited from those already occupying top-level managerial posts. The main impetus for creating the first industrial academy came not from Stalin but from the red directors with the support of Kuibyshev. The selection of A. Z. Kamenskii as the director of the Academy was hardly indicative of Stalin's hand in the matter. An Old Bolshevik who sympathized with the Left Opposition in 1925 and 1926 and who was known for his dissident views within the party, Kamenskii had been a member of the first club for red directors and an organizer and director of its courses of instruction. If the appointment of the fiercely independent Kamenskii represented anything, it was above all a bow to the red directors.[25]

As Kamenskii later described it, the major goal of the Academy was to train executives "in general technical-economic knowledge, to be literate in a general factory sense." Like those who attended the courses for red directors, the Academy's students had difficulty handling even simple technical or mathematical subjects. General educational subjects accounted for more than 90 percent of the failing grades. The original study program included a number of courses on managerial functions, as well as a course on NOT. Members of the Academy staff wanted to increase the amount of time devoted to these subjects, but because of the difficulties trainees experienced in mastering arithmetic and introductory technical subjects, "time did not suffice."[26]

Rather than training managers in Scientific Management, a more concerted effort was made to train specialists as factory consultants. At Bekhtirev's Institute for the Study of the Brain, a series of NOT courses was conducted for factory specialists, including training in chronometry, norm-setting, and office technology. The approximately one hundred students who began this program in April 1925 were better educated and less inclined to party membership than the red directors; only a quarter were party members, and nearly four-fifths had graduated from high school, including one-fifth who had finished college.[27]

None of these programs, however, could compare with the vast training empire built by TsIT during these years. At the end of 1922 TsIT began the experimental training of workers at its Moscow laboratories. In 1923 these courses were expanded to include the training of "instructors," workers versed in TsIT's methods who would be capable of spreading them through their pedagogical and consulting activities. By the end of 1925 approximately one thousand instructors working in 108 cities had been trained. By then TsIT was experimenting with a new program intended for training not simply consultants, but future "heads of production" who would be "true social engineers for building production collectives of a new type."[28]

But the most ambitious and controversial of TsIT projects was the application of Scientific Management to the mass training of an industrial work force. Developing its own methodology based on the work of Taylor, Gilbreth, and Gantt, TsIT viewed training as the essence of rationalization. The purpose of training, Gastev believed, was the creation of "a new type of employee," one whose habits and instincts had undergone "adjustment" (*ustanovka*) to the technical requirements of machinery and tools. "We assert," he wrote, "that to reform contemporary production one must not only reform organizational processes, but also remake the contemporary human employee; we also believe that the best educator of the contemporary employee is the machine."[29] In accordance with these ideas, TsIT subjected work motions to an excruciatingly detailed analysis, divided motions into their constituent parts, determined the most rational approach for performing tasks, and then developed models that allowed skilled workers to be trained in three months.

As the Soviet economy recovered in 1924 and 1925, industry

experienced a severe shortage of skilled labor. In 1924 TsIT formed a joint-stock company (Ustanovka) to train skilled workers and provide consultation to enterprises. Ustanovka proved so successful that within a year its earnings covered its own operating costs as well as those of TsIT. In late 1925 Narkomtrud and the metalworkers union commissioned TsIT to train ten thousand metalworkers, and soon similar proposals poured in from all over the country. By the middle of 1927, with assets of over a million rubles, Ustanovka had trained more than 4100 workers employed at three hundred plants and possessed a network of eight training bases capable of training up to six thousand workers annually.[30]

This rapid expansion brought TsIT into direct conflict with the educational bureaucracy, which, jointly with the economic commissariats, operated a network of six hundred factory-workshop schools (FZU). Charged with providing workers not only with vocational training but with a general education as well, the FZU programs were infamous for their inefficiency and costliness. Industrial executives expressed doubts concerning the effectiveness of FZU production training and viewed the enterprise schools as burdens on their plants. In 1925 the three-year and four-year FZU programs were graduating twelve thousand workers a year at a cost of 1500 to 2000 rubles per student; TsIT's three-month programs, by contrast, trained workers at the same or slightly lower skill levels at a cost of only 200 rubles per student.[31]

Sensing the vulnerability of Narkompros, Gastev embarked on a campaign to seize control of labor training. In 1923 Dzerzhinskii's Commissariat of Railroads approached TsIT with the idea of using TsIT's labor-training methods at its FZU schools. Within three years 125 transport schools were using TsIT's techniques. In the summer of 1925, on the initiative of VTsSPS, an interagency commission was created under Narkomtrud to look into the matter. Arguing that "the FZU school must be regarded not as an educational issue, but as an economic one," the commission endorsed TsIT's approach. According to one observer, the conclusions of the commission "provoked a lengthy discussion," in which the trade union hierarchy, Dzerzhinskii, and Kuibyshev sided with TsIT. The result was a Central Committee decree in March 1926 that provided for the expansion of TsIT's training network and wider use of TsIT's methodology within the FZU network.[32]

A heated bureaucratic and ideological struggle for control of FZU training followed. In the summer and fall of 1926 Gastev proposed a plan for reform of the FZU school that envisaged greater control by TsIT and a revamping of the entire FZU curriculum. In a memorandum to the Sovnarkom commission established to study the issue, he argued that the FZU school was "a form of popular education suitable for the children of factory workers," but "harmful to the function of training a labor force."[33] Led by Lunacharskii and Krupskaia, Narkompros viewed Gastev's plan as an attempt by TsIT to seize full control of the FZU network, to deprive workers of the opportunity to receive an education, and to subordinate education to purely economic tasks. The struggle to prevent TsIT from encroaching on the FZU school was joined by Komsomol and VSNKh's Department for Professional-Technical Education, then headed by red director Kamenskii. Presenting the red directors' position, Kamenskii called into question the effectiveness of TsIT's training methods and accused Gastev of seeking to seize control of worker education. He argued that the FZU network could be made more effective if control over it was given to economic managers rather than TsIT. Both Komsomol and Narkompros shared the fear that Gastev would strip the FZU school of ideological and political training and would eliminate mobility opportunities for working-class youth.[34]

Gastev countered by accusing his opponents of "inciting an entire campaign against TsIT" and of harboring bureaucratic pretensions of their own toward the FZU school.[35] After a series of drawn-out deliberations, in November 1926 the investigatory commission of the Sovnarkom concluded that direction over several FZU schools should be transferred entirely to TsIT and that attempts to block the introduction of TsIT's methods should cease. Throughout this period Gastev's control over worker education steadily increased. When the First Five-Year Plan was announced in 1928, it provided for training 112,000 workers in TsIT training bases—more than a third of the projected total of new workers to be trained during the plan period.[36] But with the heightened atmosphere of class struggle that accompanied industrialization and collectivization, the issue of worker training once again became politicized, mushrooming into a political battle that decimated both sides in the controversy.

The Commissariat of Organization

Lenin's plan for reorganizing the NKRKI had aimed not only at establishing a national center for Scientific Management, but also at transforming the NKRKI into a model commissariat for the entire state apparatus, a living example of the principles of Scientific Management in action. In this spirit, among party circles of the twenties, the NKRKI was dubbed the "Commissariat of Organization." Few experiments in the history of organizational science rival the scope and magnitude of its effort to promote efficient public administration. Were a similar organization created in the American government today, it would combine the functions of numerous governmental, corporate, and private undertakings: the Office of Management and Budget, the Internal Revenue Service, the Civil Service Commission, the General Accounting Office, the Bureau of Standards, dozens of executive commissions, and hundreds of private consulting firms and teams of efficiency experts. The activities of the NKRKI cut across all institutions in the Soviet hierarchy— educational, economic, administrative, and military; in Kuibyshev's words, the expanse of NKRKI activities was "frightening."[37] Yet, paradoxically, the Commissariat of Organization quickly turned into an administrative nightmare, confirming Downs's observation that any attempt to control the activities of one large bureaucracy tends to generate the rise of another with similar distortions.[38]

Throughout the 1920s the NKRKI was subjected to a confusing whirlwind of reorganizations that epitomized its insoluble dilemma as an antibureaucratic bureaucracy. Simply from the end of 1923 to the end of 1926 the commissariat underwent seven major reorganizations. The structure that emerged from this dizzy game of bureaucratic musical chairs included three departments directly engaged in rationalization: Labor and Production, Accounting and Bookkeeping, and Administrative Technology. The Department of Labor and Production at first was charged with coordinating all NOT work at industrial enterprises, but this soon proved an overwhelming task. In practice its activities narrowed to devising research methodologies, gathering information on standardization, consulting on psychotechnics (particularly for the Red Army), and developing instructional materials on NOT for training programs. The

Accounting and Bookkeeping Department developed new accounting procedures and provided consultation to commissariats and enterprises in this area. The Department of Administrative Technology was engaged in rationalizing administrative structures, simplifying paperwork, and developing systems for managing flows of information.

From the beginning the Department of Labor and Production, under the leadership of Radus-Zenkovich, found itself in difficult straits. Not only did it suffer from an absence of skilled personnel, but its broadly defined goals prevented it from concentrating on any one task in depth. Radus-Zenkovich's close association with the enemies of TsIT left him in a precarious position within the commissariat; in 1925, when Gastev's influence was at its height, he was transferred to Belorussia to head the local NKRKI organization. Thereafter many of the functions of his department devolved upon SOVNOT, and later (after SOVNOT became inactive) upon smaller operational groups within the NKRKI. The Accounting and Bookkeeping Department, under the guidance of the former actor and Chekist P. N. Amosov, also suffered from a lack of skilled personnel; not until the latter part of the decade did it play an active role in production rationalization.[39]

The Department of Administrative Technology, headed by Elena Rozmirovich, was the most energetic and powerful of the three. The former wife of Aleksandr Troianovskii, the first Soviet ambassador to the United States, Rozmirovich had joined the Bolshevik clan in 1904 and was a trusted member of its inner core. At the outbreak of the war, she allied with Bukharin and participated in his aborted attempt to publish a new party newspaper, *Zvezda*.[40] In 1915 Rozmirovich returned from abroad, only to be arrested and exiled to Siberia. When the revolution broke out, she made her way back to Petrograd and played an active role in the Bolshevik seizure of power. After the revolution she occupied a number of posts, eventually becoming chairman of Glavpolitput', Trotsky's instrument for enforcing discipline on railroad workers. It was in this capacity that her attentions were first drawn to Scientific Management. In 1922 she joined the NKRKI and became head of its new section for administrative technology. Rozmirovich immediately surrounded herself with Taylorists, including employees from TsIT, and began to rid the NKRKI of the followers of Fayol, who, under the leadership of N. Vitke, had captured the commissariat's Bureau for Normalization. In the ideological struggles over NOT in 1923 and 1924, Rozmirovich was a firm defender of Gastev and engaged in a heated polemic with Kerzhentsev over "the basic error and practical harm" of his positions.[41]

Like Gastev, Rozmirovich was infatuated with the notion of transferring the rhythms of machine technology to processes of labor, and, in particular, to managerial labor. In the mid-twenties both she and Gastev were drawn to the assembly-line innovations of Henry Ford; both saw in Ford's coordination of highly specialized labor operations the practical realization of Taylor's dream. "Fordism," as the new production method was known, elicited a heated debate within the NOT movement not unlike that which had occurred over Taylorism. As Lenin had argued in *State and Revolution*, Rozmirovich believed that the application of assembly-line methods to managerial affairs would make possible an enormous simplification of managerial processes—eventually rendering them accessible to any literate worker. Automation and mechanization, she wrote, would reduce management to "pressing the corresponding buttons of this automated apparatus and thereby causing the automated movement of the entire managerial conveyor belt." The logical conclusion of industrialism was the full mechanization of the managerial process and the eventual elimination of administrative leadership as a special command function.[42]

In keeping with this philosophy, Rozmirovich's Department of Administrative Technology attempted to upgrade office technology, improve documentation and accounting systems, and rationalize organizational structures. In 1924 it began developing a full classification of administrative posts—work which eventually led to the creation of the first *nomenklatura* lists in the state bureaucracy.[43] But the enormous range of tasks performed by the department proved too much for its overburdened staff. Rozmirovich's response was to divide responsibility between applied and theoretical work. In January 1926, after a year of lobbying, an Institute for Managerial Technology (ITU) was created to develop methods of documentation and accounting, establish norms for managerial work, and design organizational structures. The ITU was intended to complement the other arm of Rozmirovich's department—the State Bureau for Organizational Construction (Orgstroi), which opened in December 1924 as a consulting center in the field of office technology and organizational design. Created as a joint-stock company, Orgstroi's consulting groups were headquartered in eight cities around the country.[44]

Rozmirovich's department acted as a coordinating body for agency and enterprise rationalization groups. In April 1923 VSNKh issued a circular calling for the creation of enterprise rationalization organs. In the years that followed, these divisions grew into a confusing mishmash of units—rationalization bureaus and departments, NOT bureaus and sections, experimental stations, and so on. The most common of these units was the *orgburo*. In December 1925 after a lengthy discussion on the chaotic state of enterprise rationalization, the Fourteenth Party Congress designated the orgburo as the basic unit of rationalization in Soviet industry. By the end of 1927 over 200 orgburos, 52 of which were located in Moscow, had been established. By that time Moscow's orgburos alone had carried out more than 1300 projects aimed at rationalizing paperwork, accounting procedures, and administrative staffs.[45]

Though orgburos formally were under the authority of their own enterprises, the Department of Administrative Technology acted not only as a clearing house for information on them, but also as their major defender against the encroachments of agency superiors. Rozmirovich convened frequent conferences and, beginning in December 1927, weekly meetings of orgburo members at her institute. A broad range of issues, from enterprise rationalization to the latest managerial innovations in Germany and America, were discussed at these sessions.[46]

From the viewpoint of the experts who created it, this network of institutions seemed an efficient structure for realizing the principles of Scientific Management. In reality it overlooked a basic and enduring problem in Soviet administration and in organizations in general: that the behavior of individuals cannot be "rationalized" against their will. From the beginning, relations between the NKRKI and plant managers were tense. Point One of the NKRKI Charter emphasized that the commissariat's authority in rationalization was limited to arousing interest in NOT among production executives and to rendering consultation; actual implementation of rationalization measures was left entirely in the hands of agencies and enterprises. Many managers, sensitive to any encroachment on their powers and prerogatives, were critical of the NKRKI's plans for creating NOT bureaus at plants. At the Second Conference on NOT in March 1924, a resolution was approved prohibiting the NKRKI from introducing rationalization measures against the will of plant executives.[47] A year and a half later, at the First All-Union Conference on Rationalization, N. V. Arkhangel'skii, director of the Moscow Club for Red Directors, warned that measures "worked out by a special organ for rationalization can be put into practice only by a decision of plant management and the directing board of a trust," and "in no instance can be dictated from outside."[48]

The desire of plant executives to protect their authority from outside encroachment left the NKRKI with no powers of enforcement. At most, it was capable of compelling recalcitrant managers to explain their actions; but except for persuasion, it possessed no administrative or financial incentives to ensure that factory executives would pay attention to rationalization. Constant foot-dragging by plant management frequently led local NKRKI organs to try to impose rationalization over the heads of managers. As early as October 1923, NKRKI officials were incensed at "the scabs of routine, stagnation, and inertia" in the attitudes of managers toward NOT. At a conference five months later rationalizers complained that enterprise directors were frustrating attempts to apply NOT at their plants and were protected in this by provincial party authorities, who controlled the hiring and firing of local NKRKI personnel. A number of NKRKI executives lobbied for the centralization of appointments in the commissariat, but this was rejected by Kuibyshev as interference in local party affairs.[49] Throughout the 1920s, before centralized direction of industry had been fully consolidated in Soviet Russia and when some industries were being given great latitude in decision-making, the organizational environment of Soviet administration contained strong disincentives for administrators to take rationalization seriously and led to constant friction between efficiency experts and managers.

Nowhere was this more evident than in the treatment accorded the orgburo and other enterprise rationalization groups by plant executives. In 1925, only a year after the first orgburos appeared, rationalizers complained about "the insufficient recognition of the need for permanent work on rationalization and almost a complete lack of information on the character and significance of the work of orgburos on the part of administration." Three years later Rozmirovich observed that "executives of agencies and economic organs often are indifferent to the organization of an orgburo in their institutions, do not render proper support" to them, and "fail to help them overcome bureaucratic inertia." This could be explained, she wrote, "by the fact that rationalization measures in the majority of cases touch upon the habits and interests of employees who often have a direct material stake in preserving the existing situation." As a result, "the opinion that a permanent organ for rationalization is unnecessary is still very widespread among managers and administrators."[50]

Examples of the antagonism between orgburos and enterprise executives abound in the press and specialized literature of the time. A director of one large enterprise ordered the orgburo at his plant to cease all chronometrical activity, since, in his words, "this is not TsIT here, and all that work is quackery in any case." Enterprise directors closed down orgburos in their plants, supposedly in the name of cutting costs and "rationalizing" production. At a conference on rationalization in early 1928, speakers noted "the abnormal fact that in conducting the campaign for a regime of economy, the first to be cut back on are the rationalization organs." In many instances, orgburos were loaded down with paperwork to keep rationalizers from poking their noses into plant affairs. In other plants, the factory director would select the least promising and least capable personnel to staff the orgburo as a way of ensuring that the unit would be weak.[51]

The efficiency experts were not feared by management alone. As one report noted in 1927, "the broad mass of employees relate to orgburos either indifferently or with fear, as a 'cutter of staffs.' " Specialists treated the rationalizers "either sarcastically or with outright hostility," particularly in those cases "when the orgburo . . . uncovers mistakes by specialists in work organization and technology." Despite attempts by Rozmirovich to mobilize party support behind orgburos, in general they remained dangerously isolated from party organizations. In the Ukraine, for instance, only 9 percent of orgburo members belonged to the party. In most cases, although plant party cells were sympathetic to their goals, party officials refused to render aid to orgburos and were caught in the crossfire between managers and rationalizers. Even the local party apparatus at times viewed the orgburo as a "competitor and a parasite, capable only of pronouncing foreign words." As one report noted, "the *instruktor* of an *orgotdel* or *inspektor,* having visited an outlying organ and suggested that 'such-and-such a shortcoming be eliminated,' believes that he too is engaged in 'rationalization,' and that therefore the orgburo is a parasite, totally unnecessary in the institution."[52]

The case of a certain engineer Vadetskii, head of the orgburo at the Stalin Metallurgical Plant in the Donbass, illustrates the extremes to which these antagonisms could sometimes go. Before arriving in the Donbass, Vadetskii had worked for eleven years in America, where he became an ardent follower of Scientific Management. His tireless efforts to uncover instances of mismanagement and waste at the Stalin plant aroused the ire of senior management and the hatred of the entire factory. He and his staff were locked out of the plant's shops, were ostracized and shunned throughout the enterprise, and were "terrorized" with physical threats. Accused by management of having "washed our dirty linen in public," Vadetskii was removed from his post and transferred to a low-paying position; he subsequently became ill and committed suicide—the victim of a lost war for efficiency.[53]

In response to abuses such as these, in August 1928 the NKRKI and VTsSPS issued a joint statute aimed at upgrading the role of the orgburo. It attempted to define the orgburo's legal position, declared its right of inspection, and outlined its conditions of work. A special fund was created in enterprises for encouraging rationalization measures. Soon afterwards, VSNKh decreed that all trusts and large enterprises were obliged to establish orgburos. None of these documents, however, gave precise instructions regarding the structure of orgburos, their volume of work, the training their personnel should receive, or the funds to be allocated to them. More important, the decrees were greeted with skepticism by plant managers, who complained that they would let loose "dozens and hundreds of people who have become acquainted with matters [of rationalization] for the first time 'on a shock-worker basis' [and who] will carve anew the managerial structures of the enterprise based only on their common sense or, in the best of circumstances, their study of the literature on the issue."[54] In the end, the documents gave little relief to the embattled rationalizers.

During the twenties, in part because of friction with economic organs, the NKRKI withdrew from direct interference in plant rationalization and confined its activities to observation, research, and consulting work.[55] This reorientation accelerated when Ordzhonikidze assumed leadership of the commissariat. But even in the performance of these more limited functions, the NKRKI confronted enormous obstacles. By the late twenties, efforts to contain the growth of Soviet administrative staffs already had a long and sordid history. As early as 1921 TsIK had ordered slashes in managerial staffs; but when the NKRKI investigated the matter in April 1922, it discovered that "not only has a significant cutback in staffs not occurred, but there is every reason to assert that the opposite is true." After its 1923 reorganization the NKRKI devoted considerable attention to cutting excessive staffs—a task once described by Kuibyshev as "the rude axing of protruding boughs."[56] Kuibyshev's axe, however, was a blunt instrument. Although the NKRKI supposedly achieved cutbacks of 28 percent during 1923 and 1924, later studies revealed that this was largely the result of reclassifying personnel and that throughout these years managerial staffs had actually grown instead of declining.

A report to Ordzhonikidze in November 1926 on the efforts of the Department of Administrative Technology to keep track of the growth of staffs complained that the department had only four people engaged in this task; "naturally," the report concluded, "there could be no serious . . . checking of the requirements of agencies under these conditions." Rozmirovich's department analyzed the staffs of ten state institutions and recommended total cuts of 13.4 percent in administrative personnel. A subsequent report observed that "very quickly, a number of objections against the cuts began pouring in" from executives. Eventually the targets were revised downward. By the beginning of 1927, despite the campaign to cut staffs, the number of office workers in the Soviet Union had actually increased by more than forty-three thousand. As Ordzhonikidze complained at the time, "dozens of commissions were formed and staffs were cut, but after a new count it turned out almost every time that staffs had increased."[57]

These and other instances of managerial resistance led the Department of Administrative Technology to look to the West, in particular to the German model of functional management, as a way of reducing staffs through the reorganization of the entire bureaucracy. The idea was to eliminate several levels of management by introducing semi-independent functional departments (in German, *dezernats*). This system had already been tested, with Dzerzhinskii's approval, in the Commissariat of Railroads. But it had encountered strong managerial resistance, particularly from heads of trusts, who, in trying to protect their powers, complained that the idea contradicted the principle of one-man management laid down by Lenin.[58] A number of Rozmirovich's ideas found their way into measures adopted by TsIK and the Sovnarkom in June 1927 for reorganizing industry. This reform, based on a report by Ordzhonikidze and supported by Kuibyshev, sought to squeeze trusts by decentralizing operational and functional authority to the enterprise level. At the same time, central direction over the activities of trusts was strengthened. But two years later, when the NKRKI checked into the situation, it found that the reform remained largely on paper, having been successfully resisted by trusts in a large number of cases.[59]

The NKRKI hardly fared better in its efforts to simplify paperwork and documentation procedures. Beginning in 1924 it developed a number of innovations in this area: substituting card systems of documentation (then popular in the West) for the old register system that prevailed in Russian administration; reducing the number of signatures required on documents; devising uniform systems of paperwork; introducing labor-saving office technology; and reorganizing communications systems within and between departments. In a number of cases these measures had a perceptible impact.[60] Yet, judging from the statements of Soviet leaders, excessive paperwork and incoherent documentation grew at an exponential rate throughout this period and remained an acute problem. In May 1926 Dzerzhinskii proclaimed: "I participated in the suppression of counterrevolution; I helped to restore transport. But I am powerless against this flow of paper. I am trying all the time to cut back on paperwork, but the more I push, the more it swells."[61] In December of that same year, Ordzhonikidze related the case of the Moscow Broadcloth Plant, whose report to VSNKh on its activities consisted of thirteen thick volumes costing a total of 1.3 million rubles—three times what the prerevolutionary owners of the plant had spent on record keeping. "It's bad enough," he said, "that these people write, make fools of themselves, grow stupid, and don't even understand what they are writing, but even we are not in a position to find out what is written in them . . . We beat Denikin, Yudenich, Wrangel', and every other counterrevolutionary scoundrel, but we are slowly drowning in paperwork."[62]

A study conducted by Amosov's department in 1925 found existing accounting procedures in Soviet administration to be chaotic, expensive, and of little use to anyone. New procedures developed by the department and adopted by the Sovnarkom in 1924 were ignored in favor of agency accounting systems. More drastic measures were introduced in April 1927. Although these reforms resulted in reductions in paperwork, Soviet historians later observed that many officials, fearing that improved procedures would lead to staff cuts, and "guided by a false understanding of agency interests," sabotaged the measures by "covering up the possibilities for simplifying accounting forms and presenting false information about the state of cutting back on accounting."[63]

In December 1925 the Fourteenth Party Congress warned against the danger that "the worst elements of our bureaucratic apparatus, covering themselves with the camouflage of rationalization work," would "discredit the very idea of rationalization." By the end of 1926 a report to Ordzhonikidze on the state of the NKRKI's rationalization efforts admitted that "the employees [of the NKRKI] who are now fulfilling this work have already grown accustomed to behaving toward it in a bureaucratic way [*pochinovnich'i*]."[64] The same problems continued to appear in the NKRKI's work throughout the twenties. In 1921 and 1922 a concerted effort was made to control the excessive proliferation of interagency commissions. Two years later Kuibyshev put forth a similar proposal: that the number of interagency commissions be slashed by 40 percent. In 1926 another NKRKI study pointed out that 40 percent of interagency commissions could be eliminated. All this time the very agency that was proposing cuts in interagency commissions was itself demonstrating "a passion for numerous commissions"; contemporary Soviet historians consider this to have been one of the NKRKI's "major mistakes."[65]

Kuibyshev found running the NKRKI's rationalization efforts so frustrating that he pleaded to be transferred to another post, referring to the NKRKI as "that madhouse."[66] His successor, judging from his speeches, found the task no less difficult. By 1928 signs of disillusionment with the rationalization movement were rampant inside and outside the NKRKI, expressed not only in the large number of critical articles that appeared in the press but also in a drop in interest in rationalization generally.[67] By this time it was clear that the forces of organization within the Commissariat of Organization had suffered heavy losses and were already in retreat.

The Bureaucratic Economy

In their scope and reach, Soviet attempts in the 1920s to infuse administration with the principles and methods of Scientific Management far surpassed any of the concurrent efforts directed by Western governments. Rationalizing education, combating excessive lines at stores, improving the sorting of mail, reorganizing the harvesting of potatoes, and even curing syphilis were all subjects of experimentation and research conducted by Scientific Management enthusiasts at state expense. One report of early 1925 observed that "at present there exists no branch of state activity which the principles of NOT have not penetrated." A survey conducted by the NKRKI found that, of 119 Moscow institutions questioned, 72 percent were conducting some kind of rationalization work and 67 percent of these were maintaining constant contact with one of the centers of Scientific Management research.[68]

Even politically sensitive areas felt the impact of the organizational charts and stopwatches of the NOTisty. Shortly after the NKRKI's reorganization, E. M. Yaroslavskii sent a note to Kuibyshev calling for the organization of a NOT brigade to rationalize the work of the party collegium of the Central Control Commission. Kuibyshev consented and asked Rozmirovich to supply the personnel. In October 1924 the Tatar *obkom* officially commissioned Burdianskii and his institute to engage in research on record keeping and paperwork in the regional party organization. Whether party administration was successfully rationalized in these cases is not known; Kerzhentsev noted the existence of "an extreme skepticism toward NOT in the ranks of our party," a sentiment which, he said, was "far from dead" in 1925.[69] There is no reason to believe that efforts to rationalize party administration did not encounter the same problems, patterns of resistance, and ideological controversies that were exhibited in the state bureaucracy.

The military also played a prominent role in the early NOT movement. Defense applications of Scientific Management drew support from top-level military commanders, including Trotsky, Frunze, and Tukhachevskii. Enthusiasts of Scientific Management in the military participated extensively in the work of SOVNOT and even organized a special military center under SOVNOT in 1925. In addition to the work conducted by military rationalization organs, a large number of civilian NOT research institutes engaged in military research on a contract basis. In 1922 the Psychotechnical Laboratory of TsIT established close ties with the Moscow Aviation School in designing aptitude tests for would-be military pilots. In the late 1920s this cooperation expanded as groups of military instructors were trained by TsIT. Similarly, Rozmirovich's institute conducted extensive rationalization work in the military and provided consultation on documentation and accounting systems.[70]

Despite Russian backwardness, Scientific Management penetrated the provinces to an extraordinary degree: the old Russian settlements of Kaluga, Vologda, and Voronezh; the Caucasian cities of Vladikavkaz, Tiflis, and Baku; the Central Asian towns of Tashkent, Kokand, and Kizil-Arbat; and such Siberian outposts as Tiumen, Chita, Tomsk, and Omsk. In view of the level of development of these regions, the movement frequently bore a superficial character. As a representative of the Siberian NKRKI observed in February 1924, "We have such places, for example, as Oirotia and the Buriat-Mongolian Republic, where there are absolutely no skilled people, and yet it is suggested that they be concerned with NOT."[71]

The results reaped from all this effort were disappointingly meager. It is true that many enterprises reported large ruble savings from NOT.[72] TsIT estimated that its labor-training methods saved the state four million rubles over several years. The Ukrainian division of Orgstroi reported savings of three hundred thousand rubles in 1928. That same year Rozmirovich proudly recited that five orgburos alone had reaped annual savings of 3.5 million rubles.[73]

But there are reasons to approach these figures with skepticism. For one thing, no commonly accepted methodology existed for measuring the savings accrued from rationalization. Those who attempted to develop such a methodology at the end of 1925 frankly admitted that measuring the effects of rationalization "is extremely difficult, and sometimes simply impossible, because it requires continuous and thorough observations for which the rationalizer does not have time." In most cases crude estimates of potential rather than actual savings were made by the rationalizers themselves, who obviously had an interest in presenting the rosier side of their activities.[74] National statistics on productivity and rationalization collected by TsSU and VSNKh were the laughing stock of the party. TsSU claimed that by the early twenties industrial productivity had exceeded prewar levels while wages lagged behind. VSNKh asserted the opposite: that wages had grown more quickly than industry had recovered. On various occasions, Dzerzhinskii called the statistics collected by both agencies "a joke," "nonsense," and "black magic."[75]

Considerable evidence exists of the widespread falsification of rationalization figures by the economic bureaucracy, particularly toward the end of the decade when pressure from above to cut costs was increasing. At the Seventh Congress of Trade Unions in December 1926 Ordzhonikidze complained that "some are trying to conduct a regime of economy on account of a single electric light bulb unscrewed somewhere in the corridor, or in the places where workers wash, or they are trying to conduct it on the basis of cutting back on one night watchman or messenger." He admitted that "even more serious perversions" than these had taken place. In a conversation with one manager he was told: "Do you really think we actually give correct information? Not at all. We maintain a special staff of five or six people in order to lie our way around [*otbrekhat'sia*] all those demands that you present to us."[76]

The most convincing evidence of the inefficacy of NOT comes from those who were directly responsible for its application: managers and management experts. What stands out in their testimony is the extent to which the organizational environment of Soviet administration was profoundly inimical to rationalization. In the 1920s the activities of enterprises were largely an extension of their trusts, and under the prevailing conditions of a mixed economy the motivations of trusts varied considerably. Some trusts worked on a loosely defined profit motive, buying and selling on a regulated market. But even here the profit motive was subject to frequent interference from above. In 1925 Dzerzhinskii complained about the planning agencies' standard practice of lowering the prices of goods produced by any enterprise that managed to achieve a profit.[77] Under such circumstances, even those enterprises that enjoyed greater autonomy had little incentive to operate efficiently. Other trusts acted as little more than extensions of VSNKh; they maximized plan targets in output units in a fashion that differed little from later Soviet practice. And since plan targets were often set chaotically during these years and frequently reached enterprises only toward the end of the planning year, many trusts lacked any operational guidelines whatsoever.

Beginning in 1925 a gradual centralization of control over economic activity took place in conjunction with the industrialization drive and the regime's fears that market activity would eventually overwhelm the state sector. Hefty taxes were imposed on private entrepreneurs, and the markets that remained came under increasing central regulation. Within state industry systematic central control over the production and distribution of goods accelerated, and by 1927 the party announced its intention to create a nationwide economic plan that would integrate the development of all branches of industry.[78]

As a result, any incentive that might have existed for rationalization was gradually suffocated. Even earlier the NOTisty had earned the reputation, perhaps deservedly, of engaging in sky-high theorizing that had little to do with actual production problems. Kuibyshev chastised NOT enthusiasts for describing their work in "dry, bureaucratic language, frozen with foreign words."[79] In the view of many practitioners, the NOTisty searched for cure-alls for the problems of the economy and ignored the specifics of production situations. No single system of rationalization methods, managers correctly pointed out, could possibly apply in all circumstances, since "a system which might give brilliant results at one plant could seriously undermine the situation in another."[80]

Over the course of the decade relations between rationalizers and managers deteriorated further. Early in 1926 one NOT enthusiast felt it necessary to respond to charges that "one encounters the scum of officialdom [*nakip' chinovnichestva*] and the manners of bureaucratic pen pushers among NOT employees." In early 1928 at a Moscow conference on rationalization, Ordzhonikidze decried the poor relations between rationalizers and managers and argued for finding "a common language." Nevertheless, the relationship continued to be marred by tensions. One shop head at the Stalin

Metallurgical Plant, describing rationalization efforts at his plant, observed: "We've been working here for thirty years without rationalization, and we will work here thirty more without it; all this is a kind of fad." Another shop head commented: "If it were my decision, I'd chase all of you rationalizers out of our factory with a dirty broom."[81]

The rationalizers found their work no less frustrating. Reports to the NKRKI on NOT work habitually noted "a great apathy" on the part of enterprise executives and local leaders toward rationalization. This skepticism often resulted in difficult working conditions. In their dealings with the Kazan Institute, factory managers insisted that the institute not be paid a single kopeck unless it could prove that its innovations were having a positive effect, thus placing the institute in difficult financial straits. Some rationalizers were fired from their jobs and taken to court by plant directors for failing to deliver their promised improvements in production.[82]

Even more dangerous than the risks of failure were the perils of success. Like his cousins in the West, the Soviet rationalizer was the most hated man in industry; he was the target of hostility, scorn, and physical threats. As one newspaper account bluntly put it, "Rationalizers and employees of technical norm-setting bureaus, as a general rule, are the least respected personnel at enterprises."[83] Victor Kravchenko, a Soviet manager who defected to the West during the war, described how he, as a young rationalizer in the late 1920s, "won myself a good many powerful enemies" by his rationalization efforts. The animosity of those he criticized "in some instances pursued me for years."[84]

In 1927 Gastev wrote of "the tragic despair of the rationalizer." "Even in those cases when his work results in a certain organizational victory," Gastev observed, "the rationalizer encounters enormous opposition." "He is opposed by the director; he is opposed by the chief engineer; to a large degree he is opposed by the foreman; he clashes with the opposition of the workers; in addition, he is hindered by endless conferences." Conflict between the rationalizer and the factory director was "inevitable," for "at the rationalizer's every step, the manager expects criticism and an insult to his pride"; any criticism was considered by the director as "an encroachment on his personal freedom" and "an exposure of the intimate and personal aspects" of his work. Gastev noted that plant directors were inclined to oppose rationalization even "when they themselves are its initiators." "If the cause of rationalization is supported by the trust . . . then the plant administration often struggles with this trust as if it were an enemy."

Gastev called the idea that workers oppose rationalization only under capitalism "an unjustified lie." Even in Soviet Russia, "if one approaches a worker with a chronometer or any other kind of apparatus measuring the speed of work, the instinct of defense is absolutely inevitable."[85] Newspaper reports occasionally noted that "in the shop one often hears disapproving remarks by workers concerning one or another of the measures of Scientific Management adopted for improving production." Although the Soviets attempted to mobilize workers in favor of rationalization by setting up economic commissions and production conferences at plants, a survey in 1926 found that only a small percentage of workers (10 percent) ever participated in these voluntary units.[86]

By the late 1920s the workers' instinctive distrust of rationalization took on more violent manifestations. Workers tossed bricks at rationalizers employing chronometry and evicted them from their plants. In the Donbass, miners threw lumber down the shafts as a form of protest against rationalization, even though lumber was in short supply at the time. An attempt to introduce Taylor's system of functional foremen at a glue plant in 1928 (an innovation expected to save a quarter of a million rubles) resulted in production sabotage by workers and lower-level managerial personnel. That same year the decision to close a factory in Vladimir province as part of rationalization efforts touched off a violent occupation of the plant by three hundred workers, who beat up the plant director and clashed with the police. By then it was clear that what one newspaper called "a serious antirationalization mood" was sweeping the country.[87]

The NOTisty undoubtedly had some success in improving the operations of particular organizations. Due in part to their efforts, industry recovered to its prewar levels by the end of 1926. But all too often the effects of their innovations were either temporary or were quickly overwhelmed by other serious defects of Soviet administration. As one newspaper report on rationalization concluded in 1928, "The achievements of rationalizing one factor of production are swallowed by the minuses of another factor." A survey of rationalization in RSFSR commissariats made at the end of 1929 observed that "as before, people seem to swarm and something appears to get done, but everything remains on paper, and the force of paper in these narkomaty is truly great."[88]

The persistence of low productivity, red tape, bloated staffs, and excessive paperwork was hardly the fault of the NOTisty. It was endemic to a broader system of bureaucratic management which defied remedy. When Kuibyshev transferred from the NKRKI to VSNKh in 1926, he convened a meeting of industrial executives to explore why rationalization efforts were not yielding the expected results. "What's wrong?" he asked them. "Why is there such inertia on the part of managers in using new discoveries and rationalizing proposals?" According to Kuibyshev's biographers, "the managers themselves suggested the answer. Many of them in frank conversations candidly admitted: 'With this rationalization there is such red tape and drawn-out proceedings that one has to ram one's head through all of the obstacles! If one seriously occupies oneself with it, then no time will be left for the fulfillment of production programs.' "[89] Ordzhonikidze's explanation in December 1926 for the unchecked growth of administrative staffs was that it was bound up with "the very nature of our system, our organization, and the work which we conduct in our institutions."[90] Paradoxically, Ordzhonikidze was very much a part of that system. In July 1927 he pushed through a resolution prohibiting agencies and enterprises from using any savings that might accrue from rationalization. Instead, these funds were to be transferred to the central government for financing industrialization.[91] Ordzhonikidze's action was indicative of a profound misunderstanding of organizational processes; it eliminated one of the few incentives for managers to engage in rationalization. Yet, it was very much in keeping with the entire spirit that had guided Bolshevik economic policy for the preceding decade and that had called a bureaucratic economy into being.

3

. . . . . .

Stalinism as Antibureaucracy

The struggle against bureaucracy is the most important sector on the front of class struggle.

—*Resolutions of the Sixteenth Party Congress, June 1930*

Stalin once described 1929 as "the year of the great break [*god velikogo periloma*]."[1] It was then that full-scale collectivization was begun, industrial plan targets were raised to impossible levels, a campaign unfolded to impose discipline upon the work force, new controls were placed on specialists and administrators, and a broad-ranging purge was unleashed in the industrial hierarchy. "Class warfare" was waged against "capitalist elements" in the city and the countryside, and "cultural revolution" was declared in education and the arts. Subversive "wrecking groups" composed of specialists from the old regime were accused of sabotaging industry in the service of foreign enemies. And Stalin's personal predominance over the Soviet system was affirmed, as his last major rivals were evicted from the leadership.

Although the frictions between Soviet rationalizers, on the one hand, and ideologues, administrators, and workers, on the other, were not a direct cause of the violence unleashed by Stalin at the end of the 1920s, they did contribute in several ways to the political, social, and economic atmosphere that made Stalinism a viable alternative in Soviet Russia. In view of the tension and even violence that plagued the relationship between the rationalization movement and nearly all sectors of industry—managers, specialists, and workers—it was hardly a coincidence that members of the Scientific Management movement were prominently represented among the thousands of specialists accused of wrecking activities in the late 1920s and early 1930s. The atmosphere of resentment and mistrust toward rationalizers that ran throughout the industrial hierarchy flowed easily into specialist-baiting and the perpetration of witch hunts.

This potentially explosive situation coexisted with considerable dissatisfaction within the political elite over industrial performance and the pace of economic development. The inability of industry to meet consumer demand led in 1928 to a "goods famine." Not only did consumers have to wait in long lines to purchase the simplest items, but peasants, with no goods to buy for their money, withheld grain from the market, eventually giving rise to more forceful methods of grain requisitioning. Although most sectors of industry had recovered to prewar levels by the end of 1926, production of some heavy industrial goods continued to lag. In 1927 industry as a whole experienced a growth slump—a source of anxiety to those in the Bolshevik movement who favored rapid development. The tone of party pronouncements increasingly shifted away from rationalization toward taking the economy by force.

Finally, party leaders showed increasing frustration and impatience with the bureaucratic diseases of the Soviet state and with the powerlessness of established means for dealing with them. Peter Blau has observed that "an unenforced rule that is regularly violated extends the discretionary power of superiors, because it furnishes them with occasions to use legitimate sanctions whenever they see fit."[2] Despite massive rationalization efforts, the campaign for a regime of economy, and the continual exhortations of politicians, bureaucratic disorders proliferated with alarming speed throughout the 1920s. As new goals of rapid industrialization were imposed upon the administrative apparatus, the gulf between administrative aspirations and performance became a major source of concern to the regime. The blame for this situation and for the continuing bureaucratic morass was placed upon three groups: kulaks, wreckers, and bureaucrats.

Stalinism was in many ways a deeply antibureaucratic movement; it drew much of its strength from its incessant attacks upon the *chinovnik* (the bureaucrat), whose ubiquitous presence and vulnerability made him an inviting target for political rabble-rousing. In this respect, Trotsky's interpretation of Stalinism as the victory of the clerk was mistaken, for although Stalinism, like Leninism, was bureaucratic in form, it was essentially antibureaucratic in content, particularly if one accepts Weber's classic definition of bureaucracy as the application of knowledge to organizational affairs. This is not to say that Stalin's rule did not result in an enormous growth of bureaucratic institutions and patterns of behavior, nor that Stalin's opponents were sympathetic to the perpetrators of red tape and pen pushing. Indeed, a large number of specialists within the rationalization movement suffered for their close association with the Right Opposition and its platform of balanced, gradual growth. But much of the broader appeal of Stalinism in the late 1920s lay in its frontal assault on bureaucratic stagnation in Soviet economic and political life and in its harnessing of the social and ideological tensions that large-scale bureaucratic organization had fostered.

Among those who supported Stalin's bid for power were the two politicians most intimately connected with the rationalization movement: Kuibyshev and Ordzhonikidze. These men viewed NOT as an integral part of Stalin's industrializing revolution; they consistently promoted the cause of rationalizers and protected them against the vicissitudes of politics. By contrast, others within the Stalin camp, including Stalin himself, have been described by Moshe Lewin as "violently antibureaucratic,"[3] perhaps bordering on what Victor Thompson called "bureautic." Thompson described such a personality syndrome in the following way:

> To them bureaucracy is a curse. They see no good in it whatsoever, but view the demands of modern organization as "red tape" . . . Bureautics fear the world beyond, the nonpersonalized world, and they fear bureaucracy because they cannot personalize it. They feel powerless in relation to it, on the "outside" . . . To him [the bureautic] the organization is a great battleground between his friends and him, on the one side, and "the rest," his enemies, on the other.[4]

Much of industrial politics in the years preceding the Great Purge can be understood as a conflict between these different approaches to bureaucracy within Stalin's own entourage—a conflict which, by the mid-thirties, led to the victory of the partisans of coercion over the partisans of rationalization.

The use of coercion as an instrument against bureaucratic distortions was not Stalin's invention. Lenin had sought on several occasions to intimidate recalcitrant officials by threatening to try them for their organizational "crimes," and Trotsky had proposed a violent program to militarize labor. But the ruthless use of violence and intimidation by Stalin and some of his associates in the name of rooting out bureaucratic sabotage and conservatism was conducted on a qualitatively different scale: as part of a coordinated, sustained disciplinary strategy that evoked a popular response among sectors of the population. To be sure, Stalin's program of imposing discipline on industry and eliminating imaginary wreckers and saboteurs was self-serving, for it justified the imposition of greater controls on society and the concentration of power in his hands. Yet, this self-serving lust for power found fertile soil within the communist party and within Soviet society at the end of the twenties—an appeal that cannot be explained by reference to Stalin's personality and political craft alone.

Wreckers and Rationalizers

In March 1928 the Soviet press announced the discovery of a "counterrevolutionary wrecking organization" of engineers in the town of Shakhty. The Shakhty affair, as the case was known, quickly spread beyond the small mining town of the Northern Caucasus, as similar wrecking groups were uncovered throughout the Donbass. From May to July, fifty-three of the accused were publicly tried on charges of purposely installing improper ventilation and timbering in mine shafts, buying unnecessary equipment from abroad, organizing accidents in mines, and consciously damaging machinery over a period of six years. The alleged aims of the conspiracy were to lower worker productivity, fan worker discontent, and prepare the way for foreign intervention and a restoration of capitalism. After torture, sixteen confessed their guilt. Four were acquitted, eleven were sentenced to death, and thirty-eight received sentences ranging from one to ten years.[5]

A Central Committee resolution passed in April, before the trial opened, faulted party organizations, managers, and trade unions for lack of vigilance against class enemies. Wrecking activity, it said, was possible because managers lacked the knowledge necessary for managing their enterprises in depth and limited themselves purely to "general leadership." "Perversions in the system of management," the resolution added, "undoubtedly aided the long impunity of the counterrevolutionary wreckers." A second resolution approved by the Central Committee in July shortly after the trial noted that "alongside the overwhelming mass of specialists who are working conscientiously, there remain those, particularly among the more privileged elements in the past, who are directly conducting sabotage and wrecking socialist industrialization"—a fact which "all the more sharply puts before us the problem of training new cadres of red specialists for industry and transport."[6]

The Shakhty trial was the opening shot of what has been called Stalin's "revolution from above,"[7] a massive upheaval that would eventually affect all aspects of Soviet life, convulsing the factory no less than the village. In October 1928 the First Five-Year Plan was launched, setting incredibly ambitious targets for industry, targets far above those suggested by the most optimistic economists. Even these targets were repeatedly pushed upward until finally, in December 1929, Stalin ordered that the five-year plan be fulfilled in four years. The frontal assault on specialists unleashed by the regime, with its accusations of industrial wrecking and sabotage, was intended not only to deflect the population from the hardships of breakneck industrial expansion, but also to justify training new specialists committed to the Bolshevik cause and to rationalize the need for "vigilance" and increased regimentation. During the three years of witch-hunt and violence that followed the Shakhty affair, an estimated two to seven thousand of the country's thirty-five thousand engineers were arrested.[8] The terror was by no means confined to the engineering community; a large number of specialists in other professions, particularly economists, planners, and managers, were swept up as well.

Precisely how many of those arrested were connected with the rationalization movement is unclear. But if one judges according to well-publicized cases, the proportion was significant. The rationalization movement was dominated by nonparty, white-collar specialists. A 1928 survey of employees of rationalization organs in the

Ukraine showed that more than 90 percent did not belong to the party and approximately half had a higher education. A similar survey conducted in the RSFSR showed that almost three-fourths were of white-collar origin, with approximately the same percentage being nonparty.[9] Given their overwhelmingly educated, white-collar, nonparty profile, rationalizers were likely to come under suspicion as potential saboteurs at a time when the relationship between specialists and the regime was breaking down. Moreover, much of the spirit of the rationalization movement ran counter to the notion of growth at any cost that had come to dominate economic decision-making. Believing above all in a well-ordered economy rather than in storming tactics and shock brigades, rationalizers were drawn instinctively to the positions of the Right Opposition. In his "Notes of an Economist," Bukharin argued that rather than forcing the pace of industrial development and inflating capital investments, it would be better to "take decisive measures providing for a greater effectiveness of construction, greater productivity in all our production units, and much greater productivity of those new enterprises which are entering into the production process—effectiveness and productivity that seriously exceed current demands in this field."[10] It is hard to imagine that those seriously engaged in these tasks would think otherwise.

But the rationalization movement made an inviting target for other reasons as well. There was widespread dissatisfaction within the party over the lackluster results of rationalization during the previous five years. The continued presence, and even growth, of bureaucratic diseases raised questions about the effectiveness of rationalization methods for dealing with the problem. Considering that, in the bureaucratic environment of Soviet administration in the late twenties, rationalization efforts quite often failed to deliver results, it is not difficult to see how the line between legitimate rationalization and industrial sabotage could be blurred, particularly when someone was intent on blurring it. That rationalizers had already come under suspicion for importing techniques and theories that were alien to socialism helped fuel such accusations.

Animosity toward rationalizers had mounted within the industrial hierarchy in the years preceding industrialization. As production pressures on plants intensified during the industrialization drive, relations between rationalizers and industry deteriorated further.

The spontaneous specialist-baiting and violence against specialists that engulfed the country after the Shakhty affair were frequently perpetrated against those most actively involved in rationalization activities, for it was these engineers and specialists who were most resented by workers and managers. As one newspaper report, after listing a large number of cases of violence against rationalizers, admitted in February 1929: "It is a small step from a hostile attitude toward the practical workers for rationalization to violence against them . . . The rather numerous incidents of violence against specialists in the past two to three months have arisen, to a significant degree, on the basis of production rationalization."[11]

Almost immediately after the Shakhty trial, a wave of arrests hit the engineering community. New wrecking organizations were uncovered in the coal, shipbuilding, textile, machine-building, oil, rubber, and chemical industries, as well as in military production, transport, and supply agencies.[12] Among those arrested were a large number of prerevolutionary Taylorists. Nicholas von Meck, former owner of the Moscow-Kazan Railroad, had been active in introducing Taylorist techniques to the Tsarist railroad system on the eve of the war. After the revolution he had been protected by Krasin and made a consultant to the Commissariat of Railroads. When the OGPU arrested him and a number of his former employees in the fall of 1928, it hoped to stage an even more spectacular show-trial than the Shakhty case. It accused von Meck, who had advised the commissariat to increase the size of freight trains without concern for the heavier load, of seeking to wear out locomotives and railroad beds, thereby leaving the country without sufficient transport in the event of foreign intervention. (Several years later, when Kaganovich would introduce the same innovations, scores of engineers would be shot for opposing double and triple loads.) The OGPU charged that von Meck's wrecking activities were part of a broader conspiracy to restore capitalism led by former industrial owners, including, besides von Meck, Petr Pal'-chinskii, a prominent mining engineer and consultant to Gosplan, and A. F. Velichko, a military engineer. Pal'chinskii had been deputy chairman of the War Industries Committee during World War I, an outpost of Taylorist sentiment, and Velichko had been in charge of military transport during the war. All three men died in OGPU custody without having confessed their guilt.[13]

Swept up with Velichko were several other military engineers who had led the effort to apply Taylorism in the Red Army. V. A. Dyman, a former Tsarist general, had been active in the introduction of Taylorist methods into artillery production during the war. After the revolution, under Trotsky's policy of utilizing Tsarist military talent, he had become chairman of the Technical Commission of the Main Administration for Military Industry. Dyman and his colleagues, Vysochanskii and Prozorov, had formed the core of Taylorist specialists in military production in the early twenties. In 1924, on Gastev's suggestion, both Dyman and Vysochanskii were appointed members of SOVNOT; Dyman was even elected a member of SOVNOT's ruling Presidium. At that time Gastev had praised both men for their "completely unparalleled experience in mass military production." Nevertheless, Dyman and Vysochanskii were arrested in 1929, accused of "conducting systematic work toward undermining the defense capabilities of the country," and shot.[14]

Pal'chinskii died in OGPU custody, but was posthumously appointed the founder of a new wrecking group—the Industrial Party. In a new show-trial held late in 1930, eight engineers and managers were forced to confess to accusations of planning the overthrow of Soviet power.[15] All of the accused were prominent engineers from the old regime. Many had displayed sympathies for the positions of the Right Opposition. And rationalizers were conspicuously represented among them. N. F. Charnovskii was one of the most highly respected Taylorists of Tsarist and Soviet Russia. Before the revolution he had been the first to introduce courses on Taylorism into the Moscow Technical Institute, publishing the first textbook on Scientific Management in Russia. Charnovskii was a follower of the Pole Karol Adamiecki and an admirer of Taylor and Ford. In the early twenties he had been a voting member of the directing board of TsIT, which had published one of his books on management in 1921. In 1927 another of his books was published by Orgametall, a rationalization unit with close ties to Rozmirovich. In 1930, shortly before his arrest, his book was reprinted by Rozmirovich's institute, and a series of his lectures were recommended by TsIT for the training of rationalizers.[16] In addition to Charnovskii, two other defendants at the trial had direct connections with the NOT movement: V. I. Ochkin, head of the industrial research laboratories of the Scientific-Technical Administration of VSNKh, and Sergei Kuprianov, head of the Textile Rationalization Department of VSNKh.

The defendants were accused of causing production delays in the coal, power, metals, textiles, and transport industries by freezing capital investments, creating shortages of raw materials and bottlenecks in transportation, introducing minimum standards and norms, and buying excessively expensive equipment abroad. All of these branches had been experiencing severe problems at the onset of industrialization—a fact which the prosecution spared no effort to point out. They were also the industries in which the rationalization movement had been most active. Once again the wreckers were accused of conspiring with foreign powers to prepare the way for a restoration of capitalism. The "right deviation" in the party was directly linked with the conspiracy. Although the trial abounded in inconsistencies, the message from the authorities was clear: the old intelligentsia, under the supposed guise of rationalization, was sabotaging industrialization.

Attempts were made by some within the leadership (in particular, Rykov, Kuibyshev, and Ordzhonikidze) to rein in the attacks on specialists. Kuibyshev and Ordzhonikidze, having been responsible for guiding the rationalization movement during the previous five years, were particularly concerned about the effects of specialist-baiting and arrests on plant productivity. At the Sixteenth Party Congress in July 1930, on the eve of the Industrial Party trial, Ordzhonikidze argued that "it would be a terrible mistake to behave negatively toward old specialists," the vast majority of whom "are working honestly with us," on the basis of the wrecking acts of a few.[17] In 1929 Kuibyshev similarly spoke of "the sincere devotion of engineering-technical workers to the cause of socialist construction and their high political maturity and consciousness." He placed great emphasis on the role which engineers should play in production rationalization.[18]

But throughout 1929 and 1930 the witch-hunt against wreckers, urged on by Stalin's claim that "the Shakhtyites are now ensconced in every branch of our industry,"[19] increasingly encroached on rationalizers. The defendants at the Shakhty trial were charged with purposely introducing red tape into managerial operations. In a number of the cases that followed, wreckers were frequently accused of trying to impede rationalization. In one case, for instance, the defendants were convicted of "stubbornly opposing rationalization in the rubber industry and the realization of valuable suggestions for improving production." In transport, another supposed wrecker confessed to "undermining the regime of economy by refusing to search for savings inside transport (rationalization and technical-organizational measures)." Another wrecker had allegedly attempted to "awaken dissatisfaction among the working masses with the measures taken by the Soviet government for introducing and supporting labor productivity and deliberately misrepresenting all measures aimed at achieving savings in the national economy."[20]

All of these charges could well have been true, since resistance to rationalization efforts was widespread in Soviet industry and rationalizers were unpopular among the working class. Even if they were not true in particular cases, they at least represented social phenomena. But with the arrest of such rationalizers as von Meck, Dyman, Vysochanskii, and Charnovskii, the accusation that rationalization measures themselves might be tantamount to wrecking grew frequent. In one such case, the engineer Shukhov confessed to conducting wrecking activities "under the flag of rationalization" by proposing a reorganization of railroad management with the aim of restoring private ownership.[21] A newspaper commentary published shortly after the "discovery" of the Industrial Party charged that "bourgeois economic science and bourgeois conceptions in technical issues" had become "a weapon against socialist construction."[22] The distinction between legitimate rationalization and wrecking was becoming more and more difficult to draw.

An unwitting victim of the growing confusion between wrecking and rationalization was O. A. Yermanskii, whose critical approach to NOT had always put him on the fringes of the rationalization movement. After his defeat at the Second NOT Congress, Yermanskii had continued his research and teaching activities. But he had no shortage of enemies. In 1926 TsIT devoted an entire series of articles to debunking his so-called theory of the optimum, which warned against physical exhaustion of workers as a result of the widespread application of Taylorist techniques. Even those taking the "communist" position in the debates of 1923 and 1924 lost no opportunity to criticize the former Menshevik for his unbridled opposition to Taylorism.[23] In 1928 Yermanskii published an updated version of his ideas under the title *The Theory and Practice of Rationalization*. Arguing against excessive application of piecerates and the "intensification" of work, he was especially critical of Soviet practices of norm-determination and chronometric analysis.[24] Except for his diatribes against the influence of prerevolutionary Taylorists in industry, Yermanskii's book seemed strangely out of step with the times. Appearing on the eve of the party's announcement of the First Five-Year Plan, with its intensified pace of development, his "physiological" and "unmarxist" approach was quickly criticized for artificially limiting industrial growth.[25]

At a meeting of the Communist Academy in December 1929 Yermanskii was attacked by Shatunovskii, Shpil'rein, and others from the "communist" fraction of the mid-twenties, whose influence within the academy soared as "class struggle on the rationalization front" became a reality. Early in 1930 they were joined by their old allies Burdianskii and Kerzhentsev, the latter becoming the academy's deputy chairman. In June 1930 Yermanskii, along with two other former Mensheviks (the economist V. A. Bazarov and the historian N. N. Sukhanov, whose early praises for Taylorism had been criticized by Yermanskii) were expelled from the academy as part of a general attack on the influence of Mensheviks and the so-called Deborinite tendency. Leading the assault against Yermanskii, Burdianskii characterized his work as "the activity of a wrecker of production" and charged that Yermanskii and his theories "had always served as a brake to the cause of socialist rationalization."[26]

What was surprising about the case of Yermanskii was not that he was removed from the academy, but that he managed physically to survive despite the accusations against him. The same cannot be said of his former Menshevik companions removed with him, Sukhanov and Bazarov. Sukhanov was arrested within a month of his expulsion; in March 1931, he, along with thirteen other former Mensheviks, were charged with wrecking activities in yet another of the infamous show-trials of the time. Among the other defendants, mainly economists and managers by profession, were V. G. Groman, who, together with Bazarov, had been the major defender of balanced growth within Gosplan, and I. I. Rubin, the elder statesman of the discipline of economics. Bazarov, who was mentioned at the trial as a participant in the wrecking operation but who himself was not a defendant, was arrested in 1931 and tried separately.[27]

Although Yermanskii's name was mentioned at the trial by chief prosecutor Krylenko as a participant, with Sukhanov, in the counterrevolutionary group,[28] and although nearly all of the former Mensheviks, particularly those of Yermanskii's stature, were rounded up by the OGPU in the early thirties, Yermanskii was never formally charged with any crime. Not only that, but shortly after the Menshevik trial, a fourth edition of his book was published in fourteen thousand copies. The new edition included a special addendum entitled "A Reply to My Critics," in which he lashed out against all those who had questioned his approach and participated in his removal from the academy. Arguing that "people foreign to Marxist scientific thought and to technical-production practice have predominated" in rationalization, Yermanskii accused his opponents of repeating the formulas of Bukharin, of exhibiting "not a petit-bourgeois, but a pure capitalist, grand-bourgeois ideology," and of committing "mechanistic," "antidialectical, that is, non-Marxist, sins."[29] Burdianskii was particularly angered by the republication of the book, as well as by the favorable review it received in the journal of the red directors, *Predpriiatie*. He charged Yermanskii with wrecking through the publication of his "harmful," "Menshevik" theories and asked why Yermanskii had not been arrested, like his Menshevik compatriots.[30] But Yermanskii's brazen attacks did not abate. In 1933 another edition of his book appeared that essentially repeated the arguments for which he had been expelled from the academy.

Obviously Yermanskii had protectors in high places. Could he have cooperated with the OGPU in the Menshevik trial and provided key evidence used by the police in fabricating charges against his former friends and comrades? Such duplicity was possible, considering the opportunist streak in Yermanskii's character noted by his Menshevik colleagues. It does seem clear that someone found Yermanskii's survival and his continuing attacks upon Taylorists useful, for they undermined the authority of the rationalization movement and its sponsors. In the early years of industrialization, the Scientific Management movement was embroiled in two major policy disputes—one over worker training and the other over administrative reorganization—that reveal the forces mounting against rationalizers and their political protectors, forces that were successfully harnessed by Stalin for his own ends.

Cultural Revolutions

What is often called Stalin's third revolution was not a coherent policy program but a confusing array of alliances. This appears most vividly in the intricate politics surrounding educational policy. One of the main conclusions Stalin rushed to draw from the Shakhty affair was the need to speed the recruitment of new specialists from the working class. Blaming Narkompros for its inertia and conservatism, in July 1928 he pushed through a proposal, over the objections of Lunacharskii, Rykov, and Bukharin, to transfer several engineering vuzy to economic commissariats. During the next two years a heated battle was fought over control of higher education, eventually resulting in the transfer of all engineering programs to managerial control by 1930.

Kuibyshev was among Stalin's closest allies in his attacks upon Narkompros. As one of the masterminds behind the First Five-Year Plan, he had earned a reputation as a "super-industrializer" and a defender of high rates of capital investment in heavy industry. Kuibyshev believed that in order to meet manpower needs, education had to be subordinated to the interests of industry. Curricula should be stripped of their humanistic orientation and focused more narrowly on practical industrial problems. Moreover, the period of study in engineering programs should be shortened in order to speed the flow of newly educated cadres to an expanding economy starved for managers and technicians.[31]

If Kuibyshev favored subordinating education to the needs of the industrial revolution, Komsomol, his ally on the issue of control over higher education, viewed educational policy through a different prism. In the spring of 1928, responding to Stalin's calls for class vigilance and for the training of a new Soviet intelligentsia, Komsomol directed its fire against the educational establishment. Accusing Lunacharskii and the Narkompros bureaucracy of displaying "opportunism" in educational policy, the Komsomol leadership raised the banner of cultural revolution and lobbied for opening classroom doors wider to working-class youth. Closely mirroring the views of Komsomol were those of a band of radical agitators and propagandists who sought to rid the arts, sciences, and schools of bourgeois influences. To them, cultural revolution meant nothing less than the remaking of man, the ideological and cultural uplift of an entire generation of working-class youth.[32]

The attacks on the educational establishment led by VSNKh, Komsomol, and the Culture and Propaganda Department of the Central Committee (Kultprop) followed three years of intensive controversy between Narkompros and TsIT over worker training. Gastev occupied a delicate position in the struggles over educational policy in 1928. As a worshiper of the engineering profession, he opposed the growing violence against specialists that engulfed the country. A number of Taylorists with ties to Gastev were victims of this terror. Yet Gastev undoubtedly found some pleasure in the barrages unleashed against his old rival Lunacharskii. After all, had he himself not been charging Narkompros with the sins of Oblomovism and mismanagement for the past five years? Like the young rebels from Komsomol and Kultprop, Gastev had been putting forth his own version of cultural revolution for more than a decade. In contrast to the vision of these young upstarts, he had championed a radically different transformation: the remaking of man in the image of machine. With the onset of industrialization, such ideas found fertile soil within portions of the political and economic elite. The shortages of skilled labor that plagued Soviet industry in the mid-1920s had worked in TsIT's favor in the past, providing the impetus for the rapid expansion of its training empire. The First Five-Year Plan, with its ambitious targets for industrial growth, would undoubtedly bring an even sharper need for skilled labor and for TsIT's rapid training techniques.

With VSNKh attempting to wrest control over higher education from Narkompros, Gastev proposed similar reforms for worker training. Kuibyshev had always been a close supporter and personal friend of Gastev. He had been Gastev's chief sponsor within SOVNOT and was a frequent visitor to the Gastev home. In April 1928, shortly after the discovery of the Shakhty conspiracy, Kuibyshev circulated a note to the Sovnarkom in which he advocated the transfer of the entire FZU network to the control of VSNKh, narrowing FZU curricula to the needs of training a skilled work force quickly by TsIT's methods, and training new, young workers en masse rather than mature workers already engaged in production. The proposal, which was based on Gastev's recom- mendations, was supported by the trade union chairman, Mikhail Tomskii, and Commissar of Labor O. Yu. Shmidt—both personal friends of Gastev.[33]

The note touched off a political furor. At the Eighth Komsomol Congress early in May 1928, Gastev came under fire from the Komsomol leadership, who saw the FZU school as the major avenue by which young proletarians might acquire the basic knowledge necessary for further education and advancement. Particular outrage was expressed at Gastev's suggestion that employment be reserved for new workers only after they had reached the age of eighteen. The so-called *bronia,* or reservation system, which had been in effect for youngsters since 1922 was, in Komsomol's view, the keystone of the factory-school system. A form of work-study, bronia provided financial support for working-class youth who sought to improve themselves through study in the FZU school. In his address to the congress, Komsomol General Secretary Chaplin accused Gastev of taking a "non-Marxist position" and of "thinking of the worker in a Fordist manner." "The basic argument," he said, "comes down to this: will the worker be an appendage to a machine, or a conscious participant in socialist construction?" Komsomol Secretary Segal charged Gastev with aiming to create a "labor aristocracy" and holding back the proletariat from cultural advancement—accusations which had been leveled at Gastev during the debates over trade union policy in the early twenties. A resolution on the subject, though not mentioning Gastev by name, criticized attempts "to transfer Fordism and methods of capitalist rationalization to Soviet soil" in the field of worker education.[34]

The strong stand taken by Komsomol against Gastev was warmly greeted by Narkompros, which had long accused Gastev of these same sins, but which had been unsuccessful in containing the expansion of TsIT's power over worker training. Its head, Lunacharskii, did not share Stalin's assessment of the traitorous motivations of bourgeois specialists; he believed that the wrecking disease was limited in scope and that measures should be taken to draw specialists closer to the regime. He dissented with Stalin over the need to introduce preferential quotas for the working class into higher education.[35] For these views, Lunacharskii was attacked and ultimately removed from the government. But on issues of worker training, his positions coincided with those who were raising the banner of cultural revolution. At the end of May, Lunacharskii lauded Komsomol's attacks on Gastev and labeled his opponent "a communist Ford." Kuibyshev, Tomskii, and Shmidt, he said, had been drawn into supporting Gastev's technocratic "fantasies" by the prospect of using the FZU schools to lower wage costs.[36]

Gastev nevertheless continued to press his case. At a VTsSPS Presidium meeting at the beginning of June, he put forth a program for the complete revamping of the FZU network; this plan envisaged the transfer of the entire FZU network to VSNKh, the introduction of instructional-training shops employing the TsIT method in all FZU schools, and their eventual transformation into a system of labor institutes patterned after TsIT.[37] Speaking against the proposal at the meeting were Lunacharskii and S. Kaplun, a representative of Komsomol. Kaplun was a longtime critic of TsIT and had been a member of the "communist" fraction in the debates over NOT. His presence at the meeting was indicative of the overlap between the coalitions opposing TsIT at the time of the Second NOT Conference and those opposing it in 1928. Not long before, Kerzhentsev had been named deputy head of Kultprop, where he played an important role in conducting cultural revolution in the arts. Kerzhentsev was a close associate of Lunacharskii from their Proletkult days and a personal friend of Krupskaia. Both Krupskaia and Lunacharskii had supported Kerzhentsev in the debates over TsIT in 1924.[38] For Kerzhentsev it was not a far leap from his views on NOT as a mass movement to his support of a thorough cultural revolution in Soviet life. After a lengthy debate the trade union leadership supported TsIT's position. Lunacharskii was rebuked by Tomskii for his attacks on Gastev, and a decision was taken to hand over the drafting of legislation on the matter to a commission headed by trade union secretary A. I. Dogadov, a supporter of Tomskii and TsIT.[39]

The politics of worker training in the spring of 1928 can be understood as a conflict between two notions of cultural revolution as old as the Russian revolution: one grounded in the industrial world that the regime was in the process of creating; the other based on the Marxist vision of egalitarianism and upward class mobility, a view which was reinvigorated as a result of the renewed atmosphere of class warfare. The conflict between these two cultural revolutions was used by Stalin to consolidate his power over the trade unions, VSNKh, and the educational bureaucracy.

During the summer of 1928 a realignment occurred within the Politburo. Rykov and Bukharin were joined by Tomskii in opposing Stalin's policies toward the countryside and his attempts to raise industrial plan targets precipitously. By the fall Stalin spoke of the danger of "right opportunism," and by February 1929 the split was openly proclaimed. The leadership struggle left Gastev straddling both sides of the conflict, torn between his patrons Tomskii and Kuibyshev. Stalin consciously sought to drive a wedge between Tomskii and Kuibyshev and to split the industrialist coalition. In a letter to Kuibyshev in August 1928 he accused Tomskii of planning to insult the VSNKh chairman and of improperly criticizing VSNKh on issues of rationalization; he called Tomskii "an evil person" who was "not always fair" in his tactics.[40] While sowing the seeds of discord between Tomskii and Kuibyshev, Stalin was simultaneously attempting to penetrate the trade union leadership by proposing Kaganovich as a candidate for the VTsSPS Presidium. When Tomskii tried to block Kaganovich's election, he was joined by a number of TsIT supporters, including Dogadov and members of his commission. Thus, as Tomskii's authority came under attack, the VTsSPS commission on worker training was swallowed by leadership politics.[41]

In the fall of 1928 the publication of TsIT's report on worker training to the Dogadov commission gave rise to sharp criticism of Gastev. "*Gastevshchina,*" Krupskaia wrote in *Pravda*, "has now become a threat," and "youth, which has its entire life ahead of it, cannot sit quietly by and watch such a 'rationalization' " of education. A Komsomol Plenum at the end of October criticized VSNKh, the trade unions, and Gastev for their "narrowly managerial approach" to worker education and called for "a decisive struggle against these harmful tendencies."[42]

Gosplan chairman Krzhizhanovskii attempted to resolve the dispute by summoning an All-Union Conference on Issues of Labor Force Training, to which representatives of the warring parties were invited. According to later accounts, the meeting resulted in a stalemate along well-defined positions, with VSNKh, TsIT, and Narkomtrud pitted against Narkompros, Komsomol, and Gosplan.[43] But by April 1929, when the Sixteenth Party Conference convened to approve the First Five-Year Plan, Kuibyshev and Krzhizhanovskii had reached a compromise over the heads of the combatants. It called for training 216,000 workers in FZU schools and 112,000 in TsIT's training programs. Komsomol objected outright to the deal. In his speech before the conference, the newly elected Komsomol General Secretary, Aleksandr Kosarev, formerly a member of the Presidium of Kerzhentsev's Time League, spoke forcefully against any compromise. Kosarev criticized Gastev for his "capitalist, Fordist approach" to labor issues and for producing "cadres who are trained like animals, incapable of thinking, reasoning, generalizing, and working."[44]

Kosarev's line was rejected in favor of the compromise package. But the heat generated by the conflict and the incessant attacks upon Tomskii and the trade union hierarchy undermined Gastev's position. In June 1929 Tomskii was removed from the leadership of VTsSPS and replaced by Nikolai Shvernik, a former NKRKI official and an ally of Stalin. Shvernik was an outsider to the disputes over labor training; he had little interest in their ideological intricacies or even in alleviating shortages of skilled labor. But he had been charged by Stalin with consolidating his hold over the trade union bureaucracy, and he was eager to put an end to Komsomol's attacks on what had become his organization.

Sensing that with the change of leadership at VTsSPS, TsIT's position had become untenable, Kuibyshev did his best to save Gastev. Shortly after Tomskii's ouster, he made a complete turnabout, publishing a letter recognizing the correctness of the Komsomol line in order to assuage the young rebels. But Komsomol, seeing first blood, was not satisfied. The youth leadership wanted nothing less than a full reversal of government policy and a confession from Gastev of his errors. At a Komsomol conference at the end of June, Komsomol Secretary Segal charged Gastev with trying to smooth over the conflict. "Gastev," he said, "has now taken the position that 'I won't touch your FZU if you don't touch my TsIT.' " Right Opposition member N. A. Uglanov, by then in charge of Narkomtrud, defended TsIT against recommendations by Komsomol radicals that the institute be liquidated. Gastev himself addressed the meeting and proposed that the conflict end. But Segal vowed "to struggle until he [Gastev] repudiates his mistakes."[45]

Strident attacks upon Gastev followed. The party's theoretical journal, *Bol'shevik*, lashed out at "the harmful and socially danger-ous 'philosophy' " which he preached, and his theories were lumped together with other "neo-bourgeois and petit-bourgeois" positions on labor issues.[46] RAPP leader L. L. Averbakh, brother-in-law of police chief Yagoda and a major proponent of cultural revolution, charged Gastev with defending "bourgeois and anti-Marxist theories," seeking to create "an aristocracy of engineers," and "dreaming of subordinating man to machine." Gastev, he wrote, "wants to build the house of proletarian culture on the prac-tice of Ford and Taylor" and was "a direct apologist of the negative features of capitalism."[47] A special Komsomol task force was as-signed to investigate TsIT, and the future of the institute appeared to be in jeopardy.

That Gastev survived such attacks testifies to the support he enjoyed from elements within Stalin's entourage. By the end of the year the influence of the industrialists had revived. In December 1929 Lunacharskii was removed from the leadership of Narkom-pros, and in January 1930 all higher technical institutes were trans-ferred to the control of VSNKh. Shortly before Lunacharskii's re-moval, in early December 1929, a Central Committee decree on worker training, instead of excoriating TsIT, sanctioned the rapid expansion of all forms of worker training in view of critical short-ages of skilled industrial personnel.[48] Although Komsomol radicals continued to call for the dissolution of TsIT, by June 1930 Kuiby-shev had come to Gastev's rescue by issuing a decree approving still broader applications of TsIT's methods.[49]

What is usually referred to as Stalin's "Great Retreat" (the aban-donment of cultural revolution in favor of more conservative social policies) is often traced to Stalin's speech, given in June 1931 before a gathering of managers, in which he condemned specialist-baiting and called for the rehabilitation of bourgeois specialists. As a result, class quotas favoring the proletariat in higher education were abol-ished, the course of study was lengthened, and those preaching cultural revolution were removed from office.[50] The outlines of this shift were already evident in the struggles over worker training in 1930 and in the complete reversal in official attitudes toward TsIT in early 1931.

In November 1930 a major shake-up occurred within the Soviet government. Gosplan chairman Krzhizhanovskii was replaced by Kuibyshev, and Ordzhonikidze was transferred from the NKRKI to the leadership of VSNKh. Soon the fortunes of TsIT changed radically. In January 1931, in a fit of self-criticism, the Ninth Komsomol Congress officially condemned efforts by the Komsomol leadership to eliminate TsIT and declared that short-term forms of training "should exist." That same month trade union leader Shvernik praised TsIT's "great work in training and retraining the work force" and called for wider application of its methods. Shortly afterward Gastev was awarded the Order of Lenin and joined the party. A pair of decrees approving contracts between enterprises and TsIT for training workers was issued. By this time Krupskaia was warning of an imminent "collapse into Gastevshchina."[51]

In May 1931, after hearing a report from Gastev on TsIT's activities, VSNKh ordered that it be placed under "special observation" and that its methods be spread to other branches of industry. A minor bureaucratic scuffle followed between Shvernik and Ordzhonikidze for control over TsIT. This dispute was resolved in October by a Central Committee decree transferring control over TsIT from VTsSPS to VSNKh in the hope of eliminating "the opposition of sluggish and conservative elements" holding back the application of TsIT's techniques. As part of this reorganization, TsIT's stationary training bases were closed and its training activities were concentrated in enterprises.[52] It would not be long before the reforms proposed by Gastev would be adopted as government policy. In 1933 complaints were raised that too many graduates from FZU schools were bypassing production altogether, preferring to enter the vuz rather than to work on the factory floor. This was precisely the cause for which the proponents of cultural revolution had fought and against which Gastev had crusaded. But in 1933 policy took a decidedly conservative turn toward subordinating worker training to the short-term needs of industry. In September the government decreed that the period of study in FZU schools be cut from two years to six months, that study plans be emptied of general preparatory subjects, and that they be oriented instead to the narrower task of imparting factory skills.[53]

Despite the final vindication of his position, Gastev's past errors were not forgotten. Even after his rehabilitation, his long-standing critics continued their attacks. In an address to the Communist Academy in May 1931, Burdianskii accused Gastev of having taken "clearly mistaken positions" and of building his methods on "naked empiricism" and "uncritically interpreted Taylorist views." He reminded his audience of Gastev's connections with the wrecker Charnovskii and of his social-engineering machine, which, Burdianskii said, had been supported by "the old opportunist leadership of VTsSPS"; "one cannot help counterposing the ideology of this group to orthodox Marxist-Leninist methodology." Gastev might have "moved forward in recent days," but it would be all the more necessary "to help him and TsIT stamp out those mechanistic deviations which are still there."[54] In the early thirties Gastev still enjoyed sufficient protection to ignore such offers of "help" from Burdianskii and his ilk. Others within the rationalization movement were not so fortunate.

A Fatal Reform

Apart from the wrecker and the right opportunist, there was no more hated a figure in Stalin's third revolution than the recalcitrant bureaucrat. In addition to the need to train a new intelligentsia, Stalin drew three other lessons from the Shakhty affair: administrators had lost touch with the masses; consistent policy implementation was sorely lacking; and the conditions under which managers worked were hindering them from fulfilling their duties. Shortly after the April 1928 Central Committee Plenum, war was declared on bureaucratic perversions, which Stalin described as nothing less than "a manifestation of bourgeois influence over our organizations."[55] But very quickly two approaches to the struggle against bureaucratism emerged: one based on mobilization and discipline, the other on managerial technique. Beginning in 1928 Komsomol organized "light cavalry" raids on enterprises and institutions to exorcise red tape and purge inefficient officials. By the spring of 1929 the idea of casting out the bureaucrat was adopted as official party policy. At the Sixteenth Party Conference a purge of the state apparatus was proclaimed to remove "rotten elements who are perverting Soviet laws, colluding with the kulak and the NEPman, hindering the struggle against red tape . . . and behaving arrogantly and bureaucratically toward the real needs of the toilers." In a year's time the party had removed more than fifty thousand officials from office.[56]

Along with these frontal assaults on bureaucracy, VSNKh, the NKRKI, and VTsSPS stepped up their efforts to reinvigorate the troubled rationalization movement. In the summer of 1928 these three organizations undertook a coordinated campaign to upgrade factory rationalization units. In August a TsKK Plenum decreed that industrial rationalization should "acquire special, paramount, and decisive significance." The meeting called upon the NKRKI and VSNKh to take joint measures to broaden the network of rationalization institutions, to reorganize the industrial hierarchy, and to convene a Third Conference on NOT in order to mobilize rationalizers around the new tasks posed by industrialization. In the winter of 1929 the NKRKI announced a campaign to cut paperwork costs in central state institutions by 30 percent, and the Central Committee issued a call to party organizations to take immediate steps to cut costs, raise productivity, and improve labor discipline. At the Sixteenth Party Conference in April several delegates spoke in favor of a special five-year plan for rationalization.[57]

One topic on which a consensus developed within VSNKh and the NKRKI was the need to introduce functional principles into industrial organization. Rozmirovich had long been the principal advocate of borrowing from German and American experiments in this field. Mimicking the critiques of line management then so fashionable abroad, she blamed the hierarchical French system of line organization practiced in Soviet industry for creating excessive red tape and generating distrust throughout the managerial apparatus. A report written by her department at the end of 1926 concluded that "one can cut staffs somewhat, eliminate one or another unit of the apparatus, replace eight or nine hierarchical levels with five or even four, but all the same the line system . . . does not allow for the possibility of loosening the grip of red tape, bureaucratism, *chinovnichesto* of the worst sort, and the costliness of the apparatus."[58]

In the years preceding industrialization Rozmirovich and her institute had paid particular attention to recent administrative reforms in America. There a centralized Bureau of the Budget had been created with broad-ranging powers over budgetary and planning matters. On the basis of this work and a reading of Taylor, the

ITU developed its own scheme of organization, reducing all managerial activities to the three basic functions of planning, accounting, and organization. Rozmirovich advocated the centralization of these three functions in a single organ. At first the idea was to merge Gosplan and TsSU with the NKRKI. But when this scheme ran into stiff opposition from planning organs, the focus shifted to creating a single center within VSNKh for planning, organization, and rationalization.[59]

Rozmirovich and her institute shaped a series of administrative reforms in accordance with this rigid, and now discredited, understanding of organizational structures. In December 1929 the Central Committee enacted a far-reaching structural reform of industry. The task of drawing up these proposals had fallen jointly on an NKRKI commission chaired by Taylorist Abram Gol'tsman and the Scientific-Technical Administration of VSNKh, whose Scientific Council was in the hands of prerevolutionary specialists. Gol'tsman, a close friend of Rozmirovich, had led a commission to Germany in the summer of 1929 to study the organization of German industry. The commission returned with enthusiastic proposals for applying German methods of functional organization to Soviet industry.[60] Though a number of disagreements developed between the NKRKI and VSNKh over details, the functional scheme of management, a decentralization of operational responsibility, and the need to integrate science and rationalization work more closely with production formed the basic assumptions of both sides. The draft proposals of the NKRKI and VSNKh suggested stripping trusts of their direct powers over enterprises and reorienting their work toward "issues of technical leadership, rationalization, and reconstruction." The functions of main administrations (*glavki*) were to be transferred to branch associations (*ob'edineniia*), which would be given a high measure of operational authority over enterprises. Trusts and associations were to be organized "primarily along functional lines."[61]

The main issue in contention was the organization of VSNKh itself. The NKRKI theses, in accordance with Rozmirovich's ideas, called for concentrating planning, organization, and rationalization in a single center to provide closer integration of the technical and economic sides of management. The result would be the creation of a superdepartment in VSNKh, the Planning-Technical-Economic

Administration, formed by merging two key VSNKh units—the Scientific-Technical Administration and the Planning-Economic Administration. This organizational giant was to be assigned the tasks of planning industry, coordinating the activities of associations, developing technical policies, overseeing scientific research, and supervising the exchange of information on standardization and rationalization, including the assimilation of foreign innovations. VSNKh, on the other hand, called for preserving the independence of the Scientific-Technical Administration as a separate technical and rationalization staff for industry, upgrading its powers, and placing it on an equal footing with the Planning-Economic Administration.[62] In the end Rozmirovich's proposal for a unified functional organ won Kuibyshev's support.

Kendall Bailes has pointed to a considerable overlap between those who participated in drafting the VSNKh theses on reorganization and the defendants at the Industrial Party trial a year later— in particular, Charnovskii and Ochkin. The VSNKh draft proposal drew immediate criticism for its glorification of the bourgeois specialist. Particular scorn was leveled at its assertion that "the future belongs to the managing engineers and engineering managers," a line which was ascribed to Bukharin. The phrase found its way as well into the accusations against the defendants at the trial, who were charged with trying to set up a government of engineers under which "the leading role in the management of the country and national economy" would be "in the hands of engineers." Bukharin, who was appointed to head the Scientific-Technical Administration in June 1929, played a role in drafting the reform.[63] Although Rozmirovich championed the creation of a superdepartment within VSNKh rather than an upgrading of the Scientific-Technical Administration, her close association with Bukharin and Charnovskii was not overlooked by her opponents. In the aftermath of the Industrial Party trial, Rozmirovich and her institute would be accused of having abetted the wrecking activities of Charnovskii and of propounding a "Bukharinist" line on organizational issues.[64]

Equally as damaging as her friendship with Bukharin and Charnovskii were the disappointing results of the 1929 reforms, which by any standard were an organizational fiasco. They created enormous frictions between VSNKh and the thirty-five newly created branch associations. The associations had been put on independent economic accounting (*khozraschet*) and were told to maximize profits. But they remained subordinate to the VSNKh hierarchy and possessed the same rights as the liquidated glavki whose place they had taken. In the majority of cases associations were created by mechanically combining the managerial staffs of glavki and differed little from their predecessors. The new associations came into continual conflict with local and republican industries, whose activities they were supposed to supervise.[65] A preliminary report issued in May 1930 noted that direction over these industries had actually weakened as a result of the reorganization. Another problem centered around the newly created Planning-Economic-Technical Administration, which grew at an enormous pace. It soon encompassed most of the functions of VSNKh and became, in the eyes of many, "a *narkomat* within a *narkomat*." This central functional department was quickly overloaded with demands—a situation which diluted VSNKh's leadership over the economy. Rather than reducing bloated staffs and simplifying organizational structures, the reform resulted in an increase in the size, cost, and complexity of the managerial apparatus. In less than a year administrative costs in industry increased by between 15 and 35 percent.[66]

Hints of dissatisfaction surfaced in July 1930 at the Sixteenth Party Congress, when Kuibyshev was blamed for the unsatisfactory state of rationalization. In his major address Stalin criticized "gaping holes in the field of rationalization," which he called "a shameful spot" on the party's record. A number of speakers were more explicit in their criticism of the VSNKh chairman. After Kuibyshev delivered a long harangue on the need to make rationalization "the basic task of the day," he was chided by Kaganovich's brother, Mikhail, then a member of the Presidium of the TsKK. Kuibyshev, he said, "usually brings out this rationalization on solemn occasions . . . like a good dish which he is serving for hors d'oeuvres." He accused VSNKh of setting up rationalization organs and overseeing their dissolution in the name of "cutting staffs." "Wreckers," he warned, "have been holding back rationalization, and it is not accidental that Vysochanskii, Miliukov, and others sat at the head of rationalization in military industry"—a branch of industry over which Kuibyshev formally presided.

In contrast to Stalin, Ordzhonikidze argued that some successes in rationalization had been achieved. But he was sharply critical of the way in which VSNKh had put the 1929 reforms into practice. "Together with VSNKh," he noted, "we conducted a reorganization of industrial management . . . But I should say that as a result of this reorganization, instead of simplification we are receiving more muddle, and instead of lowering expenses we are receiving an unconditional rise in costs." His deputy, Zatonskii, added that the basic idea of the reorganization was "correct, but it is being implemented poorly." In many cases "things turned out worse than they were before," with industry suffering from "parallelism, enormous hitches, and an excessive concentration of all functions in the higher levels." The resolutions of the congress expressed approval for the reforms, but noted that they were not being implemented "quickly enough or energetically enough." The Central Committee was called upon to take measures "to correct the observed shortcomings" and to "finish work on reorganizing industry in as short a time as possible."[67]

A month before the congress Rozmirovich's institute published a new version of its plan for reorganizing industry. It stressed the importance of a total reorganization on purely functional lines, concentrating power in central "sectors" organized along functional principles and eliminating intermediate units.[68] These same ideas had been approved by the Sixteenth Party Conference a year before. The resolutions of the Sixteenth Party Congress ignored them. Moreover, in an unusual move the congress dropped Rozmirovich from the TsKK presidium and subsequently from the NKRKI collegium. In a statement clearly aimed at her functional scheme, Ordzhonikidze observed that although it was necessary to borrow extensively from American and European technology, that did not mean that "we should in any way transfer the managerial system of capitalist states to our Soviet state. Managerial technology, of course, we can and should borrow from them, but we cannot and should not borrow their managerial system." Shortly after the congress the NKRKI issued a resolution on Rozmirovich's institute that condemned attempts to "borrow mechanistically the experience of Europe and America," but that expressed approval of the institute's efforts to mechanize accounting procedures.[69]

The failure of the 1929 reorganization may have been one of the causes contributing to Kuibyshev's removal from the chairmanship of VSNKh in early November 1930 and his transfer to Gosplan.

Kuibyshev had been the major sponsor of the functional reforms, and he was in the midst of a heated battle to save Gastev's institute from liquidation. Two weeks after his successor, Ordzhonikidze, assumed office, he reorganized the central VSNKh apparatus once again, abolishing the cumbersome Planning-Economic-Technical Administration and investing its power in a series of branch and functional sectors. But functional sectors continued to interfere directly in the activities of plant managers, and branch sectors proved incapable of providing effective leadership over industry. The structure of VSNKh gradually drifted back toward its pre-reform organization, as evidenced by the reestablishment of glavki in fall 1931. Managerial subunits proliferated, and lines of authority grew more and more complex. In early 1932 VSNKh itself was divided into separate commissariats. Two years later, in March 1934, the continuing remnants of the functional system were criticized and fully liquidated, and the branch system that predominates in Soviet industry to this day took its place.[70]

These changes left Rozmirovich and her institute defenseless against a growing onslaught of criticism. Ordzhonikidze distanced himself from her in 1930, although he understood the value of her work. The same cannot be said of Ordzhonikidze's successor at the NKRKI, Andreev. Shortly after assuming his duties, Andreev reoriented the work of the NKRKI away from rationalization and toward inspection of the state apparatus. In the NKRKI's plan for 1931, composed in December 1930, rationalization was hardly mentioned.[71] Ordzhonikidze was highly critical of Andreev's denigration of rationalization. In February 1931 he told a group of managers that "rationalization measures giving a colossal effect have been abandoned, and even up to this time we are having quarrels over whether rationalization cells are needed at enterprises."[72] Within weeks of Ordzhonikidze's departure for VSNKh, a meeting was held at the ITU and Orgstroi at which "a basic change in the ideological positions" of these organizations was discussed. Rozmirovich was removed as the institute's director, and her organizational theories were attacked on ideological grounds.[73]

In January 1931 the new leadership of the NKRKI convened yet another meeting, an All-Union Conference on Improving the State Apparatus, to subject the activity of the ITU and the rationalization movement to a more thorough raking. Presiding at the meeting was

V. Ya. Grossman, a signer of the Platform of the Seventeen in 1924 and an ardent opponent of Rozmirovich, who was then a high TsKK official. The ITU was accused of engaging in "fruitless scholarly exercises," of reducing rationalization to a "narrow technicism," and of being guided by "foreign and harmful theories." "Recently," one critic observed, "much bourgeois rubbish and theoretical garbage have managed to make themselves felt in the basic aims and methodological approaches" of rationalization institutions. Particular scorn was reserved for the institute's dogmatic understanding of organizational design, in which "no other structure besides the functional [approach] was recognized." These shortcomings, the accusers asserted, were not confined to the ITU, but were endemic throughout the rationalization movement. A warning was issued to those "whiners among the rationalizers who try to convince us that they were confused and that their former positions have been repudiated, but give nothing in place of them." "Such a position," it was said, "must be viewed only as a form of opposition to the new in the form of the defense of the old."[74]

The fallout from the turn against the ITU spread quickly. In the aftermath of the Industrial Party trial, accusations surfaced that bourgeois specialists were wrecking under the guise of their scientific activity. Among the fields in which such charges were leveled in early 1931 were rationalization technology, the reorganization of railroad management, and accounting methods—three areas closely connected with the work of Rozmirovich's institute.[75] Only six months earlier Ordzhonikidze had given his approval to the ITU's efforts to mechanize accounting procedures. But in the spring and summer of 1931 the banner of "ideological struggle on the accounting-theoretical front" was raised, and a purge was conducted among accounting rationalizers.[76]

By the summer of 1931 Burdianskii noted that "a most brutal class struggle" was being waged in the field of rationalization theory. He directly connected Charnovskii's wrecking activities with ideological deviations in NOT. In addition to naming his old enemies, Gastev and Yermanskii, Burdianskii rattled off a long list of Scientific Management scholars and practitioners who were guilty of "mechanistic and idealistic" errors. One scholar was charged with imbuing his courses on rationalization with "100 percent Taylorism, without any correction for Soviet conditions."

"One could take this course in Chicago, if of course he would be allowed there." Others were "uncritically borrowing methods of capitalist norm-setting" more suitable to "London or Ohio" than the USSR. For those who sought to remain untouched by politics, Burdianskii's message was clear: "If you say that you are not engaged in politics, but you are conducting economic standardization, that means you are conducting capitalist standardization." Special scorn was reserved for Rozmirovich's institute, which, Burdianskii said, had become "a center for anti-Marxist, bourgeois conceptions" in rationalization theory.[77]

In the mid-twenties Rozmirovich had spared no effort in attacking Fayolists within the NKRKI, whose views on the primacy of administration she contrasted with Gastev's emphasis on automation and mechanization. In 1930, when Rozmirovich came under attack, the Fayolists emerged to play a part in her ouster and subsequently dominated the editorial board of the institute's journal. But in early 1932 the Fayolists themselves were attacked for underestimating the role of technology in production, for elevating management into a separate caste within society, and for narrow "practicism." Yet another purge rolled through the ITU, as Rozmirovich's purgers were themselves removed for their "harmful" theories.[78] All publishing activity by the institute ceased, and in August 1932 the NKRKI ordered the institute's staff cut, its affiliates liquidated, and its journal and publishing houses transferred. Not long afterward the Institute for Managerial Technology, the NKRKI's center for the rationalization movement, was closed. When Lenin's "Cheka for Organization" was dissolved on Stalin's order at the end of 1933, ostensibly because it no longer was relevant to the problems of Soviet administration, the rationalization movement was little affected, because two years earlier all of the NKRKI's rationalization activities had either been abolished or been transferred with Ordzhonikidze from the NKRKI to VSNKh.[79]

From Rationalization to Coercion

A small coup occurred within the NOT movement during the first years of industrialization. The old specialists who had dominated the movement for the previous fifteen years were removed, and new faces appeared. A number of these new leaders had been members of the "communist" fraction in NOT in the early twenties. Others were recruited from opportunist or ideologically orthodox elements who occupied middle-level administrative or research posts in NOT institutes. The Stalinist rationalizers represented a younger generation than the Gastevs, Yermanskiis, and Rozmiroviches. Many traced their roots to the critical or underprivileged within the rationalization movement. Burdianskii, for instance, never forgave Gastev for the official favor which TsIT had enjoyed over his own institute in 1922 and 1923. His outbursts against Gastev and Yermanskii bore all the marks of a personal grudge. Some of the Stalinists, including Burdianskii, maintained contacts with the secret police. In early 1931, for example, he discussed the wrecking activities of Charnovskii with Vyshinskii, then presiding judge at the Industrial Party trial and later chief prosecutor at the show-trials of the late thirties.[80]

Drastic changes occurred in the early thirties in the composition of the rationalization movement. A study of Moscow rationalizers in July 1931 found that nearly half of those surveyed were entirely new to rationalization work and had no prior experience in the field, while another 12 percent had less than a year's experience. A large proportion of these new rationalization cadres were party members. By and large, they lacked the education of their predecessors, as evidenced by a sudden rise in the proportion having only an elementary-school education.[81]

A marked decline in the quality of rationalization cadres was but one manifestation of the demoralization of the NOT movement during this period. The first two years of the five-year plan had brought a rapid growth in the number of factory rationalization units. At the same time their effectiveness noticeably deteriorated. An NKRKI decree in September 1930 decried what it saw as "the nearly total collapse of rationalization organs in industry." Most of the blame was placed on "managers who view rationalization as something secondary."[82] Even before the industrialization drive the Soviet bureaucracy had been inimical to the rationalizer. But with the inauguration of the First Five-Year Plan, with its extremely ambitious production targets, yet another wedge was driven between the rationalizer and the manager. The plan was concerned above all with achieving industrial growth as quickly as possible. Therefore, among the confusing array of targets given to the manager, the primary criterion upon which his work was judged was fulfillment of the gross output indicator. At the same time, the rapid pace of industrial growth led to extreme bottlenecks in the supply of raw materials and semifinished products. Enterprise managers devoted much of their energy to obtaining basic supplies and had little time or incentive left for production rationalization.[83]

A large portion of the materials used at the plant were wasted in the chase for figures. An American engineer from General Motors who visited twenty-five Soviet plants in 1929 was struck by "the entire swamps of filth" in which the Soviet factory was submerged. According to the visitor, "so much raw material and waste was discarded around factory buildings that they could have sufficed to supply production for weeks on end."[84] In 1929 and 1930 a noticeable decline took place in the quality of industrial production. Under pressure to fulfill quantitative output indicators, plant managers frequently consented to the production of low-quality and, at times, useless merchandise. Nearly a third of all steel rails, a sixth of all tires, and a seventh of all coal produced in 1930 had to be discarded as waste. The quality of wood supplied to the tractor industry was so poor that nearly half had to be thrown away, and waste in the textile industry frequently reached 40 percent. Plans for cutting costs and increasing productivity were met by only half. Kuibyshev complained at the time that nearly the entire growth in productivity was due to growth in capital investment and not to any increase in plant efficiency.[85]

The centralization of bureaucratic authority that accompanied industrialization flooded the enterprise with new waves of paperwork and red tape and led to growing interference by central organs in the plant director's work. An examination of the typical work schedule of an enterprise manager in 1930 revealed that six working days of every month were consumed by meetings outside the factory, and the volume of paperwork that he was expected to process during the remainder of the month prohibited him from paying regular visits to the plant's shops.[86] In 1931 Ordzhonikidze noted with consternation that whenever anything went wrong at an enterprise, the enterprise director was summoned to Moscow, where bureaucrats in the central offices of industry would attempt to rationalize production from afar.[87]

In this situation the methods of the rationalizer became increasingly irrelevant to the daily rhythms of Soviet industry. The logic of the Stalinist industrial system required, not efficiency experts, but *tol'kachi* (pushers) capable of cajoling employees to produce ever higher quotas, hiding shortcomings from superiors, and coaxing managers of other plants to provide them with sufficient raw materials to keep assembly lines churning. The regime was not uninterested in productivity. On the contrary, it issued a constant flow of edicts intended to focus the attention of managers on the problem. The funds budgeted to plant rationalization organs actually increased in 1930, in some instances even tripling. But in the vast majority of cases this money was spent by enterprises for other purposes, and factory managers, under the pressure of the plan, tended to ignore rationalization organs altogether. A report on the state of rationalization efforts in the Russian republic in the fall of 1931 observed that in most regions rationalization organs ''are in an embryonic condition, are not fully staffed, their employees are used for other purposes, and rationalization work is conducted in fits and starts.'' Enterprise directors, the report noted, viewed rationalizers ''as a reserve force to substitute for operational employees who are absent.'' ''Not only does the leading staff of institutions not participate at all in rationalization work . . . but it does not believe in its benefits and sometimes initiates its liquidation.''[88] S. I. Syrtsov, the head of industry in the Russian republic, who was later evicted from the party for his participation in a new right deviation, pointed to the hypocrisy of the regime's rationalization policies. ''We bind a man hand and foot with all kinds of rules; we drive him into a bottle, cork it up, and put a government stamp on it; and then we go around saying, 'Why doesn't this man show any energy or any initiative?' ''[89] In June 1931 Stalin lamented that ''the concepts of 'a regime of economy,' 'the cutting of nonproductive expenses,' and 'the rationalization of production' have long gone out of style.'' Ordzhonikidze echoed these sentiments, observing that the notions of ''a regime of economy'' and ''the quality of production'' had ''disappeared from our everyday lexicon.''[90]

Stalin's answer to the irresponsiveness of the bureaucratic machine was to coerce the chinovnik to perform, or as he put it in June 1930, ''to smash bureaucratism in our institutions and organizations'' and to ''liquidate bureaucratic 'habits' and 'customs.' ''[91] To put an end to the high turnover of workers that was plaguing industry, a decree was issued in October 1930 that forbade the free movement of labor. Soon there followed a whole series of laws which, in their reactionary spirit and punitive character, rivaled the worst cases of exploitation that could be found under capitalism. When a crisis in the nation's railroad system appeared in 1932 and 1933, causing even greater shortages of materials and equipment in industry, prison sentences were introduced for employees who violated labor discipline. Stalin's loyal henchman, Kaganovich, was dispatched to clear up the mess, which he accomplished by summarily shooting several thousand railroad engineers. Elsewhere in industry, workers and managers were held legally responsible for accidents and negligence at the plant, as well as for damage done to instruments and equipment. The death penalty was introduced for theft of socialist property, and drunkenness on the job or failure to appear for work on time could be punished by dismissal or imprisonment. For producing goods of poor quality managers were in theory subject to five years in prison. Overconsumption of electricity or failure to meet one's supply obligations were considered infractions of the law. These laws were liable to considerable variation in enforcement. Any attempt to enforce them thoroughly would have quickly eliminated the entire managerial apparatus, since plan fulfillment largely depended on these practices. But throughout this period the police presence on the factory floor grew tremendously, as ruthless searches for wreckers and saboteurs became a matter of routine. Lower-level managers were particularly subject to such investigations.[92] The intention of this wave of violence was as much to intimidate as to apprehend. In essence, coercion and storming substituted for organization and efficiency.

The last thing Stalin wanted under these circumstances was an independent corps of industrial executives capable of voicing dissent over the difficult conditions under which they worked. The rudiments of such a political force had already emerged by the late 1920s and had been institutionalized in a series of professional organizations: the clubs for red directors, the courses conducted under their auspices, and the new Industrial Academy. In 1929 these institutions became centers of opposition to Stalin's increasingly violent policies. Many on the instructional staff and in the student body of the All-Union Industrial Academy were appalled by the excesses of collectivization and expressed displeasure at the overly ambitious targets foisted upon managers. Many openly sympathized with the Right Opposition, which was in firm control of the Academy's party cell. At the end of April 1930 Uglanov himself was invited for an evening honoring the Academy's first graduation. His keynote address was greeted with long applause.[93]

This was a danger which Stalin could no longer afford to overlook and was, in any case, no longer willing to tolerate. In the fall of 1929 plans for ridding the country's top executive training institution of sympathizers with the right were laid. Toward this end the number of incoming trainees was practically doubled, rising to two hundred. Among the new trainees was a thirty-five-year-old party bureaucrat from the Ukraine, Nikita Khrushchev. A protégé of Kaganovich, Khrushchev was sent to the Academy to supervise its purging. He never graduated from the program, but, during the fifteen months he spent there, was engaged entirely in party work. The staff and students of the Academy were aware of Khrushchev's purging responsibilities; on at least one occasion, he later recalled, the party bureau "tried to get rid of me by sending me out into the countryside on a business trip."[94] Despite the efforts of Khrushchev the Academy remained a center of dissident thought for a year and a half more. Only in November 1931 could the party bureau report that it had finally achieved "the ideological unity of the party organization on the basis of the general line of the party." Shortly before that, the title of the All-Union Industrial Academy was changed to the Stalin Industrial Academy, reflecting Stalin's ultimate triumph over the troublesome trainees.[95]

As Stalin was consolidating his hold over dissident managers, far-reaching changes were occurring in the entire academy program. The number of academies expanded until, by the end of 1932, there were twenty-three such institutions with an enrollment of nine thousand.[96] Changes took place in the curricula as well. In May 1931, in accordance with his newly proclaimed slogan, "Technology decides everything," Stalin summoned the party secretary of the All-Union Industrial Academy to his office and ordered him to devote no less than 80 percent of the program to technical and engineering disciplines.[97] Throughout the early thirties the academy programs continued to be racked by scandal and political intrigue. In the spring of 1932 the director of the Stalin Industrial Academy, A. Z. Kamenskii, was severely reprimanded by Stalin for firing two professors implicated in wrecking activities. Although Kamenskii had apparently been trying to protect the Academy's staff from fallout from the accusations, he was warned that his actions contradicted the spirit of the party's new line toward bourgeois specialists and was told that similar actions in the future would result in his removal.[98] In December 1932 the suicide of Stalin's wife, who had been a trainee at the Academy since 1929 and was due to graduate shortly, cast another shadow over the institute. Nadezhda Allilueva was said to have sympathized with the opponents of her husband, and Stalin's pressures on her fellow trainees and teachers may have contributed to her decision to shoot herself.[99] Shortly after her death Kamenskii was removed from his post, and members of the staff were brought to trial for sabotage.

While Stalin was emasculating the academy programs, he was also stripping the clubs for red directors of their independence. In the late 1920s these clubs were evolving into professional organizations for an increasingly assertive managerial elite. Under the influence of Moscow party chief Uglanov, who exercised control over the Moscow club, particular attention was placed on activating rationalization work among the club membership and on building bridges between managers and rationalizers. In May 1927 the Moscow club was reorganized to attract broader managerial and engineering forces. A special Office for the Scientific Organization of Industrial Production was created, and ties with rationalization institutions in Germany and America were established. More than 250 managers and engineers participated in the various commissions of the club's Sector for Rationalization. Training courses sponsored by the clubs were revamped to emphasize rationalization issues.[100]

But as with the Industrial Academy, the influence of the Right Opposition, and especially Uglanov, troubled Stalin. In April 1930 he ordered all clubs for red directors to be dissolved and their courses transferred to trusts and enterprises. Enterprises were in no position, however, to supply the courses with instructional staff or adequate facilities. Study programs varied from plant to plant, and a considerable change took place in the student body. By the end of 1930 approximately half of the trainees attending the courses had no executive experience, and although a majority of them were illiterate, the programs offered no general preparatory training.[101] The number of courses and trainees actually increased over the next two years. But at the end of 1932 the crippled programs were eliminated altogether.

While managerial retraining programs were being purged, reorganized, and eliminated, an enormous expansion was taking place in higher technical education. In 1928, when the First Five-Year Plan began, the Soviet Union possessed only 26 higher technical educational institutions with 48,000 students. By the end of the plan period in 1933, higher technical education had multiplied several times over, with 270 institutions training some 233,000 students. In the year 1930 alone, 188 new technical institutes opened their doors. By and large, the training that new engineers received was narrowly specialized, highly politicized, and of poor quality. Changes aimed at broadening the basic knowledge of the engineer were introduced in 1933.[102] But Scientific Management, which in any case had never been taught widely in engineering institutes in the twenties, was largely ignored in these reorganizations.

By the mid-thirties instruction in NOT was offered at a total of seven vuzy throughout the country, and instructional time was limited by law to 110 hours. In these institutes, courses on NOT were usually allotted only a half or even a third of this time. As one NOT instructor put it, in the vast majority of engineering institutes the discipline was "clearly undervalued," its role in engineering curricula "totally insignificant." By then the few NOT instructors who remained had little or no education themselves. Their stilted presentations drew heavily upon the categories of political economy and frequently caused students to "complain about the dullness and superficiality of instruction." As a result, many students came to believe that "there is nothing for them to learn in this discipline."[103] In many respects they were correct, for not only had the subject been emptied of all content, but it was strangely out of place in the Stalinist industrial system. The Stalinist manager's lack of economic and managerial training may have seemed anachronistic, but it was well suited to a system that increasingly relied upon coercion as its motivating force and that aimed at pushing rapid economic growth at the cost of efficiency and quality.

4

. . . . . .

The Triumph of Violence

*There is no such thing as the last revolution; the number of
revolutions is infinite.*

—*Eugene Zamiatin, 1924*

It is difficult to find any rationale for the bloody orgy unleashed by
Stalin in the middle thirties. Stalin's unbalanced personality, his
desire to eliminate real or imagined opponents, the unscrupulous
character of those who surrounded him, the Bolshevik legacy of
terror, and the sweeping powers of the secret police have all been
cited as causes. Indeed, no explanation would be complete without
reference to all these factors, and this chapter makes no pretense to
substituting for any of them. In the late 1930s, terror and violence in
Soviet society became ends in themselves, sweeping up anyone and
everyone into their own logic. Rather, what interests us here is the
twisted thought process by which the use of coercion as a strategy
for rooting out bureaucratic resistance can transform itself into an
instrument for wholesale and indiscriminate mass murder.

In communist systems violence has rarely been conducted in the
name of violence for the sake of violence; rather, it has been

"rationalized by theories contrived to 'prove' the increasing need for coercion."[1] What has made these theories potent political forces has been that they have usually been grounded in a certain social reality. It was not difficult for the practitioners of violence in Soviet Russia at the end of the 1920s to turn rationalizers into wreckers and managers into saboteurs, for within the bureaucratic context of Soviet administration at the time, the lines had already been blurred. Rationalization fostered organizational tensions throughout the industrial hierarchy, and in spite of the best intentions of rationalizers, control over the activities of the bureacracy remained elusive. In the eyes of the populace and the regime, the actual results of rationalization differed little from what a real wrecker (if such a mythical beast ever existed) might have sought to accomplish.

Large-scale bureaucratic organization contains an inherent potential for introducing confusion between legitimate organizational activity and criminal behavior. Not only does bureaucracy necessitate the violation of its own rules in order to fulfill its missions, but in practice the difference between efforts to rationalize bureaucracy and purposeful sabotage may often be only a matter of intent. At the Industrial Party trial, Charnovskii vehemently denied charges that he had needed to resort to wrecking activities under the guise of rationalization. To the prosecutor's chagrin, he explained that "no wrecking activities were ever necessary," since "all one had to do was carry out the *appropriate actions* and everything would happen on its own."[2]

This same dynamic continued into the 1930s, undermining political trust in the bureaucracy and leading to a mounting spiral of violence. In his study of industrial bureaucracy Gouldner described how the attempts of a new manager to discipline workers through the strict application of rules and close supervision released "a vicious cycle" of sanctions, resulting from the manager's growing isolation from the organization and the activation of his defense mechanisms. Eventually, this deteriorating situation led to a strike.[3] Coercion once used is not easily abandoned. Because the effects of coercive measures as a strategy of compliance are usually short-term, those who employ them are tempted to raise the level of force. Leaders in the process of instituting rapid and far-reaching changes in an organization frequently resort to sanctions and are often led to engage in the firing of personnel, for widespread resistance is a natural response to change.[4] In his efforts to root out bureaucratic resistance, Stalin had purged the Soviet bureaucracy twice, in 1929 and in 1933, in both cases dismissing tens of thousands of officials. He had raised plan targets to impossible levels in order to goad industry into performing and had introduced coercive measures to combat labor indiscipline and managerial foot-dragging. Finally, he had unleashed a witch-hunt against imaginary saboteurs and wreckers who were holding back production, cowing the technical and managerial elite into submission.

But rather than curing the disease, centralization and coercion bred still more resistance. The excessive pace of industrialization caused severe bottlenecks, the production of poor-quality goods, and a lack of concern for cutting costs. Centralization of decision-making led to floods of paperwork and hampered managerial initiative. And the use of violence caused managerial and technical personnel to eschew risk taking and try to protect themselves from the fist of the regime. These natural administrative reactions in turn fed Stalin's sickly mistrust of the bureaucracy, isolated him still further, and led to even more violent attempts to break through the bureaucratic resistance that impeded his every step and which, paradoxically, he exacerbated by his own actions.

According to accusations made at the time, "an incessant and ruthless struggle" was waged against bureaucratic perversions from 1936 to 1938. The entire bureaucracy and the remnants of the rationalization movement were said to be permeated with wreckers and spies. Under orders from "the despicable Trotskyite-Bukharinist espionage ring," foreign agents had consciously introduced "confusion and muddle into the organization of wages," attempted "to hold back the growth of labor productivity and to break up the Stakhanovite movement," "defended the absence of personal responsibility," and "fought against increasing the intensification of labor."[5] These charges were not entirely absurd. Wages were in a confused state, many attempts had been made to hold back the Stakhanovites, and administrative perversions continued as before. The absurdity of the purges lay not in the fact that these conditions did not exist, for they were inevitable and all-pervasive characteristics of bureaucratic organization, but rather that normal organizational resistance and bureaucratic confusion were defined as crimes against the state and Comrade Stalin. More-over, given the centrally planned character of the Soviet economy, no one could avoid committing these crimes in the everyday course of affairs. It was impossible to escape guilt.

Terror has been defined as "the attempt to alter the structure of society at a rapid rate and from above through forceful administrative devices."[6] In the case of the Great Purge, the main object of change (other than the destruction of several hundred of Stalin's old personal rivals) was the bureaucracy itself. All sectors of the Soviet bureaucracy—the party, the military, Komsomol, and even the police—were engulfed by the purge; the managerial and technical elite was one of the primary targets and the earliest victims. By the mid-1930s Stalin faced no direct threat from the managerial elite, or, for that matter, from any other part of the bureaucracy. Although some within the leadership (in particular, Kirov, Kuibyshev, Kossior, Rudzutak, and Ordzhonikidze) had expressed reservations about Stalin's violent policies and attempted to rein in his authority in 1934, that challenge was defeated. That some within the leadership had unsuccessfully challenged Stalin's authority cannot explain, however, why Stalin chose to engage in the systematic elimination of the entire administrative elite.

There was a twisted administrative logic behind the purge, a mode of psychotic managerial thought that posited that by eliminating the bureaucracy the sources of bureaucratic resistance would be eliminated as well. Having threatened, coerced, and cajoled the bureaucracy for a decade, Stalin apparently decided that the only way to get what he wanted out of it was to liquidate it entirely and replace it with new administrators and specialists, cadres who would not hide behind excuses of "objective" limits or barriers to their work and who would, in Kaganovich's words, "carry out any task . . . assigned to them by Comrade Stalin." As Jeremy Azrael suggested, "Stalin's ominous slogan of 1935—'everyone can be replaced'—was transformed into a directive—'everyone must be replaced.' "[7]

The Revolt against Rationality

Terror is based on the assumption that resistance to change is rooted in the character of people, not in the character of organizations. Under such an assumption the rationalization movement appeared not only as trivial medicine for the diseases of bureaucratism but as part of the disease itself. Many of the top leaders of industry, themselves targets of the purge, had been closely involved in the NOT movement. These men were more than political protectors of management experts. In many cases they had become imbued with the outlooks and values of the rationalizers and had grown enamored of their technocratic schemes. Organizational technique is predicated upon the kind of stability and predictability which mass violence renders impossible. As Stalin's increasingly violent administrative practices encroached upon their bureaucratic domains, these industrialists were led by both bureaucratic duty and administrative ideology to resist Stalin's authority.

Nearly every industrial official who in any way had been involved with the NOT movement in the 1920s and 1930s was systematically eliminated by Stalin between 1935 and 1938. By the early thirties much of Kuibyshev's authority had already been undermined by his attempts to protect Gastev and Rozmirovich and by his close association with their politically controversial projects. If one believes the accounts later given at the Moscow show-trials, Kuibyshev was the victim of willful murder by his doctors, presumably on Stalin's order, in January 1935, shortly after the Kirov assassination.[8] Another of Gastev's sponsors, Tomskii, committed suicide in 1936 in anticipation of his arrest and trial. Piatakov, who had played a key role in the NOT movement as Ordzhonikidze's deputy, was arrested in September 1936 and tried at the second of the infamous Moscow show-trials. From 1932 on, Ordzhonikidze, as VSNKh chairman and later as People's Commissar for Heavy Industry, increasingly played the role of protector of the NOT movement. He provided a safe haven for Gastev and his institute in the early thirties, and during these years a number of new rationalization institutes were established under his aegis. Ordzhonikidze's authority, however, would not last forever. His death in February 1937 (reportedly from a heart attack, but now known to have been suicide) removed the final buffer that had protected rationalizers from the depredations of the NKVD.

In the second half of the thirties the Soviet rationalization movement and its sponsors were engulfed by a new type of politics that saw no limits to the possible and no boundaries to the permissible.

During these years the remnants of the Scientific Management movement became a lightning rod for violent attacks against managers and management experts. The main instrument for these attacks was the Stakhanovite movement and its offensive against the production norm. The notion of the production norm was central to the Scientific Management movement. But how production norms should be established had been a subject of controversy since the days when Taylor resolved that norms should be set at the pace achievable by "a first-class man." All methodologies suffered from inconsistencies. All contained an enormous potential for abuse, as well as for sparking worker dissatisfaction and protest. And as the Hawthorne experiments revealed, even the most "scientifically determined" work norms easily floundered upon the social fabric of the enterprise if they did not take the informal group dynamics of the work environment into consideration.

In socialist society, where remuneration is supposed to be based upon the principle of "from each according to his labor, to each according to his work," production norms play a much more important role than under capitalism. Indeed, in communist systems there are few alternatives to widespread norming activities, since most communist systems utilize piece-rates (rather than time-rates) as their major method of wage payment. Moreover, in centrally planned economies, where the types of goods to be produced, the volume of output, the price of products, and the cost of labor are determined by planners rather than by the market, there are few ways to compare the performance of workers, managers, factories, and even whole industries without formal production norms. It is not surprising, then, that since 1918, when Gastev and his allies in the metalworkers union created the first socialist norm-setting bureaus, the production norm has occupied a sacrosanct place in all communist economies.

But throughout Soviet history (and communist history in general), the practice of norm-determination has evoked considerable controversy. Despite the acrimonious debates over piece-rates and chronometric norm-determination in the early years of Soviet power, the regime remained committed to employing chronometric techniques of norm-setting as widely as possible. During the 1920s the practice of chronometric norming expanded rapidly. By the middle of the decade the technical-norming bureau had become an integral part of the Soviet enterprise, and piece-rate payment had been extended to more than half of the labor force.[9]

Throughout this period tensions remained high over technical norm-setting. As in the West, norm-setters were hated figures throughout Soviet industry, and much of the violence of the early industrialization drive on the factory floor was directed against them. Persecution of the practitioners of chronometry became a common occurrence. Lower-level managers frequently prevented them from entering factory shops, fearing the effect they would have upon workers, and norm-setters were forced to take chronometric readings in secret for their own safety. Because of the tenuous position of the norm-setter in the factory social system, few individuals were attracted to the profession. According to one report of the early thirties, engineers "who happen to land in the technical-norming bureau make every effort to leave for production as soon as possible."[10]

On the whole, Soviet norm-setting practices were highly inconsistent. Despite the continual urgings of the regime to the contrary, technically determined norms created on the basis of chronometric observation encompassed only a small proportion of the norms in operation; the overwhelming majority of norming decisions were made arbitrarily, or—as the practice was commonly called—*na glazok* (by eye). In many cases these "unscientific" methods were favored by workers as security mechanisms against speedup, and social pressures to engage in them were strong. The regime, however, continually condemned norm-determination na glazok, for it lowered norms to the level of the average worker, diluted the role of wage incentives, and undermined labor discipline. Attempts were made to develop a systematic chronometric methodology and to hasten the training of norm-setting cadres. Norm-setters were exhorted to create norms that were "maximally technically feasible" and based on a thorough study of labor gestures. But by and large these measures had little effect upon a situation whose causes lay in the enterprise social system and in the method itself.[11]

It was in this context that Stalin condemned what he called "left-wing leveling [*uranilovka*] in the field of wages" in his famous "Six Conditions" on the operations of industry in June 1931. Wage-leveling, Stalin asserted, destroyed worker incentive and blurred the distinction between skilled and unskilled labor. To eliminate this evil "the old tariff system must be smashed," and new norms based upon a wider scale of wage differentials must take its place.[12] Following Stalin's speech, the entire conduct of norm-determination was reorganized. A "progressive piece-rate system," which increased tariff rates on a sliding scale according to the level of above-norm production, was introduced throughout Soviet industry. Tariff tables were revised to reflect sharper wage differentials, and a national Committee for Standardization, chaired by Gastev, was established to coordinate norming activities nationwide.

Research on norm-determination, at first under Narkomtrud and later (after Narkomtrud was abolished) under Ordzhonikidze's Commissariat for Heavy Industry, expanded in the ensuing years, as did the number of norms governing the operations of the Soviet enterprise. In 1935, in one plant alone, the rhythms of production were guided by more than thirty-five thousand norms.[13] But problems continued to plague norm-determination. At the Seventeenth Party Conference in January 1932 norm-setters came under attack for "perversions" in norming practices. In a number of instances in which progressive piece-rates had been introduced, wage increases outpaced gains in productivity. Mikhail Kaganovich called the existing state of affairs "a parody of technical norm-setting"; "in practice," he said, "we have no norm-setting as such, but only endless conflicts."[14] Two years later Gastev, the chief norm-setter of the country, confessed that "there is hardly another country in the world which produces more chronometric work than ours, the majority of which is used for display rather than for analysis."[15]

The unsatisfactory state of norm-determination made it a field ripe for accusations of sabotage. The first such charges emanated not from the regime but from the working class, and in particular from its better performers. During the early years of the industrialization drive the shock-worker movement, organized on the initiative of Komsomol, had been critical of norm-setting practices. *Udarniki* (shock workers) pledged to overfulfill output norms, proposed their own "counternorms" to those currently in place, and with the regime's support lobbied for orienting norm-determination toward the "best worker" as opposed to the "average worker."[16] The Stakhanovite movement that emerged in 1935 from the shock-worker movement differed from its predecessor only in the virulence of its attack on norm-setters. In one shift the Donbass miner Aleksei Stakhanov dug 102 tons of coal under an established norm of 7 tons; several weeks later he was said to have dug a world record of 227 tons. Soon other miners were breaking Stakhanov's record, producing 400, 500, and 600 tons of coal per shift; the norm then in operation in the Ruhr valley was 14 tons a shift, and in England 11 tons.[17] With chronometers measuring every move, speed kings in other branches of industry emulated Stakhanov's feats.

Stakhanovism, with its glorification of speedup and its cult of record breaking, bore a formal resemblance to Taylorism. In reality it was the antithesis of everything the Scientific Management movement valued. Stakhanovism was not based on Taylorist methodologies, but developed as a protest against time-and-motion techniques, which were charged with placing artificial, "scientific" limits on production. In place of "scientifically determined" norms based on a thorough analysis of labor gestures (something which was physically impossible to achieve, in any case), Stakhanovism stretched the pace of work beyond the limits of the humanly possible. Rather than a method of organization, Stakhanovism was little more than a grizzly experiment in how much the human body and industrial equipment could endure. Its hothouse conditions could hardly be replicated on a mass scale. The secret of the Stakhanovite's success lay in a division of labor that was strictly subordinated to supplying and servicing individual record breakers. Managers immediately realized the movement's fraudulent assumptions; an individual worker might be easily supplied, but an entire factory was a different matter! An excessive work pace could not be maintained for more than several hours, for it would exhaust the work force, undermine morale, and wear out equipment. Little wonder that from the beginning managers and rationalizers resisted the Stakhanovite movement, and that Stakhanovites were ostracized by their fellow workers for raising output quotas.[18]

Ordzhonikidze greeted the Stakhanovite movement as a protest against the bureaucratic stagnation and inertia that had frustrated his leadership of heavy industry. In April 1935, several months before Stakhanov's labor feats became known, he criticized managers for hiding behind "so-called technically justified norms." Many of these norms, he asserted, were outdated and arbitrarily determined and had become a limit to further economic growth. Ordzhonikidze made it clear that he was not against norms in general, but only against rampant abuses of norms that "strengthen our current backwardness." He viewed the achievements of the Stakhanovites as an opportunity to pressure recalcitrant managers into performing. In a telegram congratulating Busygin for his labor feats in the automobile industry, Ordzhonikidze praised the Stakhanovites for demonstrating "just what the so-called technically justified norms of our bureaucrats in the departments of labor and the technical-norming bureaus are worth." Managers who refused to aid in organizing the Stakhanovite movement because they feared higher plan targets were the movement's "incorrigible enemies."[19]

By fall 1935 the Stakhanovite movement had spread to the major industrial centers of the country through the influence of the media and the organizational energies of party leaders. By November, when the First All-Union Conference of Stakhanovite Workers in Industry and Transport convened, the movement had become nationwide. The conference took place in an atmosphere of self-indulgent celebration. But behind the rhetoric lay a more ominous message to administrators and rationalizers. Ordzhonikidze warned managers who were dragging their feet to take the lead in organizing the movement or face removal. Existing norms were obsolete, he said, because norm-setters had slavishly followed the teachings of prerevolutionary professors and the example of capitalist countries. By demonstrating that the technical rules of the capitalist world did not apply to socialist workers, Stakhanov had "beaten all our scientists and the scientists of Europe and America." This did not mean, Ordzhonikidze continued, that the Bolsheviks had nothing to learn from Western technology and organization, but only that capitalist norms should not be considered a limit beyond which socialist workers could not venture.

Others were more extravagant in their accusations. Kaganovich announced that "hostile elements" and "class enemies" were attempting to hold back the Stakhanovite movement by propagating "a theory of limits," spread by "a whole group" of specialists who "supported and defended one another." In the weeks before the conference Kaganovich had already been using the achievements of the Stakhanovites as an excuse to purge "scholarly good-for-nothings'' from the institutes and offices of the Commissariat of Railroads for their "unscientific limit theories." Stalin cited Kaganovich's example of delivering "a jolt in the teeth" to conservative specialists as the proper way to deal with the opponents of the Stakhanovite movement when persuasion failed; he warned that similar methods would have to be applied in other branches of the economy. But to those who suggested that technical norms should be done away with entirely, Stalin answered that such a path would be foolish, since they were "a great regulating force" without which "a planned economy would be impossible." Nor should norms be set, as some had proposed, at the levels achieved by the Stakhanovites, but rather somewhere between the Stakhanovite records and current norms. Soon afterward, work norms around the country were revised upward by more than a third.[20]

The Stakhanovite movement arose only eight months after the assassination of Kirov, the event which set the Great Purge in motion. Though thousands were arrested in the aftermath of that crime, there were limits to the number that could be implicated in the death of one man. The Great Purge attained its murderous momentum with the reappearance of charges of industrial wrecking and sabotage in the months following the First All-Union Conference of Stakhanovites (November 1935), when thousands of managers and specialists were dismissed and arrested on the charge of sabotaging the movement. The slightest equipment breakdown, spoilage of materials, or industrial accident became fair game for the secret police. Ironically, the Stakhanovite movement and its speedup pace served only to accelerate such disruptions, for which managers were held accountable with their lives. Many complained to Ordzhonikidze, who attempted to render aid. At a gathering of heavy-industry managers in June 1936, he criticized the excessive turnover of executive personnel at plants, the loss of control by his commissariat over appointments, and the charges that managers were sabotaging production, which he called "nonsense."[21] But by that time matters were beyond the control of Ordzhonikidze and were being dictated by the *vozhd'* himself. On instructions from above, the secret police continued their investigatory work in industry, unmasking supposed wreckers and spies on trumped-up charges of bureaucratic sabotage.

As the founder of Soviet norm-determination, Gastev was one of the major targets of the Stakhanovite movement and its revolt against industrial rationality. After TsIT's political troubles in the early thirties, he and his institute lived a precarious existence, constantly subject to attack, yet protected by powerful patrons from feeling the regime's full wrath. But unwittingly Gastev's rationalization activities helped set in motion the forces that eventually caused his downfall. In 1931 and 1932, when his standing within the party had been partially restored, Gastev championed the notion of functional organization in the work place. Under the system devised by TsIT each work station, usually encompassing several machines, was divided into a series of functional operations centered on servicing the production process. The method was tested at TsIT's experimental factory, where production more than doubled in the course of two years. TsIT's functional method was applied extensively in the early thirties in the textile and defense industries, as well as at a number of the country's major industrial projects. The importance of the method was recognized in a series of party and governmental decrees in 1930 and 1931.[22]

But from the first, TsIT's functional organization met strong resistance from skilled workers. Under the new system workers were forced to move back and forth from machine to machine to perform their functions. Skilled workers with considerable production experience often found themselves performing operations that were new and that required cooperation with unskilled workers, generating friction between the two groups. The result was a high level of turnover among skilled workers at plants where the functional system was in operation, as they sought jobs at plants that did not employ TsIT's method. Significantly enough, the Stakhanovite movement, which was largely composed of young, skilled workers, employed the opposite principle: instead of dividing tasks functionally, as TsIT did, labor was strictly specialized according to work operations and centered around servicing the skilled worker. Thus, one of the sources of Stakhanovism can be traced to the widespread dissatisfaction of skilled workers with TsIT's functional methods.[23]

At the Seventeeth Party Conference in January 1932 the leadership of light industry, where nearly half of all enterprises had been put on TsIT's system, was criticized for forcing application of the method without proper preparation. The September 1932 Central

Committee Plenum decreed that, beginning in 1933, application of the functional method should cease.[24] Nevertheless, the disorganization created by the method plagued light industry for years. At the Seventeenth Party Congress in January 1934, when all functional schemes of organization came under attack, Gastev's system was lumped together with Rozmirovich's unsuccessful reorganization of the state apparatus, and both were condemned as foreign and irrational schemes. Hinting that support for these discredited approaches could still be found in high places, Kaganovich complained that "many of our managers and leaders, although they are honest and good, do not understand the genuine difference between the organization of management in our country and its organization in bourgeois countries."[25]

Without the backing of Ordzhonikidze in the face of these attacks, TsIT undoubtedly would have met the same fate as the ITU, disbanded in the early thirties. Support for TsIT's functional method had originally come from VSNKh, which, at a meeting of its Presidium in April 1931, had given the green light to the method's application. In January 1932, when VSNKh was split into several branch commissariats, TsIT was placed under the control of Ordzhonikidze's Commissariat of Heavy Industry, where it acted as a consulting organ for forty of the largest enterprises in the country.[26] But with the rise of the Stakhanovite movement and the growing attacks upon norm-setters, TsIT soon found itself on the defensive again.

Since the late 1920s Gastev had been critical of norm-determination procedures, which in many cases he himself had been instrumental in establishing. He clashed on several occasions with planners and norm-setters over their "unscientific" approach to the problem. In 1932, when the norm-determination hierarchy was overhauled, he was appointed head of the All-Union Committee on Standardization, created to provide methodological leadership in this area. Several years later, when Ordzhonikidze attacked outdated norms, Gastev was one of the commissar's chief advisers on the issue. The widespread use of faulty methodologies in norm-setting, Gastev wrote in mid-1935, was but one of the manifestations of the "bureaucratization of NOT" in the Soviet Union. Existing norm-setting procedures artificially divided work motions into their separate elements and introduced a significant degree of

bias into norm-determination. Even before the rise of the Stakhanovite movement, Gastev complained that the norms then in effect
had "lost their veracity," for they had been left untouched for long
periods of time.[27] In January 1936 Ordzhonikidze issued a decree
praising TsIT for its past services to industry and ordering it to act
as a national coordinating center "for servicing the Stakhanovite
movement."[28]

Not all, however, agreed with Ordzhonikidze's decision. In April
1936 TsIT's sister institution, the Central Institute of Labor of the
Commissariat of Light Industry, was accused of devising artificially
low norms and was dissolved on order of the Central Committee as
"an organization holding back the development of the Stakhanovite
movement." The proper authorities were instructed to "review all
the so-called scientific works, handbooks, and textbooks published
by the institute and to withdraw those unfit" for public consumption.[29] Not long thereafter, Gastev was stripped of his leadership
of the All-Union Committee on Standardization, which was dissolved.[30] At the end of 1936 TsIT finally managed to publish a guide
to Stakhanovite methods of organization. But immediately after
Ordzhonikidze's suicide the book was criticized for giving vent to
TsIT's pretensions to leadership over the movement, for containing
"a number of perversions" on labor issues, and for a passing reference to Piatakov, then under arrest as an "enemy of the people."
Calls were issued to withdraw the book from circulation.[31]

Ordzhonikidze's successor in heavy industry, Kaganovich, subjected TsIT to growing repression and restrictions. The institute
was forced to abandon all its projects but those connected with the
machine-building industry, and TsIT training programs were revised to emphasize political and ideological instruction instead of
practical, hands-on training with instruments and tools. TsIT employees increasingly encountered police harassment and arrest.
Then, in 1937, TsIT was transferred from the Commissariat of
Heavy Industry to the newly created Commissariat for Defense
Industry, where it was put to work designing production lines and
training workers for aircraft factories. Gastev attempted in vain to
save his institute and protect his personnel. In September 1938 he
himself was arrested and sentenced to ten years in the camps,
where he died in 1941.[32] Soon after Gastev's arrest, TsIT was trans-

ferred again, this time to the newly created Commissariat of the Aircraft Industry. At the end of 1940 the twenty-year-old Taylorist institute was dissolved, and its remaining personnel and equipment were turned over to the Scientific Institute for Technology and the Organization of Production of the Aircraft Industry (NIAT).

"Cadres Decide Everything"

In 1935, in a symbolic reassertion of the primacy of politics over administration, Stalin revised the party's slogan "Technology decides everything" to read "Cadres decide everything." Implicit in this shift was the assumption that the root cause of Soviet administrative problems lay not in an absence of technique, skill, or organizational capacity, but in the political character of men. In accordance with this shift, the Scientific Management movement was treated as part of a broader wrecking conspiracy aimed at turning problems of politics into narrow problems of administration. Unlike the effect of the Great Purge on the party and state bureaucracies, no new generation, no Class of 1938, replenished the ranks of the Scientific Management movement. Rather, it was subjected to a quick and painful death.

One branch of rationalization that came under heavy assault was industrial psychology. As in the West, Soviet research in this field had developed in two directions: investigation into the physiological processes of work and fatigue (labor physiology) and work on identifying the talents and skills of personnel (psychotechnics). Labor physiology, which dominated industrial psychology in the early 1920s, came under attack at the end of the decade for its "mechanistic" denial of human consciousness. Pavlov's physiology and Bekhtirev's reflexology were criticized for their excessively biological interpretations of human behavior; they were accused of denying the mutability of human nature, which the regime was then in the process of altering. These theories, which had always been controversial, had been frequently used by opponents of industrial speedup to counterpose labor "intensification" to rationalization. With the rise of the shock-worker movement and the imposition of breakneck industrial plans, labor physiology was prohibited from exploring the sources of work-place fatigue. Scholars instead were instructed to study, as one source put it, "all methods capable of increasing the work capacity of man," such as production gymnastics, introduced in Soviet enterprises in 1930.[33]

Developed largely in Germany and America, labor physiology's sister field, psychotechnics, was subject to considerable scientific abuse; it gradually lost popularity among Western researchers in the 1920s. But in the 1920s and 1930s, when psychotechnical research was on the decline in the West, the field flourished in Soviet Russia under the umbrella of the NOT movement. As in the West, Soviet psychotechnical research was not immune from charges of abuse. At the Kazan Institute in the early twenties psychotechnical researchers were accused of administering tests aimed at proving the racial superiority of Russians over Tatars; the scandal led to a heated controversy and to a purge of the institute's psychotechnical laboratory.[34]

In spite of such controversies, the Central Committee convened a meeting in the fall of 1922 to discuss the development of psychotechnics; a small group of communist psychotechnical researchers, most of whom were employed by the Department for the Preservation of Labor of Narkomtrud, persuaded party leaders of the need to sponsor psychotechnical research aimed at "increasing productivity and the maximum use of human resources." Indicative of the tenuous nature of the party's support, the meeting resolved to place psychotechnical research under "the attentive control of the party."[35] During the remainder of the decade, Soviet psychotechnicians conducted extensive work on the sources of industrial fatigue and the identification of qualities necessary for industrial leadership. In addition, psychotechnicians engaged in a wide variety of military-related research, including an investigation into the skills of airplane pilots and an examination of factors influencing test scores of students drafted into the Red Army. Krupskaia, in particular, was a strong supporter of psychotechnical research in the country's school system and of its use in career counseling of students.[36]

Unlike other branches of NOT, psychotechnics fared well during the first years of the industrialization drive. In fact, Soviet psychotechnics developed so extensively that Moscow was selected as the site of a convention of the International Psychotechnical Association in August 1931. I. N. Shpil'rein, a member of the "communist" fraction in NOT and the most prominent communist spokesman for psychotechnics, was elected president of the international society. Others within the "communist" fraction, such as Burdianskii and Torbek, supported psychotechnics as an alternative to TsIT's "biological" approach to labor training. A Psychotechnical Society was established in 1927, and the Communist Academy organized its own Section for Psychotechnics in 1930. By the end of 1929 more than a hundred thousand Soviet citizens had been subjected to psychotechnical testing of some sort.[37]

Shpil'rein's connections with other members of the "communist" fraction, many of whom played important roles in conducting "cultural revolution" in the late twenties, saved him from disgrace when psychotechnics came under attack at that time for its "excessive industrialism." The sons of kulaks and hostile elements, it was charged, were selected by some psychotechnicians for command posts in the military; psychotechnical testing was said to favor the bourgeoisie and to discriminate against the working class.[38] In May 1931 an All-Union Congress on Psychotechnics and the Psychophysiology of Labor, called to prepare for the forthcoming international conference hosted by the Soviets, was the occasion for a personal attack on Shpil'rein. Stalinist philosopher M. B. Mitin charged him with failing to distinguish between capitalist and socialist psychological approaches. Particular scorn was reserved for Shpil'rein's adoption of the "idealistic" theories of the German psychologist Wilhelm Stern. TsIT's psychotechnicians A. A. Tolchinskii and N. D. Levitov were criticized as well for their indiscriminate "application of bourgeois tests . . . containing elements of anti-Semitism." Once again the charge surfaced that psychotechnicians were seeking to prove the "mental backwardness" of particular national groups—this time Turks and Uzbeks.[39] Shpil'rein confessed to his mistakes and renounced his former positions. When the international psychotechnical congress opened in Moscow in September 1931, foreign guests were shocked by the extent to which their Soviet hosts sought to distinguish between capitalist and socialist psychotechnics.[40]

Despite virulent attacks such as these, psychotechnics continued to survive. But beginning in 1934 a new wave of opposition against psychotechnical testing in the educational system appeared. Foreign psychotechnicians conducting work in Moscow were warned to conclude their work. Psychotechnical testing in the factory and the classroom was curtailed. The Psychotechnical Society was disbanded, the training of psychotechnicians ceased, and journals in the field were shut down. The final blow came in July 1936, when the Central Committee issued its decree "On Pedological Perversions in the System of the People's Commissariat of Education." The document accused Narkompros of engaging in "pseudo-scientific experiments and numberless investigations on pupils and their parents in the form of senseless and harmful questionnaires, tests, etc., long since condemned by the party." Only one week before the decree Krupskaia had publicly defended psychotechnical testing as having "great significance" for "a whole number of professions." But as the purge moved into full swing, psychotechnics was accused of being a groundless and sinister attempt to hold back the education and promotion of new cadres from the working class. Psychotechnical tests, the July decree charged, were aimed at "proving the special giftedness and the special right to existence of exploiting classes and 'superior races,' and . . . at proving that the working classes and 'inferior races' are physically and spiritually doomed."[41] Soon Shpil'rein himself was arrested and accused of Trotskyite sympathies; he was never heard of again. Numerous other psychotechnicians were swept up with him, and all laboratories in the field, including those engaged in industrial research, were closed. Burdianskii, who had led the Stalinist attacks upon the Scientific Management movement in the late twenties, was arrested as well for supporting the "false science" of psychotechnics. He died in prison in 1938.[42]

Even that portion of the NOT movement that most carefully toed the regime's line experienced repressions similar to those that rocked TsIT and psychotechnics. After the dissolution of Rozmirovich's institute in the early thirties, the leading role in the field of production automation and organizational design fell to the Central Research Institute for the Organization of Production and Management of Industry of the Commissariat of Heavy Industry, known by its initials, TsIO. TsIO was created at the end of 1931 for designing assembly-line systems in the machine-building industry. When the new institute opened its doors in 1932, much of its personnel was recruited from the former employees of Rozmirovich's institute, including some who had participated in the purging of the ITU.

TsIO and its Ukrainian affiliate specialized in the design of production dispatcher systems. Such systems, prevalent in Soviet industry in the 1930s, established a series of special control and communications centers (dispatching services) to coordinate planning and production in plant subunits and to maintain a continuous work flow within the enterprise. Each dispatching service was connected by telephone to several integrated assembly lines, whose activities were coordinated by the dispatcher to prevent bottlenecks. Work on designing dispatcher systems had been conducted in the late twenties at Rozmirovich's institute. At that time, on the basis of a study of similar practices in the West in the railroad industry, dispatcher systems were applied to the Soviet railroad network. But in the early thirties, when production bottlenecks within and between plants became an acute problem, attention was turned to applying dispatcher systems more broadly. By 1934, with the aid of TsIO, more than fifty-six heavy-industry enterprises were in the process of implementing dispatcher systems. By 1937 several hundred enterprises, mainly in the machine-building, metalworking, chemical, and coal industries, were using the new system.[43]

The dispatcher system met strong resistance from plant management. David Granick wrote of the tendency to use dispatchers as *tol'kachi,* as agents for obtaining needed supplies. Often dispatching services were staffed by enterprise tol'kachi who were entirely ignorant of production processes. Dispatching services duplicated the work of enterprise planning bureaus, creating endless friction. In general, dispatchers were forced to adjust to the existing rhythms of the enterprise and "remained on the fringe of administration." Despite the lackluster performance of its dispatcher systems, TsIO enjoyed the favor of the political leadership in the mid-thirties, even while other NOT institutes were being eliminated or harassed. This was largely due to the appeal that the dispatcher system held for centralizing managerial control and to the presence of a strong core of Stalinists on the TsIO staff. In November 1937 all industrial commissariats were ordered to reorganize their central operations to introduce the dispatcher system in their *glavki.* The *glavk* dispatcher, it was said, was to become "the *central figure*" of the economic apparatus and a "living link" between enterprises and the commissariat.[44]

As a further indication of the regime's confidence in TsIO, it was the only institute permitted to engage in theoretical work aimed at developing a "socialist theory of management."[45] Beginning in 1937 the institute's publications spewed forth a torrent of rhetoric against Trotskyite-Bukharinist "spies" and "wreckers," who were said to have disorganized production through their sabotage activities and their "harmful and foreign" organizational theories.[46] Yet TsIO did not entirely escape the upheavals of the late thirties. At the end of 1935 a number of projects were curtailed, and in 1936 the institute went through a wrenching reexamination of its methods in light of the Stakhanovite movement. During these years the leadership of the institute and its Ukrainian affiliate was purged, as were a number of staff members, for being partisans of "the Menshevik theory" of "active limitations" on production. Those involved in the institute's attempts to develop management theory came under attack in 1938 for underestimating the role of technology in rationalization.[47] The TsIO project on management theory was in fact the last of its kind in the Soviet Union for the next twenty-five years. In 1940, when the Commissariat of Heavy Industry was dissolved, TsIO, the only rationalization institute that the regime had trusted to any extent, was liquidated as well.

While NOT institutes were being closed and rationalizers shipped off to the camps, Yermanskii, the sworn enemy of the Taylorists, not only survived the purge years but survived them well, considering his former political associations. He had retired from teaching in 1934 at the age of sixty-eight. But in 1935 and 1936, when attacks on the norm-setting community commenced, the regime found a willing partner in this longtime critic of Soviet Taylorists. According to one contemporary source, in 1937 and 1938 Yermanskii "conducted a fierce struggle against . . . the ideologies of limitations that had developed and had defended the methodology of so-called 'technically based' norms." In particular, he was said to have played an active role in attacking Gastev and TsIT.[48] The former Menshevik, who eight years earlier had been expelled from the Communist Academy, was even permitted to publish a new book. While ostensibly dealing with the Stakhanovite movement, the work spared no effort to criticize the evil proponents of "limit" norm-setting: Taylor, his disciple Carl Barth, and all those "uncritical minds" who had imported these foreign theories, "our professor-specialists in metal cutting, all of whom were connected with the fetishized teachers of our Katkovs, Glebovs, and Besprozvannyis—Taylor and Kronenberg.'' Yermanskii himself did not escape criticism; his book took two years to clear the censors, and even then it was prefaced with a warning that portions of it were not orthodox.[49] Nevertheless, he remained immune from the grasp of the secret police. In his final vindication over his opponents, the onetime pariah of the rationalization movement died a natural death in 1941 at the ripe old age of seventy-five.

The School of Life

Despite the violent attacks upon rationalizers during these years, several attempts were made to revive NOT instruction. In 1936 Krupskaia sent a note to Ordzhonikidze and Andreev bemoaning the fact that ''in recent times NOT has been removed from school curricula because of the vagueness of the subject and the absence of a textbook.'' On numerous occasions, she said, Lenin had insisted that NOT be introduced throughout the Soviet school system, but somehow the great leader's wish had been forgotten.[50] Only a year earlier TsIO had undertaken the task of compiling a textbook for NOT instruction at machine-building vuzy. But with the inauguration of the Stakhanovite movement, those teaching the few remaining NOT courses at vuzy were accused of ''not emphasizing the special features of the socialist organization of production'' because of ''an underevaluation and insufficient knowledge of the teachings of Marx-Engels-Lenin-Stalin as the single theoretical basis for the science of the organization of production.''[51] A deadly purge swept through the ranks of NOT instructors. Indicative of the confusion that followed, TsIO's project for composing a new management textbook dragged on for more than two years. The final product was stilted in its presentation and relied heavily on quotations from Stalin. Even so, it came under fire almost immediately for failing to devote sufficient attention to the Stakhanovite movement and refusing ''to denounce completely 'theories' and views in the field of the organization of production that are inimical to Marxism.''[52]

By 1938 management science remained a discipline in name only. A guide for instructors of courses on production organization published in that year by the Ordzhonikidze Engineering-Economics Institute (one of the few vuzy where the discipline continued to be offered) reflected the degree to which NOT had been swallowed by Stalin's cult. "Some people," it noted, "have had pompous daydreams about creating a true Marxist theory of the socialist organization of production . . . as if the necessary theoretical basis for the science . . . did not already exist." To the contrary, the authors argued, such a science did exist in the works of Comrade Stalin, who "with exceptional depth has worked out issues of economic management and the organization of labor under the dictatorship of the proletariat." Therefore, it was "indisputable that the next task in the area of developing our discipline consists not in conjuring up a special theory, but in the deepest and most conscientious study of that already existing theory developed in the works of Marx, Engels, Lenin, and Stalin and in a thorough study of the broad practical material which we have in light of this theory."[53]

Throughout this period executive training bore a narrowly technical orientation. In 1936 only a small proportion (14 percent) of enterprise directors had a higher education.[54] The vast majority were *praktiki*, lacking any formal education beyond high school. In the early thirties a number of training programs were created to provide praktiki with a rudimentary technical education; in all of them, training in the managerial disciplines was absent. One such program, whose goal was to impart a part-time technical training to factory managers, was the FON (*Fakul'tet osobogo naznacheniia*), or Special-Purpose Faculty. The first FON was established in 1931 at the Bauman Higher Technical Institute on an experimental basis. By the end of 1932 there were eleven such programs, six of which were located in Moscow. But a spot check conducted in 1933 revealed that three-quarters of those attending FON programs were not executives at all, but rather would-be vuz students who used the training as a preparatory school for college.[55] In general the level of instruction at these programs was poor. In May 1934 the FON programs were accused of "not coping with their task of making every manager an engineer" and were abolished; their assets were transferred to a new set of executive training programs, the Institutes for Upgrading the Qualifications of Managers (*Instituty povysheniia kvalifikatsii khoziaistvennikov*), known by their initials, IPKKh.

Like the FON, the IPKKh provided managers with part-time engineering instruction devoid of economic or managerial training.

Unlike its predecessor, the IPKKh was more successful in attracting executive personnel to the classroom, since trainees were commandeered by their commissariats. Even so, the IPKKh programs experienced their own problems. Out of the seven thousand trainees who attended from 1934 to 1936, 70 percent had only an elementary school education. Since the short IPKKh programs could not cope with the needs of such students, the period of study was extended to four years in 1936—making them little different from part-time vuzy. Even before the Great Purge, turnover among IPKKh staff and administrators was high. In 1934 and 1935, 40 percent of IPKKh directors were replaced.[56] The IPKKh programs survived the Great Purge, but in 1941 after Hitler's invasion they were disbanded due to the war effort.

The industrial academies were subjected to a thorough purging and reorganization. In the fall of 1935, not long after the Stakhanovite movement appeared, Stalin decided that Stakhanovite workers should be admitted in large numbers to vuzy, trained as engineers, and promoted to leading executive posts as replacements for the red directors.[57] In March 1936 Zhdanov announced that a special enrollment of Stakhanovites would take place at the Leningrad Industrial Academy. Of the new trainees, 57 percent came straight from the workers' bench; another 37 percent were foremen or brigadiers; the remaining 6 percent were shop heads or assistant shop heads. Stalin liked the idea so much that in September 1936 he ordered that the incoming class at the Stalin Industrial Academy, where top-level executives for the Soviet economy were supposed to be trained, consist primarily of Stakhanovites rather than managers already possessing executive experience.[58] Gravely wounded by political intrigues, purges, and reorganizations, the industrial academies limped along until January 1941, when Stalin transferred their facilities to the vuzy.

Management-training programs that survived until Hitler's invasion ceased to function during the war. After 1945 several branch academies were reopened for retraining executives who had been away at the front. Narrowly technical in orientation, these programs were eliminated in August 1956, purportedly because they had outlived their purpose. Similarly, a number of Institutes for Upgrading Qualifications (IPK) were reopened after 1945. But unlike their predecessors, they were entirely devoted to training engineering and technical personnel, not managers. When Khrushchev abolished most central ministries in his *sovnarkhoz* reform of 1957, all but two IPK were disbanded.[59]

During the remainder of Stalin's rule, a stifling, dogmatic ideology encroached upon what was left of the managerial discipline. The few books on industrial management published during these years confined themselves to a formal, constitutional description of Soviet government, a list of six or seven features of party doctrine on administration, and quotations from the collected works of Comrade Stalin. The "objective laws" of socialist society were said to determine the behavior of executives, independent of their conscious knowledge or skills. Coercion was portrayed as a legitimate means for goading managers into action. One textbook warned executives that violations of the technical and design specifications confirmed in an enterprise plan were criminal offenses and would be prosecuted accordingly. The same textbook credited Stalin with having "raised Lenin's directives on organizational leadership to a new, higher level," and with having "enriched and developed them as applied to new tasks of socialist construction."[60]

At least one major attempt was made to revive the managerial sciences after the war. Nikolai Voznesenskii, Stalin's top economic administrator, had been working on a book entitled *The Political Economy of Communism* before he was arrested and shot in 1949. As a party executive in the Donbass in the mid-twenties, Voznesenskii had been exposed firsthand to NOT methods, which were widely applied there during those years. Voznesenskii's unfinished book called for, among other things, a renewal of serious work in the economic and managerial sciences. Though he was dismissed in March 1949, his work was not publicly criticized until December 1952, when ideologist Mikhail Suslov bitterly attacked the philosopher P. N. Fedoseev for having described Voznesenskii's earlier book, *The War Economy of the USSR*, as a "valuable contribution to Soviet economic science." Much of Stalin's last work, *The Economic Problems of Socialism*, was devoted to an attack on the ideas of Voznesenskii and the economist Leonid Yaroshenko, who were accused of promulgating unorthodox views on economic science. Yaroshenko, in particular, was charged with seeking to create a political economy that dealt more realistically with managerial problems. He was accused of equating communism with "the scientific organization of productive forces" and of aiming to fashion a "Universal Organizational Science" in imitation of Bogdanov. Stalin declared at the time that "problems of the rational organization of productive forces, the planning of the national economy, and so forth, should not be the subject of political economy, but rather should be the subject of the economic policy of executive organs." In other words, managerial problems should be in the hands of politicians and top-level administrators rather than scholars. The behavior of the industrial executive, Stalin asserted, was guided by "economic laws" that "operate independently of human will."[61]

The fundamental thrust of Stalinist administrative thought was to deny legitimacy to managerial authority by denying that bureaucratic administration required specialized knowledge beyond a technical and ideological education. Throughout this period and up to the late 1950s, a new orthodoxy reigned on the subject of executive training, one which contrasted sharply with that laid down by Lenin in his final works. Rather than aiding managers, education beyond an understanding of plant technology was considered of little aid in learning executive skills, which, it was said, could only be acquired through on-the-job experience. According to one party textbook on personnel policy, "The art of leadership can only be mastered by active participation in political life and in the practice of communist construction . . . There are no schools and no books that can create an executive; he advances and is tempered in the process of life itself, at work." "The school of life, the school of practical activity," another party text proclaimed, "is the best way of examining, training, and tempering personnel."[62] Managers were left on their own to discover through costly trial and error what worked and what did not work in production. As I. V. Paramonov, an industrial executive of the Stalin years, later reminisced: "All of us, the first Soviet managers, learned to manage industrial enterprises, construction projects, trusts, larger economic organs, and Soviet institutions by our own personal mistakes."[63]

Such "mistakes" could cost the enterprise director his freedom and his life. More frequently, violations of plan fulfillment were punished by dismissal. In 1939 in the ferrous metals industry alone more than 2600 executives and specialists were removed for failing to fulfill their production plans.[64] The enormous turnover in managerial posts during the Great Purge was unusual for the Stalin years only in its scope and in the consequences suffered by its victims. Both before and after the purge, turnover among managerial personnel was extremely high. In 1934, several years before the fury of the secret police descended upon the Soviet manager, Gastev complained that so many executives had been changed during the previous few years that TsIT's organizing brigades "could not have a very strong effect" on production. Two decades later, in 1955, Bulganin similarly criticized the high level of turnover among factory directors, which in some branches had reached annual rates between 40 and 50 percent.[65] The aim of these and other disciplinary measures was to ensure by means of intimidation that managers would never lose sight of their personal responsibility for the fulfillment of their weighty tasks. Managers, Stalin said at the Seventeenth Party Congress in 1934, were to hide no more behind excuses of "objective" conditions which supposedly prevented them from carrying out their plan assignments; rather, failure was to be directly attributed to the managers themselves, who were to bear the blame for the shortcomings of the economic system.[66]

Disciplinary campaigns, because of their effect on morale, the high cost of enforcing bureaucratic rules, and the tensions that they foster in organizations, tend to be of short duration. Any attempt to sustain them over a long period of time is likely to lead to an escalation of sanctions, a bloated enforcement apparatus, and even to a spiral of violence. In addition to the Great Purge, a series of waves of violence occurred during Stalin's rule, each accompanied by new and more forceful measures of coercion. The introduction of draconian labor and management legislation by Stalin in the early thirties may have been successful in squeezing more output from recalcitrant managers and workers for a time. But in 1933 transportation and production bottlenecks caused a sharp drop in economic indicators. New purges swept through the industrial bureaucracy, and brute force was applied on the country's railroads in order to clear up the situation. After 1933 Soviet industry experienced three consecutive years of outstanding growth. But beginning in 1937, due largely to the purge, economic growth fell sharply, improving only slightly by the outbreak of the war. In response, Stalin turned once again to draconian measures. In December 1938 workbooks for recording infractions of labor discipline were introduced.

Unjustified absence from work for more than twenty minutes was subject to criminal prosecution. Managers who failed to apply the new law found themselves facing yearlong prison sentences. In June 1940 these regulations were amended to include "loafing," and workers were legally prohibited, under the threat of arrest, from changing jobs. In July 1940, in response to the continuing production of poor-quality goods under the pressures of the plan, violations of quality indicators by managers were made a criminal offense. Several months later another decree called for the prosecution of managers who introduced changes in the technical specifications of products without the direct approval of their superiors. New waves of arrests followed to demonstrate that these laws were to be taken seriously. Although many of these statutes and other measures intended to enforce discipline fell into disuse in the early fifties, they remained legally in force until 1956, when they were quietly repealed.[67] The periodic conduct of disciplinary campaigns by Stalin and the codification of legal sanctions for violations of bureaucratic rules constituted a massive attempt to institutionalize coercion as an administrative strategy for rooting out bureaucratic inertia.

In many cases disciplinary measures forced managers and laborers to work more conscientiously and even to perform the seemingly impossible. Throughout the Stalin years the Soviet Union recorded impressive rates of economic growth. Moreover, the country successfully mobilized its economic resources to defeat its technologically superior Nazi opponent. But although Stalin's war against bureaucracy was successful in raising output indicators, it paradoxically intensified the very resistance against which it was directed. The many studies of Soviet managerial behavior during these years testify to the ways in which a political economy of force generates its own subtle forms of resistance.[68] The threat of removal, or even the extreme penalty of death, for failure to fulfill plan targets only exacerbated familiar bureaucratic distortions. All considerations except the fulfillment of the quantitative gross output indicator had to be brushed aside, for it was on this thread that the life and livelihood of the director hung. Cutting costs, producing quality goods, introducing new technologies, engaging in experiments, or even meeting contracts to one's customers not only ran counter to the prevailing system of incentives, but such behavior could also ruin a manager because it threatened the strict fulfillment of the output plan by which his fate was judged.

The regime's public statements continually praised the risk-taking, cost-conscious, and innovative manager, and penal sanctions were introduced to discourage poor-quality production. But in practice both incentive and penal policies made such behavior unprofitable and self-injurious. In the face of rampant shortages of materials and labor, factory executives hoarded huge caches of supplies and hired additional workers in order to avoid being caught shorthanded. Both poor performance and excessively good performance were punished by the logic of the system, for in the latter case one was rewarded the following year with still higher plan targets. The Soviet executive quickly grasped that only through engaging in illegal and semilegal practices (revision of the planned mix of output, "creative" accounting techniques, bribery, hidden market exchange, "family circles," and other maneuvers punishable by law) could he ensure his own survival. These were the real lessons that managers learned in the so-called school of life. And whether he risked falling on the wrong side of the law for the sake of the plan, or whether he risked nonfulfillment of the plan by refusing to engage in illegal practices, the plant director lived a precarious existence.

To his subordinates the Stalinist manager was a powerful figure— in Kaganovich's words, the enterprise's "sole sovereign" for whom "the earth should tremble" when he walked onto the factory floor.[69] In reality the behavior of this "sovereign" was constricted by centrally determined prices, by success indicators, by endless regulations, decrees, and laws, by the ubiquitous secret police, and by the logic of the bureaucratic machine of which he was but one easily replaceable cog. Unlike the red directors, the beneficiaries of the Great Purge, whether they were in favor of or opposed to managerial professionalization, did not dare to attempt group political action on their own behalf. It is doubtful that they even thought in such terms. Rather, divisions within the elite along departmental, hierarchical, and patron-client lines fostered a spirited competitiveness among managers for access to the resources, investment funds, and political favors that were essential to their survival.[70] Managerial professionalism was alien to the Stalinist manager for good reason, for not only were such ideas considered dangerous, but the regime had also eliminated the political and organizational conditions for any potential coalition between rationalizers and managers. As with previous generations of Soviet managers, concern for the values of the rationalization movement—productivity, quality, innovation, and cost-effectiveness—was discouraged by the system of political and economic controls to which the Stalinist manager was subject. But whereas many red directors had feared the rationalization movement because it threatened to replace them, complicated plan fulfillment, and eroded their authority in the enterprise, the Stalinist manager saw the rationalization movement and the values it represented as a luxury that he could afford to contemplate only at the risk of jeopardizing his freedom and his life.

Yet, in spite of the mortal blows the rationalization movement received, a tiny contingent of rationalizers, hidden in the nooks and crannies of Stalinist research institutes, survived these years of violence and repression to plant the seeds for a revival of the managerial sciences. Chronometric norm-determination was practiced throughout the 1940s, though with less frequency and even greater inconsistency than in the past. The most systematic work in this area was conducted in defense industry—in particular at NIAT, where TsIT personnel who had weathered the purge and dissolution of their institute continued to work. The inventor of TsIT's social-engineering machine, N. A. Bernshtein, continued his experiments in biomechanics at the All-Union Institute for Experimental Medicine. He would eventually play an active role in the founding of cybernetics in the Soviet Union.[71] Other NOTisty who survived would provide valuable insights into the history of the NOT movement for a new generation of rationalizers searching for lessons from a forgotten past. These and other examples attest to the historical continuity of the Soviet rationalization movement. For though Stalin, in his war against bureaucracy, could vanquish individual scholars and bureaucrats, bureaucratism and the need for organizational expertise were not so easily eliminated.

PART
TWO

. . . . . .

The Second Cycle

5

. . . . . .

The Rebirth of Managerialism

True freedom of will is the ability to make knowledgeable decisions.

—*Editorial in* Ekonomicheskaia gazeta, *September 1965*

The overriding political question facing the Soviet Union since 1953, aside from how to deal with Stalin's crimes, has been what to do about the economic system Stalin created. Though the Stalinist industrial system attained many of its goals, its successes were due less to a rational use of resources than to reliance on force and on so-called extensive factors of growth: the addition of increasing numbers of inputs from the Soviet Union's enormous material and human reserves in order to achieve higher levels of outputs. By 1960 Soviet industrial output was thirty-four times higher than on the eve of the industrialization drive. But by then it was beginning to be clear that the old approaches to running industry were themselves barriers to further industrial progress.

A new set of problems connected with the increasing complexity of the economy, with shortages of new sources of inputs to fuel economic growth, and with the rise of new goals of quality, innovation, and productivity plagued industrial decision-makers. In 1937 Soviet industry was administered by five industrial narkomaty; by

1956, on the eve of Khrushchev's sovnarkhoz reform, the number of industrial ministries had burgeoned to thirty-six. Academician Glushkov's famous prediction that, barring major changes in the system, nearly the entire adult population of the country would be engaged in planning, accounting, and management by the mid-1980s reflected the growing administrative morass involved in coordinating an industrial economy which, by 1960, included forty-five thousand enterprises.[1] Even in the late twenties and early thirties the Soviet economy had experienced serious shortages of skilled labor; in the 1960s and 1970s, because of the ravages of the war, declining birthrates in the European portion of the country, and the extensive misuse of existing labor, all labor was in short supply, skilled and unskilled alike. In the early 1960s the Soviets also began to brush up against natural constraints on the availability and accessibility of raw materials, making it necessary to invest large amounts of capital in searching for new supplies and to cut waste in the use of existing stocks. Under Stalin the suppression of domestic consumption and the draining of resources from the countryside had provided Soviet planners with an abundance of capital by which to implement their five-year plans. But beginning in the 1950s and 1960s consumption and agriculture soaked up large amounts of investment, putting pressure on industry to increase the efficiency of the capital at its disposal. For all these reasons, Soviet leaders began to regard growth through efficiency rather than growth through expansion as a top priority.

It was in this context that, after a hiatus of twenty-five years, the Soviet Union once again looked to the West, and in particular to the descendants of the Scientific Management movement, for inspiration in dealing with its industrial problems. In the 1950s and 1960s the offspring of Scientific Management, management science, underwent enormous growth in America and Western Europe. In less than a quarter of a century the number of U.S. business schools multiplied almost seven times (from 163 in 1956 to 1100 in 1979), and the number of students training in these programs increased more than twelve times (from approximately four thousand in 1956 to fifty thousand in 1979). By the early seventies almost one in five top executives of corporate America, as well as 40 percent of those receiving promotions to high-level corporate posts, held an

MBA degree.[2] In the postwar capitalist countries the managerial specialist, working as either consultant or educator, became a central figure in the conduct of business. Thousands of private consulting firms emerged, draining off the best and the brightest from American business schools. Managerial consultancy was transformed, in the words of one Dutch expert, into "an operation of such magnitude and specialization" that it had become "the domain of high-calibre experts" and "a product supplied to top management, rather than . . . a product of top management."[3]

Given the prominence of the managerial sciences in the capitalist world, it was only logical that in a time of economic difficulties the Soviets should feel a strong attraction to these doctrines. Since the first wave of Soviet interest in capitalist managerial techniques, the Scientific Management movement had undergone significant changes in packaging and approach. In a reaction to Taylorism and its excesses, the focus of managerial thought at first shifted from the study of worker gestures, labor physiology, and functional organization to a "human relations" approach, emphasizing the social preconditions for productive labor. But by the 1950s a plethora of schools and approaches had emerged, described by some as a "management theory jungle."[4] Many of the new methods and techniques traced their origins to the movement founded by Taylor. In some cases old techniques were applied in more sophisticated forms in fields which were new in name only. Modern executive testing was not far removed from the abandoned discipline of psychotechnics, and Henry Gantt, had he been alive and familiar with the use of computers, would certainly have recognized his own work in what goes by the name of operations research. The computer, with its capacity for rapid processing of information, represented a revolutionary breakthrough in organizational technology; yet the goals of office automation, of coherent and efficient documentation systems, and of speeding and streamlining organizational communications were pursued for decades before the first computers came into existence. Management science as it emerged after the war was strongly affected by systems theory and the behavioral revolution. Many of the fundamental assumptions concerning organizational behavior changed drastically as a result of these influences. But the underlying purpose of management science was never far removed from that of Scientific Management. Both were attempts to develop intellectually complex techniques for coordinating human behavior in organizations.

Much of the politics surrounding the rebirth of management science in the Soviet Union in the 1960s and 1970s resembled the controversies that had plagued the Scientific Management movement in the early 1920s. Proponents of a managerial strategy again encountered resistance from ideological elites, who accused them of acting as a bridgehead for an alien, capitalist, work culture. To overcome this opposition, advocates of managerialism, like earlier generations of NOTisty, relied on the support of powerful patrons within the leadership who hoped that new organizational techniques would multiply productivity and enhance their control over organizational processes. And like their predecessors, the new management experts were seriously divided, both over their approaches to the subject and over the role which technique should play in economic policy. As in the past, these divisions hardened into a series of political, bureaucratic, and ideological struggles for control over the managerial discipline—conflicts which were to determine the shape of Soviet administrative policy for two decades.

Soviet management scientists trace the rebirth of their discipline to 1962. In that year, during nationwide discussions over economic reform, proposals surfaced for establishing an independent science of management, for borrowing managerial techniques from abroad, and for training industrial executives in this new branch of knowledge. Official recognition that a special discipline of management did indeed exist was not granted until three years later, and the controversies surrounding management science continued for at least a decade more. During this period significant changes occurred in national administrative strategies and in the purposes of management science as they were interpreted by politicians. If in the early sixties the management-science movement was part of the broader movement for economic reform in the Soviet Union, by the mid-seventies it had become a counterreform movement, as rationalization substituted for structural decentralization. From the late 1950s to the early 1970s two sets of overlapping struggles were waged: the first, between those who proposed that a new science of management be established and those who, for bureaucratic or ideological reasons, sought to prevent it from emerging; and the second, among the supporters of management science for control over the new discipline and over the direction of administrative policy. These conflicts were not confined to the pages of scholarly journals or to academic conference rooms, but were closely connected to power struggles waged in the Kremlin. Behind them lay the broader issue of de-Stalinization in the economic system.

"Harebrained Schemes" and Administrative Secularization

It is a paradox of Soviet history that Khrushchev, the man removed by his colleagues for his "harebrained" administrative schemes, oversaw the rehabilitation of administrative science in the Soviet Union. Khrushchev's administrative strategies were, to say the least, full of contradictions.

On the one hand, he emphasized the need for administrative and labor discipline and championed popular participation in administration. He established comrade courts, neighborhood vigilante groups, and people's control commissions to enforce law and order in the factory and on the street. He fired bitter tirades at managerial officials for their "conceit and complacency . . . and their loss of a sense of responsibility for the work entrusted to them."[5] A number of his policies were intended to strengthen party control over managerial cadres—in particular, the dismantling of central ministries and reorganization of industry under territorial *sovnarkhozy* (economic councils) in 1957, and the division of the party apparatus into industrial and agricultural sectors in 1962. Khrushchev promoted mass participation in administration as a means for holding administrators accountable and for attacking managerial resistance. Since his political enemies were concentrated in the industrial ministries, this mix of disciplinary and mobilizational strategies was as much a matter of expediency as of conviction. But many of these projects were ill planned and ill conceived, and they resulted in considerable confusion. The failure of Khrushchev's administrative policies and the opposition they engendered were major causes of his removal in October 1964.

On the other hand, measures aimed at diluting the extreme centralization of the Stalinist economic system by granting factory directors broader operational authority were enacted in 1955, and under Khrushchev's leadership a gradual secularization in the relationship between science and ideology took place. It was this policy, in particular, which led to the first stirrings of a revival of Taylorist research in Russia. At the July 1955 Central Committee Plenum, industrial executives were taken to task for their lack of attention to production standardization and automation and for the unwieldy size of the industrial bureaucracy. Particular scorn was reserved for the chaotic state of affairs in norm-determination. On-the-spot inspections had revealed that the norms used to govern identical work in different ministries varied as much as 40 percent. As in the past, it was charged that "tariff scales and rates have become obsolete," and "norms are not being established on the basis of technical achievements and the experience of advanced workers, but are, rather, artificially driven below the level of wages."[6] In May 1955 a State Committee for Labor and Wage Issues, chaired by Kaganovich, was established to address these problems. Ironically, it was Khrushchev's rival, Kaganovich, one of the leaders of the attack on "limit" norm-setting in the mid-thirties, who was to bear the heat for the unsatisfactory state of norm-determination in the 1950s.

Not long after the July Plenum the Council of Ministers decreed that an Institute of Labor should be organized under the State Committee for Labor and Wage Issues. The title of the institute, patterned as it was after TsIT, showed that almost twenty years after Gastev's death the memory of him and his institute was still alive. Shortly after the death of Stalin, Gastev's son had raised the subject of his father's rehabilitation with procuracy officials. According to the younger Gastev, appeals were also made to Andreev and Shvernik, both of whom had been involved in the work of TsIT in the 1920s, as well as to Molotov. But only after June 1956, when Kaganovich was removed from the State Committee for Labor and Wage Issues, did the Gastev family receive a positive reply. Then Gastev's son was summoned by the new committee chairman, Aleksandr Volkov, a Khrushchev protégé, and asked to provide information about TsIT and his father for an internal report on the relevance of TsIT's work to contemporary problems.[7]

Throughout 1957 articles by former TsIT employees appeared in the journal of the Institute of Labor, some referring to Gastev and TsIT directly and calling upon researchers to utilize the "positive experience of the past." In November the State Committee for

Labor and Wage Issues officially rehabilitated TsIT and paid homage to "the great service" performed by the institute in developing the Soviet economy. Gastev's ghost, it seems, had returned to haunt his enemies, for one of the charges brought against Kaganovich shortly after his removal from power in 1957 was that he harbored "dogmatic" views on issues of labor organization and had attempted to hold back the development of research on norm-determination.[8]

In the years following the Twentieth Party Congress, chronometric norm-determination experienced a revival in the Soviet Union. The works of Taylor and Ford once again were praised, and new interest was displayed in analyzing foreign research.[9] Yet, as the Soviets looked westward after two decades of isolation, they quickly realized that their old Taylorist methods were no longer in fashion. At the Twentieth Party Congress Mikoian had criticized the state of Soviet research on the capitalist West, and in particular, on economic trends in Western economies.[10] Soon an Institute of the World Economy and International Relations (IMEMO) was organized to provide systematic analyses of developments in capitalist countries. One of the first tasks of the institute was to translate a series of reports, written by a delegation of British economists and engineers, on American managerial organization—the first published materials on capitalist managerial techniques made available in the Soviet Union for more than two decades.[11]

In the meantime other scientific disciplines closely related to NOT were emerging from the shadow of Stalinist orthodoxy. In the late Stalin period cybernetics had been labeled "a science of obscurantists" by conservative ideologists. By 1954, however, its merits were being openly discussed in the press, and in 1958, with the founding of a Scientific Council on Cybernetics under the Academy of Sciences, the field was officially recognized as a legitimate area for scientific inquiry.[12] Economics underwent a similar process of secularization in the late 1950s. At the Twentieth Party Congress Mikoian led the call for a revival of the economic sciences and criticized economists who relied on the dogmatic formulas of Stalin. Heated debates broke out between conservative political economists and the proponents of quantitative approaches over the meaning of the law of value under socialism and the use of mathematical modeling in planning and price formation. In 1958 barely a dozen Soviet specialists were investigating mathematical modeling in planning and management; within three years more than forty institutes were engaged in such research. By the late 1950s the standing of economics had been restored to the point where the regime could announce a major campaign for "economic literacy" among Soviet managers. Part-time courses were organized under local party organizations and vuzy, and the first Soviet textbooks on industrial economics since the 1930s were published.[13] These textbooks contain some of the earliest assertions in the post-Stalin period that managers should be taught the discipline of management.

In the early 1920s the conflict over trade union authority had provided the initial impetus for Lenin's and Trotsky's efforts to organize the Scientific Management movement. In the early 1960s political divisions within the leadership once again placed these issues on the agenda. A strong rivalry developed between Suslov and Il'ichev, Khrushchev's main ideologist. Il'ichev attacked by raising the Voznesenskii case at the Twenty-Second Party Congress in 1961. He indirectly accused Suslov of conservatism and dogmatism in economic theory and cited as evidence Suslov's role in repressing Voznesenskii. Suslov is said to have countered in an unsigned article in *Pravda* in which he called "groundless" the assertion that "no important works on political economy, philosophy, and history were printed" during the Stalin years.[14]

The Suslov-Il'ichev rivalry coincided with the rise of Aleksei Kosygin to the party's inner circle. A lifelong industrial administrator, Kosygin became a major sponsor of reformist economic ideas. That he had a direct role in organizing the revival of managerial research in the Soviet Union is beyond doubt. In 1961 his son-in-law, Dzherman Gvishiani, was permitted to establish a Laboratory for Problems of Management under the Philosophy Department at Moscow State University (MGU). Support within MGU came from Rector Petrovskii, who had taken the lead in developing mathematical economics at the university. But the Philosophy Department, as well as the scholarly community in general, was deeply divided over this new addition. Three years later the laboratory was transferred to the more congenial atmosphere of the Economics Department.

Like its predecessors of the 1920s, the MGU laboratory at first barely survived. It was staffed by only eight people and was given "no concrete research topics or assignments," since its primary purpose was to justify its own existence. Gavril Popov, later head of the laboratory and dean of the university's Economics Department, wrote of these early days: "The fact was that then the very idea that management would be an independent field for research needed substantiation. It was necessary to explain in general terms the problem itself and only afterward choose topics for research." Petrovskii nursed the controversial laboratory by providing it with "five years of 'freedom' " from the normal responsibilities of university organizations and by insulating it from the attacks of conservative ideologues. The staff spent most of its time examining foreign management literature and rediscovering the history of past Soviet efforts to import NOT in the 1920s.[15] The laboratory's first product, Gvishiani's book *The Sociology of Business*, was simultaneously a critique of Western managerial techniques and a plea for their applicability to Soviet conditions.[16]

At the end of 1962 Khrushchev advanced his plan for dividing the party apparatus into industrial and agricultural sectors—a reform aimed at injecting the party more deeply into economic administration. The scheme was particularly repugnant to conservative *apparatchiki* and ideologues, who feared that it would weaken the party's control over society by turning it into a loose collection of economic managers. In support of Khrushchev's plan a previously unpublished first draft of Lenin's pamphlet of 1918, *Urgent Tasks of Soviet Power*, was suddenly "discovered" and given broad publicity. In it Lenin had argued that the party was in need of "economic organizers" rather than "political agitators" and, in a reversal of the usual formula attributed to him, had contended that "political tasks occupy a place subordinate to economic tasks." The document also contained one of Lenin's most favorable evaluations of Taylorism and its potential for preparing the road to communist society through rationalization.[17]

Soon after the appearance of this document, public proposals for reestablishing management science began to surface. N. Adfel'dt, the newly appointed head of MGU's Laboratory for Problems of Management, called the traditional engineering education of Soviet industrial executives "clearly inadequate" for the tasks they performed. Learning administration through on-the-job experience was "often unsystematic, its deficiencies only partially offset" by the "general background, talent, and intuition" of managers. Executives were plagued by the diseases of bureaucracy, overloaded with trivial issues, and saddled with inefficient staffs. Training in the art of administration, Adfel'dt said, "could become a real remedy for ailments of this sort."[18] One month later an editorial in the planning journal *Planovoe khoziaistvo* obliquely cited "the experience of choosing directors in a number of countries" in support of training young college graduates "of a broad profile" in "the practice of economic leadership."[19]

In mid-October in an address to the Academy of Sciences, Il'ichev formally proposed the development of "a science of planning, a science of management of the national economy in accordance with the recommendations of Lenin." Deploring "the vestiges of a dogmatic, talmudic attitude toward theory," he criticized Stalin's treatment of Voznesenskii for "leading objectively to a divorce of economic theory from national economic practice." Academician A. I. Berg, chairman of the Academy's Scientific Council on Cybernetics, cited the general trend toward quantification in economics as proof that management was already becoming an independent branch of scientific activity. Recalling the NOT movement of the 1920s and its prominent role in formulating economic policy, Berg argued that the time had come to reestablish "a science of the organization and management of labor." "This science," he said, "is not included in our list of social science disciplines anywhere, and books and journals on it are not being published." In Berg's formulation the new discipline was to be an extension of cybernetics, which he called the direct "heir and successor" of the NOT movement.[20] In support of this claim Berg organized a commemorative meeting in early November 1962 to mark Gastev's eightieth birthday, where he called upon cyberneticians to "continue the work begun by Gastev and Kerzhentsev."[21] At the November Central Committee Plenum, Khrushchev publicly lent his support to the proponents of the new managerial discipline and advocated borrowing from capitalist managerial experience. "Why don't we use that which is rational and economically profitable from what the capitalists have?" he asked. "In the conditions of a planned economy, all this could be realized more simply and easily than under conditions of capitalist competition."[22]

In 1963 practical work on management science began. A Soviet delegation headed by V. Lisitsyn, deputy chairman of Gosplan RSFSR and a close associate of Kosygin, was dispatched to Harvard Business School. Lisitsyn returned home with proposals to create similar institutions throughout the Soviet Union.[23] Soon Soviet scholars were dispatched to American business schools to study American managerial practice. In Moscow instructors from the Ordzhonikidze Engineering-Economics Institute undertook the design of a computer-aided accounting system for the Likhachev Automobile Plant. In Minsk a Central Research Institute for the Organization and Technology of Management was established to investigate plant automation and to design management-information systems.[24] In Sverdlovsk a NOT plan, subjecting workers to systematic chronometric observation, was drawn up at the Urals Chemical Machine-Building Plant; within a year and a half more than four hundred enterprises in the province were engaged in similar projects. In Novosibirsk NOT laboratories were created with the help of researchers from the Institute for Economics and Organization of Industrial Production of the Siberian Division of the Academy of Sciences, which also convened a conference of local researchers and managers on the subject.[25] In May 1963 Gvishiani, recently appointed deputy chairman of the State Committee for the Coordination of Scientific Research, organized a Scientific Council for Problems of the Scientific Basis of Management, whose purpose was to "coordinate and determine the directions of research" on management throughout the country. At the council's first meeting in July, he observed that "the necessity of systematically retraining the executive personnel of enterprises" had "already been recognized" by the political leadership; the main task of the council was "the creation of a textbook on management science."[26]

But objections to a managerial discipline soon appeared. In early 1963 A. Birman, pro-rector of the Plekhanov Institute of the National Economy, published a pamphlet entitled *Some Problems of a Science of Socialist Management*, in which he lamented that "one can hardly find a book where . . . it is clearly written how one should manage, for example, a state machine-building plant, a grain *sovkhoz* [state farm], or a division of Gosbank." Birman's plea for "a science of how to organize the management of a socialist economy . . . and the leadership of the national economy" was considered so controversial by the publishers that in the preface they warned that much of the brochure had "a polemical character, and far from all the proposals in it can be considered indisputable." Birman himself commented on the conservative opposition to a managerial discipline that was coming from political economists who claimed, like Stalin, that the activity of executives was governed by objective economic laws.[27] Similar signs of foot-dragging were evident in February 1963, when Gvishiani addressed specialists on the capitalist economies at the Academy of Sciences concerning "the task facing Soviet scientists, of making a complex analysis of management problems." Gvishiani's speech was devoted to an analysis of American management theories and management development. "It would be useful," he argued, "to borrow in a critical manner all the valuable things that have been accumulated in this field abroad, and above all in the United States." But "some scientific institutions," Gvishiani indicated, were "underestimating the significance of questions of managerial organization" for the Soviet economy.[28]

Among the supporters of managerial research, differences quickly appeared over the direction that the discipline should take. In October 1963 at a general meeting of the Academy of Sciences, Il'ichev once again railed against "dogmatism" in economic thought and supported the development of "a science of management of the development of socialist society," which he called "a Leninist science." His idea was a policy-oriented political economy of socialism, a branch of knowledge that would research "the conscious use of the action of the most important laws of development of socialist society."[29] Reform-minded economists similarly advocated an administrative science closely linked to managerial practice, a body of knowledge which, in Birman's words, lay somewhere "between branch economics and theoretical political economy," but one aimed at providing managers with the skills and knowledge they needed in order to assume greater decision-making authority. These differences coincided with the so-called Liberman debates, in which calls were issued for far-reaching economic decentralization and for using profit as the major criterion for judging enterprise performance. Allusions to the need for economic reform frequently appeared alongside proposals for a science of management and for professional training for executives. According to Birman, the development of such a science could not be carried out under the guidance of political economy, which was "concerned only with general theoretical conceptions of the economic laws of socialist society and does not give any concrete idea about either the mechanism of their appearance or the ways of mastering these laws."[30]

Conservative philosophers and political economists took issue with both of these conceptions. At the October 1963 meeting of the Academy, P. N. Fedoseev, head of its Institute of Philosophy, criticized a number of economists for their "narrow empiricism" and for displaying "elements of managerialism and technocratic theory" in their work.[31] An article published in *Kommunist* on the eve of the meeting had noted that a number of economists, "in particular, political economists," opposed the notion of a political economy of socialism, arguing dogmatically that "the study of productive forces is a task of the technical sciences only."[32]

Other academic disciplines also staked their claims on the new science. In 1963 and 1964 Soviet jurists argued that administrative law should serve as the basis for management science, since management pertains not only to economics but also to the organization of the entire state apparatus and to "all spheres of social life." The controversy stirred by Khrushchev's division of the party apparatus gave impetus to the jurists' assertions. In contrast to Khrushchev's spokesman Il'ichev, who had declared that management research should investigate "the growing role and significance of the party" in management, jurists wanted to research "the determination of which questions should be handled by state organs and which by social [party] organs, and what their interrelationships should be."[33] The new field of sociology had similar pretensions to a leading role in management science. In 1963 sociologists convened a conference at the Institute of Philosophy in order to recognize social psychology as a legitimate field of inquiry. Although they differed as to where this discipline belonged, the participants emphasized the important contributions that social psychology could make to the development of management science.[34] Finally, early in 1964 a group of conservative economists and cyberneticians, heeding Academician Berg's call for a fusion of cybernetics and Taylorist time-and-motion studies, advanced their own version of a "science of management and the organization of labor," aimed at strengthening central planning and work-place discipline through automation and norm-determination.[35]

Each of these groups sought to place its own stamp on the meaning of management and disputed with its competitors over their "distorted" interpretations. Economist Birman complained that jurists and sociologists were "objecting to developing this new section of the economic sciences" by claiming that "issues of managerial organization should be the subject of study of other scientific disciplines because they are closer to the legal sciences or to sociology." Birman conceded that "managerial issues do not only have an economic content." But "when one talks about a Teaching of Socialist Management," he wrote, "only or mostly economic problems come to mind."[36] Jurists, by contrast, criticized cyberneticians for their "completely incorrect" view that "cybernetics is becoming the successor to the scientific organization of labor and management." Rather, it was "only an important aid, a means for operative decision-making on specific issues." "One should not forget that a 'smart' machine will never be able to replace the living executive."[37] Even before serious research on management began, the reawakened management-science movement was plagued by major splits. Little wonder that in September 1964, a month before Khrushchev's removal, one observer noted with concern that "the term 'management science' is now being used in our literature in ways that are far from identical."[38]

The "Idealists" and the "Practical Men"

The political vacuum that followed Khrushchev's removal exacerbated conflicts over management science. To those who sought to effect a compromise among the warring disciplines, cyberneticians countered that any syncretic administrative science was not a true science but only a conglomeration of other sciences; true management theory, they asserted, could only be based on a general body of knowledge applicable to all systems.[39] At a conference held in December 1964 on the use of computers in management, Gvishiani criticized cyberneticians for their aggrandizing views. In the West, he said, a science of management as such did not exist, but "only particular issues of management that apply scientific methods." "Even purely formal, mathematical approaches to settling this problem require a critical attitude, since often they reflect a private-property approach in their actual statement of the problem."[40]

These disputes merged with a growing polarization within the leadership over economic reform. Kosygin, the new prime minister, viewed economic reform and management science as two sides of the same coin; if decision-making authority were to be decentralized, an idea which he championed, executives would need to be guided by knowledge in exercising their new authority. Within days after assuming his new post he unilaterally expanded the number of enterprises operating under the experimental Bolshevik-Maiak system, which eventually served as the model for the September 1965 economic reforms.[41] In his first major policy statement he called for an economic science "reflecting the laws of development of our economy and making it possible to adopt sound decisions." Kosygin envisioned a discipline geared to administrative practice. Quoting Lenin, he argued that the country was not in need of more "general arguments" but required instead "economics, in the sense of collecting, carefully verifying, and studying the facts of the actual construction of the new life." In a swipe at Khrushchev and a fillip at his conservative opponents in the leadership, he observed that Lenin had "demanded a practical, businesslike, and scientifically grounded approach to issues of economic construction; he scoffed at empty, insipid declarations."[42]

Three months later, in March 1965, the Council of Ministers established the first permanent training programs for managers since the 1930s. "By way of an exception" (a phrase suggesting less than full consensus), five faculties of organizers of industrial production and construction were to train managers under forty who had a higher education and at least five years of work experience and who had "recommended themselves well for executive work." Lasting from six months to a year, these experimental programs would teach trainees "the latest achievements in science and technology and the leading experience in the field of production organization and planning," including "the organization of labor, the use of contemporary computer technology, and mathematical methods in economic calculations." In their first year of operation the new faculties offered a thirty-hour course on management science, the first course on the subject to be taught in the Soviet Union in more than two decades.[43] A week after the promulgation of this decree, Kosygin forcefully championed greater managerial autonomy. "In the course of analyzing many important problems," he said, "we often find ourselves prisoners of laws we ourselves made, laws which should have been replaced long ago by new principles corresponding to the modern conditions that govern the development of production."[44]

As conflicts intensified over the role of expertise in economic policy, conservative ideologists struck back. In words reminiscent of the debates over the use of bourgeois specialists after the revolution, Stepanov, the editor of *Kommunist*, argued in a lengthy article in *Pravda* that "it is profoundly incorrect to equate communism merely with the fulfillment of the 'needs of the stomach,' with a narrow, pragmatic approach that is blind to the broad horizons of future higher ideals." He criticized the "narrow-minded 'practical men' who cannot see the forest for the trees, who get bogged down in details, and who lose sight of the overall picture." The task of the party was "not simply to manage the country, but to lead the country forward to the achievement of the higher historical goals of Marxism, to communism." Quoting Dzerzhinskii, he questioned those who denied the need for party controls over management and ideological training for executives:

> It is impossible to mechanize leadership and management. This work is intellectual and individual, but at the same time deeply collective and political. Enterprises and institutions do not work, but rather people; therefore one must study people, educate them, hold them more responsible in every unit for every matter, and know who does what, who is responsible for what, and to what degree. Mass educational, organizational, and political work with people is the basic content of party work, and through it influence is achieved over all sectors of state, economic, and social activity.

The party, he said, "is for concreteness and business efficiency in work, but at the same time it sharply criticizes 'harebrained scheming,' blind, mindless wallowing in trifling bustle and squabbles, whose admirers can still be found even to this day." Lest there be any doubt that Stepanov was referring to Kosygin, he summoned

Lenin to the task. "The machine eludes control: one believes that a man is there steering the wheel, but the machine does not go where it is driven . . . It does not operate quite as the man at the wheel imagines, and sometimes quite differently."[45]

Several days later *Izvestiia* responded with a long editorial criticizing "various simplified conceptions of the paths for achieving the goals that stand before us," as well as "disregard for economic laws in the leadership of the national economy." In contrast to Stepanov, who had defended ideological training for managers lest they lose sight of the party's lofty goals, *Izvestiia* emphasized the need for practical training in management science for industrial executives:

> It stands to reason that the employee who is trusted with leadership needs to know much. He should know technology and production techniques to perfection; he should know the economics of production; and he should know the laws of the scientific organization of labor. Now it is becoming more and more obvious that under contemporary conditions it is difficult for the executive to achieve substantial success if he has not mastered management science.

"The combination of business efficiency and loyalty to high ideals," *Izvestiia* declared, "is characteristic of the Soviet executive, no matter what his post . . . When all is said, the Soviet director is not a narrow-minded 'practical man.' "[46]

Parallel conflicts could be observed within the academic community. In the spring and summer of 1965 a flurry of articles staking each discipline's claim to control over management science appeared in the scholarly and economic press.[47] A four-day conference of economists and managers was held in June at MGU to discuss the issue. The resolutions of the meeting called "the formulation of a scientific theory of management" an "urgent task of the social sciences," and economic institutes were to play "a decisive role in the elaboration" of this theory. But political economists, reflecting the strains between "idealists" and "practical men," convened a separate session. N. A. Tsagalov, a political economist from MGU, conceded that management science was "different from political economy," but he insisted that "only political economy can serve as a scientific basis and as a starting point for management theory." The main task of political economists was to "develop a theory of management of socialist production on the basis of political economy."[48]

While the Moscow conference was drawing to a close, *Literaturnaia gazeta*, then a stronghold of reformist economic thought, published a fanfare review of a new book, *Organization and Management*, by V. I. Tereshchenko, an American management consultant who had returned to his native Ukraine in 1960. The book described Tereshchenko's experiences working in corporate capitalism and emphasized the importance of Western managerial practice for his newly adopted homeland.[49] The article, entitled "The Gain from Trifles," was a scathing attack on the Stepanov line, including a reference to Stepanov's portrait of the state as a "machine out of control":

> There are still some idealists in our country who have faith, as we all once had, in the saving power of "emergency" work through enthusiasm. They have learned no songs except the old one about the cudgel: "a cudgel may be easy to handle, but a machine is not." It [the machine] cannot be politically mature or immature. You must invent it and build it and accomplish big tasks. But to solve these problems people must be at their best. They must have peace of mind, and they must be cheerful and efficient. They must not be disturbed in their work either by poor organizers or by personal worries. These things affect a person's state of mind and hence his labor productivity. "Trifles" can be irritating . . . These "trifles" are so important and so numerous that they are the object of the special science of the organization and management of production.

Noting "a certain contempt for the so-called nonproductive sector" of the economy in some circles, the reviewer cited the example of management consultants in the West, where "whole regiments of 'nonproductive workers' " were engaged in "studying production and making recommendations." Tereshchenko's book, it was said, "shows us what we can adopt and learn from the organization of production in the most advanced capitalist powers." "We must not forget Lenin's words that it is never shameful for someone to learn something good from someone else."[50]

A number of writings at the time recalled the fortieth anniversary of the Second All-Union Conference on NOT, which had put an end to the bitter squabbles over NOT in the 1920s through Kuibyshev's intervention. With analogous battles brewing in the 1960s, the prospect of a similar resolution from above appealed to many. Proposals were raised for a Third NOT Conference to sort out the divisions among management scientists.[51] V. G. Afanas'ev, head of the Department of Scientific Communism at the Central Committee's Academy of Social Sciences, called for a compromise and an end to the conflict. Jurists, he said, were trying to "reduce management science to the administrative and legal regulation of various fields of social life." Cyberneticians "believe that management science is above all the formalization of social processes, a description of these processes in the language of cybernetics, even though not all these phenomena can be subjected to a mathematical treatment." Economists wanted to "limit the sphere of activity of management science to economics, to the national economy." A true science of management could only be developed on the basis of "the joint efforts of representatives of the most varied sciences." He proposed a syncretic discipline of the "scientific leadership of society," which, he hoped, would provide common ground on which the warring disciplines could unite. But Afanas'ev's appeal fell on deaf ears. Philosophers immediately responded by citing examples of "managerialism" among economists and cyberneticians and asserted that only "scientific communism" could serve as the basis for management theory.[52]

When Kosygin announced the final details of the 1965 reforms, he emphasized the need for an independent discipline of management science. The rapid development of the economy, he said, "will inevitably bring forth in the future more and more new problems in improving management," requiring "the resolute overcoming of the lag of research in this field." In an oblique criticism of Stalin, Kosygin called the abolition of executive training in the Soviet Union "a grave mistake" and declared that "the system for upgrading the qualifications of executive personnel that used to exist and that had proved itself in practice must be restored." When the decree instituting the reforms was published in October, it envisaged stepped-up efforts to train industrial executives "so that this personnel might know well the economics of industry and how to analyze the work of enterprises."[53]

In December 1965 a general meeting of the Academy of Sciences formally recognized management science as a legitimate field of scientific inquiry. The meeting heard a report on the subject by A. M. Rumiantsev, the reform-minded former chief editor of *Pravda*. Rumiantsev advocated a specialized managerial discipline in which the economic sciences would play "the leading role." He recognized the need for other academic disciplines to participate in its development, but criticized "the incorrect notions" put forward by political economists, conservative philosophers, and cyberneticians. Some "opportunists," Rumiantsev said, were trying to portray the economic reforms as "alien to Leninism" and had put forth their own "abstract" and "universal" notions of management. But management issues were "above all problems of economic and production relations." Noting the enormous attention to management in the West, Rumiantsev argued that "we should not and cannot simply brush aside this research for the reason that it concerns a sphere of the capitalist economy that operates according to its own economic laws and is inapplicable to our reality." Such research "also has practical significance for us." In its resolution on Rumiantsev's speech the Academy delegated to economists and jurists the responsibility for "reworking the theoretical problems of NOT and the scientific basis for management of the national economy."[54]

At the Twenty-Third Party Congress held three months later the party gave official recognition to the new discipline when it called upon executives to "use the latest information on management science."[55] The phrase was subsequently cited as proof of the final defeat of efforts to prevent the discipline from being established. "Not all that long ago," Adfel'dt observed shortly after the congress, "verbose quarrels were conducted over management science: does it exist, and is it necessary?" Opponents of management science "did not want to see the requirements of life itself and, not finding this educational discipline with an unfamiliar title in the sanctioned list of university departments, boldly denied the very possibility of such a science." But "now, when we have the decisions of the Twenty-Third Congress in which the necessity of 'using the latest information on management science' is directly mentioned, the recent enemies of this relatively young science must become accustomed to it, understand it, and think about its urgent problems."[56]

Complex Approaches

In June 1966 an All-Union Scientific-Technical Conference on Problems of Managing Industrial Production, attended by over a thousand managers and specialists from more than five hundred organizations, convened in Moscow. The first convention of its type since the Second NOT Conference, it had been called to mobilize established scientific disciplines around the challenge of developing a new administrative science. As one of its organizers later recalled, the meeting "addressed representatives of various sciences with an appeal to gather material relating to management in their spheres and to present it for examination." Instead, it became an arena for competing approaches, as the discussion "disintegrated into subsystems, with the existing classification of sciences serving as the basis for division."[57]

At the section on organizational problems, cyberneticians continued to assert that "only cybernetics can serve as a general science of management." Economists countered that "cybernetics does not encompass the entire broad and varied range of issues that relate to the field of managerial organization." Jurists argued that only on the basis of the legal sciences "is it possible to work out such problems as the distribution of rights and responsibilities between various subdivisions . . . or issues of discipline in the work of the apparatus, or the interrelationship between administration and rank-and-file employees." And philosophers emphasized the need for *partiinost'* (party mindedness) in administrative theory and for a critical attitude toward bourgeois organizational theories.[58] Many of the participants, Gvishiani observed in his keynote address, "had pretensions toward one another," and "sometimes a lot of energy is wasted on scholastic discourses and definitions in which the basic substance of actual processes is overlooked." He called upon "all scientists and specialists to move from declarations of the importance of management science to the concrete study of its various and complicated problems." Management science could not be developed on the basis of "separate and independent research" by each discipline; it required "a harmonious, 'systemic' character" and "information from the most disparate branches of knowledge." In Gvishiani's words, management science should rely on "a complex approach [*kompleksnyi podkhod*]"—a catchword that was to become the rallying cry among those who sought to mute conflicts over administrative policy.[59]

In the years that followed, management science made enormous strides in the Soviet Union. In December 1966 the Central Committee issued its decree "On Measures for Ensuring the Further

Growth of Labor Productivity in Industry and Construction''—the equivalent of a manifesto for the management-science movement. Noting that "in recent years the rate of growth of productivity in industry and construction in our country has fallen," the document called upon ministries and agencies to "take into account the leading domestic and foreign experience in working out concrete organizational-technical measures" for improving productivity. Beginning in 1967 such measures were to be confirmed by each agency in the design of new enterprises. The Academy of Sciences and the Ministry of Higher Education (Minvuz) were instructed to broaden research aimed at applying "the methods of the scientific organization of labor." Minvuz was to create at selected vuzy a series of "problem laboratories" modeled on that at MGU. It was to introduce courses on management into engineering programs and to commence training management specialists. Ministries and agencies were to begin production of computer technology and to oversee its managerial applications. A special Scientific-Methodological Center was established under the State Committee for Labor and Wage Issues to coordinate all managerial research. In August 1967 yet another decree cited the work of the Sverdlovsk party organization in sponsoring NOT work at its enterprises as a model for emulation. Party organizations were called upon to review NOT work in their regions. Ministries and agencies were to speed up the application of the latest domestic and foreign managerial innovations. Soon provincial party organizations began to organize conferences to discuss ways to hasten the application of new managerial techniques. Some local party organizations established their own methodological councils for NOT, made up of specialists from local plants, that were to apply Scientific Management within the party apparatus. In all, between 1965 and 1968 more than thirty separate conferences were held to discuss the development of managerial research.[60]

But by the end of 1968 conflict over the new science of management was still apparent. As one source described the situation, "we . . . often hear the question: what kind of science is this management science? How many years did we get along without it and nevertheless the national economy developed successfully?"[61] In 1967 Rumiantsev again attacked those who sought to narrow management science to the study of cybernetics or political economy.

Management, he said, "should not be reduced to cybernetics," since "cybernetic mechanisms are only tools of human labor, including managerial labor, and cannot 'substitute' for man himself." At the other extreme, Rumiantsev indicated, stood those who aimed to "turn management science into a 'double' for political economy." If political economists were to contribute to the development of the new discipline, political economy itself would have to be transformed into an empirical science.[62]

In 1966 and 1967, as permanent institutes were established, these conflicting views were engraved into the institutional structure of management research. Five separate organizations were assigned the task of acting as national coordinating centers. The Institute of Labor of the State Committee for Labor and Wage Issues, with its emphasis on norm-determination, saw the managerial hierarchy in traditional Taylorist terms. Gosplan had gathered conservative planners, economists, and norm-setters at its Research Institute for Planning and Norms. Both the Institute for State and Law and the Central Economic-Mathematical Institute of the Academy of Sciences were engaged in coordinating managerial research—the former under the dominance of jurists, the latter under the influence of mathematical economists. And the Ministry of Higher Education had organized a broad array of laboratories, institutes, and training programs. By 1968 approximately eighty *vuzy* were engaged in NOT research, and in 1967 the Ministry of Higher Education had established a Commission for the Scientific Organization of Management, whose purpose was "to make suggestions for the improvement of scientific work in the field of management science." Its first order of business was the publication of a textbook suitable for teaching management to industrial executives.[63] In the words of one observer, each of these bureaucracies was "waging its own line in management theory" and believed that "management is its own field of study."[64]

The participants in these disputes referred frequently to the experience of the NOT movement of the 1920s to justify their claims. When a collection of Gastev's works was published in 1966, the editors prefaced it with the proposal that a Labor University, similar to that advocated by Gastev in the 1920s, be established. Other works called for a revival of a central coordinating organ for NOT research similar to SOVNOT. In 1968 the editors of Kerzhentsev's republished writings lauded this opponent of Gastev for criticizing "those engineers and organizers of NOT who continue to rediscover Taylorism as it exists in America." Still others, noting the parallels with contemporary cybernetics, argued that the criticisms leveled at Bogdanov at the Second NOT Conference for interpreting NOT as "a holistic system" had been entirely unfounded.[65] Precisely because participants saw the relevance of past conflicts to their present situation, these historical analogies were a potent means of legitimating their positions.

At the end of the sixties a major realignment occurred within the Soviet leadership that affected the outcome of these struggles. Throughout the 1960s the dominant group in the management-science movement had been closely connected with Kosygin and his efforts at economic reform. These reformers saw management science as a necessary concomitant of economic decentralization, which in their view would create the need and the conditions for the rational application of organizational techniques. But the idea of importing management techniques from abroad was not the monopoly of reformers alone. It also appealed to many opponents of reform, who saw these techniques as an alternative to economic decentralization. As Joseph Berliner has described this outlook: "To hold this view is to feel secure in the belief that there is no need for vast reforms that may let loose who knows what economic convulsions and what kinds of political dissolution that may threaten the hegemony of the party itself. Our system works perfectly well, is the implication of this view; we need only to teach our managers the tricks that the best capitalist managers have learned, and then the fundamental superiority of our socialist system will become manifest."[66]

Differences over economic policy permeated the debates on management science. Shortly after the First All-Union Scientific-Technical Conference in 1966, Gvishiani observed that although the gathering had "devoted great attention" to the September reforms, some participants had misunderstood their actual meaning and were inclined to make judgments about their inefficacy too quickly. Confusion had resulted, Gvishiani said, as to whether the reforms were intended to centralize or decentralize management. Some management scientists were attempting to divorce management science from a policy of economic decentralization. But it had been his father-in-law's reforms, Gvishiani declared, that had made it possible to apply Scientific Management methods to the economy. Reform and management science should be viewed as inseparable elements of a complex set of measures creating "the basis for an uninterrupted improvement of the entire productive-economic activity of enterprises."[67]

By the end of the decade, with the Kosygin reforms mired in bureaucratic intransigence and the leadership's attention focused on Czechoslovakia, where managerial reformers had strayed beyond the bounds of what the Kremlin could tolerate, Kosygin's economic policies came under attack from conservative elements in the party leadership. Brezhnev had remained conspicuously silent about the revival of management science and had been in the forefront of those calling for greater "responsibility" and "discipline" on the part of industrial administrators. At the Twenty-Third Party Congress in 1966, where Kosygin spoke in favor of importing capitalist managerial techniques and executive training, Brezhnev called instead for improving "the ideological and theoretical training" of managers. Even earlier, in October 1965, he had reminded industrial executives that they "should not only be managers, but leaders of the masses as well"—a line reminiscent of Stepanov.

At the December 1969 Central Committee Plenum, Brezhnev delivered his first major policy statement on industrial management, lashing out at the indolence of economic executives. Managerial problems, he said, "are primarily political problems, not technical problems." Making only passing reference to economic reform, he concentrated on the enormous rationalizing potential of management science. Management, he said, was "turning into a science, and this science must be mastered as quickly and as thoroughly as possible. Even those who occupy high posts of command need to study it thoroughly." In the years since the 1965 reforms, he observed again in June 1970, "we ourselves have learned much." It was time to "look more broadly" at the ways in which the economy might be improved. "The solution to many of our economic problems should be sought at the juncture between scientific-technological progress and progress in the matter of management."[68]

About this time the party began to issue a series of edicts redefining the aims of administrative strategy. In October 1969 the Central Committee announced its intention to bring the costs of the managerial apparatus under control. Cuts of 1.7 billion rubles in

1970 were to be achieved through the application of computer technology and the reorganization of managerial structures. One year later the Central Committee outlined a plan for improving management through a far-reaching computerization of the economy. It envisaged the creation of a series of management-information systems that would be linked to a national computer network.[69] Management scientists closely associated with Kosygin's program of reform warned against attempts to "narrow" rationalization to the application of "various technical means for automating management"; expensive computer technology, they noted, could affect production only when the proper organizational conditions had been created for its use.[70] But increasingly economic policy was moving away from reform and toward recentralization.

Political conflict over administrative strategy surfaced again at the Twenty-Fourth Party Congress in March 1971. In his main address Brezhnev spoke of the "opportunities for improving management" in the coming five-year period as consisting of "an increase in the level of knowledge and professional training of our personnel . . . and the rapid development of management science and computer technology." But "the political side of the matter," Brezhnev added, "is also very important." Rather than being the domain of economic experts only, management issues were matters of concern to "all party, Soviet, and economic organizations." The party had acted correctly in enacting the 1965 economic reforms; but the reforms "by far did not manage to solve all our problems." The emphasis in rationalization policy should be placed instead on training professional managers, applying computer technology, simplifying and reorganizing managerial structures, and fusing science with production. For Kosygin, by contrast, the 1965 reforms were not only "correct" but were "the furthest development of Leninist principles of socialist management." They were not to be viewed as "an occasional act" but as part of an overall strategy of modernizing management. The next five-year plan, he said, would witness a broader application of the principles of the reforms, which required "further refinement and development." Although Kosygin endorsed computerization and the simplification of managerial structures, he devoted a large part of his speech to the need for improving the economic incentives and plan indicators that governed managerial behavior.[71]

Brezhnev has been called "the artful synthesizer" for his ability to preempt his opponents by staking out compromise positions.[72] His turn toward a conservative managerial strategy in the late sixties and early seventies was one example of this skill. Brezhnev used an issue first raised by Kosygin as a weapon against Kosygin and the proponents of structural reform. He also discovered a platform around which he could forge a consensus within the leadership: rationalization without reform. Even party ideologist Mikhail Suslov, previously reluctant to recognize management as an independent science, rallied to the cause. The growing complexity of the economy, he told a gathering of social scientists in 1971, "puts very high demands on the managerial apparatus and requires full and precise information about the underlying process of management, an uninterrupted analysis of incoming information, and its timely and correct use." But Suslov added that the proper direction of managerial research was "a complicated issue." He called upon political economists and philosophers to "make a significant contribution in this matter" by "participating in working out the theoretical problems of management." Suslov criticized those attempting to confine management science to narrowly practical and empirical issues; the term "management," he said, should be interpreted "in its broadest sense—from the individual enterprise to the enormous scale of the entire country," and "moral-political factors" should be treated on a par with "economic factors" as instruments of rationalization.[73] By the end of 1972 the pursuit of a managerial strategy had been effectively severed from efforts at economic decentralization. From then until the mid-1980s a gradual recentralization of authority would be combined with efforts to rationalize production on the basis of organizational techniques.

Emerging consensus within the leadership required consensus within the management-science community. But by 1972 there were no signs that bickering among management experts had abated. As one scholar put it: "Although people are using the same words—methods, management, and so forth—in essence they have very different things in mind." Researchers still largely spent their energies in justifying their claims to the field rather than in conducting concrete research. "Economists write about the management of socialist production; jurists talk about the socialist state, seeing management of the economy as one of the forms of state management; and cyberneticians are interested in the laws existing under any form of management."[74] Much as Kuibyshev had imposed consensus upon the Scientific Management community at the Second NOT Conference, Brezhnev effected a compromise at the Second All-Union Scientific-Technical Conference on Problems of Improving the Management of Industrial Production, which convened in Moscow in the spring of 1972. The visible presence of a number of high party and state officials seemed intended to aid agreement among the bickering scholars. In his keynote address, Gvishiani outlined the major claims of each discipline over management science. As before, he proposed "a complex approach" that confirmed the right of all disciplines to participate in management research. "The process of management of social production," he explained, "is a complicated, complex phenomenon which can find adequate expression only in a conglomeration of scientific research that takes into account both the general and the specific features of the system being studied." This time the meeting "unanimously supported" Gvishiani's "complex" formulation. According to the conference resolutions, "no one even raised the possibility of conducting research on the management of social production from the position of a particular, single science or 'through the prism of one's own scientific specialty,' though even today there are still proponents of such views."[75]

The Second All-Union Conference marked an important turning point in the development of Soviet management science. "Complex approach" and "systems approach" would henceforth become the buzzwords around which the management-science community would unite. But deep differences remained. Empiricists continued to argue that management was an art rather than a science, called for professional managerial institutions, and spoke of the growing significance of the "subjective factor" in administration—that is, the role of leadership as an integrating function.[76] Cyberneticians, by contrast, were critical of "antiscientific" statements claiming that "a special science such as management science does not exist at all, that management is more of an art than a science, and that knowledge is not required for success in management, but experience or, at best, skill acquired by purely empirical means."[77] The Second All-Union Conference created no new converts and witnessed no prominent defections from any side of these controversies. But by persuading the warring factions to agree to disagree and to get down to business, it precipitated a second golden age of Soviet Scientific Management.

6

. . . . . .

The Science of Victory

*On the fronts of construction of a communist economy,
comrades, the science of victory is in essence the science
of management! Therefore, studying management science
and, if necessary, restudying it is becoming one of the highest priorities of our personnel.*

—*Leonid Brezhnev, June 1970*

In the 1970s Soviet management experts turned their attention to
demonstrating the reputed superiority of socialist management science, which, freed from the fetters of capitalist greed, was expected
to increase productivity several times over. That there is such a
thing as socialist management science, and that it contains a more
potent magic than capitalist management science, has been a myth
propagated by successive generations of NOTisty and their political
supporters. In reality, the content of socialist management science
in both the 1920s and 1970s has differed little from that of its capitalist counterpart.

It is true that the Soviets have been selective, or, more properly
stated, inconsistent, in the management methods they have adopted
from abroad. But it is also true that Soviet management science has
been largely, if not wholly, borrowed from the West. Soviet management scientists have contributed no new ideas and no distinctive

approaches to the subject, nor are they likely to do so in the future, considering the chaotic state of management in that country. Western management scientists who visited Moscow in the 1970s in search of gems of organizational wisdom returned home disappointed. American participants in officially sponsored exchanges were so disillusioned by what they discovered that they unilaterally terminated their activities with their Soviet colleagues in the fall of 1979—only four years after the exchange began. For Soviet management experts, however, the capitalist corporation has always represented the paragon of efficiency, the basic model from which they have drawn their inspiration and their methods.

Rather than being a consistent body of thought, Soviet management science has been a curious mix of capitalist organizational theories and Marxist-Leninist dialectics. This combination has not been lacking in conflicts, controversies, and tensions. Western management science has made no secret of its economic, political, and cultural assumptions. It developed in societies in which the notions of individual freedom, of the acceptability of social conflict, of state intervention in the economy, and of the prerogatives and privileges of the professional manager are quite different from those on which communist ideology, political structure, and economic practice rest. Though some of the theories and techniques which Soviet management scientists borrowed have fitted their political culture and administrative practice, others have been at odds with ideological orthodoxy and with dominant political and administrative interests. At times, under pressure from above, Soviet management scientists have had to water down their borrowed theories to accommodate these forces. In other instances management science has been divorced from the realities of the Soviet context, simply because its theories and techniques were predicated upon assumptions foreign to Soviet practice.

As unethical as the behavior of the capitalist corporate executive in the pursuit of profit may be, management science has been referred to in the West as "the conscience of the profession."[1] In importing managerial techniques, Soviet management scientists also imported a professional managerial ethos, which, though not entirely at odds with Soviet political culture, has not been entirely at ease with it either. The basic claim of Soviet management professionalizers has been simple; as one management scientist put it at a conference in Tallin in 1972, "In any sphere of human activity—in economics, politics, military affairs, art—where one must solve complex, principally new problems, amateurs are not needed, but professionals."[2] Throughout the 1970s the Soviet regime permitted the propagation of this type of professionalism in the training class-room and the media, and support for the ideas of management professionalizers could be found in high government circles.

But if it were carried to its logical conclusion, managerial profes-sionalism would involve major changes in Soviet political and ad-ministrative practices, in the career paths of officials, and in the role of politics in economic decision-making. Party conservatives have at times accused proponents of managerial professionalism of seek-ing to divorce management from the purview of the party, aiming to turn managers into a separate technocratic caste, and propagating "foreign" ideologies. Were management treated as a fully separate profession, independent of ministerial boundaries, agency control over socialization, recruitment, and selection activities would be eroded, and personnel would flow more freely between economic units. The professional-management generalist is a common phe-nomenon in the capitalist business world, where there has been a considerable degree of horizontal executive mobility, manifested in the emergence of managerial markets and corporate head-hunting agencies.[3] He has never been a popular figure in public bureaucra-cies with strong administrative agencies, since agencies tend to view generalists as a threat to their autonomy. When Soviet man-agement scientists adopted the model of the managerial generalist from American business and attempted to apply this model in a nonmarket context, they inevitably ran into opposition. Managerial professionalism was also bound to have a differential impact on managers themselves, since it aimed at promoting the "best and the brightest." As in the 1920s, many managers opposed professionali-zation as a threat to their careers and their positions, while ideo-logues opposed it on the ground that it threatened to cut off chan-nels of social mobility.

In all these ways a professional managerial ethos imported from the West conflicted with the hierarchical environment of Soviet administration and with ideological goals and dogmas. Frustrated in their efforts to professionalize management, management scientists advocated still more radical technocratic schemes and further political intervention from above. But although managerial professional-ism found some support within the political hierarchy, far-reaching professionalization was blocked by powerful opposition. As much as Brezhnev might have proclaimed management science "the science of victory," it was not the victory of professionalism over hierarchical domination that he had in mind.

The Politics of Executive Training

Differences over management-development policies had emerged immediately after the Kosygin reforms went into effect. These conflicts focused on what, where, and when managers should be taught. In 1965 part-time courses, sponsored by local party organizations and conducted at enterprises and vuzy, were organized to explain the reforms to production managers. Some within the party viewed these courses as precursors of a nationwide network of management schools. In October 1965, V. Pavlov, then secretary of the Moscow city party committee, gave his support to proposals for transforming courses for plant directors at eighteen vuzy in Moscow into faculties of organizers. These new faculties, like the five already in existence, would train managers for a reserve for promotion to higher posts.[4] At the Twenty-Third Party Congress in March 1966 Kosygin hinted at a similar proposal for establishing business schools at colleges to train young managers.[5] A number of speakers at the First All-Union Scientific-Technical Conference also advocated expanding the faculties of organizers into a network of management schools, introducing management-science courses into engineering and economic vuzy, and requiring that all new managers receive a managerial education before being assigned to their posts. The resolutions of the conference called upon Minvuz, which had been given the task of drafting a proposal on executive training jointly with branch ministries, to "work out a plan for creating a unified system" for training managerial personnel.[6]

Two months later, when Minvuz unveiled its draft, a heated discussion ensued. Instead of endorsing the proposals of Kosygin and others for management schools, Minvuz had placed the prerogative to create training programs in the hands of individual agencies. A. Bogomolov, a member of the ministry's collegium, explained that a "harmonious" training system required that each ministry control the content of instruction within its own branch. This was to be achieved through reviving the Institutes for Upgrading Qualifications (IPK), abandoned by Stalin in the 1930s, but now to be resurrected to service agency personnel. O. Kozlova, rector of the Ordzhonikidze Engineering-Economics Institute and a proponent of managerial professionalism, openly disagreed with the Minvuz draft. Representatives of the union republics also dissented; they favored territorial interbranch programs that would maximize their control over trainee selection. Representatives of the branch ministries responded by accusing proponents of interbranch training of fostering "parallelism" with their own work.[7]

To some party circles the entire debate smacked of "narrow professionalism" and bureaucratic maneuvering. An editorial in *Ekonomicheskaia gazeta* called for "a proper mixture of branch forms . . . with territorial forms" and declared that whatever form training took, it "should come under the unremitting control of party organs."[8] After ten months of bargaining, in June 1967 the Council of Ministers established a national system for retraining executives and specialists in management science, new technological developments, computer technology, and planning techniques. A compromise was effected by granting legal status to both branch and interbranch forms of training.[9]

The arguments hardly ended there. Within months of the decree, management scientists called not only for compulsory training of executives in a nationwide network of management schools, citing the American business school as a model, but also for a Higher Academy of Management, patterned after the Industrial Academy, for training top-level industrial executives. These proposals received the support of Minvuz, whose Commission for the Scientific Organization of Management was dominated by advocates of management professionalism. Under the influence of these advisers, the leadership of the ministry embraced the cause of interbranch training.[10] Management experts expressed puzzlement that the political leadership was dragging its feet on the issue: "Readers had practically unanimously supported suggestions" for interbranch management schools at universities and vuzy. "Now no one appears to be objecting to these suggestions, but their practical realization is going very slowly. What is the problem? Apparently, the core of the problem of improving management in the economy is not yet clear to everyone." Echoing this line, a *Pravda* editorial of March 1970 complained that it was "impossible to acknowledge as normal the fact that the leading universities of our country do not have management schools."[11] But instead of setting up management schools, in February 1971 the State Committee for Science and Technology opened an Institute for Management of the National Economy (IUNKh) that would provide top-level industrial executives with three-month refresher courses in management science, computer technology, and planning methods.[12]

That proposals for creating business schools had been endorsed on the front page of the party's newspaper and yet failed to be acted upon could only have been the result of conflict within high party circles. There is evidence that Brezhnev and Kosygin held divergent views on the issue. Both supported the creation of IUNKh for retraining top-level administrators: Brezhnev spoke of the need for such a program at the December 1969 Plenum; and Kosygin, at the opening ceremony of the new institute, emphasized "the great importance of enabling leading cadres to refresh their knowledge in connection with the greater tasks facing the country's economy."[13] But whereas Kosygin at the Twenty-Fourth Party Congress called for "broadening and improving the system for training and retraining managerial personnel at all levels," Brezhnev praised the party's new efforts at "retraining" economic executives and reminded managers that "the basic method of study was and remains, of course, independent work."[14] At the end of 1971 Suslov noted that the problem of training personnel "skilled in contemporary methods and means of management" was "a complicated issue."[15]

Differences over managerial training within the leadership mirrored similar divisions among scholars and administrators. One source observed in 1971 that "arguments are being conducted about whether executives in general need special training." "Some scholars and executive praktiki," it was said, "do not believe that management is an independent profession and maintain that the executive should be, above all, a specialist in a particular field." According to this view, "the experience of work with people and of solving production tasks . . . gathered over the years gives the executive the right and the opportunity to occupy a post." Others, by contrast, "believe that executive activity is an independent profession having its own specific features and requiring its own kind of professional knowledge and skills, and that in principle executives can be trained in vuzy, even those who do not have very serious experience in production."[16] Similar arguments against business schools surfaced at the Second All-Union Scientific-Technical Conference in 1972. According to Gvishiani, some delegates argued against management schools on the grounds that "the abilities to manage appear in people later than other abilities, and are formed not only by theoretical upbringing but also by accumulating practical experience." Still others opposed management schools "for purely ethical considerations, since the right to leadership should be earned by practical, fruitful work."[17]

Opposition to management schools was also rooted in a bureaucratic struggle for control over personnel recruitment. In his study of European public administration Brian Chapman concluded that ministries and agencies usually favor the recruitment of older executives, since later recruitment permits agencies to "insist on their own requirements, specify their own ranking systems, and refuse to collaborate in attempts to classify their specialists together with the specialists of other ministries." The likely consequences of agency control over training and recruitment are to restrict the competence of administrators to specific agency matters and to reinforce barriers of communication between rival agencies.[18] In the politicking over the 1967 decree, industrial ministries lobbied for their own branch IPK programs and opposed interbranch training precisely for these reasons. But having won the right to their own programs, most ministries proceeded to ignore them and consciously undermined efforts to train executives in a generalist science of administration.

By 1981, 66 branch programs with 134 affiliates had trained more than 1.6 million executives and specialists.[19] But each ministry shaped curricula, trainee selection, and the quality of instructional facilities in accordance with narrow agency goals. According to the June 1967 decree, Minvuz was to establish curriculum guidelines for all executive training institutes through its Scientific-Methodological Office. In 1970 it specified that at least 32 percent of instructional time should be devoted to management science. But branch IPK programs, ignoring these guidelines entirely, oriented instruction toward engineering disciplines. Soviet newspaper accounts consistently described these programs as "overloaded with narrow, agency, technical themes," devoting only a minute portion of time to general issues of management or economics. In fact, most of the branch IPKs trained managers and engineers in the same classrooms.[20]

Each ministry sought to become an island unto itself, confining flows of personnel between agencies by limiting managerial socialization to agency issues. Recognizing the danger this posed, in 1971 the party decreed that ministries should "seriously review study plans and the organization of all work" in their IPKs and "significantly increase the instructional time for economic issues." In December 1971 a group of deputy ministers was summoned to the Central Committee Secretariat and rebuked by V. Medvedev, then deputy head of the propaganda department, for the absence of management science and economics in their IPK curricula.[21] Two or three ministries increased the managerial content of their training programs as a result of these pressures. But in the ensuing years the majority of ministries actually decreased the proportion of study time devoted to management science. By the end of the decade, *Pravda* editorials were still criticizing branch IPKs for the "small amount of attention . . . paid to studying the methods and practice of planning, analysis of the results of enterprise production activity, and the educational functions of leadership."[22]

Most branch ministries, desiring to devote as many resources as possible to areas directly influencing plan fulfillment, were reluctant to pour funds into executive training. By the late seventies only twenty out of fifty-six branch IPKs possessed their own study quarters; the overwhelming majority were situated in rented school buildings. In Moscow alone there were "dozens of these institutes, belonging to various agencies and departments, each finding shelter as best it can." Many of the buildings "failed to meet elementary sanitary norms," and classrooms were often "unfit for conducting instructional lessons." Some ministerial programs had no laboratories, classrooms, or offices. Other programs spent an enormous sum of money for equipment, but because of lack of classroom space, had to offer instruction in two separate shifts. In several IPKs one or two floors of rented school buildings served as living quarters for trainees. In most institutes, however, trainees had to rent their own apartments—a difficult undertaking in the city of Moscow—because their ministries had failed to allocate funds for dormitory space.[23]

Western business corporations generally consider corporate in-house training the most successful type of management development, since company programs can be successfully tailored to the specific work needs of trainees.[24] But in the absence of market mechanisms, the dominance of in-house branch training programs aggravates traditional administrative weaknesses by reinforcing barriers of communication between agencies. As Soviet educational administrators described the problem: "Waste in instruction naturally leads to waste in management; having gone through IPKs like these, managers are prone to departmentalism in preparing plans, experience difficulties when their decisions clash with the decisions of executives from adjacent factories, and are not able to comprehend complicated problems in a complex way."[25] The very institutions which were supposed to be teaching Soviet executives the art of management had themselves become paragons of bureaucratic mismanagement.

Attempts to force ministries to correct these problems were frequent throughout the sixties and seventies. Only in isolated cases did they succeed. In September 1975 the Ministry of Finance circulated a letter to ministries asking them to "take measures toward creating the necessary material base for instruction" at their IPKs. The letter was ignored, and two years later it was reported that "achievements have been rare." Minvuz's Scientific-Methodological Office likewise wrote "hundreds of letters in order to turn the attention of ministries to the needs of the IPK." But reports indicated that by and large ministries "take these 'methodological nurses' into account very little and act according to their own minds." As one management educator declared in 1974, "today, in fact, no one defends the interests of the IPKs."[26]

In contrast to branch IPKs, managerial educators refer to inter-branch programs (interbranch IPKs, faculties of organizers, and IUNKh) as "the prototype of a special school for the *professional education* of executives."[27] Compared with the multitude of agency programs, there are still relatively few interbranch training institutes in the Soviet Union. In 1972, in a bow to management professionalizers, the number of faculties of organizers was expanded from five to eleven, the faculties were accorded permanent status, and differentiated instruction was introduced. Factory directors were to upgrade their qualifications in three-month programs, while those on the reserve for promotion were to study for six months. By

1981 the faculties had trained approximately 20,000 executives and were turning out another 3,200 graduates every year. By then six interbranch IPKs had also been established under union republic councils of ministers. Usually involving three months of instruction, these programs were charged with training republican reserves for promotion to management posts. In 1978 the three-month IUNKh retraining program for top-level executives had also been reorganized. It was incorporated into an Academy of the National Economy, which included a new two-year program for training a reserve for promotion to top-level posts. By 1983 approximately 3,500 executives had graduated from the Academy's three-month retraining program at a rate of 300 annually. Moreover, 300 had finished the Academy's two-year program, with about 100 graduating each year.[28]

According to Soviet sources, instruction in interbranch programs has focused "not on agency narrowness, not on technology, but on the broad study of the leading experience in the fields of management and planning, the latest achievements of science and technology, the organization of labor, and social-psychological problems of management." At the faculties of organizers, for instance, 67 to 90 percent of instructional time is devoted to subjects of an interbranch character, and 35 to 40 percent is spent studying management science. At the Academy of the National Economy the study program covers "a wide range of issues concerning management," including managerial applications of computer technology, new decision-making techniques, managerial psychology, economics, and statistics.[29] As opposed to ministerial IPKs, where lecture halls are usually "crowded" with fifty to a hundred people, interbranch programs conduct lessons in groups ranging from ten to thirty and utilize so-called active methods of instruction (business games, the case-study method, role-playing exercises, and so forth). At the Latvian Interbranch IPK only 40 percent of instructional time is spent in lectures. At the faculty of organizers of the Belorussian Institute of the National Economy active methods occupy 20 percent of the program.[30] Most interbranch programs are well supplied with dormitory space, classrooms, and technical equipment. Most have their own computer facilities, consisting mainly (in the late seventies) of second-generation hardware, but in some cases including RIAD-series third-generation computers. Located at the leading vuzy of the country, the faculties of organizers have been able to use an existing material and scholarly base. At the faculty of organizers of the Ordzhonikidze Institute of Management, for example, trainees are housed in "a spacious dormitory" only a few blocks from classroom buildings and have access to the excellent computer facilities of the institute.[31]

Nevertheless, as islands of managerial professionalism in a sea of bureaucracy, interbranch programs have not entirely escaped agency barriers. The selection of trainees has been shaped by ministries and agencies, and they have been reluctant to condone the absence of their employees from production for training purposes, since this could threaten the immediate fulfillment of production plans. In the mid-seventies, for instance, the Ministry of Oil used only a third of its places at the faculties; the ministries of the Electrotechnical Industry, of Industrial Construction, of Ferrous Metallurgy, and of Light and Food Machine-Building used even fewer. In 1977 the three-month training programs in all eleven faculties of organizers fulfilled their admissions plans by only 69 percent, and the six-month programs for training a reserve for promotion by only 60 percent. Minvuz accused branch ministries of failing to exercise proper control over trainee selection, while branch ministries blamed Minvuz for distributing the number of places allotted to them either too late or "without prior agreement."[32]

According to Soviet law, every manager, no matter what his rank, is supposed to attend an executive training program at least once every six years. Yet studies conducted in the 1970s indicated that only 8 percent of the country's industrial executives were undergoing some kind of training each year, so that managers would be trained only once every thirteen years, assuming all were attending. As an in-house report prepared for the Ministry of Higher Education in 1976 revealed, "a significant portion" of the managerial elite had escaped the classroom altogether. Another internal Minvuz report compiled two years later complained that many ministries were artificially inflating the number of trainees attending programs without paying attention to who was attending. "In a number of cases, a rather low level of organization is hidden behind the large figures of people studying." In many ministries trainees were selected according to "whether they have a family or whether their absence will hurt production." In some cases "enterprise executives simply ignored the instructions of their ministries to send particular employees to instruction." Trainees arrived in the middle of the semester or were recalled in the midst of a training session because they were needed in production. Low-level, poorly qualified personnel were at times sent to train in place of their superiors.[33] To overcome this resistance, management educators proposed that "there should be a law that every executive should have an organizer's diploma." Others called upon the party to intervene, requesting "strict party control over the selection of the contingent of trainees."[34] Thus, bureaucratic resistance to managerial professionalism generated calls for political intervention and fed the rise of still more far-reaching professionalizing schemes.

Pink and Not Quite Expert

The executive training classroom has been a major base for propagating an ideology of managerial professionalism in the Soviet Union. At the Academy of the National Economy, for instance, top-level executives are taught that "knowledge," "training," "experience," and "natural-born abilities" are all necessary for executive activity. At the faculty of organizers of the Plekhanov Institute of the National Economy, where I observed enterprise executives being trained for three months in the fall of 1979, trainees were told that good leadership requires "intellect" and "special features in the executive's personality." Managers were exhorted to play an active role in bringing about administrative professionalization. As one lecturer declared, "We have already come to the time when the enterprise should concern itself with and influence the training of specialists." Business schools and systems for the professional evaluation of executives, trainees were told, were necessities in the modern world. At the end of one lecture, trainees were asked to list the features that an ideal executive should possess. After listening to this lecture, one young trainee wrote a course project on managerial recruitment and training. He concluded that two-year interbranch management schools should be established at Soviet universities.[35]

Managerial professionalism has coexisted precariously with political authority, at times becoming the target of official attack. In 1973 in the party's theoretical journal *Kommunist*, Vladimir

Shcherbitskii, head of the Ukrainian party organization and a Brezhnev protégé, criticized excessive professionalism among management experts. "In some works recently published on issues of management," he charged, "one encounters the theoretically bankrupt and completely unfounded thesis of the separation of managerial activity into some kind of special sphere, being the privilege of a certain social stratum [*prosloika*]." Such assertions, "independent of the intentions of their authors, are fundamentally mistaken and contradict the entire system of life in our society." Though a "critical" borrowing of management ideas from the West was legitimate, Shcherbitskii said, "some Soviet scholars working on problems of management theory sometimes try to create certain abstract schemes that have a seemingly general character, but which are really only a mechanistic borrowing of bourgeois conceptions." Fedor Burlatskii, a prominent sociologist with connections in high circles, has also written of "the tendency toward technocratic totalitarianism" found in some Soviet works on management; and party philosopher P. Fedoseev warned against the danger that excessive managerial professionalism might lead to "bureaucratic and technocratic" distortions. According to Soviet sources, in the late seventies calls for professionalization of management encountered "a decisive objection" from those who accused management scientists of defending "managerialism," an ideology that "has appeared in foreign countries."[36]

Reflecting these tensions, Soviet management science has been a curious mixture of native and foreign, of political and professional. Soviet management-training programs typically include courses not only on foreign management experience but also on ideological and political themes, such as the economic and foreign policies of the party and civil defense.[37] At times the regime has imposed explicit restrictions on the activities of management scientists, lest they become too independent. More frequently, management scientists have devised their own means of self-censorship in order to avoid conflict with the authorities. They have been in the forefront of those who "unmask" and criticize foreign management theories, while at the same time calling for their extensive use. The result has been a management science which is neither fully red nor fully expert.

More than any other field, management psychology, with its

guiding assumptions about human behavior, challenges basic tenets of Marxist-Leninist ideology. Before 1966 management psychology was not even recognized as a legitimate field of scientific inquiry in the Soviet Union. Social psychology was labeled an "unfounded and antiscientific" approach by ideologues, who argued that "the problem of the relations created between people in the process of production is basically not a psychological problem, but a social-political one in the broadest sense of the word." At the 1966 Scientific-Technical Conference several speakers criticized the "underevaluation of psychological factors" that had predominated in Soviet managerial thinking. But while the conference included separate sections on cybernetics, law, and economics, no such legitimacy was accorded to psychology.[38] In the years that followed, management educators took the lead in establishing management psychology as an integral part of the new science of administration. Instructional materials on the subject were developed, and by the mid-1970s courses were being taught in most interbranch training programs. By then it was widely accepted that "the executive needs knowledge to help him create normal relations between people, an atmosphere of good will and mutual exactingness, and healthy competition in the work place—that is, to create what has now come to be called a normal psychological climate in the collective."[39]

But controversy continued to shroud Soviet work on management psychology. Textbooks for executives note that though a significant amount of research on the subject has been conducted, "a general unity of opinion on many key theoretical issues of management psychology as a science has not yet been worked out."[40] Another textbook used for training top-level executives at the Academy of the National Economy is prefaced with the caveat that the author's treatment "is not generally accepted, though it lies within the mainstream of work by Soviet scientists." The author, it is said, "exaggerated the significance of social-psychological aspects" of management due to an "understandable professional enthusiasm." Nevertheless, executives are advised to read the text, since it is "useful for solving managerial problems."[41]

The central notion of all management psychology is the concept of leadership. Today the words *lider* and *liderstvo* have become integral parts of Soviet managerial jargon. But in a society in which personality cults have left deep scars, the acceptance of these terms, as one management scientist explained, was not gained without "conflicts." "It was not clear whether in general it was possible to study leadership scientifically in Marxist social-psychology."[42] Today that acceptance has been won, but an uneasiness over the subject remains. In contrast to the West, where Freudian and Adlerian approaches constitute lively fields of inquiry, these theories have remained anathema in the Soviet Union. The one field of psychology the Soviets saw fit to borrow was human relations theory.

Human relations theory focuses on the role that small informal groups play in satisfying the emotional and psychological needs of organizational members. In reality, it fitted no better into Marxist assumptions about human motivation than other branches of psychology. As one Soviet management scientist has admitted, "In the theory of 'small groups' put forward by American psychologists, an attempt is made to move away from class as the basic social group of society."[43] But whereas other branches of Western psychology focus on the more controversial human drives of power and sex, the implicit aims of human relations theory have a long tradition in Russian and Soviet political cultures. Scholars have observed that human relations theory is based on a "noncoercive communications concept of social control," one which attempts to utilize "control mechanisms generated and internalized by the individual" for the attainment of organizational objectives.[44] Given the widespread existence of informal groups in Soviet administration and the emphasis on noncoercive control in post-Stalinist Russia, Soviet managers have been urged to study human relations theory despite its ideological heresies, since it is said to be useful for "improving production and management."[45]

But human relations theory can also be interpreted as a justification for tolerating the many illegal and semilegal practices in which Soviet administrators routinely engage. Some management textbooks assert that the presence of informal relations within organizations is "unavoidable." "Basically, it is a positive thing," one textbook observes. "The informal structure gives business relations flexibility." At the Academy of the National Economy trainees are taught that informal relations result from inflexible hierarchical organizations, which make it "difficult to fulfill one's functions as prescribed and to fulfill assignments if one simply follows the specially approved procedures and decrees." Under such circumstances, "personal contacts, acquaintances with employees of other subdivisions, communication with them during leisure hours, and other factors that are formalized with difficulty often help."[46] At the Plekhanov Institute trainees were told that large hierarchical organizations have a number of inherent disadvantages, such as a dispersion of decision-making responsibility, an absence of risk taking, contradictory instructions from disparate sources, a lack of clarity over rights and responsibilities, and interunit rivalry over limited resources. Because of this, one lecturer explained, such familiar bureaucratic diseases as family circles, *blat,* agency narrow-mindedness, and localism take root. "I don't have to ask the managers in this room whether they have ever engaged in these activities," the lecturer remarked. "Every manager can answer for himself whether or not he engages in them every day."[47]

Like managers in any highly centralized organization, Soviet managers are continually pulled between the behavior desired by superior bureaucratic authority and the role requirements needed to motivate their subordinates. These conflicts pose special problems for Soviet management psychology. There is greater ambivalence in Soviet scholarly works about whether executives should seek to become informal leaders than one finds in Western social-psychological literature. On the one hand, ignoring informal relationships leads to the isolation of the executive from his subordinates and impedes his ability to accomplish tasks. Some Soviet textbooks argue that "in order to influence employees through the system of informal relations, the executive should occupy a worthy place in it." In this view the ideal situation occurs "when the official executive is simultaneously the unofficial leader." On the other hand, too much attention to informal relations and too close an identification with the informal authority structure undermines bureaucratic discipline and leads to a situation in which the executive's allegiances are co-opted. Executives are warned that "there is a sad history of research in which poorly educated social psychologists proposed changing the executive of a collective, referring to the fact that he was not the actual leader." The leader need only be attractive to his subordinates, but the executive must possess a knowledge of the regime's goals and the ways in which they can be achieved. Good leaders, it is asserted, do not always make good executives; rather, "it is more often the other way around."[48]

Hierarchical duty and political expediency define the limits to which executives should tolerate informal groups. If an informal group has not harmed plan fulfillment but has been a constant thorn in the executive's side, the executive should not attempt to dissolve it. Such attempts in the past "not only did not lead in a number of cases to the desired result, but [they] can even encourage greater [group] solidarity." Much depends on timing, since "at the early stages of the formation of an informal group the obstacles created [by the executive] may be sufficient, but at later stages they will solidify the group." When the behavior of an informal group conflicts with the goals of plan fulfillment, repression is appropriate. As one textbook declares, "If the group of employees does not hinder the fulfillment of official duties, then there is no need to interfere in its affairs." Indeed "a particular group can serve as a support for the executive in progressive undertakings." But "if the behavior of any group interferes with the general business, the executive cannot be indifferent toward what is connecting its members."[49]

Individuals who do not conform, executives are told, can be controlled through psychological pressure and, if need be, repression. Top-level executives at the Academy of the National Economy are taught that the "ultimate form of nonconformism is negativism—the total rejection of the norms and values of the collective." Such behavior can lead to "a voluntary moral isolation of the person in the collective, which looks upon the person as 'foreign' and causes a distressing sensation of psychological discomfort." Such persons must be made either to "leave the collective . . . or to accept ([that is,] force oneself to accept) the collective's norms." In those cases in which "negativism . . . expresses itself in opposition to the collective's efforts" (that is, dissent), "social-psychological methods can turn out to be ineffective" (in other words, police action is appropriate).[50]

Soviet textbooks lean heavily toward endorsing consultative and autocratic management styles. "Liberal" executives are described as "weathervanes," as "sand" in the hands of their employees. A "liberal" style almost always "ends in failure" and "brings a definite harm" to the enterprise by causing "total disarray in the work of the collective." At the Plekhanov Institute future factory directors were told that "liberal" executives suffered from neurotic disorders, since they feared direct contact with people and avoided punishment when punishment was due.[51] Top-level executives at the Academy of the National Economy are taught that a "liberal" management style allows "a great deal of independence and opportunity for individual and collective creativity." But trainees are warned that a "liberal" style is almost always inappropriate for modern industrial production and might be used successfully only in scientific research institutes. "Autocratic" management styles have also been condemned for creating "a psychological barrier between the executive and his associates." At the Plekhanov Institute "autocratic" executives were criticized as a "socially maladapted" type; Khrushchev's "subjectivism" (rather than Stalin's "cult of personality") was cited as the major example of an autocratic style. Khrushchev, executives were told, "did not listen to specialists and thought he always knew what was best."[52] But an "autocratic" executive style is said to have the advantage of a quick "force of influence." It is condoned under conditions of organizational crisis, in newly established organizations, when an executive's authority is insecure, when there is a lack of discipline or unity, or when a situation has turned "dangerous." "Even if the leadership is not always pleasant," one textbook notes, "people want to have a decisive and energetic executive who is able to take full responsibility for decision-making." An indecisive executive "who does not know what he wants and hides behind the democratism of 'collective opinion' never achieves success."[53]

The Case Study and the Business Game

It is one thing to explain in abstract terms how executives should approach decision-making; it is quite another to effect changes in their actual behavior and role definitions. In the West, active methods of instruction, such as the case-study method, business games, role-playing exercises, and sensitivity training, have been used to accomplish these goals. But active methods of instruction create a number of difficulties in the context of Soviet administration. Not only do they assume that managerial activity is a creative and empirical craft dependent on skills of independent judgment and executive discretion, but they also require an atmosphere of free inquiry and broad experimentation in the classroom and the factory. Both the Soviet administrative system and educational system have traditionally lacked these conditions. The empirical approach which proponents of professionalism have espoused has frequently conflicted with the realities of Soviet administrative and political centralization.

The most widely applied form of active instruction in Soviet management training is the case-study method. In the 1970s several collections of case-study exercises were published,[54] and a number of interbranch training programs established their own methodological offices for writing case exercises. Yet compared with the West, where managers analyze between twenty and several hundred case exercises in the course of training, the case study is still used on a modest scale in the Soviet Union, where in the best of programs three to six cases might be analyzed over a three-month period. This minimal use of the case method has been due to the difficulties encountered by management scientists in composing case exercises and to the cultural obstacles the method has met in the classroom.

Soviet management educators using the case-study method understand that cases "ought to deal with events that take place in the real world." But because of agency concerns for secrecy, the type of information necessary for writing realistic cases has rarely been available, and most materials instead have been drawn from the press. The party has established explicit guidelines regarding what should and what should not be included in case exercises. Cases "should have a positive character" and should not question fundamental political and economic relationships. Class discussions of case materials are supposed to focus on "a review of the alternative courses of action in the particular circumstances."[55] But in a highly centralized and politically dominated economic system, it is often difficult to avoid touching on sensitive relationships without trivializing an exercise. Rarely is the role of local party organs in economic decision-making addressed in Soviet case-study materials; most cases deal with issues internal to the plant or with relations between the enterprise and its ministry. One Soviet case exercise, for instance, describes an *ob'edinenie* which must choose between manufacturing a consumer product at a plant located in another *oblast'* or manufacturing the same product at a less efficient plant in its own oblast'. The proposed move would have lowered overall provincial production indicators for consumer goods and normally would have been opposed by local party organs. But nowhere in the text is there any mention of local party organs or their interest in the matter.[56]

Western scholars have observed that in societies which "have strongly drawn lines of respect for authority and clearly defined social classes," active instructional techniques such as the case-study method encounter cultural obstacles.[57] Soviet instructors using the case-study method have been advised "not to stifle discussion with opinions that are too categorically stated until the proper time" (that is, the end of the lesson), but they have not adapted easily to a passive role in the classroom. As for Soviet managers, they are unaccustomed to free interchange of opinions in a public setting and do not adjust quickly to the freewheeling class participation required by the method. One Soviet description of a case exercise revealed that the majority of trainees "listened very little to one another during discussion." Trainees "attempted to express their thoughts in eager rivalry and then began to exchange ideas with their neighbors. Since there were forty people in the classroom, it was difficult to follow the course of the discussion." In general "the lesson was very confused." I observed the same confusion during a case exercise at the Plekhanov Institute. Trainees were intimidated by the case-study format. Many sat awkwardly silent, fearing to speak their minds; others noisily interrupted their colleagues in order to attract the instructor's attention. Few opinions were challenged, and the instructor, a graduate of Harvard Business School experienced in the use of case-study techniques, had to play the role of provocateur to prevent the lesson from stagnating.[58]

Another form of active instruction borrowed from the West is the business game (*delovaia igra*). In 1975 a national conference on business gaming was held, leading in the 1980s to the publication of a handbook on Soviet business games.[59] The acceptance of the business game was not achieved without a struggle. As Soviet gamers have observed, "There is still no single opinion on what a business game is." A major disagreement concerns whether conflict is a necessary element of a game. One game designer has written that games "can only be designed and conducted according to management situations in which a conflict lies at their base—that is, there must be no fewer than two participants whose interests at least partially do not coincide." But others, emphasizing the dogma that under socialism competitive and conflictual relationships are "very atypical," have advocated games designed for individuals in which each player competes only against himself. Most game designers have adopted the point of view that "the process of interaction between various enterprises and agencies" should be modeled into games, including simulation of "the defense and interconnections of particular interests among separate groups of trainees," which can aid in understanding "opposing positions" and in integrating agency interests with the goals of the state.[60]

Business games have been applied on only a modest scale in the Soviet Union in comparison with the United States, where, within a few years of the appearance of the first computer-simulated games in the late 1950s, more than a hundred games, played by thirty thousand executives, had been designed.[61] By contrast, it was not until the middle 1980s, almost two decades after the design of the first computer-simulated Soviet business game, that a comparable number of games were in operation in the Soviet Union. The slow spread of business gaming has been due less to ideological restrictions than to organizational inertia. Most Soviet games have been developed in academic institutions, where qualified personnel capable of their design are concentrated. But games developed at the university and in the research laboratory encountered bureaucratic obstacles to their application in training classrooms. A survey made in 1982 revealed that only 11 percent of Soviet business games were used on a regular basis in instruction and that the use of games outside the walls of their designing institutions was "extremely rare."[62] Moreover, most Soviet business games have not been designed for computer use. Manual games, though cheaper, are more difficult to organize, require more time for play, are clumsy, and are not easily transferred from one institution to another.

What is taught by a business game—Soviet or American—depends largely on what its designers decide to put into it. In the United States an oligopoly market structure is typically modeled into games. As one group of American gamers has stated, "there is no justification for the market structure other than [that] it produces realistic behavior and the mechanism has some semblance of plausibility . . . the choice of relationships to be employed is largely a matter of judgment on the part of the game designer."[63] Market structures and competing firms are obviously irrelevant for Soviet business games. But as a result, all Soviet games contain a number of methodological difficulties. In the West the criterion of profit is typically used to judge the performance of players. In the Soviet system there is no such overarching performance indicator that integrates all aspects of production. Instead, production plans typically contain dozens of performance indicators, each of which is viewed by the state as legal and binding in theory, although in practice emphasis is placed on one or another portion of the plan. If, as the gaming format assumes, the performance of players is to be judged and compared with that of other players, piecemeal indicators from the plan, such as gross output, must be used as in real life. This means that a business game simulating a centrally planned economic mechanism is likely to be either highly unrealistic, isolating economic activity from its broader administrative milieu, or dysfunctional, reinforcing a narrow focus on one goal among the many goals performed at the plant and supporting forms of economic behavior that the regime itself condemns. Soviet business gamers admit that the problem of evaluating performance in a game is "the key problem" they face. The vast majority of Soviet business games have sought to simulate a particular production function rather than general managerial processes, which in some cases can do Soviet managers more harm than good.[64]

Frequently managers are asked to engage in game behavior which runs counter to longstanding managerial practices. For instance, in the game "Enterprise-Ministry," which simulates the planning process of an entire branch, each actor attempts to maximize his enterprise's profits by choosing the mix, type, and quality of goods produced. But in real life the performance of enterprises is rarely judged by profit indicators, which in any case vary considerably with the price-setting policies of the center, but rather by output indicators. In the game, when the final variant of the plan is achieved, the period of play is over and the plan is said to be fulfilled. In real life, plan targets continue to be the object of negotiation and adjustment throughout the entire planning period, and plan fulfillment is never achieved as effortlessly as it is in this laboratory exercise. Another business game, one simulating supply decisions for enterprises undergoing plan corrections imposed on them from above, has the unintentional effect of teaching trainees that "plan corrections are not really that undesirable," even though the regime has tried for years to eliminate this practice. In some cases functions which lie outside the scope of authority of players in real life are modeled into games. In other cases the same game is played by both ministers and foremen, despite the obvious differences in their powers and functions. A management specialist from Yaroslavl, after playing a business game simulating production bottlenecks, came to the conclusion that "it is easier for the manager to take over the machine himself and eliminate breakdowns than to spend an enormous amount of time calculating losses and figuring out unnecessary puzzles," as the game required.[65]

As one game designer admitted, the unrealistic nature of many business games has caused managers frequently to "relate to game forms of instruction with skepticism and apprehension." The vast majority of Soviet games revolve around the problems of allocating scarce resources and eliminating emergency breakdowns in production. But in the words of one management specialist, such games often reinforce the existing shortcomings of the economy. Instead of teaching managers "not to permit these malfunctions, which interfere with the normal course of production, and to know how to prevent them," they teach executives the very familiar skills of how to adjust to the disorders endemic to the planning system. "One would think," she concluded, "that industrial executives, having a whole arsenal of 'fire-fighting' tools for eliminating production bottlenecks at their disposal, have little if anything to learn from such games."[66]

Professionalization from Above

The 1950s and 1960s brought a major transformation to management recruitment in the United States. In 1959 two reports, one sponsored by the Ford Foundation and the other by the Carnegie Corporation, concluded that the business profession had failed to attract "the best and the brightest" to its ranks. Studies had shown that standardized test scores of students in undergraduate business programs fell significantly below those in liberal arts programs; better-educated college students from high-income family backgrounds were more inclined to go into the so-called free professions than to embark on a business career, while children of clerical and factory workers predominated among undergraduate business majors. A broad reorganization of management education followed. Standards for admission to graduate business schools were tightened, and a national entrance examination was introduced. A campaign to attach the standards and status of professionalism to management raised the prestige of managerial work and attracted better-educated candidates. As William Whyte observed, the campaign to professionalize management was more than simply "a sugar-coating, a more attractively packaged indoctrination"; rather, it was "a manifestation of a deep change in the organization's view of what *kind* of man it wishes to achieve."[67]

In the Soviet Union, management professionalizers have expressed similar concerns over the low quality of candidates attracted to the managerial profession. At a conference in the early seventies Soviet management scientists, in words reminiscent of their American counterparts, complained that, among all Soviet professions, management had had one of the lowest rates of growth in the proportion of its members having a higher education.[68] In the mid-thirties only 14 percent of Soviet enterprise directors had a higher education, and between 40 and 49 percent had a primary school education or less. Although after Stalin's death the rate at which graduate specialists saturated the industrial bureaucracy increased, by 1965 only a third of Soviet enterprise directors had a higher education, and as late as 1970 that figure had risen to only 42 percent.[69]

The Soviet Union produces the largest number of graduate engineers in the world. Yet, ironically, the overwhelming majority of these engineering graduates prefer to work in research and design institutes rather than in management, even though the salaries, power, and privileges of managers are greater than those of engineers and scientists. Surveys of engineering vuz students indicate that only 10 percent even consider embarking upon a managerial career; many graduates "flatly refuse to become managers." Managers frequently complain that, "of the small number of talented, well-equipped graduates in the sea of mediocrity, few want to go into management." A sociologist recently observed, "The better graduates are assigned to research institutes, and the average ones to the shops."[70]

The failure of Soviet management to attract the best and the brightest has been due largely to the low prestige of the managerial profession. Although Soviet industrial executives receive relatively high salaries, have a large number of material privileges, and enjoy a considerable amount of power, their social status has not been commensurate with their income, standard of living, or authority. A 1962 survey conducted in Novosibirsk indicated that only 2 percent of high school students regarded wages as a major factor in choosing a profession. By contrast, 45 percent responded that "the creative nature of the work" was an important consideration. Interestingly enough, Soviet surveys exploring why executives are attracted to managerial work show that they, unlike these high school students of predominantly white-collar backgrounds, let material factors (in particular, wages and living conditions) weigh heavily in their decisions.[71]

The low prestige of managerial work has been in part the result of the disdain with which Russian society has traditionally regarded commercial activity. But it has also been related to the risks and lack of independence associated with managerial work. Management in the Soviet Union, because it is a political profession, bears all the risks attached to Soviet politics. Success has depended on plan fulfillment, and plan fulfillment has depended less on good organization than on the ability of the manager to coax neighboring plants into delivering supplies, to wheedle lower plan targets from the ministry, to mask conditions at the plant from outsiders, and to obtain critical support from superiors and local party authorities. The low prestige of managerial work has been buttressed as well by conscious policies of the regime. Management has constituted one of the major paths of upward mobility in Soviet society. This was no less true in the 1930s, when more than half of the directors of heavy-industry enterprises were of working-class origin, than it was in the mid-1980s. At the Twenty-Fourth Party Congress in 1971 Brezhnev proudly recited that over half of the directors of the largest enterprises in the country had begun their careers as workers or peasants. The engineering vuz has been one of the major paths of upward mobility for students of working-class background. While students of white-collar background predominate in Soviet universities, law schools, teachers colleges, and music conservatories, students of working-class background have been in the majority at engineering and economics institutes.[72] Relatively open admissions policies have permitted workers to rise through the managerial hierarchy at a comparatively late age. A significant proportion of factory directors have made use of part-time and correspondence education, which has allowed them to work while studying.

The traditional preference for promoting managers with experience in lower-level line posts has also favored the rise of managers from the workbench. The low-level line posts have been particularly unattractive to graduate specialists because of the low salaries (at times, 20 to 30 percent less than the skilled workers they supervise) and the face-to-face contact with workers they require. Soviet surveys indicate that only 3 percent of production engineers express a desire to become foremen, and managers complain that "you can't even entice them into the shop by rolling out a red carpet." Although the foreman is one of the chief recruiting grounds for future managers, only 5 to 10 percent of foremen are college graduates, while the number of praktiki among them ranges from 30 to 60 percent. Even at the level of shop head, only a third have a higher education, while more than a quarter are praktiki.[73]

Proponents of managerial professionalism have recognized that these career patterns make it difficult to promote a capable executive corps. Much as Whyte saw managerial professionalism as signaling profound changes in organizational man, Soviet management professionalizers have argued that "the transition to new methods of management frequently requires not simply the upgrading of qualifications, but the enlistment of a new type of employee." They have called for "hastening the process of saturating industry with executive personnel having the necessary scientific knowledge" and thus "increasing the prestige of administrative work."[74] During the 1970s management scientists attempted to forge a new Soviet managerial man through national legislation. In particular, they lobbied for reform of management education, legal regulation of managerial careers, and professional procedures for the selection and evaluation of managerial personnel.

According to one source, proposals for revamping the management-training system in the early seventies were both "numerous and diverse." At the Second Scientific-Technical Conference in 1972 a number of delegates spoke in favor of management schools, and the resolutions of the conference called upon the State Committee for Science and Technology, Minvuz, and other agencies to "review the issue." A follow-up conference in Tallin proposed similar measures. "The [job of] economic executive in socialist production," one delegate argued, "is a special profession, no matter whether this is subjectively recognized or not"; the creation of management schools in the Soviet Union was "an inevitability."[75] Both Minvuz and the State Committee for Science and Technology, with their responsibilities for supervising interbranch training, were natural allies of these ideas. Administrators from Minvuz have disclosed that issues of executive training were "regularly reviewed" at meetings of the ministerial collegium throughout the seventies; and top-level executives within the ministry, including former minister Yeliutin, were accused by branch ministries of harboring biases against branch training. Yearly reports compiled by Minvuz routinely called for reform of management training, including the creation of business schools. Minvuz had a vested interest in this project, since any new management schools would have expanded its own influence over branch ministries. In 1973 it established a special working group to "prepare proposals for improving the system for upgrading qualifications."[76]

In the mid-seventies managerial professionalizers launched a public campaign to reform executive training. Throughout 1976 and 1977 proposals for "Business Universities," described as "the logical outgrowth of the scientific-technological revolution," appeared with unusual frequency in the popular, party, and specialized press. The basic idea behind the campaign differed little from the motivations of American management educators in the late fifties. As one advocate put it, "If we want to have healthy forests, we must first care for the earlier undergrowth."[77]

This campaign touched off a heated bureaucratic and ideological struggle. Administrators from Minvuz supported the idea that "preliminary study ought to be obligatory before assignment to an executive post," and they accused branch ministries of seeking to "supplant the interbranch training of executives." Ministerial officials in turn charged Minvuz with attempting "to attract enterprises into their arms, establishing an unhealthy competition with branch IPKs." "Surely it is cheaper and quicker," they argued, "to 'bring up to condition' specialists who are already trained and who have production experience than to produce them anew from the first course in vuzy and wait while they accumulate experience."[78] One management educator reminisced that, only twenty years earlier, proposals for management schools "would have been perceived as risky." That management scientists were no longer risking their necks was indicative of the extent to which their ideas had penetrated party circles. A number of regional party secretaries echoed calls for the reform of executive training.[79] But others within the party apparatus, reflecting a traditionalist view, feared that management schools would erode party control over managerial recruitment and choke opportunities for social mobility. As the first secretary of Perm obkom, Boris Konoplev, argued, "It is difficult to imagine an institute or faculty that could immediately train seasoned factory directors." Managers should be "selected from the large mass of specialists and leaders of the lower ranks of production and be armed with the latest theories and the leading experience of management," but "for this there already exists a far-flung system to retrain managerial personnel." It was the party's responsibility "to aid their growth, patiently and consistently correcting them when the need arises."[80]

During the summer of 1977 the Politburo examined alternative proposals on executive training. The outlines of a decision were already in place by September, when a *Pravda* editorial reminded managers that the successful fulfillment of their duties was "impossible without mastering management science," but that "the major means for uninterrupted replenishment and renewal of skills" would remain "self-education." In November a government decree preserved ministerial control over training, but it called on ministries to take "urgent measures" to improve their programs. Minvuz's authority over branch programs was enhanced; its Scientific-Methodological Council, soon upgraded to a division, was to enjoy "large rights" over executive training, and its decisions were to be "binding for all ministries and agencies."[81] In 1979, in an attempt to force branch IPKs to increase the amount of managerial instruction in their curricula, the Scientific-Methodological Division ordered that all IPK study programs must receive its approval before they could be used. This sparked an uproar of protest from branch IPK personnel, who argued that standardized study programs could not take into account specific agency needs and circumstances.[82]

But instead of management schools, the leadership established the Academy of the National Economy, a two-year program for training a reserve for promotion to top-level management posts. Central Committee Secretary Ivan Dolgikh explained the rationale behind the institute at its opening ceremonies. Although other forms of executive training had "demonstrated their value and must continue to be used," the party had decided that these programs "should be supplemented with a more thorough training for top-level executive personnel."[83] Throughout the late seventies and early eighties, proponents of managerial professionalism continued to call for management schools.[84] But in the conservative atmosphere of the late Brezhnev era, fewer ears within the aging leadership were willing to listen.

The second area in which professionalizers sought national legislation was that of the legal regulation of the managerial career, or as one management scientist put it, "to fix by law the method of choosing and training organizers of production in all branches of the economy, regardless of their level." Suggestions were made for a nationwide system of career models, allowing "everyone to know beforehand what stages he must go through and what length of time is required to become a shop head, chief engineer, director, or general director." Others advocated laws restricting managerial posts to those with a higher education. Still others proposed that graduation from a faculty of organizers be made a legal requirement for becoming an enterprise director.[85] The systems for training and selecting executives in the Soviet Union have been described as "two wheels rotating independently of each other; there have been some successful attempts to connect them more or less, but basically the wheels turn discordantly." Since the mid-sixties some effort has been made to identify promising candidates for management positions and to provide them with training. But only a small proportion of executives on these reserve lists for promotion go through any preparatory training at all, and only about half of all promotions within the managerial hierarchy are made from the reserve.[86]

Legal regulation of personnel assignments has been a touchy subject, since any laws governing personnel selection restrict the power and flexibility of party and state officials in filling nomenklatura positions. In the late 1960s the State Committee for Labor and Wage Issues, at the prodding of management scientists, drew up new occupational handbooks governing the assignment of executives. But when the new job descriptions were published, they turned out to be so fuzzy that almost anyone could have been assigned to a managerial post without violating them. Though calling for the hiring of executives with special training, the documents went on to note that "persons who have not had the special training or the period of experience set forth by these occupational requirements, but who possess enough practical experience and have fulfilled the occupational duties given to them, can be kept at their posts or are allowed to fill a post at a given enterprise." Critics of the handbooks charged that officials at the State Committee "were suddenly frightened by their own decisiveness and quickly took a step backward."[87]

In the absence of national legislation, a piecemeal approach dominated. A number of ministries pursued unwritten policies of hiring only graduate specialists for managerial posts. Yet, in the words of one journalist, an examination of the Soviet industrial executive corps in the mid-seventies presented "a very motley picture: directors with and without diplomas; directors suited for our fathers and grandfathers; directors with a deep understanding of the problems of the scientific-technological revolution; and those trying to adapt to the scientific-technological revolution with old baggage." Throughout the seventies the rate at which vuz graduates replaced praktiki among enterprise directors remained low—approximately 1 to 2 percent per year.[88] Even this slow pace of change aroused considerable anxiety, however. Letters appeared in the press from frustrated workers complaining about the prevalent attitude that "with a diploma one is able to become someone, perhaps even a minister, and without it one can attain only the highest rank of worker." Most studies concur that "the times of swift promotion from the workbench have passed," and that in the future the problem of mobility opportunities for workers in the managerial apparatus will "become even more acute and pressing."[89] At higher levels of the bureaucracy, the need for education has already become a barrier to upward mobility. By contrast, the middle and lower levels are still populated to a significant degree by those lacking diplomas, and in the absence of legislation they are likely to remain so for some time.

Throughout the 1970s management scientists called for the introduction of managerial degrees, ranks, and titles to raise the prestige of management. One proponent of professionalization wrote, "Diplomas, titles, badges, and other attributes should teach the executive to respect instruction and define the level of his skills." Suggestions were even made to resurrect the old Tsarist Table of Ranks, with the modification that rank be based upon possession of a degree in management science rather than upon years of service.[90] Along similar lines, management scientists championed a national system of certification for managerial personnel. In 1969 personnel certification (*attestatsiia*) began as an experiment in the Ministry of the Construction Materials Industry. The idea was to produce a periodic evaluation of all personnel, including managers, in order to weed out incompetents, identify promising employees, and select those who were in need of further training. In October 1973 the Council of Ministers "recommended" that similar certification systems be established in national and union republic ministries. But the system contained loopholes designed to preserve party and ministerial discretion. Each ministry was instructed to draw up its own list of personnel subject to certification, and executives on the nomenklatura of top-level party and state organizations were specifically exempted. As one management scientist later complained, "A rather strange situation exists in which rank-and-file workers and members of the middle levels of management undergo certification, while those managerial executives on the nomenklatura of higher organizations are not subject to certification at all."[91]

In 1977 it was revealed that 26 percent of managers and specialists in heavy industry had never undergone certification. In a number of industries the list of those targeted to be certified included only 30 percent of executives and specialists in the branch. Even where certification was practiced, patron-client relationships frequently turned it into a farce. In the Ministry of the Construction Materials Industry, where the original experiment had been conducted and all managers were periodically reviewed, only 2,000 (1.5 percent) of the 130,000 employees who underwent certification in 1972 received below-average evaluations. The ministry's certification process was subject to considerable abuse. In one case a glavk attempted to cover up for one of its plant directors by supplying the ministry's certification commission with false information. Although the fraud was subsequently discovered, the certification commission merely recommended that the executive undergo re-certification within a year, at which time he was duly certified. The connection between certification and personnel decision-making was also weak. At one industrial plant in Gorki only eight out of the forty-three employees who received negative evaluations were fired. The remainder were simply asked to undergo certification again.[92]

The final area in which proponents of professionalization attempted to alter recruitment practices concerned the procedures for selecting and evaluating executives. Since Lenin's day it has been accepted party doctrine that industrial executives are selected according to both professional and political qualifications. But these principles have been put into practice in various ways. On his deathbed Lenin called for the use of tests and examinations to check the professional competence of personnel. By contrast, Stalin emphasized the political side of the formula and rejected the use of professional tests, destroying the field of psychotechnics in the process. As a result, few formal rules—other than the nomenklatura system, which specifies which party and state organs are to participate in personnel decision-making—govern the selection of Soviet industrial personnel. This informality has aided centralization within the bureaucracy. As Blau and Schoenherr point out, "insufficient rather than excessive standardization of personnel practice seems to foster the development of a rigid authority structure with responsibilities centralized in the hands of top management."[93] The absence of formal selection criteria also opened the door to the burgeoning of patron-client relationships, thereby lowering the professional quality of the executive corps. Management scientists meeting in 1972 declared that "the professionalization of management places the design of an appropriate system of evaluation . . . for executives (according to their abilities, knowledge, and skills) on the agenda of the day." One management scientist observed, "Today it is evident that the necessity of designing a scientifically based system for evaluating personnel is arising"; methods guaranteeing "maximum objectivity" should replace procedures based on "personal memory and personal impressions" only.[94]

Management scientists looked to the capitalist corporation as a model for professional personnel procedures. By the late seventies more than two thousand American corporations and government agencies had established personnel assessment centers, where candidates for executive positions were subjected to a barrage of tests, mock exercises, and interviews designed to elicit their managerial talents. Most corporations maintain comprehensive personnel records detailing the interests, careers, and performance of managers, and a number of companies have devised elaborate point systems for evaluating personnel. All of these methods, in one form or another, were proposed for adoption in Soviet industry by Soviet management experts.

A number of management scientists bemoaned the fact that existing systems of personnel documentation in Soviet industry were "so simplified that it is very difficult to get any real facts from them." They suggested the use of computer-aided personnel systems capable of storing large amounts of information on the professional qualifications of executives. Some even argued that computers could be used to weed out potential candidates for job openings. Some published books detailing how point systems could be used for evaluating personnel. Others proposed tests, mock exercises, and assessment centers for identifying executive talents. Rector Shorin of IUNKh insisted that computer-aided personnel evaluation was an inevitable by-product of the scientific-technological revolution. "We have become accustomed to airplanes, rockets, and television . . . gradually our psychological stereotypes against using computers for personnel work will also break down."[95]

But opposition to these evaluation methods pervaded the party and the bureaucracy. As Soviet management scientists came to recognize, "Those employees who count on a step-by-step advancement on the basis of length of service or seniority are usually against a system of evaluation that accentuates the differences among employees." Older executives and praktiki were particularly wary of the new techniques.[96] More important were the objections raised within the party. Even younger and more professionally oriented apparatchiki were unwilling to sacrifice their personnel privileges for the sake of promoting formal professionalizing schemes. G. P. Bogomiakov, often considered a representative of the younger generation of co-opted specialists within the party apparatus, accused proponents of professional selection of seeking to "formalize a problem which by its very nature cannot be formalized." For Bogomiakov the haphazard personnel practices of the party were "of much more practical use than all the advice and articles on the 'computerization' of personnel evaluation, point systems, tests, computerized personnel documentation, and so forth." "The essence of the party method" in personnel selection "is an *individual* approach" relying on "an analysis of concrete situations and not on general speculative schemes."[97] In the face of this kind of opposition, professionalizers retreated, calling only for "broad-ranging experimentation." As one textbook for top-level personnel admitted, "The problem of evaluation methods still awaits its resolution."[98]

7

. . . . . .

The Irrational Rationalizers

A Soviet manager participating in a cultural exchange was invited to run an American corporation while its president was on vacation. On his return the American manager asked his Soviet friend how things had gone. "Fine," the Soviet manager replied. "First, I bought all the raw materials on the market, before our competitors could get them. Then I hired five hundred extra workers, in case the party asks us to help with the harvest this fall. Finally, whenever a customer came to my office, I chased him away and told him never to come back."

—*A Soviet management scientist, 1980*

The Brezhnev era began with a spate of optimism about the potential of management science. Scientific management was to solve, in the words of one specialist, "any problem that hampers the economy or is a bane to our life." Training in management science would be "the magic key" that would "open the doors to the storehouse of hidden reserves."[1] During these years (1965–1982) an army of management experts was unleashed upon society. Several hundred research institutes, encompassing the labor of tens of thousands, were established, as were hundreds of training programs to which tens of thousands of managers were dispatched.

221

Simply from 1965 to 1975 almost 3000 articles and 760 books were published on management issues. As one Soviet journalist recently recalled, "In the sixties and seventies the problem of management gained such popularity that it frequently came to be called 'the problem of the century.'"[2] So fascinated was the Brezhnev regime with management science that the country was no longer said to be "ruled," but to be "scientifically managed."

As in the 1920s, Soviet management experts had a profound impact on national administrative policy. Decree after decree on management to some extent reflected their influence. As in the twenties, imported management techniques penetrated every imaginable sphere of activity: the administration of schools, factories, hospitals, libraries, laboratories, army units, grocery stores, museums, collective farms, and local governments. Personnel from the Ministry of Defense accounted for 10 percent of trainees at the faculties of organizers in the early 1980s. Including trainees from defense production ministries, those with military connections made up nearly 21 percent. Even the police recognized the relevance of management science for their work; in the early eighties the Ministry of Internal Affairs of Kazakhstan sent 215 of its personnel to train at the faculties. Since Kazakhstan is still a major center of labor-camp activity, it seems likely that management science even penetrated the remaining outposts of the GULAG.[3] Beginning in 1972, a course on scientific management was regularly taught at the Central Committee's Higher Party School. Local party organs established their own councils of management experts to rationalize the party apparatus.[4]

Mark Twain once wrote that nothing so needs reforming as other people's habits. It has been the task of the management expert, in both the East and the West, to do just that. The most difficult part of the management expert's job is not diagnosing problems, but persuading people to change their behavior. Under market conditions the final arbiter of the correctness of an expert's recommendations is profit, determined by the interplay between consumer satisfaction and cost-effective production. In the hierarchical environment of central planning, where the requirements of bureaucratic discipline (expressed in the obedient fulfillment of production plans) frequently conflict with the goals of productivity, cost-effectiveness, and product quality, management scientists have found the reform of managerial habits a formidable task. As in the past, some proposals of Soviet management experts brought positive results in practice. But nearly every scheme encountered serious resistance, results were often temporary, and the gains of rationalization in one corner were frequently overwhelmed by irrationalities arising in another. Moreover, management specialists exhibited many of the same irrationalities as the managers whose activities they were supposed to rationalize. Despite massive efforts by the Soviet government to improve administration, economic performance declined precipitously over the 1970s. Under these circumstances management science increasingly resembled a catechism divorced from reality.

The Classroom and the Factory

Evaluation of management training has always been a black art. No scientific methodology for it exists, nor is it likely one could ever be designed. One American management scientist working in this area has noted that "more evaluation research has been carried out with reference to management education than in other fields of education." In spite of such studies, as a French management scientist observed, "paradoxically, we know more about management development techniques and tools than about their impact in many organization environments." Western researchers probing the issue have uncovered abundant examples of the unanticipated and dysfunctional effects of training.[5] It may be, as is claimed in some of these studies, that the sources of business success are exogenous to the classroom and are to be found in the innate skills of managers or in the surrounding marketplace. Nevertheless, studies comparing managers before and after training have demonstrated some positive effects of training. One American management scientist observed that "despite our limited knowledge and understanding of cause and effect in the training process, organizations with trained managers tend to be more effective than those with untrained managers."[6] Few, however, would claim that training alone is a sufficient condition for success.

In contrast to the hundreds of such studies in the West, research on the effectiveness of Soviet management training has yet to be undertaken. Managers have occasionally been surveyed, while still in the classroom, on the usefulness of instruction; but the timing of these surveys as well as their mixed results make it difficult to draw conclusions.[7] There are also the standard recitations of management educators concerning the large ruble savings supposedly amassed as a result of their efforts. The director of the IPK of the Ministry of the Construction Materials Industry claimed that as a direct result of training each enterprise sending trainees to the institute in 1973 saved between 20,000 and 100,000 rubles. But if training so improved management in the branch, why did its economic performance, in terms of growth both in output and in productivity, lag significantly behind the average rates of the rest of industry during the 1970s? In another case the Study Combine of the Ministry of Light Industry of Estonia claimed that the course projects of its first group of trainees had saved some 3 million rubles. But surveys conducted five years later showed that only 16 percent of trainees reported that their course projects had brought significant improvements to their plants. Another 17 percent had not even attempted to put their projects into practice, and 47 percent said that their projects had either had no effect or had actually worsened the position of their enterprises.[8] The IPK of the Ministry of the Construction Materials Industry and the Study Combine of the Estonian Ministry of Light Industry are among the better organized programs for managers in the Soviet Union. One can only guess at the situation elsewhere.

To probe the effectiveness of instruction one must look beyond the din of these figures to managerial behavior in the classroom and the factory. The deeper one examines this, the more aware one becomes of the enormous tension between manager and management scientist. The typical reaction of many managers to their management teachers has been, in the words of a retired enterprise director, that "one senses that they themselves have never managed enterprises or construction projects."[9] Trainee evaluations of management programs frequently include "such uncomplimentary words as 'a scholarly approach' . . . 'a poorly thought-out selection of information,' and 'an absence of pedagogical skills.'" Often "brilliant vuz teachers with a lot of experience shrink before the demanding auditorium, where there are seated not students, but executives, sometimes of the highest rank and broadest knowledge."[10]

Many management instructors simply don't care whether their lessons are applicable to trainees. According to one report, when an enterprise director questioned one of his teachers about how he could put the information given on systems theory into practice at his plant, the scholar replied, "That's not my problem."[11] A common complaint among trainees at the Plekhanov Institute was that instruction too often bore an exhortatory tone. According to one trainee, "We are all experienced executives. We already know that it is necessary to preserve the environment, to cut costs, and so on. So when they read lectures to us about this, it's not telling us anything that we don't know already. You can't just tell us these things; you must show us *how* to accomplish them." Lectures at the Plekhanov Institute frequently assumed the form of agitation sessions. Once when a retired executive from Gosplan devoted a lecture to reading aloud the latest party decree on industry from *Pravda*, trainees read newspapers, chatted loudly, and wrote letters to their families. After forty minutes several trainees requested that the class end early—an entreaty that was granted after some protest by the lecturer. Another observer witnessed an open confrontation in the classroom between theorist and practitioner. Only ten minutes into a lecture, a frustrated manager rose and shouted: "Enough! I've had it with theory. All this philosophy just flies right by me. Explain what you mean in concrete terms or forget it."[12]

Management educators have found their work no less frustrating. They have frequently complained about the difficulty of trying to "overcome the barrier of prejudgment" among trainees, when "the trainee thinks that he has known for a long time what he is being taught." One management scientist found the following attitude typical of older trainees: "Leave me in peace with your science of organization and management! I have two years to go until my pension. I've worked well all my life, and I will work just as well in the future. Just try and take my place and manage differently!" Another management educator observed: "As a rule, the experienced executive already has a certain style and method of work which perhaps are not always effective and do not always answer contemporary requirements, but which have served him well for a number of years and have helped him achieve success." As a result, he "does not always accept unconditionally" what he is taught, nor does he "accept all the recommendations of science as the irrevocable truth, even if they are supported by the fact of their successful application in practice." Paradoxically, "the life and production experiences" that are "the professional wealth and support" of the executive become "a barrier to his acceptance of the new."[13]

The assertion of Soviet management scientists that "it is always easier to train and retrain younger people"[14] can also be heard in Massachusetts, London, or Frankfurt. But for a number of reasons, the "barrier of prejudgment" has been a more serious problem in the Soviet Union than in the West. For one thing, very little training of young managers takes place in the Soviet Union. The overwhelming majority of programs cater to experienced mid-career executives. Older trainees approach training with skepticism not only because of habit, but also because they are less inclined to take instruction seriously. Anyone entering a Soviet management classroom cannot help being struck by the atmosphere of indifference in the auditorium. Soviet executive training programs make extremely light demands on trainees. The few assignments which the executive is given are usually ignored. Absenteeism is a serious problem, and instructional staffs are under pressure to ignore poor attendance or performance. Grade inflation is pervasive.[15]

The indifference of managers and management scientists is only a microcosm of a broader set of institutional relationships that engulf both manager and management scientist. Friction between theory and practice is common in executive training programs. A Dutch management scientist has written of the problem of reentry, which occurs when managers "find that the philosophies of their training clash with those prevailing in the company, and when their newly learned techniques seem impractical in view of insurmountable constraints." Such conflicts have also engendered frustration among Western managers and have even caused them to seek new employment opportunities.[16]

In the Soviet case the problem of reentry and its manifestations in the classroom may be likened to a profound clash between organizational cultures. As Western researchers have come to recognize, "to remove a person from his role set, tell him in a training program or executive interview that he should change his behavior, and then return him" to his organization "burdens him with a double responsibility." Not only must he change his own behavior, but he must also change the expectations and behavior of those with whom he interacts.[17] For precisely this reason Western experts have shifted their attention away from the individual to the group or organization as a whole. But Soviet attempts to change the behavior of industrial managers have taken place within an organizational context in which the role requirements of the organization as a whole have remained unchanged and are frequently at odds with the behavior envisioned in managerial theory.

Efforts to encourage employee participation and more open decision-making styles have often been frustrated by the hierarchical environment and authoritarian political culture in which Soviet managers operate. Although they are taught that important decisions should be made on the basis of a discussion of alternative courses of action and specialist advice, Soviet research into decision-making patterns in the late 1970s revealed that "executives very rarely use the multivariant method" and in the majority of cases "prepare only one variant of a draft decision." Although executives are taught to confer broadly with their subordinates when making decisions, Soviet scholars themselves admit that "many executives of enterprises, and also shop heads and foremen, feel that their superiors rarely confer with them in preparing decisions and do not take into account the specifics of their work."[18] At the Plekhanov Institute during a discussion of the art of motivating employees, managers were asked to "behave like a Georgian manipulating a saleswoman at a store"—an ethnic stereotype linked with black-market wheeling and dealing. Ostap Bender, the wily swindler of Ilf and Petrov's comic novel *The Twelve Chairs*, was held up as a conscious model for managers. To Ilf and Petrov, Bender was a satirical character, a spoof on the NEPmen of the 1920s who aimed to get rich quickly through shady activities. But in the absence of a market culture and its inherent need to persuade customers of the worthiness of products, instructors necessarily had to use semilegal black-market activities as models of persuasive behavior.[19]

What Soviet management scientists have referred to as the barrier of prejudgment has often been a euphemism for more deep-seated conflicts between the behavior envisaged in management theory and the actual role requirements of managerial practice. At the Plekhanov Institute a lecturer with thirty years of managerial experience spent several hours haranguing trainees over the considerable waste of raw materials and the enormous number of unfinished construction projects in Soviet industry. "All this is known to you," he scolded them, "but all the same the situation is not corrected!" Later the same lecturer told how, when he was a manager, a construction firm had tried to pressure him into declaring one of his new buildings completed, even though water pipes had not been installed and the building was not usable. In the end the local party authorities ordered him to sign the declaration, lest the situation reflect poorly on them. (As it happened, the building in which the lecturer spoke was itself a victim of the lagging construction industry: the construction of a new building to house the Plekhanov Institute's training program had dragged on for more than a decade.) Trainees were given several detailed lectures on office technology, documentation systems, and methods of handling paperwork; but finding the material of little interest, they requested that class end early. At the end of one such lesson a trainee raised his hand and asked why, if the time of the plant director was so precious and every rationalization of document-handling so important, the Soviet government didn't provide managers with more secretarial help. The lecturer could give no satisfactory explanation.[20]

A lecture describing the 1979 indicator reform elicited a chorus of questions from trainees. This reform sought to eliminate the common practice of double and triple counting in the fulfillment of production plans by introducing a new indicator, normative net output, to guide managerial behavior instead of gross output (the *val*). But trainees expressed skepticism over whether the new indicator would have any effect. "Why didn't the new decree take into account that the results of applying new technology are usually not evident until three to five years after its introduction?" "Why should managers be concerned with applying new technologies if their efforts are not reflected in their bonuses?" "Should managers attempt to introduce new technologies even if they do not bring about a palpable economic effect?" It is impossible to imagine mid-career corporate executives in Western Europe or America raising such questions. Even the lecturer responsible for presenting the reform as "serious" and "profound" was forced to admit, in the face of this barrage, that he doubted whether much would change as a result of it. In fact, little did; not quite four years later, press reports indicated that the val still dominated Soviet economic practice and that normative net output had actually exacerbated administrative problems by confusing the role requirements of managers.[21]

At the Plekhanov Institute a case-study exercise on the Shchekino experiment, a well-known economic innovation of the 1970s, was the occasion for reflection on the conflict between bureaucratic discipline and rationalization in the Soviet context. The primary idea behind the Shchekino experiment was to provide material incentives to executives for rationalizing managerial structures, improving labor productivity, releasing excess workers for employment elsewhere, and stimulating technological innovation. In the experiment, the wage fund of an enterprise was fixed at a stable level, and savings in wages gained through rationalization were paid to the remaining employees in the form of additional salaries. As a result of these innovations, within a short time the Shchekino Chemical Combine tripled its volume of production, quadrupled its labor productivity, increased the average salary of its employees by 45 percent, and released 20 percent of its work force.[22]

After discussing the reasons for the experiment and how it was organized, the instructor asked for a show of hands from those who would have attempted the experiment if they had been director of the Shchekino combine. The trainees unanimously voted in favor of the experiment, either out of a desire to appear "progressive" or out of genuine enthusiasm. But if the purpose of this exercise was to reinforce risk-taking behavior on the part of managers and to demonstrate the worthiness of such experiments, it failed. As discussion of the experiment proceeded, the manager-trainees brought to light a host of problems. Several raised the point that managers in the Soviet system need to employ superfluous labor resources as a safety factor in the event of emergencies; without them, they said, the enterprise would find itself in serious trouble whenever a critical situation arose. At the Shchekino combine, once the enterprise's administrative structure had been rationalized and superfluous personnel had been released, the enterprise had used up a large part of its internal reserves for improving production, and further gains in productivity required retooling the plant with costly new technologies. To maintain high rates of growth in productivity and to meet plan targets, management had to seek an additional 40 to 45 million rubles of investment from Moscow. Several trainees commented on the risky political dependencies that the Shchekino method assumed. Without help from local party authorities and from the ministry in obtaining investment funds and supplies, they observed, the Shchekino method would fail. In fact, the Ministry of the Chemical Industry had been reluctant to provide additional funds for technical reconstruction of the Shchekino combine and had only been persuaded to do so by the Tula regional party committee, which had actively promoted the experiment.

A number of trainees pointed out the dangers of embarking on such an experiment as long as enterprise plans were set according to the standard practice of "planning from the achieved level" (that is, according to the enterprise's record during the previous plan period). The initial successes of the experiment caused the Shchekino combine's plan targets to rise to unrealistically high levels. When these targets could not be achieved, the bonus fund of the enterprise started to decline, and the incentive for rationalization was lost. The only recourse left to the enterprise was to "beat out" (*vybit'*) lower plan targets from the ministry. Trainees emphasized the importance of enjoying the personal support of ministerial superiors in obtaining such favors, to prevent well-intentioned attempts at rationalization from leading to disaster.

Reflecting on the case materials, the director of a newly opened computer plant said he would not attempt to introduce the method at his enterprise because it would require too much time and effort to retrain and reassign the employees released from their jobs. This would also entail an enormous distraction from the primary goal of management—plan fulfillment. By the end of the discussion, group opinion had turned sharply against the experiment; a second show of hands on whether managers would be willing to use the method expressed an overwhelming "Nyet." Thus, a case exercise intended to promote rationalization activities by managers ended by alerting them to the dangers which rationalization posed to plan fulfillment. As one trainee sarcastically summed up the group's opinion: "If you could guarantee the experiment's success, I'd try it; if not, I wouldn't."[23]

The continual need to demonstrate hierarchical obedience by

fulfilling gross output indicators leaves Soviet managers with little incentive for rationalization. One newspaper account observed that "under ordinary conditions managers have no reason to be concerned with management, and what's more—with Scientific Management." As a plant director described his dilemma: "Even if I fulfill the plan by 98 percent, but save 10 percent of the metal or, say, eliminate two hundred jobs, I still may get fired. So is it worth working on such things?" When the general director of the giant Likhachev Automobile Works in Moscow, P. D. Borodin, was asked if he used management theory in his work, he replied: "We ourselves create our own theory."[24]

Neither ignorance nor tradition is a sufficient explanation for such attitudes and behavior. The cause must be sought in a web of social relationships that is embedded in the structure of bureaucratic hierarchy and is highly resistant to change. As Berliner noted in his study of innovation in Soviet industry, "With the best stock of techniques teachable by the best business school in the world, the Soviet manager obliged to operate in the social structure of the Soviet economy would soon find himself making the same kinds of economic decisions as are widely criticized in the Soviet literature today. If the problem is that nobody cares, the fault is not in the people but in the structure of the system."[25]

Clients and Experts

No management expert can afford to ignore the politics of the institutional environment in which he works. He must rely upon a constituency within his organization—a client whose interests he serves and who acts as his major support in enacting change. But within the bureaucratic context of Soviet administration, it is unclear who that client is. Should the management expert serve the interests of the party, the ministry, the factory director, or the shop? Or is he supposed to serve some abstract notion of efficiency without regard for the interests of any constituency? Like the Soviet manager, the management specialist has been ensconced in a web of hierarchical relationships marked by conflict between the role requirements of bureaucratic discipline and the requirements of rationalization.

The Soviet Union is one of the few countries in the world which still speaks glowingly of traditional Taylorist techniques. Despite the demise of Taylorism in the West, much of the Soviet effort to apply management science over the past twenty years has centered on the classical approaches of Scientific Management, rationalizing the individual work station through time-and-motion analysis and sweeping principles of organization. In one year (1969) alone more than 600,000 NOT proposals encompassing the activities of some 5.5 million people were implemented in Soviet industry. These measures supposedly resulted in the release of 214,000 employees, saving the state 545 million rubles. National legislation establishing factory departments and laboratories for NOT was enacted in 1968. In 1970 ministries began to draft agency NOT plans, and in 1971 a national plan for NOT was included in the draft for the Eighth Five-Year Plan.[26]

As in the 1920s, it was difficult to judge the effect of all this activity. Aside from the question of the accuracy of reported figures, there was little consistency in the ways in which savings from NOT were measured. One study of the 1970s listed at least twelve different ways of measuring the savings accrued through NOT; another study listed six.[27] Rarely did evaluations take into account the costs incurred in rationalization. Although in 1969 NOT specialists were said to have saved the state 545 million rubles, the cost of these projects totaled 363 million rubles. In general the payoff from NOT measures was not great. In Moscow every ruble invested in rationalization in the early seventies yielded a one-time average return of 1.29 rubles—a rate of savings that was condemned as too low at a 1973 conference. At least a fifth of the NOT measures implemented in 1969 had a negative payoff, and during the seventies the effectiveness of investment in NOT at plants and enterprises fell. Thus, while in 1969 each ruble of investment was said to yield a one-time savings of 1.61 rubles in return, by 1972 studies indicated that this rate had dropped to 1.39 rubles.[28]

Not surprisingly, the same problems that had plagued the work of factory rationalization units in the 1920s reappeared in the 1970s. By the late sixties administrative perversions of NOT had already become a source of concern. A study of rationalization units in the Ukraine noted that "despite broad popularity," NOT was being applied "slowly" because of "elements of conservatism and opposition." Writing in 1971, S. S. Novozhilov, deputy chairman of the

State Committee for Labor and Wage Issues, observed that there were "still many enterprises that look upon NOT work as the latest 'campaign,' and that permit a superficial approach" to rationalization, "often leading to a vulgarization of the very idea of applying the scientific organization of labor." In words reminiscent of Ordzhonikidze, he criticized executives who sought to "substitute trivial organizational measures" for thorough economizing. A Moscow conference on rationalization in 1973 complained of "serious shortcomings" in the rationalization work of the capital's enterprises. That same year a plenary session of the Sverdlovsk regional party committee criticized "inertia-bound executives and those who make a lot of noise while avoiding serious work" aimed at improving managerial operations.[29]

As in the 1920s, the proliferation of plant rationalization units resulted in a confusing array of organizations. Specialists noted that these units were often organized "in an intuitive manner," leading to "a significant and unjustified lack of coordination." The staffs of NOT laboratories and departments varied in size from two to thirty-five. Their employees lacked specialized training and had acquired whatever knowledge they possessed "through trial and error." Accordingly, the quality of those working in these departments was low. A survey of Ukrainian local industry in the early seventies revealed that only a quarter of plant NOT employees had a higher education, and many had only a high school education or less. Bonuses for those who introduced rationalization measures were minimal. A study of four Moscow machine-building plants found that the average bonus for rationalization measures ranged from twelve to twenty-one rubles per person. At many Moscow enterprises no bonuses were paid.[30]

In the 1920s enterprise directors who sought to outmaneuver rationalizers had often assigned production and clerical tasks to rationalization units to keep them out of the way. Studies in the late 1970s showed that 40 percent of the time of the factory NOT specialist was spent on tasks that were not included in his job description.[31] As in the 1920s, rationalization units were attractive targets for enterprise executives who were under pressure to cut costs. NOT specialists were usually the first to be fired when staffs were cut. In 1973 plant directors in Moscow were criticized for "undervaluing the role of NOT departments and permitting their unjustifiable cutback." Some enterprises, it was said, were "mechanistically slashing and even liquidating" their NOT departments. A decade later a large number of enterprises did not even have special departments for NOT. In those that did, the departments normally consisted of one or two specialists, and were understaffed to the point where they could have only a marginal impact on production. According to one report, by the mid-1980s managers had "so actively cut back on NOT departments" that "all that is left of them are horns and hoofs [*rozhki da nozhki*]."[32]

In addition to the factory NOT specialist, a new figure appeared on the industrial scene: the professional management consultant. Management consultancy is still in its infancy in the Soviet Union; as a recent article pointed out, consultants "are still a rarity for the large majority of enterprise directors." In the late 1970s a conference in Tallin on consulting attracted 250 attendees.[33] A few special consulting enterprises were established to design, install, and service management-information systems. And in isolated enterprises in-house consulting services were created. In the 1960s and 1970s several consulting centers also appeared, such as MGU's Center for Problems of Management, Academician Aganbegian's Institute for the Economics and Organization of Industrial Production in Novosibirsk, and R. Kh. Iuksviarav's consulting group at the Tallin Polytechnic Institute. But such centers are exceptions and are capable of servicing only a handful of enterprises. In sharp contrast to the West, where management consulting has become a multibillion dollar industry, there are practically no independent consulting firms or organizations in the Soviet Union; for most consultants that activity is a sideline to their regular teaching or research work. As one Soviet management consultant pointed out, "Almost no one among those engaged in management consulting is a consultant in the pure sense; for everyone, this activity is supplementary, not primary."[34]

The spread of management consultancy has been blocked in part by the uncertain legal status of the profession. There is no category of "management consultant" in official occupational lists. There are no legal regulations to govern relations between consultants and enterprises, and no uniform methods of payment. One management consultant has reported that "because of the organizational limbo of consulting activity . . . enthusiasm for consulting work has waned among some specialists." Similarly, the lack of special training has led to the prevalence of "self-taught" consultants and has "raised doubts" among managers about the utility of consulting work.[35] In 1974 the Ministry of Higher Education established an experimental program at the Ordzhonikidze Institute of Management in Moscow to train "engineer-economists in the organization of production management," who were to act as management consultants working "alongside the director." Many management specialists publicly advocated the expansion of such programs. But Rector O. V. Kozlova noted the existence of "a definite psychological barrier, disbelief, and sometimes simply misunderstanding" among party and government officials concerning "what such specialists will do in production."[36]

Even more important have been the bureaucratic barriers to consultants in production. A readiness among managers to discuss problems openly is a prerequisite for consulting activity. In the Soviet system such openness is a direct threat to an enterprise director's position, for it reveals to his superiors the problems of his plant and the reserves he has managed to hoard. According to one manager, the first question that occurs to a director who is considering asking consultants to visit his plant is, "Will they discover the negative sides of our activity and make them known to the whole world?" R. Kh. Iuksviarav, the founder of management consultancy in Estonia and a graduate of American business schools, has commented that usually management consultants are hired "by those executives who recognize the gaps in their knowledge and are not embarrassed to ask for help from outside." He added: "In my experience such executives are still rare; more often one encounters those who admit their need for additional knowledge only to themselves and are afraid to speak of it aloud." A management consultant from the Estonian Ministry of Light Industry has written of the contradictory administrative claims to which he and his colleagues are subject: "We are not able to use in our reports to the ministry the information we have received in confidential conversations at the enterprises we advise, and sometimes we are reproached for not reporting certain information." Iuksviarav has written that enterprise directors have at times attempted to "use our work . . . as a shield against inspectors and higher-level commissions, as proof of their supposedly 'close' contacts with science.'' This same sensitivity about the uses to which the consultant's information might be put has caused another consultant to observe: "There is a conviction among professional management consultants that it is wrong to suggest one's services to an organization; one should be there only on invitation."[37]

Not only have enterprise directors feared to wash their dirty linen in public, but frequently the most important problems facing them cannot be ameliorated at the plant level. Academician Kantorovich once likened the most powerful Soviet plant directors to "free birds in snares, hemmed in by countless prohibitions, limitations, obligatory permits, and agreements at numerous levels for what seem to be the most elementary undertakings." Studies have shown that enterprise directors spend at least half of their time dealing with problems external to the plant—in particular, with the issues of supply and delivery of materials. Between a fifth and a third of the director's decisions involve the execution of instructions received from higher authorities, two-thirds more are operational decisions, and only 5 to 10 percent are considered by management experts to be "creative." As a recent article in *Pravda* pointed out, "Frequently everything is assigned to the factory now from above: what and how much to produce, at what price, with what level of wages, who should be the supplier, to whom and when the product should be delivered, how much profit should be obtained, and so forth."[38]

Although Soviet management consultants may be able to identify the problems plaguing an enterprise, the solution to these problems often lies in the hands of outsiders. In the words of one consultant, "Management consultants work at the level of the enterprise and association, but many managerial problems go far beyond the bounds of the single enterprise. The field of activity of the consultant remains narrow, and his opportunities for aiding the enterprise are modest." Often rationalization decisions at the plant level turn out to be impossible to implement without corresponding changes in higher managerial organs. A group of management specialists in the Ukrainian coal industry, after analyzing the work of several enterprises, concluded that the number of officials directly subordinate to each mine director exceeded manageable levels several times over. But their recommendations for alleviating the problem could not be implemented, for they would have required reorganizing the entire managerial structure of the ministry.[39]

Frequently plant production continues to lag even after the latest managerial innovations are introduced, either because the enterprise does not receive timely support from above or because other plants fail to deliver supplies on time. In the late seventies, specialists from Academician Aganbegian's Novosibirsk institute engaged in a thorough reorganization of a tractor plant according to principles of program management. Although the new system succeeded in rationalizing the plant's internal operations, its full effect could not be realized because the innovations stopped at the factory gates. The enterprise received supply deliveries on an irregular basis, disrupting production and raising "doubts" in the minds of managers about the worth of the new system. As the plant director concluded, "If a systems approach is carried out only within the confines of an enterprise, the obstacles . . . can still turn out to be traditional." Attempts to apply program management methods to the construction of power lines along the Urengoi gas pipeline were less successful. Though they brought initial results, within a year the enterprises involved had "utterly failed" to fulfill their production plans because superior authorities had neglected to provide the experiment "with minimum basic working conditions."[40]

With enterprises caught in such horizontal and vertical webs of dependence, the pressures to engage in traditional economic practices have frequently been overwhelming. In the late seventies two dozen engineers from an atomic power station attempted to apply program management methods to the construction of new power facilities. Six months after the reorganization, labor productivity at the construction project had increased several times over. But within a short time the group "had found it necessary for various reasons to return to the old ways." When the specialists tried to interest senior ministerial officials in the project, they were "politely thanked for their extremely timely proposals," but they never heard from the ministry again.[41]

At the plant the base of support for the consultant's work is usually narrow, at times resting precariously on the will of a single official. Such was the case with a project initiated by MGU's Laboratory for Problems of Management at what was described as "a solid Moscow organization." In the words of Gavril Popov, director of the laboratory, "We worked there for five years, created a new methodology, and implemented the first part of the project.

Then all of a sudden a sad event occurred: the manager of the organization, a proponent of creative cooperation with science, died. From that moment on our work was no longer needed, and our partners do not want it continued." Another management consultant has written of "the riddle of implementation" that "is familiar to every consultant." Enterprise officials "may gladly work with him, and the results may be satisfactory; but as soon as he leaves the factory walls his partners resume their usual daily behavior."[42]

The Soviet management consultant is as much a part of the administered economy as is the manager. He exhibits the same forms of bureaucratic behavior as his managerial counterparts. The management consultant has borne only slight responsibility for the quality of his proposals, and often consulting organizations have operated with no less disorganization than the managers whose behavior they have been asked to rationalize. Take, for instance, the case of the Volgograd Scientific-Research Institute for Management-Information Systems, responsible for the design and introduction of management-information systems in the country's tractor and farm machinery industry. In the early seventies the institute was subordinated to a research and production association in Moscow as part of a nationwide effort to promote the integration of science with production. The institute's staff soon found itself spending thirty-five man-years annually on business trips to Moscow. Central authorities in Moscow constantly reorganized the unit, redefined research projects, and "loaded us down with assignments bearing no similarity to the institute's specialization." Little wonder that in eight years of activity the association had "produced almost no articles bearing any similarity to a management-information system."[43]

Among plant managers, consultants have a reputation for abstract and wooden concepts that bear little resemblance to reality. P. D. Borodin, general director of the Likhachev Automobile Works, has described himself and his colleagues as "especially practical people removed from theory." He once invited a team of management experts to his plant to study its managerial structure. After a quick tour, the experts promptly announced that the plant's organizational structure was "outdated and designed so that not one automobile could be produced under it." Borodin recounted the angry exchange that followed.

Borodin. If you will, automobiles are nevertheless coming off our assembly lines, and rather successfully. The plan is always being fulfilled.

Consultant. Your automobiles are illegitimate. According to theory they have no right to come off the assembly line.

Borodin. What do you suggest?

Consultant. Here is the single correct structure.

Borodin examined the plan and concluded that "under that structure not a single automobile could come off the assembly line!" He summarily rejected the proposals and threw the management "experts" out of his office. The moral of the story: "These theoreticians are so nagging. Everything for them is according to pure science. But we start from actual reality."[44] In another instance, a consultant related how a colleague delivering a lecture at a plant was noisily interrupted from the back of the room with the question: "And have you yourself ever worked in factory management or in the shop?" The specialist's response was no less antagonistic: "Is it really necessary to choose a criminal investigator from among former criminals?"[45]

The Wheel of the Treadmill

During the 1970s "USSR Incorporated" experienced a dizzying series of bureaucratic vicious circles, described by Western experts as a "treadmill of reforms."[46] The causes of this wasted motion lay in what Mikhail Gorbachev later called the "peculiar psychology" that pervaded the Brezhnev leadership—a psychology which aimed "to improve things without changing anything."[47] The science of management was the main source of inspiration for this psychology—the wheel of this endless treadmill of administrative rationalization.

The management expert appealed to the Brezhnev leadership by his promise to rationalize administration without reforming it, to impart to Soviet management, by some process of sympathetic magic, the organizational culture of capitalism without incorporating the principles of the marketplace. The scope of Soviet efforts to rationalize administration in the 1970s was impressive. The results were considerably less. Some projects undoubtedly had positive effects. But there is also evidence that, contrary to their intended results, most of these measures either were not properly implemented, were absorbed by the bureaucracy, or ended in producing as much confusion as before. In the words of a Soviet journalist, "If someone coordinates the adoption of the scientific organization of labor, both on the scale of branches and in the entire national economy, other organizational activity is without aim or direction. And when the extremely expensive matter of adopting management-information systems at enterprises . . . is undertaken, there are almost no instances in which a new organizational order is simultaneously developed."[48]

Applications of management science on a national scale during this period fell roughly into five categories: establishing standards and norms; overhauling organizational structures; redefining lines of responsibility; improving information flows; and upgrading organizational technology. In 1972 and 1973 a series of party and governmental decrees outlined, in familiar words, "serious shortcomings" in norm-determination practices. At many enterprises outdated and artificially low norms were in effect; overfulfillment of norms in some branches exceeded 40 percent. Shortcomings in norm-determination, it was said, were a cause of "overexpenditure on wages and violations of the proper relationship between growth in productivity and wage increases." Ministries and agencies were ordered to engage in a systematic review of norming practices.[49]

The scope of the review that followed was extensive. By 1978 revised norms had been established for 80 percent of industrial workers and 58 percent of technical and administrative personnel. But within a short time complaints were raised again over excessively "liberal norms that do not stimulate a growth in productivity, but serve only as a means for raising wages." By the early 1980s most production norms had once again become outdated and were set at artificially low levels. Many factories were easily able to overfulfill them by 20 or 30 percent; norm overfulfillment in construction in 1980 averaged 50 percent.[50] Not surprisingly, the same problems that had accompanied industrial norm-setting in the early seventies had reappeared.

Attempts to establish quality control standards had a similar history. In 1972 the Soviet Union introduced a national system for rating product quality. Certification commissions within ministries were to assign each product a quality category that was subject to review by the State Committee for Standards. The highest category was to be reserved for those products equal or superior to the best Soviet and foreign models. In the Tenth Five-Year Plan (1976–1980) quality indicators based on the percentage of goods ranked in the highest category were introduced into national economic plans.[51]

Like work norms, the determination of product quality is hardly a science. In market systems the consumer is the ultimate arbiter of these decisions; in centrally planned systems they must be made administratively, through product testing, through a cumbersome system of opinion surveying, or simply arbitrarily. In the Soviet case the producer, in the form of the ministry and its quality control commissions, was asked to rate the quality of his own product, and obviously each ministry had an interest in inflating the number of its products in the highest category. Every year the State Committee for Standards would reject two thousand applications for certification in the highest category and would withdraw certification from more than a hundred products. But its capacity to subject the hundreds of thousands of products circulating in the economy to a systematic review was limited. To receive the state committee's approval for a product, dozens of documents and official signatures had to be collected. Despite these obstacles, the number of products listed in the highest quality category grew steadily, until in some branches the proportion reached 40 percent. The decision to classify a product in the highest quality category was often made arbitrarily, "sometimes on the basis of impressions of foreign-made goods." As one expert observed, "No one at the enterprise or the branch level knows precisely when an item has reached obsolescence."[52]

The repeated attempts in American public administration to find a magic formula for coordination through reorganization have been referred to as "the twentieth-century equivalent of the medieval search for the philosopher's stone.''[53] The idea that the tensions and ambiguities of bureaucratic roles could be overcome by tinkering with administrative charts has been a guiding assumption of rationalization efforts throughout Soviet history. Unlike the situation in the 1920s, when schemes for reorganization revolved around functional and line approaches, proponents of structural reorganization in the 1970s relied on a new import: systems analysis.

The cornerstone of Soviet efforts to overhaul the bureaucracy was the creation of all-union, republican, production, and scientific-production *ob'edineniia* (associations). The ob'edineniia reforms aimed at: establishing rational lines of supply and communication by grouping enterprises around integrated product lines; eliminating superfluous layers in the chain of command by introducing three levels in place of four, five, or six; stemming the growth of managerial staffs by pooling managerial resources; fostering technical innovation by grouping research and development facilities together with production units; and rationalizing central ministerial staffs by redistributing functional and line authority within agencies.[54] In some agencies responsibility for the design of the reorganization was given to branch centers for the scientific organization of labor and management. In other cases outside management consultants were hired to oversee the process.

By 1978 60 percent of Soviet industrial enterprises had been reorganized into ob'edineniia. Estimates of the number of administrative personnel released ranged from eighty-three to ninety-two thousand, and claims of savings extended from 1.5 to 17 billion rubles. Despite these claims, later reports revealed that the number of managerial personnel in the Soviet Union actually increased by more than three million from 1975 to 1983![55] It is now clear that much of the supposed rationalization of the ob'edineniia reforms remained on paper. In a number of branches, small associations containing one or two plants were established, so that a parallel managerial apparatus was plastered on top of the old. By 1981 the Ministry of Chemical and Petroleum Machine-Building had created forty production and scientific-production associations encompassing only seventy-seven enterprises. In all, nearly eighteen thousand enterprises had joined ob'edineniia by 1981. But 42 percent of them remained independent, retaining not only their separate legal status but most of their managerial staff as well.[56]

Significant increases in management staffs also took place as a result of the transformation of glavki into union and republican industrial ob'edineniia. In several years central ministerial staffs had grown in size by an average of 100 to 250 employees. In most ministries the reorganization of glavki into ob'edineniia amounted to a simple change of nameplates on office doors. One account admitted, "In their styles and methods of work, as well as in their rights and responsibilities, many ob'edineniia are little more than the former glavki, only slightly refitted." Staff reductions mainly affected lower-level personnel. The result was a "disproportion" between "cuts in the managerial staffs of lower-level organizations and a noticeable increase in the staffs of higher-level organizations." Widespread deception was also practiced. Managers supposedly released as a result of reorganization were in many cases reclassified to technical jobs. In other instances inflated sums of rubles were allocated for administrative staff salaries, only to be reduced later as part of a ministry's target for staff reduction.[57]

The impact of the ob'edineniia reforms on productivity was at best ambiguous. Enterprises were often grouped into associations in a haphazard way. Foot-dragging by managers reluctant to surrender the independent legal status of their enterprises led to delays in implementation. And because of political pressures, territorial and agency boundaries were usually preserved. As a result, full specialization along integrated product lines was rarely achieved.[58] In the early seventies, when the number of enterprises participating was still small, ob'edineniia generally achieved higher growth rates in output and labor productivity than industry as a whole. But by the early 1980s, after the reforms had become widespread, questions were raised about their effectiveness. It turned out that enterprises remaining outside associations often performed better than those that had joined. At the national level, experts concluded, "the flow of written information has increased, as has the volume of daily work in the ministries and the all-union ob'edineniia." Technical and economic indicators had "not only failed to improve, but have actually worsened." In some branches, such as in the Ministry of the Coal Industry (one of the first agencies to embark upon the reorganization), voices were raised in favor of a return to the prereform ministerial structure. In the early eighties the ministry actually disbanded a number of the ob'edineniia it had organized only ten years earlier. One economist recently cited these reforms in a long list of failed structural reorganizations in the Soviet economy, including the 1929 reforms, which were in many ways similar in approach and outcome. The ob'edineniia, he explained, had "brought some results, but, it seems, far fewer than those that were possible and that were needed."[59]

Another major reorganization similarly rooted in systems theory was the use of program-management methods. Attaching special status to a program is not a new idea in Soviet administration; GOELRO, Lenin's electrification plan, and Khrushchev's Virgin Lands Program have been cited by Soviet authors as the predecessors of the special-purpose and integrated regional development programs of the mid-1970s.[60] But what distinguished recent program management from these crash campaigns of the past was the scope of the effort to provide integrated coordination for tasks that cut across agencies and territories.

Based on American and French experience in program budgeting and also on corporate principles of management by objectives, a rash of management programs appeared in the Soviet Union in the 1970s. The aim of these programs was to overcome agency barriers that have traditionally plagued Soviet industry and hindered solutions to interbranch problems. Program management has been most closely associated with the proponents of "optimal planning," particularly with Academician Nikolai Fedorenko, its most prominent spokesman. Using formal mathematical modeling, optimal planners argued for a series of long-term integrated development programs based on projections of future trends and on the construction of goal-trees.[61] The program approach was not accepted without controversy. Some critics, Fedorenko observed, accused its proponents of seeking to supplant the branch approach to management, and conservative economists charged that program management was a "neo-positivist method" torn out of its bourgeois American context. But since 1966 twelve territorial-production complexes have been established to coordinate regional economic development. Energy, machine building, food, consumer goods, and transportation were chosen as subjects of comprehensive special-purpose programs. Fifteen similar programs were selected as part of the Eleventh Five-Year Plan (1981–1985), which also included plans to draft 40 special-purpose programs for the development of specific fields of science and technology and 120 programs for the application of major technical innovations.[62]

In designing special-purpose programs the Soviets encountered the same problems that accompanied program budgeting methods in American public administration during the 1960s. It was difficult to generate a consensus over how goals should be determined and ranked, how resources should be allocated in programs, and how programs should be evaluated. Even more challenging were the problems associated with the implementation of programs once the pulling and hauling of the agencies concerned with their design had ended. A Soviet management textbook comments that "more often than not, only certain requirements of the program approach are being realized—in particular, mostly in the stage of planning programs and less in the stage of implementation." In general, special-purpose programs were "designed and implemented on the basis of traditional management methods" and did not entail a restructuring of administrative authority.[63] In the best of cases, coordinating responsibility was vested in interagency commissions under either the Council of Ministers or Gosplan. Such was the case with the food and energy programs through the mid-1980s. But the branch planners who dominated Gosplan were reluctant to reorganize around the programs concept, and branch ministries obstinantly refused to surrender their prerogatives to a superior coordinating authority. For a large number of programs, coordinating commissions either were not created, existed in name only, or were paralyzed by agency rivalries. The problems generated by these political interests explain why, in the post-Brezhnev period, the idea of establishing "superministries" has appealed to scholars and politicians.

Most territorial-production complexes were not blessed with interagency commissions, but were instead the responsibility of one ministry chosen to act as "head ministry," overseeing implementation. By the late sixties agency barriers had left deep scars on the first territorial-production complex in Bratsk-Ust-Ilimsk. According to one economist, "Roads and other lines of communication were not built on time at Bratsk. A significant quantity of timber was burned off in clearing the area that was to become the bottom of the Bratsk reservoir. All these mistakes were repeated at Ust-Ilimsk." The city of Bratsk itself was turned into "ten separate agency worker settlements, each remote from the others and poorly linked.'' In the aftermath of this and other fiascos, management scientists proposed the establishment of coordinating centers under Gosplan or the Council of Ministers for each territorial-production complex.[64] But through the mid-eighties only one program (the West Siberian) was allowed to form such a center, as agencies successfully blocked efforts to impose order on their activities from above.

As a result, many of the same problems that plagued the Bratsk program reappeared in later projects. In the early eighties the building of the Kansk-Achinsk Territorial-Production Complex, a major coal development project in East Siberia, fell significantly behind schedule because there was no authority to coordinate the activities of the dozens of ministries and agencies involved in its construction. At the Timan-Pechora Territorial-Production Complex in European Russia, where energy and forest resources are being tapped, 30 to 40 percent of the timber has been discarded as waste, and the cost per ruble of production of timber has been two to three times higher than the average for the branch as a whole—the result of the failure to consolidate and coordinate the work of hundreds of small timbering concerns subordinated to dozens of different agencies. In the case of the West Siberian Complex, for which interagency commissions were established, coordination of the program has been a time-consuming and difficult process. Interagency commissions have grown considerably in size and have been slow to react to problems. Moreover, at times agencies have simply ignored the commissions' decisions that have not been to their liking.[65] Although less is known about the fifteen national special-purpose programs, there is no reason to believe that the situation differs significantly. As one academician observed, ''Special-purpose programs are broken up and scattered among numerous small agency entities'' as a result of ''confused organizational structures deeply rooted in our industry.'' These same organizational structures, he noted, ''render such fine concepts as 'systems analysis' meaningless.''[66]

The Abacus and the Computer

One of the striking parallels between the NOT movement of the 1920s and that of the 1970s is the degree to which the dominant paradigm in both eras was the attempt to mechanize human activities as much as possible—to eliminate what the Soviets call "the subjective factor" in management and replace it with the automatic reflexes of a well-oiled administrative mechanism. If Gastev sought to transform human nature by training workers to respond to the rhythms of the machine, and Rozmirovich attempted to automate administration through the application of office technologies, their heirs have demonstrated a similar penchant for extravagant and utopian technological solutions to organizational problems.

Beginning in the late sixties and early seventies, as administrative strategy shifted from decentralization to recentralization, the leadership's faith in the redeeming possibilities of managerial technology replaced their former emphasis on structural reform. Technocratic dreams of eliminating the role of men in administration through the use of complex technologies penetrated the halls of power. As opposed to economic reform, most business technologies had the advantage of not directly threatening power relations; with some important exceptions they could be bent to accommodate nearly any authority structure, though certainly not without cost. Unfortunately for the Soviets, the technical requirements for office technologies have always been easier to master than the organizational conditions necessary for their proper use. Their effectiveness depends as much, if not more, on the efficiency of the organizations that design them and apply them than on the efficiency of the machine. No office machine, no matter how complex or expensive, is likely to yield significant improvements in productivity if an organization is incapable of fostering productive behavior among its employees.

The latest in the long line of office technologies imported from the West has been the computer. No country in the world (with the possible exception of the United States) has shown so deep and abiding a fascination with the computer as the Soviet Union. The potential of computer technology as a rationalizing force has captivated the imagination of both politicians and management experts, and since 1971 it has played the central role in Soviet efforts to improve the efficiency of the economy. Work on the first Soviet computer-aided management-information system began in 1963 at a Moscow automobile plant with the help of a team of experts from the Ordzhonikidze Engineering-Economics Institute. Not until the latter half of the sixties, however, did the technology begin to spread on any significant scale. By 1970 more than 400 automated management systems of various types were in place; 150 management-information systems had been installed in enterprises, and another 19 within ministries and agencies.[67]

Soviet enthusiasm for computerization reached its height in the early 1970s. At that time investment in computer technology rose sharply, increasing 420 percent in the Ninth Five-Year Plan (1971–1975) over the previous plan period. By the end of the plan 2300 automated management systems, of which 1500 were management-information systems at enterprises and 160 were located in ministries and agencies, were said to have been installed. Investment in computer automation during these years has been estimated to have been between 4.5 and 6 billion rubles, or approximately 1 percent of total planned investment in the economy. Actual costs, however, were probably much higher. It is known, for instance, that by 1976 more than 250,000 specialists, 90,000 of whom were concentrated in branch research and design institutes, were engaged in the design of automated management systems; this number was expected to grow to 450,000 by 1980.[68]

The merger of the computer with communism was not without its share of what Lenin called *komchamstvo,* or communist boasting. Under capitalism, so the official myth goes, computer applications are limited because of commercial secrets and the competition of the marketplace, which put up artificial barriers to the spread of the technology. Instead of viewing the computer as an aid, the capitalist worker inevitably fears automation since it threatens his job. Only under socialism, the Soviets proclaimed, could the full potential of computer technology be realized. Moreover, socialism would be capable of using computers more efficiently because it would be able to take better advantage of economies of scale. As Academician Glushkov, a leading expert in the computer field prior to his death in 1982, argued: "World practice shows that the larger the object for which a management-information system is created, the greater is its economic effect."[69] It was precisely this sort of "gigantomania" which led in 1971 to the announcement of Soviet plans to create a Statewide Automated System (*Obshche-gosudarstvennaia avtomatizirovannaia sistema*)—known otherwise by its initials, OGAS. The plan was to install computer systems gradually in every enterprise and institution, connecting them to a national information center under Gosplan through a pyramidal network of regional and agency management-information systems. OGAS was clearly the most ambitious Soviet rationalization project since Lenin's reorganization of the NKRKI in 1923; in scale and cost it has frequently been compared with the Soviet space program and the industrialization projects of the 1930s.

It is a truism that computers are nothing more than fast adding machines. Ironically, though the Soviets engaged in a massive effort to computerize their economy in the 1970s, few industrialized countries are as backward as the Soviets in other areas of office technology. Beginning in 1965, the Soviet Union held yearly international exhibits of business machines, where the latest in Western typewriters, word processors, intercom systems, dictaphones, calculators, and copying machines were displayed. Yet, for a variety of reasons, little of this equipment, either of Soviet or foreign make, can be found in Soviet offices. The underdevelopment of the Soviet office can in part be explained by the fact that some office technologies (such as Xerox machines, personal computers, and word processors) can also act as unofficial printing presses and uncontrolled channels of communication. Where such facilities exist, access to them is strictly monitored, and the lack of fit between these technologies and the political authority structure is likely to leave the Soviets lagging behind in the computer revolution. But the primitive technical state of Soviet offices has as often been the result of the organizational environment of Soviet administration. In many cases new office technologies are simply not relevant to the practices of Soviet administration. As one article pointed out, "If it takes a month and a half to act on a letter to a ministry, no automatic letter opener is going to change anything." Moreover, the quality of Soviet-made office equipment has been low. The Soviets have yet to produce a reliable copying machine or a typewriter that comes close to international standards. New types of business equipment have confronted the same barriers as those faced by any technical innovation in the Soviet bureaucracy. Such innovations in the "nonproductive" sphere do not directly influence the fulfillment of an enterprise's gross output plan. Therefore, enterprise directors find the benefits of installing new office equipment difficult to calculate, while the effort to do so distracts managers from their pursuit of the val. Because the regime gave top priority to the spread of expensive computer equipment in the 1970s and set specific targets for its application, administrators overlooked simpler but relevant office technologies and instead "placed their hopes on management-information systems, from which they expected miracles."[70] Enterprises outfitted with the latest third- and fourth-generation computers coexisted with offices equipped only with a manual typewriter, carbon paper, and an abacus—a curious mix of nineteenth- and twentieth-century office cultures.

The Soviet leadership did not understand the organizational complexities of their ambitious computerization plans. Because of the speed and power of computers, their potential as rationalizing instruments far surpasses simpler office technologies. But it is precisely their speed and power which make the design and application of computer systems a critical process, since the more sensitive and powerful the technology, the more likely it is that mistakes will be costly. The establishment of computer-aided management systems demands a series of interrelated and complex tasks. It includes not only manufacturing the memory system itself, which involves the use of intricate technologies that are changing quickly, but also numerous other activities: producing peripheral equipment that enables users to interact with the machine; developing software geared to the needs of the user; training hundreds of thousands of computer programmers and technicians capable of installing, programming, and operating the system, as well as managers charged with directing its uses and interpreting its data; providing infrastructural conditions for the computer system, such as adequate power supplies and modern communications facilities for transmitting data over long distances; and creating backup facilities, such as servicing units and spare parts, to keep the computer systems running. One of the striking features of Soviet attempts to rationalize their economy by means of the computer was the degree to which the organizational problems associated with central planning were reflected in the development and provision of the technology itself. As with the NKRKI in the 1920s, the massive computerization campaign aimed at alleviating bureaucratic entropy was itself mired in bureaucratic entropy.

From the beginning, responsibility for developing computer technology and overseeing its application was divided among at least eight different agencies. Among them, three separate ministries

—the Ministry of Instrument-Making, Means of Automation, and Management Systems (Minpribor), the Ministry of the Radio Industry, and the Ministry of the Electronics Industry—jointly shared the task of developing and manufacturing computer hardware and components. Though supposedly a plan was drawn up to coordinate their activities, each agency developed its own equipment designs. The result was a plethora of poorly designed, unreliable, and incompatible machines. The development of more powerful third-generation computers was delayed for several years because of foot-dragging by producers; in the words of M. Rakovskii, the deputy chairman of Gosplan who oversaw the project, the ministries producing computers, "like those in all other branches of the economy," were "interested in producing exactly the same models without concerning themselves with updating their designs." Under pressure to fulfill production plans, computers were often delivered in half-finished form. The Ministry of Railroads received several computers "in various stages of 'incompletion.'" Some had two internal memory units; others had only one. Some had magnetic drum devices; others did not. As a result, it was "impossible to write interchangeable programs" for the machines. Sometimes those responsible for developing software did not receive computers until a year and a half after a model had gone into series production. The supply of peripheral equipment lagged seriously behind the provision of memory units. Since the price of peripherals was low in comparison with the price of computer units, ministries found it easier to fulfill gross output plans by producing large numbers of computers while ignoring the production of peripherals needed for their proper use. Because of delays in deliveries, users had to undertake the manufacture of computer equipment and components themselves.[71]

A large number of computers were dumped into the Soviet economy in the early seventies, but neither the programs nor the personnel necessary for running them were available. A 1973 study of computer systems at thirty Moscow enterprises indicated that it took three to four years on average to install a management-information system. In the majority of cases the installation of each system required more than seventy man-years of labor. Enterprises and organizations were forced to develop programs on their own, leading to a considerable duplication of effort and excessive programming costs. One branch institute spent almost four hundred man-years developing software for its agency because it never received the programs promised to it. In another case an enterprise computer center spent nearly 200,000 rubles from its own wage fund to develop programs that it had failed to receive. Estimates of the costs of computer time expended on debugging programs developed by computer users ran as high as 70 million rubles a year. As one report noted, computer centers were "springing up like mushrooms after a rain," but there were "few specialists familiar with the new equipment." Frequently, those charged with running and servicing the equipment were trained on the spot. With each enterprise fending for itself, a confusing variety of incompatible programs, each written in a different language but performing similar and related tasks, appeared.[72] Thus, instead of aiding the integration of administration, computerization actually reinforced existing organizational boundaries.

With the production of third- and fourth-generation computers, the quality and supply of computer equipment improved. Nevertheless, the Soviets were still not completely successful in mastering the technical aspects of the computer revolution. In the mideighties computer producers came under fire for making false "claims concerning the quality and reliability" of their equipment. "Many instances occur," it was said, "when computers lie idle more than they run." Peripherals were manufactured that were "far from compatible in their technical parameters and programming capabilities," lowering the effectiveness of machine use and raising barriers to integration between agencies. In the late seventies a central programming service had been created under Minpribor to provide standardized software to agencies and enterprises. More than two hundred software packages were developed for management and planning. Still, the new organization was able to handle only half of the requests it received. The Ministry of the Radio Industry also established a central office for computer servicing, with branches in more than forty cities. But the unit experienced difficulties in coping with its tasks, and the servicing of equipment remained "far below contemporary requirements."[73]

Even more vexing than designing, manufacturing, installing, and running automated management systems were the organizational obstacles to assimilating the technology into managerial practice.

The earliest computer applications in the Soviet Union utilized Western techniques of operations research, such as the Critical Path Method (CPM) and the Program Evaluation and Review Technique (PERT), both developed by American corporations in the 1950s. These methods, descendants of the Gantt chart, graph the flow of a complex set of interrelated activities, providing schedules and checkpoints for guiding implementation. Known in Soviet parlance as "network planning," they became the subject of a massive campaign in the late 1960s. Attempts were made to apply them to the construction industry to schedule activities and monitor progress on major projects. But as early as March 1965 reports indicated that network-planning methods were "often running up against the indifference, and sometimes the inertia," of enterprise and ministerial officials. The problem was that the rhythms of the enterprise were typically uneven, depending on the timing of supply deliveries and subject to the practice of monthly, quarterly, and yearly "storming." And since the financing of construction projects was decided by higher authorities, the provision of funds often ran counter to the projected schedules on the flowcharts spewed out of the machine. Network-planning schedules "frequently became mere forms for the registration of events."[74] By the early seventies enthusiasm for the new techniques had waned.

Attitudes toward management-information systems similarly experienced an initial period of enthusiasm followed by deep disillusionment. According to one report, by the late seventies managers of construction organizations were "beginning to express disappointment in these systems—the same attitude they had demonstrated ten years earlier when the new method of network planning failed to meet their expectations."[75] The most common area in which management-information systems were applied at the enterprise was in statistical and accounting tasks, such as maintaining inventories, calculating wages, and bookkeeping. In the mid-seventies these operations made up three-quarters of the tasks fulfilled by all Soviet management-information systems. But in the vast majority of enterprises the computer was overlaid on old patterns of behavior. The reason for this was simple; as one source bluntly put it, "Beyond the gates of the plant, the system is powerless."[76]

Even in those cases in which management-information systems

were well designed and consistently implemented, their full assimilation into managerial practice was frustrated by constant friction between the requirements of the system and the economic behavior induced by the world beyond the plant. Academician Glushkov recounted how, when he and his colleagues installed one of the first management-information systems at the Lvov Television Plant, the system came into direct conflict with the persistent managerial urge to hoard supplies. The computer relayed the latest assignment to the plant's shops, but lower-level managers refused to believe the machine and replied that the parts did not exist. The computer, however, could not be fooled; it responded that the parts existed and supplied the precise day and hour of their manufacture, as well as the shop in which they had been stored. When officials checked this out, they discovered that the parts did indeed exist, but that the stock supervisor, realizing that they were in very short supply, had decided to hide them "for a rainy day." The new system allowed the plant to obtain record-breaking levels of output. But Glushkov himself admitted later that "much of the gain that the enterprise realized internally through the management-information system" was "lost because of poor external ties and interruptions in supply." In other cases the efficiency of computer systems has been known to wreak havoc with employee salaries and to cause irreconcilable personnel conflicts. At one plant the installation of a management-information system sparked widespread dissatisfaction among employees, for once the computer had uncovered most of the factory's existing reserves, "workers stopped receiving bonuses for overfulfilling the plan." Little wonder that a three-year study on the introduction of a management-information system at a Moscow plant discovered that computerization had been accompanied by a sharp rise in psychological stress and that half of the plant's foremen had quit their jobs in protest. The same study revealed that 62 percent of foremen and 80 percent of shop heads had challenged the recommendations of the system.[77]

In this situation, managers found resourceful ways of circumventing their computers. A construction specialist from Estonia observed that the lack of dependable information "is the biggest problem facing today's management-information systems in construction." "One user may decide to deceive the machine by entering work as completed that has not yet been started. Another may deliberately understate the amount of work that has been done in order to receive more supplies and equipment. A third, having no idea what the real state of affairs is, may resort to pure improvisation." Another specialist complained: "What is the use of 'cooking' unreliable information in the expensive kettle of an electronic computer? No matter how you add, multiply, divide, and integrate half-truths, you don't get the truth, and you don't get reliable data for management."[78] The same factors that had caused report-padding in the enterprise long before computers came into vogue frequently led to a situation in which management-information systems were loaded with false data; the circuits of the new technology merely became repositories for long-standing administrative practices.

In the early seventies, when the computerization campaign was in full swing, managers eagerly competed for the latest computer equipment in hopes of gaining progressive reputations. Expensive computers, then in short supply, were frequently applied in inappropriate ways. As one report later noted, "Indiscriminate infatuation with automated systems had the unfortunate result that they were introduced and used even in places where there was no need for them." This not only "caused great financial harm," but also "undermined faith in the effectiveness of computerization and even discredited the very idea of management-information systems."[79]

One of the main goals of the computerization drive was to cut back on excess paperwork. Estimates had indicated that in the early seventies more than 4 billion documents, containing 30 billion sheets of information, circulated yearly in the economy. The computer, it was believed, would substitute for much of this paper by streamlining communications, standardizing paperwork, speeding the processing of information, and eliminating intermediate steps in its transmission. In some cases computerization did bring positive effects. A national product classification code was introduced to aid the exchange of information between computer systems. Moreover, the State Committee for Standards introduced new regulations governing the drafting of documents "that literally anticipate everything: what, where, and how to write or type, how to date and number business documents, and how to decide the number of copies needed." Some specialists even spoke glowingly about the day when magnetic tape would replace paper.[80]

Instead, an exponential increase in the volume of documents circulating in the economy occurred. That figure was estimated in 1983 to have reached a level of 800 billion a year, or two hundred times the number a decade earlier, amounting to almost 3000 documents for every Soviet citizen.[81] In part this paper flood was caused by organizational barriers. Most ministries and agencies rarely rationalized documentation systems while engaging in computerization. When information from one computer system was transferred to another, even within the same ministry, usually it was still transmitted in paper form, making it necessary to enter the information by hand once again into the computer. Changing forms so that they were more easily fed into computers was "an extremely complicated matter"; the approval of the Ministry of Finances was required, generating still more documents. The national product classification code encountered agency foot-dragging; many agencies and enterprises introduced their own classification codes, undermining the purpose of the new system. The paper flood also occurred because computers, with their expanded capacity for processing information, naturally tend to expand the volume of information in circulation. The production of new information seriously outpaced the growth of Soviet computer capacity. Studies showed that in the early eighties two or three times more documents were prepared for enterprise management-information systems than were necessary, resulting in systems overload. Many computer systems, littered with redundant information, were churning out a shower of irrelevant documents. Most important, computerization did little to affect the circumstances which have long produced a flood of paperwork in the Soviet bureaucracy: excessive centralization. As recently as 1983 it was necessary to collect more than sixty signatures before authorization could proceed for the production of an ordinary flatiron.[82] No amount of computerization was going to eliminate excessive documentation if managers were required to produce documentation at every step.

In general, the various engineering applications of computers, such as assembly-line automation, proved a more effective source of savings than management-information systems. The average recoupment period of the former was only one-third that of the latter in the mid-seventies. More than 550 such systems were established in the early seventies, an additional 1300 later in the decade, and another 1200 from 1981 to 1983. In 1983 alone, computer-aided production automation was credited with saving the labor of more than six hundred thousand employees.[83] But like all technical innovation in the Soviet economy, the risks involved in automation were high and the benefits were often low. Enterprise managers were reluctant to install new assembly-line equipment because it disrupted the fulfillment of current output plans. And the gains from technical innovations were reflected only weakly in employee bonuses.

By 1980 branch management-information systems had been established in nearly every all-union ministry and in a third of all republican ministries.[84] But the computerization of national economic agencies also reinforced agency isolation. In the late sixties and early seventies experts clashed over how an integrated national computer network should be built. Some, such as Academician Glushkov and D. G. Zhimerin, the vice-chairman of the State Committee for Science and Technology who was responsible for overseeing the development of the system, believed that OGAS should be built from the top down and integrated on a regional basis. Others, such as Academician Fedorenko, head of the Central Economics-Mathematical Institute (TsEMI), which played a key role in designing the system, argued that the first step of OGAS should be the construction of agency management-information systems, which would serve as the flagships of the network and would only later be integrated at the top. This view eventually prevailed.

Ministries went about the task of designing their own agency systems, which in many cases were incompatible with both Gosplan's system and those of other agencies. In quest of self-sufficiency, each organization created its own computing center, leading to a rise in costs for the program. The average operating time for computer centers fell significantly below established norms, indicating that the equipment was not being used at full capacity, and studies showed that the number of personnel at Soviet computer centers exceeded international norms by an average of 100 to 200 percent. Agency computer centers, which were used primarily for the processing of routine information, were said to operate 50 percent below capacity.[85]

Although the Soviets created regional time-sharing centers in the late seventies to improve the utilization of machines, the institutionalization of computer use around agency barriers complicated the process of integrating the network at the national level. Not surprisingly, attempts to use the information contained in branch systems to support proposals in conflict with ministerial interests ran into trouble. When a certain group of computer consultants "suggested some expedient idea, but one which was considered 'unpatriotic'" from the point of view of their agency, they were "sternly reminded: 'And who is paying your salary? Whose bread are you eating?'" Frustrated by such barriers, some specialists argued that it was necessary to create a national agency to oversee the computer program, an NKRKI for computer rationalization.[86] In fact, in 1985 a new "superministry" for computerization was established to cut through these obstacles.

The most ambitious and utopian uses for computers surfaced at the national level. These centered around various ways in which computers could substitute for the organizing effects of markets. In the early sixties the optimal planning school, led then by economists Nemchinov, Novozhilov, and Petrakov, argued in favor of simulating markets by calculating shadow prices to be used in drawing up plans while simultaneously granting enterprises broad authority. Cyberneticians such as Academician Glushkov went even further, believing that the computer could substitute entirely for markets and could realize the age-old Marxist dream of eliminating the need for a money economy.

Though finding support in high circles, both of these schools were ultimately rejected in favor of the more modest, but equally technocratic, approach of social and economic forecasting championed by Academician Fedorenko. By means of linear programming, input-output tables, and mathematical modeling, forecasts could aid in drafting more accurate plans and designing specific government programs. Still, these techniques had definite limits. In the late sixties and early seventies, experimental input-output tables were compiled for several years and were utilized in composing a long-term development plan for the 1975–1990 period. But the coverage of these tables was incomplete, encompassing only 260 product groups, and the data supplied to planners by agencies required substantial reworking before they could be used. Applications of input-output tables encountered a host of methodological problems—in particular, the role of ruble-value calculations when prices were centrally determined. Planners were able to construct

tables in physical units, but since agency and enterprise plans revolved around gross output in ruble terms, physical tables were of
limited use. By the end of the seventies those involved in the effort
to apply input-output tables admitted that their work was having
little effect on planning practice.[87]

Continual delays, operational difficulties, and bureaucratic inertia plagued Gosplan's attempts to use computers for national economic planning. The first part of Gosplan's computer system did
not go into operation until 1977, more than a decade after it was
conceived. Delays resulted from differences over the proposed
functions of the system, as well as from lack of coordination between the units responsible for its design and installation. The data
used in Gosplan's information system were often incompatible, and
different methods were used to calculate similar indices. Despite
some progress in the computerization of planning, critics complained that the dominant practice among national planners remained "the outmoded approach which looks upon the formation
of plans as a process of 'meshing' drafts submitted by the various
branches."[88]

The Soviet computerization drive was an expensive proposition.
In the mid-1970s the design, equipping, and installation of an enterprise management-information system cost on the average 1.5 to
2.2 million rubles, and an additional 200,000 to 300,000 rubles were
required every year to keep the system in operation. The approxi-
mate cost of designing an agency system averaged 3 to 5 million
rubles and that of the equipment for each system 5 million rubles.
The time required to recover these costs ranged from six months to
five years, depending on the methodology used. The economic
benefit of computerization fell significantly below planned levels
and regime expectations.[89]

By the mid-1970s managers and planners were expressing disappointment over the computerization campaign. Many executives, it
was noted, had "approached automated management systems with
great hopes that have often been followed by disillusionment." This
disillusionment penetrated political circles as well, for in drafting
the Tenth Five-Year Plan (1976–1980) targets for installing management-information systems were cut in half, and emphasis was
placed instead on engineering computer applications.[90] By the early
eighties studies indicated that computer centers often were having

little positive impact on the economic indicators of their enterprises. As one expert observed, a "gap" had formed between "the capabilities of the machines" and "the low level of management-information systems." "Unfortunately, despite the large investment in them, management-information systems quite often fail to bring about improvements in enterprise management, and their economic effect remains insignificant." The actual return from investment in computer technology had turned out to be "very modest compared with its costs," and in the majority of cases computers had "usually functioned as expensive adding machines."[91]

8

. . . . . .

Discipline and Reform

*Why today, when we search for parallels with the past, do
we turn to the most difficult periods of our lives? Because
today the same concentration of national will is required.
And this time the "enemy" is much more complicated: he is
among us, he is a part of our very selves.*

—*Letter to the editor*, Sovetskaia kul'tura, *June 1987*

By the late 1970s the evolution of Soviet administrative strategies
had come full circle. Lenin had chosen a combination of delegative
and managerial strategies in response to the excessive centralization of War Communism. His heirs chose a similar approach in the
mid-sixties to counteract the excessive centralization of the Stalinist model. In both cases, because of the fears of politicians and
bureaucrats that the direction of economic activity might escape
their control, a gradual recentralization followed.

Within this shifting organizational context, far-reaching efforts
were undertaken to rationalize the industrial bureaucracy through
the application of managerial techniques borrowed from the capitalist West. In both the 1920s and the 1970s these efforts failed to
arrest the growth of bureaucratic disorders. In Gorbachev's subsequent analysis, administrative and economic difficulties, expressed
in "the inertness and stiffness of the forms and methods of manage-

ment . . . and an escalation of bureaucratism,'' mounted throughout the seventies and "brought considerable harm to our cause.''[1] In both the late 1920s and the early 1980s, as new goals were embraced by political leaders and economic performance declined to disturbing levels, the political elite was increasingly frustrated by a growing gap between administrative aspirations and administrative performance.

Rather than dealing with this frustration by altering the assumptions of administrative policy, the Brezhnev leadership, despite full knowledge of the situation, persisted in plodding along the same well-beaten path. The pseudoreforms enacted in the 1970s and the series of bureaucratic "vicious circles" evoked by these measures were indicative not of total apathy, but of the deep-seated conservatism of an elite which, above all else, yearned for stability. Brezhnev preferred to suffer the consequences of economic decay rather than assume the risks involved in attempting significant economic reform. He preferred to trust in the redeeming promise of "scientific" decision-making rather than impose discipline on the bureaucracy from on high. The result was a further decline in the economy.

The causes of this lackluster performance were complex. Those most frequently cited are the growing obsolescence of machinery and equipment, the exhaustion of easily accessible sources of raw materials, a decline in the number of able-bodied workers, and the burdens of increased investment in agriculture and defense. More properly understood, the crisis of the Soviet system in the late 1970s and early 1980s resulted from the inability of its administrative institutions to adapt to rapidly changing environmental constraints that made the effective use of economic resources imperative. It was not so much that the Soviet Union, with one-sixth of the land surface of the earth and the third largest population among nations, lacked the resources or the manpower necessary for running a modern industrial economy. Soviet scientists and engineers had invented some of the most advanced machinery in the world, and although investment growth had been scaled back, industry still received the lion's share of resources. Existing labor resources were grossly underused and misallocated, and no degree of metal shortage could alter the Soviet manager's lack of concern for the enormous quantities of metal swept out as waste every day from the factory floor. The efficiency of capital investment, measured in capital-output ratios, declined drastically during the seventies.[2] Expensive computers frequently sat unpacked in their boxes in factory warehouses or in the open air—rusting monuments to the lack of incentive for innovation.

Communist systems have a number of advantages over other political systems for tolerating economic decline and widespread organizational rigidity. Their economic organizations face no threat of bankruptcy. Their politicians need not fear being turned out of office by the ballot box. Although a number of communist systems have experienced mass revolt, there is no recorded case of a successful revolution against a communist regime. On the whole, they have demonstrated a remarkable history of staying power that contrasts sharply with their relatively poor performance as deliverers of goods and services to their populations.

But the price of stagnation has been a decline in public morale, a sense of lost purpose which, if left unattended, could develop into a major social and political crisis. In the 1920s a widespread sense of lost purpose within the party was a major element in raising Stalin to power and fueling the radical transformations that he embarked upon. In the early 1980s, under different circumstances, political, social, and economic stagnation led to what Gorbachev later described as a "pre-crisis situation."[3] Nostalgia in certain circles for the social and industrial discipline of the Stalinist past, expressed not only in the unofficial appearance of photographs of Stalin on truck windshields but also in a partial rehabilitation of the tyrant's role in official history, were but singular manifestations of protest against the festering bureaucratic malaise that paralyzed Soviet society in the late Brezhnev era.

In this situation a new generation rallied around the slogans of discipline, "acceleration" (*uskorenie*), and reform. Their strategy for inducing change straddled the past and the future. It aimed to restore what was viewed as the lost dynamism of the past while enacting reforms to confront the difficult tasks of the future. Much of the political vocabulary of this generation was appropriated from an earlier age. It called for a "sharp break" (*perelom*) with bureaucratic and social stagnation, for an end to "wage-leveling" (*uranilovka*), and for the wholesale "restructuring" (*perestroika*) of society—images which conjured up the attempts of an earlier generation of leaders to shake stagnating Soviet institutions down to their roots. Like Stalinism, the Gorbachev revolution has essentially been an antibureaucratic revolution. Its driving animus has been a broad-ranging attack against "bureaucratism," described in one recent publication as "the worst internal enemy" of the Soviet state. In Gorbachev's words, restructuring aims at "decisively overcoming the processes of stagnation, smashing the mechanism of inertia, and creating a reliable and effective mechanism for accelerating social and economic development." In equating restructuring with "revolution,"[4] Gorbachev had in mind a far-reaching cultural revolution aimed not only at remaking Soviet institutions but also at refashioning the entire Soviet psyche. Thus, what was called a "sharp break" with the past was very much in keeping with the traditions of the bureaucratic economy, according to which successive generations of leaders have been driven to impose change upon the bureaucracy from above in their quest to revitalize it.

The Indulgency Pattern

In his study of industrial management Alvin Gouldner identified what he called "the indulgency pattern," under which an aging supervisor, "Old Doug," had grown excessively lenient in his advancing years. Indulgency was accompanied by extensive patron-client relationships and the flexible application of rules concerning worker absenteeism, pilfering of materials, and dismissal of unruly employees. It also contained certain humanitarian elements, as expressed in Old Doug's practice of rehiring injured employees no longer fit to carry out their full production responsibilities. Gouldner defined leniency as "a judgment rendered by workers when supervisors temper the performance of their managerial role by taking into account obligations that would be relevant in other relationships." Leniency was not necessarily irrational; indeed, it was a primary source of job satisfaction at the plant. Neither was it free of occasional disciplinary measures aimed at securing production objectives. But when Old Doug died, perceptions by top management that things had slipped too far prompted them to instruct Vincent Peele, the newly appointed supervisor, to crack down on rampant indiscipline in order to overcome stagnating production levels.[5]

One is tempted in this story to read "Leonid Brezhnev" in place of "Old Doug"; to draw an analogy between Brezhnev's treatment of aging managers and party officials and the way Old Doug handled incapacitated factory personnel; to compare the widespread corruption, worker absenteeism, and economic decline of the late Brezhnev era with similar conditions found at Gouldner's gypsum plant; and to substitute "Yuri Andropov" for "Vincent Peele." Like Peele, Andropov attempted to revitalize a stagnating "USSR Incorporated" by cracking down on violations of organizational discipline and holding organizational members responsible for performance.

The warning signs of this shift in administrative strategy were visible years before Brezhnev's death. Throughout the late seventies the language of impatience and discipline was used with increasing frequency in official pronouncements. "Is it not the case," Brezhnev asked at the November 1978 Central Committee Plenum, "that some managerial executives take the decisions of the party and government too lightly?" Despite numerous decrees, the economy was suffering from growing shortages of metal and fuel, investments were being squandered on a burgeoning number of unfinished construction projects, and the situation on the country's railroad network, where transportation bottlenecks were preventing the punctual delivery of supplies, had grown "complex." It was time, Brezhnev observed, "to increase the personal responsibility of economic executives" and "to upgrade exactingness [*trebovatel'-nost'*] toward ministers and branch executives, particularly in those places where pressing problems are still being resolved slowly."[6]

A year later Brezhnev criticized by name specific industrial ministers who, "no matter how much you speak to them, no matter how much you appeal to their conscience or their sense of duty," refused to change their behavior. "Not all ministries and agencies," he said, "have been able to overcome the force of inertia and to implement decisively a shift in their work toward quality, productivity, and better final results." In tones reminiscent of bygone years, Brezhnev called for "a struggle against violations of labor discipline, against slovenliness, and against slackness," for "the thorough conduct of a regime of economy," and for "liquidating lack of responsibility and parasitism" in production. Drawing approving shouts from the Central Committee, he declared: "We need to find the specific guilty parties for each 'deficit' caused by negligence, irresponsibility, and bungling, and punish them." "Discipline and order," Brezhnev observed, "are always needed." "Particularly now, when the scale of management has grown enormously and the network of economic interrelationships has become more complex . . . they are especially needed."[7]

Soon afterward, decrees aimed at strengthening labor discipline, rooting out corruption and mismanagement, and upgrading the role of legal organs in managing the economy were announced.[8] Two years later, at the Twenty-Sixth Party Congress, Brezhnev once again called for "tightening up demands for plan discipline, as well as for the quality of plans themselves." He reminded economic executives that "the party has always viewed the plan as law." Nevertheless, "I will say frankly that this obvious truth has come to be forgotten." At the Central Committee Plenum in November 1981 Brezhnev warned individually no less than seventeen ministers and heads of agencies that unless the performance of their agencies improved they would face removal.[9] During his last years in office, the aging leader continually spoke of the need for upgrading administrative and labor discipline, for "demandingness" toward cadres, and for conducting "the strictest regime of economy" in industry.

But a gap was evident between Brezhnev's words and deeds. Of the ten ministers whom Brezhnev had personally reprimanded at the November 1979 Central Committee Plenum, only one was removed from office in the years preceding his death.[10] Of the seventeen top executives who were similarly warned in November 1981, none were removed from their posts by the time of Brezhnev's death one year later. Just as Old Doug preferred to give his men endless warnings rather than fire them, Brezhnev's tough rhetoric contrasted sharply with his lenient behavior.

At the end of 1981 and the beginning of 1982, public calls for upgrading discipline in the office and on the factory floor appeared with increasing frequency. A survey on labor discipline conducted by one journal noted that "a sense of concern ran through all of the responses." Some respondents, presumably those of the older generation, connected a decline in discipline with a lack of public values and sense of duty among young people. As the article noted, "You often hear such comments as, 'People aren't what they used to be.' " Others attributed labor indiscipline to the difficulties of firing workers under conditions of labor shortage, to insufficient wage incentives, and to managerial incompetence. New measures were announced for combating mismanagement, report padding, bribery, and fraud within the bureaucracy. Penalties for economic crimes were made stricter, and cases of offenders were publicized in the press.[11]

In 1982 the political coalition that had sustained Brezhnev in office for eighteen years unraveled. His own physical infirmity encouraged potential successors to jockey for power. The issues of production discipline, corruption, and bureaucratic responsiveness became the rallying cries for those challenging his authority. In early 1982 rumors that the Brezhnev family itself was tainted with corruption gained wide circulation. The uncovering of a diamond-smuggling ring including close friends of Brezhnev's daughter, Galina, within the Moscow circus breathed new force into the opposition. During the summer a second major scandal involving the civilian police chief, Nikolai Shchelokov, and Krasnodar party boss Sergei Medunov strengthened the challenge. KGB chief Yuri Andropov, in a major speech in April 1982, spoke of "the justified indignation of the Soviet people" at "cases of theft, bribery, bureaucratism, a disrespectful attitude to people, and other social phenomena." Similar words were expressed by chief prosecutor Rekunkov, who in an article in *Pravda* lashed out against rampant instances of mismanagement, corruption, worker absenteeism, and drunkenness at work. When it came to swindlers and bribers, Rekunkov declared, "There should be no room for leniency." A *Pravda* editorial, reflecting the new mood, declared that "not a single instance of laxity, mismanagement, unscrupulous self-seeking, and personal gain at the state's expense should be overlooked." The time had come to wage "a resolute struggle against instances of laxness toward the performance of official duties, against bureaucratism, red tape, deception, and favoritism."[12]

Shortly after his election as General Secretary in November 1982, Andropov called for "a more decisive conduct of the struggle against all violations of party, state, and labor discipline." Police raids were conducted against employees who lingered in bathhouses, beer halls, and shopping districts during working hours. Those apprehended received hefty fines and were reported to their factories. In the month of December similar spot raids were carried out in nearly eight hundred industrial enterprises in the province of Moscow alone.[13] In its early stages Andropov's campaign for discipline closely resembled the spirit of the Time League's national war against laziness and inefficiency. A conference of representatives of Moscow work collectives issued a citywide appeal to workers to turn in "drunkards," "slackers," and "idlers" to their superiors and the police. "We urge that an atmosphere of intolerance be created toward every violation of labor and public discipline and that absenteeism, tardiness, and unauthorized absence from work be treated as extraordinary occurrences." In the Ukraine a special form entitled "Operation Chronometer" was distributed to the population for the anonymous denunciation of loafers. Workers were encouraged to criticize their superiors for tolerating indiscipline, mismanagement, and red tape. Production meetings organized by factory party cells passed resolutions condemning the perpetrators and calling for a crackdown. At the end of 1982 new legislation was enacted lengthening jail sentences meted out to speculators and embezzlers.[14]

The campaign for order in production easily flowed into assaults on bureaucratism. At the November Plenum Andropov criticized executives who spoke in catchwords about making the economy more effective, but who "do little in practice to resolve this problem." "By slogans alone," he said, "we cannot get things moving again." He singled out the transport, ferrous metallurgy, and construction industries and warned that "we should think about what kind of aid we should render to these comrades." The officials in charge of these branches had been criticized by Brezhnev over the previous four years, but had suffered no consequences. Within a month of Andropov's warning, the ministers of railroad transport and rural construction were sacked, and the minister of ferrous metallurgy found himself under attack in the press by workers from his ministry, who complained that he had tolerated chronic violations of supply contracts.[15] In the years that followed, a large number of industrial ministers and factory directors were removed from office for corruption, mismanagement, and poor performance.

A shift in the underlying assumptions of personnel policy was not officially confirmed until the Twenty-Seventh Party Congress in February 1986. Then Brezhnev's "trust in cadres" policy was openly condemned for leading to excessive leniency. As Central

Committee Secretary Yegor Ligachev explained, "It is well known that a certain trust in cadres often was replaced by us with unchecked trustfulness and, frankly speaking, lack of control." Instead, bureaucrats were to be held more closely accountable to the leadership for economic performance.[16] In a period of economic stringency, the new leadership made it known that it would no longer tolerate the kind of corrupt and ineffective economic behavior that Brezhnev had routinely overlooked.

Rationalization and Responsibility

The shift in administrative strategy from rationalization to discipline was accompanied by criticism of portions of the management-science community—in particular, those involved in computerization, norm-determination, and standardization. Since these specialists had been charged with establishing indirect mechanisms of control over the bureaucracy, the campaigns for discipline were a veiled admission of the failure of their efforts. At the June 1983 Central Committee Plenum, TsEMI was singled out for having failed to deliver on its promised improvements in production. "We expected much" from the efforts of the institute, Konstantin Chernenko observed, "but until now we are still awaiting reliable concrete research on . . . important economic problems." TsEMI and other research institutes in the social sciences, he said, had been caught up in trivial academic pursuits. A decree approved by the plenum noted that the party expected "trustworthy proposals from economists, philosophers, historians, sociologists, psychologists, and legal scholars on how to increase the effectiveness of production."[17]

Shortly after Chernenko assumed the post of General Secretary in February 1984, the Central Committee issued yet another decree critical of the state of research in management and economics. The Academy of Sciences' Institute of Economics, responsible for coordinating work on economics and management throughout the country, and a bastion of conservative economic thought, was charged with failing to exert "an active influence on the entire front of economic science and managerial practice." Again it was noted that researchers had been investigating "trivial themes" and were isolated from "economic agencies on issues of planning and on applying the results of economic research in managerial practice."[18]

A number of articles bemoaned the fact that enthusiasm for management science had "gradually died out" and been "washed onto the usual shores of the latest campaign." A certain irony was noted that, in spite of a decade of campaigns for NOT, the lack of administrative and labor discipline had once again become a major political problem. One article observed:

> Among propagandists of NOT in the twenties, one often encountered the interesting thesis that our employees lacked an elementary work literacy, a culture of labor, self-discipline, punctuality, and a sense of responsibility. And so what has happened since then? We have gone through collosal transformations . . . Nevertheless we are forced to announce a literal war against slovenliness and to struggle for elementary discipline and order. That is, as in the past, we have still not succeeded in fostering labor culture and habits of precision, punctuality, and order.

A subsequent article noted: "Unfortunately, many of the achievements of the Soviet school of Scientific Management . . . have been forgotten or reduced to zero. The level of theoretical work in this field is extremely complex, but in many areas important organizational relationships are lower now than in the 1920s."[19] Once again those responsible for norm-determination were criticized for allowing production norms, which had not been overhauled for more than ten years, to become outdated and excessively "liberal," leading to their overfulfillment by 20 to 30 percent on average. Norm-setting agencies had been "proudly reporting that nearly three-quarters of all norms in industry were 'technically justified,' but what," critics asked, "is hidden behind these words?" Outdated tariff tables and the liberal policies of wage-setting agencies, it was said, had led to rampant "wage-leveling," a practice which Andropov, Chernenko, and Gorbachev, in words not unlike those used by Stalin fifty years before, condemned as alien to Marxism.[20]

In one form or another and with varying degrees of intensity, campaigns for discipline have been pursued by each of Brezhnev's successors. But like Stalin, contemporary Soviet leaders have faced a number of obstacles in trying to sustain a disciplinary strategy. For one thing, any prolonged effort to crack down on violations of bureacratic rules fosters a search for protection by those who are targets of attack. Patron-client relationships within the bureaucracy were frequently disturbed by these assaults, impinging on powerful interests at the highest levels of the system. Evidence suggests that patronage played a role in moderating and reducing the level of turnover, particularly in the first two and a half years after Brezhnev's death. Just as managers under assault in the 1930s rallied around Ordzhonikidze for protection, so too did officials in the 1980s rely upon powerful patrons within the hierarchy to ward off attacks.

In Andropov's fifteen months in power, eleven of the country's top industrial, construction, transportation, and trade officials were retired or fired. But by April 1983 rumors circulated that some officials, frightened by Andropov's assaults on the bureaucracy, were rallying around Andropov's rival, Konstantin Chernenko, for protection. Whether or not these rumors were true, a number of top-level economic administrators who had been personally criticized for mismanagement and bureaucratic inertia survived, probably because of timely support from above.[21]

During the thirteen months in which Chernenko held power, a marked decline in turnover among industrial personnel took place. At the April 1984 Central Committee Plenum, Chernenko criticized both "ossification" and "too frequent a turnover" among personnel and hinted that some of the problems of the economy were due as much to "objective" factors as to bureaucratic inertia.[22] In contrast to Andropov's record of removals, during Chernenko's reign only three industrial ministers were retired or demoted. Mikhail Gorbachev's accession to power brought a more "demanding" approach once again, and a purge swept through the ranks of industry. In his first year fifteen industrial ministers were fired or retired—a pace of change considerably greater than that set by Andropov. These variations reflected differences of opinion within the leadership over the degree to which administrators should be held personally responsible for the problems of industry. Those differences in turn provided opportunities for administrators under fire to find protection from above.

A second factor complicating a disciplinary strategy has been the high cost of enforcement. Studies of bureaucracies have shown that efforts to crack down systematically on the widespread violation of bureaucratic rules usually require spending large amounts of effort and organizational resources for only marginal improvements.[23] In the Soviet case, given the scope of violations and the pervasive legitimacy accorded to many of them, the costs of enforcement have been high. A survey made in 1983 on popular attitudes toward sanctions against violations of the RSFSR criminal code revealed results which could only have been disturbing to the regime: 91 percent of the respondents were neutral or negative toward sanctions against workers who obtained easier work orders through bribes; 90 percent were neutral or negative toward sanctions against repairmen who pocketed money instead of filling out a work order and delivering the cash to the state; 82 percent were neutral or negative toward sanctions against petty theft at enterprises; 40 percent were neutral or negative toward sanctions against those who adjusted enterprise books so that usable materials were reported as scrap; and 25 percent were neutral or negative toward sanctions against large-scale embezzlement by store managers and against workers who overstated the volume of work they performed.[24] With public attitudes such as these, the level of force required to alter behavior in the work place would have had to be quite high and the size of the watchdog bureaucracy required to enforce rules quite large if any disciplinary campaign were to have a lasting effect. Brezhnev's heirs, unlike Stalin, wisely chose not to pay the price involved in a spiral of sanctions. As Chief Prosecutor Rekunkov, no doubt with Stalin in mind, observed in early 1983: "Life convincingly showed long ago that the strength of punishment is not in its severity but in its inevitability."[25] Nevertheless, the campaign for discipline required considerable resources and a burgeoning of the law-enforcement apparatus.

A third problem was that a high level of energy and mobilization is needed to sustain any disciplinary campaign. As a number of studies have pointed out, it is possible for disciplinary efforts to enjoy widespread legitimacy in organizations, particularly when there is a threat to survival, when the purpose is to ensure compliance with widely accepted rules of behavior, or when violators have received repeated warnings about the consequences of their behavior. But disciplinary campaigns can also generate widespread tensions within an organization, especially when measures are punitive in character or are aimed at changing commonly accepted forms of behavior.[26] To sustain a disciplinary strategy, organizational leaders constantly need to recreate an atmosphere of danger and urgency. Since Brezhnev's death a series of periodic campaigns for discipline has been unleashed, each lasting from a few months to half a year. By the spring of 1983, for example, foreign correspondents in Moscow observed a slackening of Andropov's campaign and a reversion to old patterns of behavior,[27] but during the summer new vigor was poured into the campaign—a cycle connected with the peaks and valleys of Andropov's state of health. In an effort to institutionalize discipline by harnessing peer pressure, a law on labor collectives was passed providing collectives with the right to establish their own penalties for violators. Newspaper editorials warned against attempts by executives "to relieve themselves of responsibility and to transfer it to others' shoulders." Party organizations were instructed that "the incapacity of an executive to provide for proper labor discipline in his assigned tasks . . . should be evaluated as unfitness to hold office."[28]

On assuming power, Chernenko declared that measures aimed at establishing discipline and order in the bureaucracy enjoyed popular support and would remain the cornerstone of his economic policy.[29] Yet fourteen months later Gorbachev criticized his predecessor for allowing the campaign to die. Measures aimed at checking indiscipline had brought "tangible results," he said, but "I must say frankly that recently attention to this most important of issues has weakened." In the spring and summer of 1985 measures were announced once again for rooting out mismanagement, report-padding, and fraud. The courts were instructed to toughen sanctions and to enforce punishments against managers producing goods of inferior quality, whether such behavior was perpetrated "premeditatedly or through carelessness."[30] A massive campaign against alcoholism, with stiff penalties for public drunkenness, was announced.

At the Twenty-Seventh Party Congress Gorbachev declared a decisive break with "those who hope that everything will settle down and return to the old rut."[31] But signs of complacency had already appeared in the anti-alcohol campaign only a year after its inauguration. It was observed at a special Central Committee conference in June 1986 that although the sale of alcoholic beverages had been cut by more than a third, many ministries and party organizations, "satisfied with these early partial results, have recently weakened their work aimed at eradicating drunkenness and strengthening discipline and have begun to exhibit complacency." A year later, in June 1987, Gorbachev again complained that his campaign for discipline had "faded out" and grown "stagnant."[32] Some members of the leadership believed that even more drastic measures and periodic shake-ups were needed to prevent society from drifting back into complacency; in his main address to the Twenty-Seventh Party Congress, Gorbachev revealed that "some comrades" had suggested that the party be subjected to periodic purges in order to maintain its vitality.

A fourth problem with the disciplinary campaign as a strategy for improving administration is that it has provided no positive mechanisms for guiding organizational members in their work. Corrupt, inept, and inertia-bound managers and lazy, drunk, and dishonest workers no doubt played a role in the decline in Soviet economic performance during the late 1970s and early 1980s. Without any significant economic reforms and largely as a result of Andropov's and Gorbachev's disciplinary measures, marginal increases in industrial growth and productivity were achieved. But most of the time lost by Soviet workers in production is caused not by absenteeism, drunkenness on the job, or indolence, but rather by systemic problems: disruptions in the delivery of supplies, planning errors, lack of sufficient manpower to operate machinery, broken and unrepaired equipment, or the practice of storming.[33] These problems are inherent in an economic mechanism in which attention to the needs of customers is penalized, in which technical innovation, concern for quality, and efforts to cut production costs can threaten plan fulfillment, and in which overfulfillment of plan targets results in still higher targets.

Within a centrally planned economy, it is difficult for leaders to avoid confusing violations of the law and bureaucratic indiscipline with the broader shortcomings of the economic system which induce this behavior. An *Izvestiia* editorial in February 1984 observed, "We frequently confuse the concepts of 'order' and 'bureaucratism.' " Those officials who "precisely fulfill that which they are assigned and who punctually follow the letter of documents that define their activities," no matter what the results of their labor, are not "bureaucrats," but rather "honest, obedient employees."[34] Of course, excessive rules and regulations are precisely what have hampered the initiative of management and been the major cause of the endemic disorder weakening Soviet industry.

Discipline or Decentralization

Intuitively, calls for economic reform at a time when the party was cracking down on the violation of bureaucratic rules, corruption, and inept management seemed strangely out of place in post-Brezhnev politics. Discipline and decentralization would seem to represent two distinct ways of dealing with the problems of large-scale bureaucratic organization. Discipline, on the one hand, is based on mistrust of the intentions of management, implies limits to managerial authority, and requires a large administrative apparatus to detect and eliminate bureaucratic mismanagement. Decentralization, on the other hand, requires trust, for it would loosen the bonds of bureaucratic hierarchy, erode central authority over economic behavior, and invest independent authority in managers. Nevertheless, those voices speaking in favor of economic reform were frequently the same voices that were in favor of beefing up discipline. This paradox can be resolved only by discarding the notion that economic reform meant the complete dismantlement of the Soviet bureaucratic economy. The aim of reform has not been the dissolution of hierarchy, but the creation of an economic mechanism that would foster more effective behavior in the pursuit of centrally prescribed goals and directives without the need for constant interference from above. As long as the basic framework of central planning remained in place, the aim of reform could only be a revitalization of administrative discipline, not adherence to a foreign logic of supply and demand.

Those who advocated economic decentralization while simultaneously calling for discipline recognized that disciplinary measures were likely to have only a marginal and temporary effect if the incentive structure of the economic system fostered a lack of discipline on the part of personnel. Under capitalism, the marketplace imposes an impersonal discipline through calculable and consistent rewards or punishments for those who observe or violate the rules of supply and demand. Though one can find instances of disciplinary strategies within individual capitalist corporations, politicians in market economies do not need to engage in national campaigns for discipline, to proclaim "strict regimes of economy," or to condemn the widespread practice of wage-leveling. Under conditions of market competition, those corporations that are disorganized, cannot motivate their labor forces, do not respond to consumer demand, or engage in wasteful practices are automatically punished for their behavior.

Andropov was always careful to temper his calls for discipline with a recognition of the need for some degree of economic decentralization, which he saw as a necessary condition for establishing a more spontaneous discipline than that which could be obtained through police raids and political assaults on managers. At the November 1982 Plenum he called for economic experiments aimed at broadening the authority of enterprises and associations and, if need be, "taking into account the experience of brotherly [socialist] countries." In an article published three months later in *Kommunist*, he observed that measures aimed at "improving and reshaping the economic mechanism and forms and methods of management" had "lagged behind." He spoke of "the danger of the naive beliefs of some officials" that through disciplinary campaigns and "communist decreeing" alone, the problems of the economy could be overcome.[35] A special commission was formed under the head of the new Central Committee Economics Department, Nikolai Ryzhkov, to prepare proposals for economic experiments.

Portions of the management-science community took an active part in drawing up these proposals. One group in particular gained new access to the halls of power—those management experts who had been active in lobbying for a far-reaching professionalization of management and who viewed their role as providing middle management with the tools and training necessary for exercising independent judgment. In the mid-sixties these specialists had been attracted to Kosygin's program of economic decentralization and managerial professionalism. During the next two decades they had learned that the professionalization of management was impossible to carry out without delegating considerable decision-making independence to managers. By 1983 the general outline of their proposals had already taken shape. They called for flattening the economic hierarchy into two levels by eliminating all units between the ministry and the enterprise or production association, amalgamating fifty-two industrial ministries into a smaller number of superministries, reorganizing production associations to cut across ministerial boundaries, limiting the activities of ministries to long-term, strategic decision-making, and giving enterprise directors extensive operational autonomy.[36]

But opposition to any far-reaching delegation of authority quickly appeared. In Andropov's formulation, the imposition of bureaucratic discipline on management was an essential prerequisite for economic decentralization, for decentralization would be inconceivable without trust in middle management. As Andropov put it at the November 1982 Plenum, "a broadening of independence should in all cases be combined with a growth in responsibility and with a concern for national interests."[37] But how could middle management be trusted with greater authority when the regime was simultaneously using coercive measures against managers who had abused the authority that the regime had already entrusted to them? It was not difficult for opponents of economic reform to argue that managers had proved themselves unworthy of any extensive delegation of authority and that decentralization would lead to even greater administrative disorder. As Gosplan Chairman Baibakov declared, "Rights without discipline can damage the economy."[38]

In the winter and spring of 1983 conservative members of the leadership hinted that any far-reaching delegation of authority based on foreign experience, whether capitalist or socialist, was not to be contemplated. In a major address in March, Central Committee Secretary Boris Ponomarev declared that any changes in the economic mechanism would have to accord with the "objective laws" of socialist development, which required that policies "be spared all attempts to manage the economy with methods that are foreign to its nature."[39] Fears were expressed that decentralization would insulate management from political direction and lead to administrative chaos. As a lengthy article in *Pravda* explained, decentralization "harbors the possibility that management could grow excessively isolated and lose contact with the social tasks to which, in the final analysis, its activity must be totally subordinated." There was "a danger that its specific nature will suddenly seem something that is valuable in itself, something self-contained, and that its results may come to be evaluated according to 'internal indices,' so to speak." Violations of discipline and "bureaucratic excesses" were "signs that this danger is imminent."[40]

Those in favor of maintaining economic centralization were not without self-interested backers within the managerial hierarchy. A confidential government report on economic problems that later fell into the hands of foreign correspondents noted that executives of ministries, agencies, and planning organs instinctively opposed decentralization, for they, above all others, stood to lose under any reform scheme. A number of enterprise managers as well (in particular, the less qualified, older, and less energetic executives) were apprehensive about assuming more responsibility for fear that they would be incapable of meeting the challenges posed by independence.[41]

The modest experiments in enterprise autonomy announced in July 1983 gave greater discretion to managers in disposing of plant investments and in using money saved through the dismissal of superfluous workers to increase the wages of skilled personnel. The number of economic indicators governing enterprise behavior was slashed, and enterprises were to be evaluated primarily by their output sales volume and their fulfillment of delivery contracts. Shortly after the announcement of these measures, Gosplan Chairman Baibakov sought to dispel rumors that a more thorough reform of the economic system was being contemplated. "Although we are applying measures for broadening the rights of enterprises," he told foreign journalists at an unusual press conference in Moscow, "we do not set as our task the weakening of centralized management of the economy . . . We have decided to take a circumspect approach." In much the same vein, Chernenko advocated six months later that the rule of "seven times measure, one time cut" be observed in reorganizing the economy. At the April 1984 Plenum he declared that the search for new economic structures and forms "should not deflect us from making more effective use of those managerial institutions which already exist."[42]

Although the July 1983 experiments were broadened at the beginning of 1985 to include twenty-six ministries, they fell short of the extensive economic changes that some within the management-science community had advocated. Every effort was made to create "hothouse conditions" for them by assigning priority in the delivery of supplies to participating enterprises; but many enterprises continued to experience serious supply disruptions, which complicated their efforts to fulfill delivery contracts on time. As before, enterprise plans were not always balanced with capacities, and managers had little incentive to introduce new machinery and equipment or to concern themselves with product quality.[43]

Gorbachev's accession to power was accompanied by a revival of proposals for a more far-reaching economic decentralization than that envisioned by the July 1983 experiments. In April 1985 he observed that the first results of the experiments had "not been bad," but "they cannot satisfy us completely." He called instead for "deepening" the experiments and "creating an integrated system of management and administration," beginning with "the practical reorganization of the work of the higher echelons of economic management." "Now," he said, "our conception of reorganizing the economic mechanism has grown clearer," and "persistence in working out and realizing strong measures in the economic sphere" had become "especially important."[44] In the months that followed, he gave a vague outline of the "radical reforms" which he and his advisers were contemplating—ideas that closely mirrored the proposals of management scientists two years earlier, but that had been rejected then in favor of a more "circumspect" approach. Gosplan, Gorbachev said, was to be turned into "a scientific-economic organ, staffed by the best scientists and the leading specialists" in the country. In composing national economic plans, it was not to put excessive emphasis on raw "quantitative" indicators but was instead to accord a "leading place" to "qualitative indicators" reflecting the effective use of resources, growth in productivity, and scientific-technical progress. Intermediate units between the ministries and enterprises were to be eliminated, and the ministries themselves were to limit their attention to "long-term planning and the wide-ranging use of inventions for increasing the technical level of production." They would be regrouped into new organs based on "large national economic complexes." Ministries were to be weaned of their control over operational decision-making. Enterprises would be placed on "self-financing" and "full independent accounting" (*khozraschet*), and their activities would be regulated through indirect "economic levers and incentives."

Whether Gorbachev had in mind the introduction of markets was unclear. He did speak of creating a mechanism that would "make the production of outdated and ineffective products unprofitable," that would "strengthen the influence of consumers" on producers, and that would "respect the laws of the market."[45] But other Soviet leaders insisted that reforms aim not at abandoning central planning, but rather at "strengthening" it. As Central Committee Secretary Yegor Ligachev declared in June 1985, any changes in the economy should "take place within the framework of scientific socialism, without any shifts toward a 'market economy' or toward private property." In granting greater independence to enterprises, "commodity-money relations appropriate for the socialist mode of production" should be used, and simultaneous efforts should be made to "increase the responsibility of enterprises."[46]

Proponents of reform faced stubborn political and ideological resistance to any far-reaching decentralization. During the first two years of his rule, Gorbachev was cautious in the policies that he pursued. Most innovations were purely administrative in character and resembled the familiar approaches by which the Soviets have unsuccessfully combated the diseases of bureaucracy for decades. Coordinating bureaus and superministries were introduced, and construction agencies were reorganized on a territorial basis. A national quality-inspection service (Gospriemka) was established and given broad powers to reject goods of poor quality. Large numbers of officials within the managerial apparatus were to be redeployed, and targets were set for cutting red tape by 40 percent. As one minister observed, by spring 1986 there had been "more polemics about improving management than actual reform."[47]

At the Twenty-Seventh Party Congress in Feburary 1986, Gorbachev complained that "the position that any change in the economic mechanism is viewed as a retreat from the principles of socialism" was "unfortunately widespread." Six months later, he observed that "there are those who are expressing their apprehensions" about change. "The Politburo knows about this, but I will tell you openly: they do not frighten us." Conflict over the direction of administrative policy became more heated in early 1987, when a nationwide discussion on reform took place. The role which central organs should play under conditions of decentralization was particularly controversial. The issue was still being debated only two weeks before the reforms were announced, when a special conference convened at the Central Committee. At the meeting Gorbachev noted the existence of "various approaches, various points of view . . . one should say that it is not a simple matter, and long discussions are taking place at all levels." Later, he revealed that "some people" had suggested that "we should renounce the instrument of the planned economy," but "we did not accept this, nor will we ever accept it."[48]

The law on state enterprise that emerged out of this political ordeal in July 1987 represented a departure from earlier Soviet thinking to the extent that it incorporated aspects of market mechanisms ignored by previous Soviet leaderships. But central direction over the economy, though seriously diluted, was not to be done away with entirely. The reforms were a curious (and perhaps confused) mix of market and nonmarket approaches. The behavior of enterprises was supposed to be governed rather than controlled, regulated by a series of stable "control figures" and "economic normatives" that would determine how much enterprises were to pay into the state budget, how much would be left for their own use, and to what uses that revenue could be put. But as much as half of all industrial output would continue to be planned directly from above through a system of "state orders" (*goszakazy*). Ministries were to take measures to break up the monopoly position of enterprises and to foster competition in production. Yet enterprises were to come under increasing pressure to devote attention to social tasks not directly connected with production activities, such as manufacturing additional consumer goods and building apartments.

In a sharp break with past practice, enterprises would be responsible for their own budgets and for drawing up their own plans. They would be able to rent their own property, form joint ventures, and even merge with other enterprises. And ministries would be relieved of operational control over enterprises, including material supply, which was to be concentrated in a network of wholesale supply organizations. But the extent of ministerial authority over enterprises remained uncertain. Ministries were still to be held responsible for the performance of enterprises under their jurisdiction. Planning agencies were to continue to draw up specific targets in their five-year and yearly plans that were supposed to reflect "the results, proportions, and effectiveness" of the economy. Credit would be centrally allocated by Gosbank, and prices and wages would continue to be determined from the center. Moreover, though labor collectives were given the right to elect their own leaders, their choices would be subject to the approval of higher party and ministerial authority. Thus the nomenklatura system, which has been the basis of hierarchical discipline in the Soviet economy, would remain at least partially intact.[49]

The first stumbling block which the reforms were likely to encounter was their own inconsistency. Considerable powers had been left in the hands of central administrators. Even so, these administrators were resisting any devolution of authority to their subordinates. As early as June 1986 Gorbachev had complained that "the process of redistributing rights and obligations in the economy . . . is going very poorly." "Even when only the functions of managerial organs are changed, some executives strive to preserve their command privileges by any means." A Central Committee decree in October 1986 observed that "although society in general decisively favors change," that process "is complicated, contradictory, and uneven, encountering various social-psychological and organizational barriers and meeting resistance from those who seek . . . to preserve outmoded procedures and privileges."[50]

Some began to speak openly of the "saboteurs of restructuring." As one letter to *Pravda* asserted, "If a bureaucrat . . . fails to introduce new technology and techniques, hinders the development of scientific thought and creativity among employees, and suffocates passion for work by means of indifference and formalism, then . . . this borders on wrecking and sabotage."[51] More frequently, foot-dragging was involuntary and unconscious, the product of behavior induced by hierarchical discipline and ingrained habit rather than purposeful wrecking. As Gorbachev noted in July 1986, many citizens did not understand what was being demanded of them by their new leader. "Sometimes they ask, 'What is this thing called restructuring? How are we to understand it, and how does one eat it?' . . . Of course, everyone is in favor of it, but no one knows what to do."[52] There were signs of widespread confusion within the bureaucracy over the discrepancies between the behavior envisaged in the reforms and the discipline desired by superior bureaucratic authority. The reforms were being introduced in the midst of an existing five-year plan, whose directives would have to be disregarded if decentralization was to be effective.

Faced with such dilemmas, Gorbachev and his allies took the position that successful reform required not merely a formal decentralization of authority, but a psychological "restructuring" of society as well, so that organizational members would grow accustomed to thinking independently, to taking initiatives, and to exercising greater authority. But such a cultural revolution would be difficult to achieve without dismantling the hierarchical discipline that has long served as the basis of political and administrative authority in the Soviet Union. Gorbachev spoke of restructuring as a process that would take decades, even generations. No matter how consistently this cultural revolution might be waged, the attempt to force the bureaucracy, upon threat of removal, to think and act independently would still remain a contradiction in terms, the bureaucratic equivalent of Rousseau's dictum that those who do not understand the General Will must be forced to be free. Political and administrative authority could not continue to be based on hierarchical discipline if managerial initiative and freethinking were to be fostered.

A second key issue was the extent to which the political leadership would tolerate the pluralism associated with far-reaching decentralization. Decentralization leads to greater differentiation in economic and social outcomes and erodes the leadership's control over economic processes. Successive Soviet leaderships had been led to rein in reforms precisely in order to contain such pluralism. Moreover, decentralization, if it was to be effective, would also unleash social forces which could not be easily controlled. Without allowing for greater political pluralism in society, it was doubtful that a constituency for reform could be mobilized. Gorbachev's policy of "openness" (*glasnost'*) aimed at mobilizing the population against excessive bureaucratic domination, at "awakening people to overcome the inertia and indifference that has accumulated" due to generations of bureaucratic tutelage. As Gorbachev observed, "The processes of restructuring in the economy will not work unless they are implemented in coordination with all the other spheres of life of our society—above all, the spiritual and political."[53] Such political pluralism contained obvious dangers to the discipline that underpinned the party's control over society. Yet, the party had to tolerate pluralism if it was to implement economic reform successfully.

These problems were a reflection of a schizophrenia which runs through contemporary Soviet society. The Soviet Union under

Gorbachev is a society in the midst of an inward struggle against itself, a society in the throes of the insoluble dilemma of being an antibureaucratic bureaucracy. One cannot predict what the outcome of these struggles will be—whether Gorbachev's program will amount to the beginning of a new bureaucratic cycle within Soviet administration or a bold dismantlement of the bureaucratic economy. Elements of both trends can be found in the July 1987 reforms. The purpose of reform has been to establish a spontaneous discipline that can obviate the need for constant administrative intervention from above without at the same time dissolving hierarchical authority completely. But whether a dual strategy of decentralization and discipline can be simultaneously pursued is problematic, and whether a spontaneous and coherent economic mechanism can be established without introducing markets is doubtful. The Soviet leadership continues to speak of the market as something to be feared and avoided; as Academician O. T. Bogomolov observed, "We still use the word market largely in a negative sense."[54] Yet, without markets, hierarchical conformity is likely to undermine the effectiveness of decentralization, while the pluralism that would accompany the introduction of markets would erode the bonds of political domination. The danger raised by efforts to decentralize while simultaneously imposing administrative discipline is that eventually the regime will have to choose between political change and the well-worn path of ineffective half-measures.

Conclusion

In his study of the role of the party apparatus in industrial decision-making, Jerry Hough argued that Soviet deviations from Weberian rational-technical bureaucracy "constitute an answer to real problems of large-scale organizations—problems that must receive some analogous answers in any large organization if it is effectively to fulfill the tasks given it."[1] But not all large-scale organizations successfully adapt to the problems they face, nor do all adapt in the same way. Can we, for instance, speak of the role of expertise in Soviet politics as a response to the problems inherent in large-scale organization without also speaking of Stalin's, Andropov's, and Gorbachev's campaigns for labor discipline and their struggles against bureaucratic inertia in the same way?

Throughout Soviet history discipline and expertise have been alternative means for establishing organizational order in a nonmarket economy. Neither has given a stable or effective answer to the dilemmas posed by excessive bureaucratization. As Western scholars of bureaucracy have come to recognize, there is no definitive way to create effective bureaucratic organization—no one adaptation, approach, or technique which has cured bureaucratic dysfunctions permanently. As Peter Blau once observed, "The only permanence in bureaucratic structure is the occurrence of change in predictable patterns, and even these are not unalterably fixed."[2] Neither the totalitarian nor the industrial convergence model, each with its assumption of the unilinear and unidirectional evolution of communist systems under the imperative and logic of organization, comes to grips with the inherent limits of bureaucratic organization and with the insolubility of what has come to be known as "the bureaucracy problem." Neither takes cognizance of the essential irrationality of bureaucratic structures and of the permanence of political and organizational change which bureaucracy necessitates.

A bureaucratic society is a society that experiences a constant crisis of effectiveness and therefore requires continual organizational upheaval in order to maintain its vitality. In tending toward administrative instability and cycling behavior, the Soviet system differs little from large public bureaucracies the world over, all of which have experienced a disappointing history of failed administrative reforms, tension between professional administrators and political appointees, ineffective monitoring agencies, and what Downs has called "rigidity cycles." Bureaucracies in democratic political systems are notorious for their lack of accountability, their close relationships with powerful public constituencies, their lack of responsiveness, and their waste.[3]

Western analysts have long recognized that "there are inherent limits to what can be accomplished by large hierarchical organizations."[4] Soviet leaders, as well as most other communist leaders, are only beginning to recognize this fact. What makes the political consequences of these same problems qualitatively different in the Soviet context, and in communist systems generally, is that these systems do not simply possess bureaucracies; each is in itself an enormous bureaucratic organization, encompassing all aspects of political, social, and economic life. This is the basic premise on which central planning rests and on which the political authority of communist systems has been built. It is not simply that specific administrative policies in specific administrative agencies in communist systems, like those in market systems, have been victims of a series of bureaucratic vicious circles. The evolution of national administrative strategies, and of *society itself,* has taken on the character of *one large vicious circle,* as similar problems have repeatedly appeared and as similarly ineffective solutions to these problems have alternated over time. One of the striking patterns in Soviet politics has been the way in which the Soviets "continually rediscover the same troubles and then resort to the same solutions, resolutions, prescriptions, and decrees" for dealing with these problems.[5] This broadly cyclical character of politics, in contrast to a fundamental convergence of social systems, is an essential consequence of the overbureaucratization of Soviet political and economic life. As Boris Yel'tsin, the Moscow party chief, boldly expressed the issue at the Twenty-Seventh Party Congress in February 1986: "Why is it that we continue to raise a number of the very same problems congress after congress?"[6]

Rather than evolving in a unilinear or unidirectional manner, technocratic influence in Soviet politics has shown considerable oscillation. Since the days of Saint-Simon, technocratic ambitions in politics have walked hand in hand with utopian dreams of escaping the anarchy and class conflict of markets. Perhaps no other country has demonstrated so deep a fascination with the technocratic ideologies of Scientific Management as the Soviet Union. Few governments have made such far-reaching efforts to harness the power of organizational technique as those which the Soviet government undertook in the 1920s and 1970s. Technocratic utopianism is an inherent political tendency within a planned society, for, in the absence of markets, technique is viewed as a means for establishing an elusive hierarchical discipline. To be sure, Western governments have sometimes tried to mute conflict between governmental agencies by simulating the organizing effects of markets through organizational techniques. But these schemes pale before such grandiose technocratic projects as Gastev's social-engineering machine, Rozmirovich's dreams of the total automation of production, and Glushkov's cybernetic fantasies of coordinating all economic life through universal computerization. These ideas not only emerged within the Soviet context, but they also enjoyed governmental support and were reflected in official policies. Moreover, similar phenomena have reappeared in Soviet administration over time, leaving behind a pattern of utopian technocratic politics that cannot be ignored.

Although the technocratic ideologies of management experts have at times penetrated the Soviet leadership, the influence of management experts has not been stable. This is not to say that the

Soviets have repudiated Scientific Management today, nor that some convergence with the other industrial cultures of the world has not been taking place in a formalistic sense. During the last twenty years new industrial institutions have appeared in the Soviet Union that mirror those of corporate capitalism. A number of managerial techniques borrowed from the West have become accepted parts of Soviet administrative theory, if not exactly useful tools in practice. Ideology clearly plays a smaller role in the determination of administrative policies than in the past. And the need for specialist advice in shaping administrative policy is no longer questioned.

Nevertheless, these developments have occurred within the confines of a system of authority which is based on hierarchical discipline rather than market exchange and which produces fundamentally different patterns of economic behavior from those of a market economy. Expertise is not a stable or effective solution to the overbureaucratization which central planning begets. The discipline of bureaucratic hierarchy that is the basis of central planning undermines the effectiveness of the techniques upon which the legitimacy of technocratic influence rests. Contrary to the expectations of the totalitarian and industrial convergence models, extensive influence by Soviet management specialists over administrative policy-making has not coincided with an uplift in organizational performance. The failure of organizational expertise to solve the problems of large-scale bureaucratic organizations has in turn weakened the credibility of management experts. But the difficulties they have encountered in implementing their borrowed theories have been symptoms, not causes, of the problems of Soviet administration. In both the late 1920s and the early 1980s, politicians became increasingly disillusioned about the ability of management experts to alter longstanding managerial practices and to arrest the growth of bureaucratic diseases. Management experts were vulnerable to charges of failing to deliver on their promises, and the influence of specific groups of experts was undermined. In both these cases, the penetration of government by technocratic elites was followed by the rise of antibureaucratic movements, at times violent in character. As one scholar has observed, tendencies toward group politics in the Soviet Union have been "the consequence of certain conscious decisions of individual leaders and other participants in Soviet political life, decisions which were not necessarily predetermined and which might be reversed in the future."[7] Indeed, it can even be claimed that there is a regularity about the ways in which such decisions have been reversed, as Soviet politics has been alternately punctuated by technocratic and antibureaucratic cycles.

In all these respects the Soviet experience is hardly unique. Not only do parallels exist on a much smaller scale in government agencies around the world, but similar phenomena have appeared in other communist contexts—the result of the structural features of a social and economic model which has been duplicated in numerous other national settings. Richard Lowenthal has noted "a real connection between the problem of pluralism and the problem of economic efficiency [in communist systems] in the sense that the attempt to stop at the minimum stage of consultation keeps the leadership dependent on a degree of bureaucratic centralization that prevents the degree of autonomy for the economic subsystem required for maximum efficiency."[8] All communist systems have come to recognize the need for stable administrative relationships, for mechanisms that stimulate managerial talent, and for organizational expertise. But any far-reaching delegation of administrative authority in communist systems inevitably undermines the administrative discipline upon which political and bureaucratic hierarchies rest, conflicts with the ideological goals of equality by increasing social differentiation, and creates conditions for a high variability in decision-making and for the emergence of an incipient pluralism. Communist systems continue to rely on hierarchical bureaucratic discipline as their main source of political authority and as their basic instrument for coordinating economic life. But without diluting and dissolving that discipline and without the aid of markets, all communist systems have been incapable of utilizing the talents of managers and harnessing the power of organizational techniques.

As a result of this conflict, cycling behavior—at times similar in its manifestations to that which the Soviets have experienced—has appeared in nearly all communist systems. Hungarian scholars have pointed to "a vicious circle" in centrally planned economies that results from "the inherent and irresistible tendency" toward "a constant reduplication of the systems of supervision." "Processes of decentralization dictated by demands for greater efficiency are . . . constantly counterbalanced with attempts to impose new checks (and hence new systems of control), lest any unit . . . become so effective as to be able to follow its own set of objectives."[9] Polish economists and sociologists have similarly pointed to a series of economic cycles and political crises over the past forty years, "due to the rigidity of the administrative mechanisms which distort the implementation of planned objectives and trigger uncontrolled mechanisms of accelerated industrialization."[10] Such patterns are hardly accidental; they flow from a broader institutional framework which reproduces certain patterns of behavior and certain responses among leaders and administrators.

Excessive bureaucratization has imbued communist government with a political and administrative instability and a constant tension between those who seek to uphold the authority of bureaucratic discipline and those who seek to create the political, social, and organizational conditions necessary for the effective use of expertise. Ota Šik, deputy prime minister of Czechoslovakia until the Soviet invasion of 1968 and one of the guiding spirits behind efforts to reform his country's politics and economics, has written that "it would be a special subject of research to make a list of all the reorganizations of the administrative apparatus that have so far taken place in the communist countries."[11] Indeed, the history of communist administration is littered with examples of centralization followed by decentralization, decentralization followed by recentralization, and recentralization followed by still further adjustments and shufflings. As in the Soviet Union, in Eastern Europe the excessive economic centralization of the Stalinist model gave way in the 1960s to a search for new mechanisms to harness the skills and energies of management and labor. Economic reforms were proclaimed throughout the Soviet bloc, and decentralization of administrative authority was accompanied by the emergence of management experts, new institutions for training administrators, and calls for managerial professionalization.

But tensions between bureaucratic discipline and organizational expertise remained. When public bureaucracies have decentralized and introduced quasi-market mechanisms, these arrangements have frequently turned out to be unstable, for managerial behavior is torn between the role requirements of bureaucratic conformity and those of organizational efficiency. This conflict eventually sets in motion calls for recentralization.[12] The juxtaposition of central planning and limited managerial autonomy in Eastern Europe similarly fostered conflicts between the requirements of efficiency and the requirements of bureaucratic conformity. In many cases economic performance under conditions of reform fell short of the high expectations of communist leaderships. In addition, reform unleashed dangerous pluralizing trends. In Czechoslovakia efforts to loosen the bonds of bureaucratic discipline by promulgating market reforms led to demands for political reform as well, triggering a Soviet invasion. Throughout most of Eastern Europe the economic decentralization of the mid-sixties gave way to a pattern of recentralization in the 1970s, and organizational technique increasingly came to be viewed as a substitute for decentralizing reforms rather than as a constituent element of reform. And, as in the Soviet Union, economic performance gradually deteriorated. The crises of Eastern Europe in the 1980s were due as much to national resistance against an imposed, alien rule as to economic decline, foreign indebtedness, and restrictions on domestic consumption—the results of the inability of these systems to exploit fully the talents and energies of managers and workers.

Experts can only be effective when they have the authority to exercise independent discretion and to shape decision-making—conditions which undermine the bureaucratic discipline upon which the operation of central planning and the authority of communist leaderships traditionally rest. It is not surprising that the same problems and tensions that the Soviets have experienced over the past twenty years in their attempts to import organizational techniques from corporate capitalism without also importing market mechanisms have appeared in other communist countries. In 1967 Austrian management consultants demonstrated a business game typically used to train capitalist managers to several Czechoslovak managers in Bratislava. The result was a fundamental clash between the requirements of the game and the administrative roles to which the socialist managers were accustomed. The managers showed great reluctance to cut production costs or to introduce new products, and they "demonstrated their aversion to taking advantage of the services of the firm of consultants." Observers concluded that the game had "cast light on various psychological inhibitions of our workers."[13]

All members of the Council for Mutual Economic Assistance

(CMEA), at times with the help of United Nations specialists, established their own management-development centers in the late sixties. The problems experienced by these programs were not very different from those that plagued Soviet executive training. David Granick, who visited Romania's training center in the early seventies, observed that "the students did very little of the required preparation for the classes and seemed to take their attendance at the course as somewhat of a holiday."[14] As articles in the Romanian press later revealed, narrow agency interests, much as in the Soviet case, had left deep scars on Romanian executive training. From the late sixties to the mid-seventies, approximately one out of every twelve Romanian trainees had been sent to study simply to fulfill agency attendance plans; a similar proportion had no idea why they had been sent to train, even two years after graduation. As in the Soviet Union, the institutions called upon to teach managers the art of efficiency were themselves models of inefficiency. A 1975 survey of 214 alumni of Romania's Management Development Center showed their frustration in trying to apply the knowledge they had received in the classroom. When asked whether they were using what they had learned, more than half replied either, "To a small extent," or, "Not at all." The causes of this low rate of application, the report concluded, were "largely independent of the content of instruction and the manner in which it is received by trainees" but, rather, were linked to "the general system of management and factory organization" and the skeptical reception accorded new management techniques "on the part of executives of various hierarchical levels." Of those surveyed, 51 percent cited the system of management as the major hindrance to applying what they had learned; another 20 percent identified their superiors' lack of interest in rationalization as the major impediment; and an additional 15 percent blamed the extraordinary effort required to implement rationalization measures in the face of organizational resistance.[15]

One comparative study of the adoption of ob'edineniia in East Germany and the Soviet Union found that, although resistance was considerably less in East Germany, similar forms of opposition appeared in both countries, weakening the purpose of the reform.[16] Culture and national tradition affect East Germany's ability to assimilate economic innovations. One should not overlook Lenin's repeated slurs on the Russian nation, which, he said, "has to be sworn at twenty times and watched over thirty times for the simplest things to get done."[17] Yet, even in a cultural setting vastly different from the Russian, bureaucratic structures generate comparable forms of organizational behavior. Studies of East German attempts to incorporate capitalist managerial techniques show that a bureaucratic economic mechanism is unable to stimulate managers to engage in cost-effective, innovative, quality-oriented activity.[18] The traditions of Russian culture that make effective management elusive have been sustained by an overbureaucratized system of management which, with or without traditions, elicits forms of behavior that run counter to the role requirements necessary for the effective application of expertise.

What Alfred Chandler called the visible hand of professional management has always relied on the invisible fingers of the marketplace to provide it with the decision-making independence, the social status, and the sense of a clearly defined organizational mission without which professional administration is impossible.[19] Excessive bureaucratic control over management not only undermines the legitimacy of professional management by undermining the effectiveness of the techniques that serve as the basis for professional authority, but it also has a demoralizing effect on management as a whole, lowering the prestige of managerial work and discouraging talented individuals from pursuing managerial careers. Włodzimierz Brus has observed that "the sources of the weakness of the leading personnel at different levels in the socialist countries today frequently stem not from lack of training and individual potential for development, but from the organizational situation which makes it impossible for people to spread their wings, stifles initiative and gives rise to continual conflicts between actions which conform to the imposed 'rules of the game' and rational and socially useful actions."[20] A Polish survey of young engineers in 1965 revealed results identical to those found in Soviet surveys: only 10 percent of graduating engineers in Poland responded that they would choose a job which opened the path to a managerial promotion. As one observer noted, "There is an antimanagement bias among young engineers, in the sense that they equate management with bureaucracy in the worst sense of the word."[21] The author of a recent Hungarian report, after describing the frustrations encountered by managers in a "quasi-bureaucratic" work setting, concluded that "after a certain time, the status and prestige of 'managerial work' is lowered, and as a result, it is not an attractive prospect for the worker to reach a managerial post . . . Under these conditions, one must reckon in the short run with the spread of indifferent, ambivalent managerial attitudes similar to those of workers"—expressed in a tendency toward leniency on the part of management in the face of violations of bureaucratic rules and a pervasive lack of concern for production.[22]

When managers lack the discretion to apply new techniques effectively, when they look on the management expert as the probing arm of superior bureaucratic authority rather than as an aid in achieving organizational goals, when management is incapable of attracting talented individuals to its ranks and the manager fears that the expert aims to replace him with better-trained and more capable personnel, and when the expert is himself entangled in the same organizational conditions which he is charged with rectifying, the efforts of experts can only be self-defeating. Since these experts are already under suspicion among the ideologically orthodox for importing foreign theories and because their proposals for rationalization frequently threaten agency autonomy and control, their influence is likely to be vulnerable and precarious.

It is not difficult to see how such a system might be driven to confuse conscious political resistance and sabotage with the inevitable managerial foot-dragging that excessive bureaucratization generates. At times, this confusion has been utilized by communist leaders to avoid responsibility for economic decline, to consolidate their power, and to legitimate political controls over society. The Czech Eugen Loebl, who was arrested and tried for industrial sabotage at the infamous Slansky trial of 1952, later explained his unlucky fate: "Amateurish and poorly planned economic measures had been disrupting Czechoslovakia's economy to such an extent that there were severe disturbances and strikes. The people were angered by this, and the alleged sabotages and crimes attributed to us were a plausible explanation engineered by a faction of the party leadership that was determined to survive the crisis." Communist leaders have repeatedly been able to blur the line between wrecking and rationalization, since within a centrally planned economy bureaucratic rules must constantly be violated for the sake of the plan, and the actual difference between wrecking and rationalization has tended to be only a matter of intent, not outcome. As Loebl's Russian prison interrogators explained, "Every saboteur tries to hide his crimes behind 'mistakes.' "[23]

Nor is it difficult to see how, when change is rapid and elites have ambitious, utopian goals, rationalization might be confused with technocratic counterrevolution, and coercive and mobilizational solutions might be sought for the problems generated by over-bureaucratization. Not only in Stalinist Russia, but in Maoist China as well, communist leaderships unleashed violent assaults on administrators and specialists in the name of rooting out bureaucratic inertia and expurgating "foreign" managerial practices and technocratic ideologies that had crept into administration. Like Stalin's antibureaucratic revolution, Mao's Cultural Revolution was aimed in part at the industrial administrative and technical elite, which in the early 1960s, after the fiascoes of the Great Leap Forward, had demanded more rational administration. Interestingly enough, one of the major targets of the Cultural Revolution was the piece-rate, whose widespread application in Chinese industry caused resentment not only among ideologues but within the working class as well, rather as the inconsistencies of chronometric norm-determination had fueled Stalin's Cultural Revolution in the late twenties and became a rallying cry for the Great Purge. As in the Soviet Union, the revolt against industrial rationalism was accompanied by campaigns against "capitalist management ideas," the emergence of "technocracy" in Chinese industry, and the burgeoning of administrative staffs, red tape, excessive paperwork, and bureaucratic regulations. Mao relied more heavily than Stalin on mobilizational and normative strategies in his utopian efforts to abolish bureaucracy. His was a leveling revolution, an attempt to drown bureaucracy in the sea of mass mobilization and revolutionary enthusiasm; Stalin, by contrast, had sought to liquidate bureaucratic resistance by liquidating bureaucrats. But the Chinese Cultural Revolution was not without its violence and its "militarization" of administration, expressed not only in the party's slogan, "Better troops and simpler administration," but also in the eventual use of the military to reestablish order and discipline in the factory.[24]

Distrust of managerial authority is a self-reinforcing and self-reproducing phenomenon, for it creates the organizational conditions which justify further mistrust of managers and experts. In his classic study of overcentralization in Hungarian industry, János Kornai found that excessive centralization was not only a cause of pervasive mistrust within centrally planned industry, but was "a consequence of it as well, for the nature of the contacts produced between people by this method of administration is such as to lead to ever-recurring distrust." Kornai pointed to a close connection in centrally planned systems "between the effectiveness of material incentives (and moral-political incentives), on the one hand, and the extent to which it is necessary to invoke disciplinary measures, on the other hand." He concluded that the larger the role of central coordination in economic affairs and the less capacity an economic system displays for effecting desirable behavior through material incentives, "the more it will be driven to employ methods involving coercion." The periodic application of discipline and coercion to labor and management could only be eliminated, Kornai suggested, "if instructions become much fewer in number, and if those few that remain are as far as possible in harmony with the personal economic interests of managements, instead of clashing with them."[25] The desire of communist leaders to escape the economic, social, and political pluralism of markets has fueled a temptation to seek violent and extremist solutions to coordinating organizational behavior. The Yugoslav economist Branko Horvat, commenting on Chinese and Cuban attempts to eliminate material incentives in the 1960s, has written: "Moral incentives reduced economic efficiency and made necessary police and other coercive interventions in order to induce lazy or irresponsible people to work."[26]

The penetration of communist government by technocratic ideologies and the use of coercive tactics and disciplinary campaigns against organizational inertia are but opposite sides of the same coin. Their origins can be traced to intrinsic strains within Bolshevik ideology: to the Marxist rejection of the marketplace world of capitalism, to its simultaneous glorification of the organizational and technical achievements of the machine age, and to Lenin's affection for bureaucratic discipline as a tool of revolutionary politics and social organization. But technocratic utopianism and disciplinary coercion must also be understood as desperate and extreme reactions to a tension inherent in large-scale bureaucratic organization. They are the products of an institutional structure which, like ambitious and utopian ideologies, contains the potential to generate radical responses to its deep-seated problems when it, like ideology, is instituted on an all-embracing and universal scale.

To be sure, one can find business corporations which have engaged in the equivalent of disciplinary campaigns. And technocrats, rather than traditional family entrepreneurs, have become dominant in business enterprise. But the penetration of government by radical technocratic ideologies, politically sponsored mass mobilization aimed at exorcising organizational diseases, and the use of large-scale coercion by the state as a strategy for eliminating managerial resistance are constrained under capitalism by the self-interested laws of competition, the diffuse efficiency of organization, and the limited role of governments. It is difficult to find examples in capitalist societies of national campaigns for bureaucratic discipline, of Time Leagues, of Stakhanovite movements, or of government-sponsored raids on enterprises to uncover loafers, drunks, and absentee workers. Anti-union companies have frequently been led to the mass firing of workers as a tactic for defusing worker protest, and even to the use of violence against them. But only the most feebleminded and least profit-conscious of capitalists could believe, as Stalin did, that he could rid his company of organizational resistance by liquidating its managerial staff from top to bottom, or that he could motivate his workers and managers to perform their tasks effectively by threatening them with prison sentences. Only the leaders of a system which lacks the motivational mechanisms of markets could conceive of, let alone attempt to implement, a social-engineering machine or a hierarchically organized, universal computer network.

Unlimited government is government that is unmanageable by ordinary means. It encourages extremist and often violent responses to the ubiquitous resistance it encounters. The wisdom of limited government is not, as Hayek argued, that central planning inevitably tends toward technocratic dictatorship in order to establish consensus over goals.[27] Planned societies pursue multiple and contradictory goals, and technocratic influence has been unstable because it provides no answer to overbureaucratization. Nor does the danger of unlimited government lie only in its general potential for political abuse; rather, in order to maintain its vitality, unlimited government is driven to engage in the types of policies that encourage political abuse.

In and of themselves, the instability, the cycling behavior, and the tendency toward radical administrative strategies that excessive bureaucratization imparts to communist government have not been entirely dysfunctional; they are part of a process of adaptation and change, and in their absence stagnation, inertia, and declining levels of morale are likely consequences. But cycling behavior and change through irregular and often disruptive means are not healthy for any organization. They are indicative of a profound misperception of the possibilities and limits of large-scale bureaucracy—a neurosis which, unless cured, is likely to generate the same patterns of behavior indefinitely until the logic of economic organization or the ordeal of political change intervenes. As Gorbachev himself observed in Khabarovsk in August 1986, "We will not be able to move forward if we search for the answers to our economic and technical problems in the experience of the thirties, forties, fifties, and even the sixties and seventies."[28] Without the spontaneous and diffuse discipline of markets and the social and political pluralism which markets allow, no amount of force and no degree of technique can provide communist leaders with the capacity to master the organizational revolution of the twentieth century.

Notes

Index

Notes

Introduction

1. Overbureaucratization has been defined by Brenda Danet to mean a situation in which "the organization comes to dominate the environment, or fails to respond to legitimate needs and demands of the environment." Brenda Danet, "Giving the Underdog a Break: Latent Particularism among Customs Officials," in Elihu Katz and Brenda Danet, eds., *Bureaucracy and the Public* (New York: Basic Books, 1973), p. 330. In the sense used in this book, overbureaucratization refers to the uncontrolled growth of bureaucratic institutions and forms of behavior, with its consequent effects upon the abilities of organizational leaders to achieve goals through the existing institutional structure.
2. James Q. Wilson, "The Bureaucracy Problem," *The Public Interest,* 6 (Winter 1967), 3–9.
3. Anthony Downs, *Inside Bureaucracy* (Boston: Little, Brown, 1967), pp. 158, 160, 164, 165, 166.
4. James G. March and Herbert A. Simon, *Organizations* (New York: Wiley, 1958), pp. 175–176, 185; Philip Selznick, *TVA and the Grass Roots: A Study in the Sociology of Formal Organization* (New York: Harper and Row, 1966); John Kenneth Galbraith, *The New Industrial State,* 2nd ed. (New York: Mentor, 1971).
5. Downs, *Inside Bureaucracy,* p. 163.
6. Claude Ake, *A Theory of Political Integration* (Homewood, Ill.: Dorsey Press, 1967), pp. 100–101. See also Leon Hurwitz, "Contemporary Approaches to Political Stability," *Comparative Politics,* 5 (April 1973), 449–463.

7. Samuel P. Huntington and Jorge I. Dominguez, "Political Development," in Fred I. Greenstein and Nelson W. Polsby, eds., *Handbook of Political Science,* vol. 3 (Reading, Mass.: Addison-Wesley, 1975), p. 7.

8. J. V. Stalin, *Works,* vol. 6 (Moscow: Foreign Languages Publishing House, 1953), p. 196.

9. Friedrich Engels, *Herr Duhring's Revolution in Science* (New York: International Publishers, 1935), p. 292.

10. H. H. Gerth and C. Wright Mills, eds., *From Max Weber: Essays in Sociology* (New York: Oxford University Press, 1946), p. 231; Max Weber, *The Theory of Social and Economic Organization* (New York: Free Press, 1947), pp. 337–339.

11. See Friedrich A. Hayek, *The Road to Serfdom* (Chicago: University of Chicago Press, 1944), p. 125.

12. P. J. D. Wiles, *The Political Economy of Communism* (Cambridge, Mass.: Harvard University Press, 1962), pp. 18–20.

13. Peter M. Blau and W. Richard Scott, *Formal Organizations* (San Francisco: Chandler, 1962), pp. 185, 247.

14. March and Simon, *Organizations,* p. 50.

15. Zbigniew Brzezinski and Samuel P. Huntington, *Political Power: USA/USSR* (New York: Viking Press, 1963), pp. 125, 424. See also Allen Kassof, "The Administered Society: Totalitarianism without Terror," *World Politics,* 16 (July 1964), 558–575; Paul Cocks, "The Rationalization of Party Control," in Chalmers Johnson, ed., *Change in Communist Systems* (Stanford, Calif.: Stanford University Press, 1970), pp. 153–190.

16. Galbraith, *New Industrial State;* Jerry F. Hough, *The Soviet Union and Social Science Theory* (Cambridge, Mass.: Harvard University Press, 1977); Peter C. Ludz, *The Changing Party Elite in East Germany* (Cambridge, Mass.: MIT Press, 1972); Peter H. Solomon, Jr., *Soviet Criminologists and Criminal Policy: Specialists in Policy-Making* (New York: Columbia University Press, 1978).

17. Alfred Meyer, "USSR Incorporated," *Slavic Review,* 20 (September 1961), 369–376; T. H. Rigby, "Traditional, Market, and Organizational Societies and the USSR," *World Politics,* 16 (July 1964), 539–557. Even Robert Tucker, who argued that Soviet politics should be understood as a succession of political systems, noted that it evolved "within a framework of continuity of organizational forms." Robert C. Tucker, *The Soviet Political Mind* (New York: Praeger, 1963), p. 18.

18. Peter M. Blau and Richard A. Schoenherr, *The Structure of Organizations* (New York: Basic Books, 1971), p. 136.

19. For a similar phenomenon in American public administration, see Herbert Kaufman, "Administrative Decentralization and Political Power," *Public Administration Review,* 29 (January-February 1969), 3–15.

20. Blau and Schoenherr, *Structure of Organizations,* pp. 111–139; John Child, "Predicting and Understanding Organizational Structure," in D. S. Pugh and C. R. Hinings, eds., *Organizational Structure: Extensions and Replications* (Westmead, Eng.: Saxon House, 1976), pp. 61–62.

21. Francis E. Rourke, *Bureaucracy, Politics, and Public Policy,* 2nd ed. (Boston: Little, Brown, 1976), pp. 151–152. See also Jeffrey D. Strauss-

man, *The Limits of Technocratic Politics* (New Brunswick, N.J.: Transaction Books, 1978).

22. Hannah Arendt, *The Origins of Totalitarianism* (New York: World Publishing, 1958), p. 361.

23. Child's analysis of sixty-two British firms indicated that among large companies poor performers tended to delegate decision-making less than good performers. It is not clear whether decentralization is a cause of good performance or centralization the product of poor performance; indeed, both may be true. John Child, "Managerial and Organizational Factors Associated with Company Performance," in Pugh and Hinings, eds., *Organizational Structure,* pp. 153–154.

24. Jerry F. Hough, *The Soviet Prefects: The Local Party Organs in Industrial Decision-Making* (Cambridge, Mass.: Harvard University Press, 1969); Gregory Grossman, "Gold and Sword: Money in the Soviet Command Economy," in Henry Rosovsky, ed., *Industrialization in Two Systems: Essays in Honor of Alexander Gerschenkron* (New York: Wiley, 1966), p. 235.

25. Charles E. Lindblom, *Politics and Markets* (New York: Basic Books, 1977), pp. 65–75.

26. Alvin W. Gouldner, *Patterns of Industrial Bureaucracy* (New York: Free Press, 1954), pp. 207–228.

27. Ibid.; Peter M. Blau, *The Dynamics of Bureaucracy* (Chicago: University of Chicago Press, 1963); James Q. Wilson, *Varieties of Police Behavior* (Cambridge, Mass.: Harvard University Press, 1968).

28. E. A. Johns, *The Sociology of Organizational Change* (New York: Pergamon Press, 1973), p. 133.

1. From Revolution to Rationalization

1. Margaret Dewar, *Labor Policy in the USSR, 1917–1928* (London: Royal Institute of International Affairs, 1956), pp. 37–38.

2. Adam B. Ulam, *The Unfinished Revolution: An Essay on the Sources of Influence of Marxism and Communism* (New York: Vintage Books, 1960), pp. 58–89.

3. See, for instance, Louis Duchez, "Scientific Business Management: What Is It? What Effect Will It Have on the Revolutionary Movement?" *International Socialist Review,* 11 (April 1911), 628–631; Hollis Godfrey, "Attitude of Labor towards Scientific Management," *Annals of the American Academy of Political and Social Science,* 44 (November 1912), 59–73; Robert F. Hoxie, *Scientific Management and Labor* (New York: Appleton-Century-Crofts, 1915).

4. *Russkiia vedemosti,* no. 40, 1913, p. 5.

5. *Vestnik Evropy,* no. 2, 1913, pp. 299–301, 309. See also *Sovremennik,* no. 3, 1915, pp. 89–108; Heather Jeanne Hogan, "Labor and Management in Conflict: The St. Petersburg Metal-Working Industry, 1900–1914" (Ph.D. diss., University of Michigan, 1981), pp. 83–84.

6. A. K. Gastev, *Kak nado rabotat'* (Moscow: Ekonomika, 1966), p. 19; Hogan, "Labor and Management," pp. 484–509.

7. Charles S. Maier, "Between Taylorism and Technocracy: European Ideologies and the Vision of Industrial Productivity in the 1920s," *Journal of Contemporary History*, 2 (1970), 28.

8. A. Pankin, *Nauchnaia organizatsiia truda* (Petrograd, 1914), pp. 3–4.

9. Sukhanov wrote under the pseudonym Nikolai Gimmer, in *Russkoe bogatstvo*, no. 11, 1913, pp. 132–154.

10. V. I. Lenin, *Pol'noe sobranie sochinenii [PSS]*, vol. 23 (Moscow: Politizdat, 1970), pp. 18–19.

11. Ibid., 24:371.

12. Hogan, "Labor and Management," pp. 484–509. The Aivaz plant was a center of Bolshevik support in the capital. Gastev noted that out of 2000 workers at the plant, more than 300 were "illegals" or under police surveillance. A. K. Gastev, *Professional'nye soiuzy i organizatsiia truda* (Leningrad: LGSPS, 1924), p. 11.

13. Karl Marx, *Capital*, vol. 1 (New York: International Publishers, 1967), pp. 556, 557, 553–554.

14. V. I. Lenin, *Izbrannye proizvedeniia*, vol. 2 (Moscow: Politizdat, 1975), p. 308.

15. Zenovia A. Sochor, "Soviet Taylorism Revisited," *Soviet Studies*, 33 (April 1981), 248–249.

16. Gastev, *Kak nado*, p. 7; A. K. Gastev, *Trudovye ustanovki* (Moscow: Ekonomika, 1973), p. 161.

17. Although Soviet sources acknowledge that Gastev was no longer an active member of the party after 1908, he was present at a large number of governmental meetings in the early Soviet period and was habitually referred to as comrade, a form of address reserved for party members. It appears that throughout these years Gastev lived on the fringes of the party and his membership status was unclear. Gastev did not formally rejoin the party until 1931.

18. Gastev, *Trudovye ustanovki*, pp. 159–160. Gastev later wrote about these experiences in a short story entitled "At the Trolley Depot." Aleksei Gastev, *Poeziia rabochego udara* (Moscow: Sovetskii pisatel', 1964), pp. 37–58.

19. Gastev, *Kak nado*, p. 211. See also Gastev, *Trudovye ustanovki*, p. 160; *Literaturnaia gazeta*, October 9, 1962, p. 3; Maurice Lévy-Leboyer, "The Large Corporation in Modern France," in Alfred D. Chandler, Jr., and Herman Daems, eds., *Managerial Hierarchies: Comparative Perspectives on the Rise of the Modern Industrial Enterprise* (Cambridge, Mass.: Harvard University Press, 1980), p. 134.

20. Gastev, *Trudovye ustanovki*, pp. 81, 160–161. After the failure of the Aivaz strike, a number of workers attempted to slow down the pace of production by proclaiming a counternorm to the norms introduced by administrators. But this could not be put into practice because of the efforts of norm-breakers among the workers and the inertia of old norms. After this experience Gastev began to ponder the social role played by production norms. Gastev, *Professional'nye soiuzy*, p. 13.

21. Gastev, *Trudovye ustanovki*, p. 161.

22. Gastev, *Kak nado*, pp. 19–20, 113; Gastev, *Trudovye ustanovki*, p. 161;

Pravda, June 4, 1922, p. 1; P. Petrochenko and K. Kuznetsova, *Organizatsiia i normirovanie truda v promyshlennosti SSSR* (Moscow: Profizdat, 1971), pp. 15, 25–26.

23. L. B. Genkin, *Stanovlenie novoi distsipliny truda* (Moscow: Profizdat, 1967), pp. 122–123; Gastev, *Kak nado,* pp. 19–20.

24. Personal Archive of A. K. Gastev, in possession of his son Yu. A. Gastev, typescript, "Rabota v profsoiuzakh," bk. 1, pp. 57–58, New York. The platform stated that "if the economic agony in Russia continues, then we will face the naked and definite issue of [deciding] which industrial orientation—German or American—the Russian proletariat should contemplate as its organizational contact."

25. Genkin, *Stanovlenie,* pp. 68–69.

26. Lenin, *PSS,* 36:140–142, 212–213.

27. *Narodnoe khoziaistvo,* no. 2, 1918, p. 38.

28. Lenin, *PSS,* 36:271, 311. See also Genkin, *Stanovlenie,* pp. 49, 125–126; A. Yermanskii [pseud. A. O. Gushko], *Sistema Teilora: Chto neset ona rabochemu klassu i vsemu chelovechestvu* (Moscow: Kniga, 1918). Lenin's speech was the basis of a series of articles published under the title "On 'Left-Wing' Childishness and Petty Bourgeois Morals."

29. Genkin, *Stanovlenie,* p. 128.

30. *Trudy Pervogo Vserossiiskogo S'ezda Sovetov Narodnogo Khoziaistva, 26-go maia–4 iunia 1918 g.: Stenograficheskii otchet* (Moscow: VSNKh, 1918), pp. 379–380; Dewar, *Labor Policy,* p. 39; Genkin, *Stanovlenie,* p. 149.

31. P. A. Garvi, *Professional'nye soiuzy v Rossii v pervye gody revoliutsii (1917–1921)* (New York: Rausen, 1958), p. 56.

32. Gastev, *Kak nado,* pp. 113–114; Petrochenko and Kuznetsova, *Organizatsiia i normirovanie,* pp. 25, 28.

33. Gastev, *Trudovye ustanovki,* p. 161.

34. *Istoriia SSSR,* no. 2, 1965, pp. 109–110; O. A. Pozdniakov, *Lenin o problemakh nauchnoi organizatsii truda i upravleniia* (Leningrad: Lenizdat, 1969), pp. 43–44.

35. Lenin, *PSS,* 38: 57; E. H. Carr, ed., *Bukharin and Preobrazhensky: The ABC of Communism* (London: Penguin, 1969), p. 449.

36. D. M. Kruk, *Razvitie teorii i praktiki upravleniia proizvodstvom v SSSR* (Moscow: Minvuz SSSR, 1974), p. 36.

37. Jay B. Sorenson, *The Life and Death of Soviet Trade Unionism, 1917–1928* (New York: Atherton Press, 1969), pp. 94–95.

38. *Proletarskaia kul'tura,* nos. 9–10, 1919, pp. 43, 50.

39. L. Trotsky, *Sochineniia,* vol. 15 (Moscow: Gosizdat, 1927), pp. 92–93.

40. Ibid., p. 138. Gol'tsman was defended by Trotsky against attacks by Rykov and others, who characterized Gol'tsman as an "industrialist." Although Rykov had participated in the Narym discussions with Gastev and Gol'tsman, he did not share their views on Taylorism.

41. S. A. Fediukin, *Sovetskaia vlast' i burzhuaznye spetsialisty* (Moscow: Mysl', 1965), p. 122; *Deviatyi s'ezd rossiiskoi kommunisticheskoi partii: Stenograficheskii otchet (29 marta–4 aprelia 1920 g.)* (Moscow: Gosudarstvennoe izdatel'stvo, 1920), p. 101.

42. V. I. Lenin, *O rabote s kadrami* (Moscow: Politizdat, 1979), p. 123; *Deviatyi s'ezd*, pp. 20, 41.

43. P. P. Kovalev, ed., *Nauchnaia organizatsiia truda, proizvodstva i upravleniia: Sbornik dokumentov i materialov, 1918–1930 gg.* (Moscow: Ekonomika, 1969), pp. 126–127.

44. N. S. Il'enko and K. Shamsutdinov, eds., *Nauchnaia organizatsiia truda dvadtsatykh godov: Sbornik dokumentov i materialov* (Kazan: VNII okhrany truda, 1965), p. 689. See also Kovalev, *Nauchnaia organizatsiia truda*, p. 134.

45. Leonard Schapiro, *The Origins of the Communist Autocracy* (Cambridge, Mass.: Harvard University Press, 1977), p. 256; S. N. Ikonnikov, *Organizatsiia i deiatel'nost' RKI v 1920–1925 gg.* (Moscow: Akademiia nauk SSSR, 1960), p. 93.

46. Trotsky, *Sochineniia*, 15:591–593.

47. Petrochenko and Kuznetsova, *Organizatsiia i normirovanie*, p. 46.

48. See *Pravda*, January 25, 26, 28, 29, 1921.

49. I. M. Burdianskii, *Osnovy ratsionalizatsii proizvodstva*, 2nd ed. (Moscow: Moskovskii rabochii, 1931), p. 363; Kovalev, *Nauchnaia organizatsiia truda*, p. 235.

50. B. Dvinov, "Ot legal'nosti k podpol'iu, 1921–1922" (Inter-University Project on the History of the Menshevik Movement, New York, 1955), pp. 24–25. For Yermanskii's autobiography, see O. A. Yermanskii, *Iz perezhitogo (1887–1921 gg.)* (Moscow: Gosizdat, 1927). There is a good possibility that police pressure played a role in Yermanskii's renunciation of his comrades.

51. Yermanskii, *Sistema Teilora*. On Atzler and his experiments, see Georges Friedmann, *Industrial Society: The Emergence of the Human Problems of Automation* (New York: Free Press, 1955), pp. 55, 70–72.

52. Trotsky, *Sochineniia*, 15: 593; O. A. Yermanskii, *Nauchnaia organizatsiia truda i proizvodstva i sistema Teilora* (Moscow: Gosizdat, 1922), pp. viii–ix; *Organizatsiia truda*, nos. 2–3, 1924, p. 38.

53. Burdianskii, *Osnovy ratsionalizatsii*, p. 364.

54. Il'enko and Shamsutdinov, *Nauchnaia organizatsiia truda dvadtsatykh godov*, p. 667; Gastev, *Poeziia rabochego udara*, p. 31.

55. Il'enko and Shamsutdinov, *Nauchnaia organizatsiia truda dvadtsatykh godov*, p. 166.

56. Gastev, *Kak nado*, p. 115; Yermanskii, *Nauchnaia organizatsiia truda*, pp. viii–ix.

57. Personal Archive of A. K. Gastev, in possession of his son Yu. A. Gastev, typescript, "TsIT," vol. 1, pt. 1, pp. 89–90, New York; *Istoriia SSSR*, no. 2, 1965, p. 110.

58. Schapiro, *Origins*, pp. 296–301.

59. Kovalev, *Nauchnaia organizatsiia truda*, p. 131.

60. Alec Nove, *An Economic History of the USSR* (Harmondsworth, Eng.: Penguin, 1972), pp. 96–102.

61. Gastev, *Kak nado*, p. 27.

62. Il'enko and Shamsutdinov, *Nauchnaia organizatsiia truda dvadtsatykh godov*, p. 690; Gastev, *Trudovye ustanovki*, p. 8.

63. Pozdniakov, *Lenin o problemakh,* pp. 46–50. See also Il'enko and Shamsutdinov, *Nauchnaia organizatsiia truda dvadtsatykh godov,* pp. 226–227, 249, 698.

64. *Vestnik truda,* no. 11, 1927, p. 88. See also Il'enko and Shamsutdinov, *Nauchnaia organizatsiia truda dvadtsatykh godov,* pp. 169, 210–211, 222, 226–227, 696.

65. Il'enko and Shamsutdinov, *Nauchnaia organizatsiia truda dvadtsatykh godov,* pp. 228, 676, 701–702.

66. I. M. Burdianskii, ed., *Piat' let raboty, 1921–1926* (Kazan: Kazanskii Institut NOT, 1926), pp. iii, 1; Kovalev, *Nauchnaia organizatsiia truda,* pp. 155, 159.

67. *Trud,* February 28, 1922, p. 3.

68. Il'enko and Shamsutdinov, *Nauchnaia organizatsiia truda dvadtsatykh godov,* pp. 205, 281–285; Burdianskii, *Piat' let,* pp. iii–v.

69. Il'enko and Shamsutdinov, *Nauchnaia organizatsiia truda dvadtsatykh godov,* pp. 233, 689–690; D. M. Berkovich, *Formirovanie nauki upravleniia proizvodstvom* (Moscow: Nauka, 1973), p. 91.

70. Il'enko and Shamsutdinov, *Nauchnaia organizatsiia truda dvadtsatykh godov,* pp. 158–159, 234, 675, 686.

71. *Stenograficheskii otchet X s'ezda Rossiiskoi Kommunisticheskoi Partii (8–16 marta 1921 g.)* (Petersburg: Gosizdat, 1921), p. 24.

72. Lenin, *PSS,* 54:120; 53:165.

73. Pozdniakov, *Lenin o problemakh,* p. 127. For other cases, see Lenin, *PSS,* 45:103; 53:163.

74. Lenin, *O rabote s kadrami,* pp. 206, 230.

75. Il'enko and Shamsutdinov, *Nauchnaia organizatsiia truda dvadtsatykh godov,* p. 148. See also Pozdniakov, *Lenin o problemakh,* pp. 76–77.

76. Lenin, *Sochineniia,* 33:331; Lenin, *PSS,* 45:290. Yermanskii's Menshevik past could not be entirely overlooked. In a conversation with A. I. Sviderskii, Lenin requested that Sviderskii send a team abroad to collect foreign literature on Scientific Management. To Lenin's chagrin, this task was entrusted to Yermanskii. Lenin expressed doubts that Yermanskii would properly fulfill the assignment. "He is a Menshevik," wrote Lenin, "and although his book is very good, one can detect a certain malice in it." Lenin, *Sochineniia,* 36:533–534.

77. Ikonnikov, *Organizatsiia i deiatel'nost',* pp. 13, 20, 55.

78. Lenin, *Sochineniia,* 36:522.

79. Lenin, *Izbrannye proizvedeniia,* 3:729; G. Kekcheev, in *Organizatsiia truda,* no. 1, 1924, p. 78.

80. Lenin, *Izbrannye proizvedeniia,* 3:731. See also L. F. Morozov and V. P. Portnov, *Organy TsKK-NKRKI v bor'be za sovershenstvovanie Sovetskogo gosudarstvennogo apparata (1923–1934 gg.)* (Moscow: Iuridicheskaia literatura, 1964), pp. 12–13.

81. Adam B. Ulam, *The Bolsheviks* (New York: Macmillan, 1965), p. 569.

82. *Pravda,* March 24, 1923, p. 3.

83. *Pravda,* March 18, 1923, p. 4; M. P. Shevchenko, "Deiatel'nost' kommunisticheskoi partii v osushchestvlenii podgotovki rukovodiashchikh kadrov dlia promyshlennosti (1926–1932 gg.)" (Dissertatsiia na soiskanie

uchenoi stepeni kandidata istoricheskikh nauk, Moscow, MGU, 1967), pp. 113–124.

84. *Dvenadtsatyi s'ezd rossiiskoi kommunisticheskoi partii (bol'shevikov): Stenograficheskii otchet* (Moscow: Krasnaia nov', 1923), pp. 42, 45, 174; see also pp. 113–122.

85. Quoted in Jeremy R. Azrael, *Managerial Power and Soviet Politics* (Cambridge, Mass.: Harvard University Press, 1966), p. 67.

86. *Dvenadtsatyi s'ezd,* pp. 635–637.

87. Personal Archive of A. K. Gastev, in possession of his son Yu. A. Gastev, typescript, "TsIT," vol. 3, pt. 1, pp. 298–312, New York.

88. *Voprosy Istorii KPSS,* no. 8, 1965, pp. 8–9. See also Il'enko and Shamsutdinov, *Nauchnaia organizatsiia truda dvadtsatykh godov,* pp. 230, 232, 234.

89. Gastev, *Trudovye ustanovki,* p. 223.

90. *Pravda,* June 2, 1923, p. 3; *Vestnik truda,* no. 4, 1923, p. 45.

91. Gastev, *Kak nado,* pp. 6, 193–194.

92. See P. M. Kerzhentsev, *Printsipy organizatsii: Izbrannye proizvedeniia* (Moscow: Ekonomika, 1968), pp. 313–316; Sochor, "Soviet Taylorism Revisited," pp. 246–264.

93. *Pravda,* January 11, 1923, p. 2.

94. Il'enko and Shamsutdinov, *Nauchnaia organizatsiia truda dvadtsatykh godov,* p. 235; *Trud,* January 17, 1923, p. 2. See also Kovalev, *Nauchnaia organizatsiia truda,* pp. 139–143.

95. *Pravda,* February 2, 1923, p. 1. In a letter to the Bolshevik leader, Burdianskii enclosed a review published by Gastev that positively evaluated an article by the sociologist Pitrim Sorokin; Lenin, in a review of the same article, had labeled the author "reactionary." Burdianskii used the opportunity to remind Lenin of his own "ideological struggle with the misconceived 'Social-Engineering' of the Central Institute of Labor." No reply was received. Il'enko and Shamsutdinov, *Nauchnaia organizatsiia truda dvadtsatykh godov,* p. 160; Lenin, *PSS,* 45:23–33; *Organizatsiia truda,* no. 3, 1922, p. 182.

96. *Pravda,* March 18, 1923, p. 4; O. A. Yermanskii, *Teoriia i praktika ratsionalizatsii,* 4th ed. (Moscow: Gosizdat, 1931), pp. 473–474.

97. Il'enko and Shamsutdinov, *Nauchnaia organizatsiia truda dvadtsatykh godov,* p. 676.

98. Kerzhentsev, *Printsipy organizatsii.* For Lenin's evaluation of the book, see Lenin, *Izbrannye proizvedeniia,* 3:732.

99. Kerzhentsev, *Printsipy organizatsii,* p. 366. See also *Pravda,* July 18, 1923, p. 1; July 25, 1923, p. 1; July 28, 1923, p. 3; July 29, 1923, p. 3.

100. *Pravda,* July 31, 1923, p. 3. Meierkhol'd had been a close friend of Kerzhentsev ever since they had worked together in *Proletkult.* See Yu. Elagin, *Temnyi genii (Vsevolod Meierkhol'd)* (London: Overseas Publications, 1982), p. 260.

101. Kerzhentsev, *Printsipy organizatsii,* p. 370. See also Il'enko and Shamsutdinov, *Nauchnaia organizatsiia truda dvadtsatykh godov,* pp. 683–684. At the end of 1924 the organization consisted of 800 cells with 25,000

members, 40 percent of whom were party or Komsomol members. *Voprosy Istorii KPSS,* no. 8, 1965, p. 11.

102. *Pravda,* August 5, 1923, p. 3.
103. Kerzhentsev, *Printsipy organizatsii,* p. 376. See also pp. 347–382.
104. Ibid., pp. 305, 312, 314.
105. *Organizatsiia truda,* nos. 2–3, 1924, pp. 48–89 passim.
106. Il'enko and Shamsutdinov, *Nauchnaia organizatsiia truda dvadtsatykh godov,* p. 304.
107. *Trud,* February 5, 1924, p. 2 and February 6, 1924, p. 4.
108. *Pravda,* February 8, 1924, p. 1.
109. *Pravda,* February 13, 1924, p. 5.
110. Quoted in I. Dubinskii-Mukhadze, *Kuibyshev* (Moscow: Molodaia gvardiia, 1971), p. 231. See *Pravda,* February 20, 1924, p. 2; February 24, 1924, p. 4; March 7, 1924, p. 4; March 8, 1924, p. 7; E. Rozmirovich, *NOT, RKI, i partiia: K postanovke voprosa o tekhnike upravleniia* (Moscow: NKRKI, 1926), pp. 234–243.
111. Dubinskii-Mukhadze, *Kuibyshev,* pp. 231–232; G. V. Kuibysheva et al., *Valerian Vladimirovich Kuibyshev: Biografiia* (Moscow: Politizdat, 1966), p. 216.
112. Dubinskii-Mukhadze, *Kuibyshev,* pp. 232–235. Bogdanov played the convenient role of a straw man, for even those who portrayed him as a threat admitted that his theories of creating a "universal organizing science" had few followers. See Kerzhentsev, *Printsipy organizatsii,* pp. 307–309. Because of Lenin's disdain for his erstwhile rival, Bogdanov was a safe target for criticism from all sides. A more serious challenge came from the followers of Fayol, who were entrenched in the NKRKI bureaucracy. Fayolism, with its emphasis on the science of leadership, was criticized throughout these years by both opponents and allies of TsIT for contradicting the premises of Marxism. See Burdianskii, *Osnovy ratsionalizatsii,* p. 365; Rozmirovich, *NOT, RKI, i partiia,* pp. 194–233. At times a connection was made between the "idealism" of the Fayolists and that of Bogdanov.
113. *Trud,* March 18, 1924, p. 5.
114. Ibid., March 11, 1924, p. 2.
115. Dubinskii-Mukhadze, *Kuibyshev,* p. 235.
116. *Trud,* March 11, 1924, p. 2; Il'enko and Shamsutdinov, *Nauchnaia organizatsiia truda dvadtsatykh godov,* pp. 348–349; *Organizatsiia truda,* nos. 2–3, 1924, pp. 59–60.

2. Scientific Management at the Helm

1. P. P. Kovalev, ed., *Nauchnaia organizatsiia truda, proizvodstva i upravleniia: Sbornik dokumentov i materialov, 1918–1930 gg.* (Moscow: Ekonomika, 1969), p. 33. See also N. S. Il'enko and K. Shamsutdinov, eds., *Nauchnaia organizatsiia truda dvadtsatykh godov: Sbornik dokumentov i materialov* (Kazan: VNII okhrany truda, 1965), pp. 33–34, 668–672; D. M. Kruk, *Razvitie teorii i praktiki upravleniia proizvodstvom v*

SSR (Moscow: Minvuz SSSR, 1974), pp. 60–61. A second edition of the bibliography, published one year later, referred to 4400 works.

2. P. M. Kerzhentsev, *Printsipy organizatsii: Izbrannye proizvedeniia* (Moscow: Ekonomika, 1968), pp. 331–332, 372–373, 376–377; Kovalev, *Nauchnaia organizatsiia truda,* p. 97.

3. *Pravda,* August 13, 1925, p. 5; *Tekhnika upravleniia,* no. 2, February 1926, pp. 88–99; Kovalev, *Nauchnaia organizatsiia truda,* pp. 47–48.

4. Il'enko and Shamsutdinov, *Nauchnaia organizatsiia truda dvadtsatykh godov,* pp. 391, 395–396. See also E. Rozmirovich, *NOT, RKI, i partiia: K postanovke voprosa o tekhnike upravleniia* (Moscow: NKRKI, 1926), pp. 37–38, 52; L. F. Morozov and V. P. Portnov, *Organy TsKK-NKRKI v bor'be za sovershenstvovanie Sovetskogo gosudarstvennogo apparata (1923–1934 gg.)* (Moscow: Iuridicheskaia literatura, 1964), pp. 56–57; D. M. Berkovich, *Formirovanie nauki upravleniia proizvodstvom: Kratkii istoricheskii ocherk* (Moscow: Nauka, 1973), p. 105.

5. Kovalev, *Nauchnaia organizatsiia truda,* p. 37. In addition, see *Pravda,* March 17, 1923, p. 3; G. V. Kuibysheva et al., *Valerian Vladimirovich Kuibyshev: Biografiia* (Moscow: Politizdat, 1966), p. 220; Berkovich, *Formirovanie,* p. 106. The model for these organizations was the American National Bureau of Standards, created in 1901, which attracted Gastev's interest as early as March 1923.

6. Kuibysheva, *Kuibyshev,* pp. 231–232.

7. *Tekhnika upravleniia,* no. 12, December 1925, p. 87; Il'enko and Shamsutdinov, *Nauchnaia organizatsiia truda dvadtsatykh godov,* p. 449.

8. Kuibysheva, *Kuibyshev,* pp. 237, 248.

9. *Tekhnika upravleniia,* no. 6, June 1925, pp. 3–14.

10. Morozov, *Organy TsKK-NKRKI,* pp. 37–38; *Pravda,* April 25, 1926, p. 1.

11. Il'enko and Shamsutdinov, *Nauchnaia organizatsiia truda dvadtsatykh godov,* p. 470. See also Kovalev, *Nauchnaia organizatsiia truda,* pp. 48–55.

12. I. M. Burdianskii, *Osnovy ratsionalizatsii proizvodstva,* 2nd ed. (Moscow: Moskovskii rabochii, 1931), p. 367. Although SOVNOT formally existed until the NKRKI was dissolved in 1934, there is no evidence that it ever met during this period, and it ceased to play a role in the NOT movement. Il'enko and Shamsutdinov, *Nauchnaia organizatsiia truda dvadtsatykh godov,* p. 677.

13. Morozov, *Organy TsKK-NKRKI,* pp. 39–40.

14. Il'enko and Shamsutdinov, *Nauchnaia organizatsiia truda dvadtsatykh godov,* pp. 426–428, 453–454, 474–475.

15. See Sheila Fitzpatrick, *The Commissariat of Enlightenment* (London: Cambridge University Press, 1970).

16. Survey results cited in *Literaturnaia gazeta,* no. 45, November 5, 1975, p. 11.

17. Il'enko and Shamsutdinov, *Nauchnaia organizatsiia truda dvadtsatykh godov,* pp. 229, 247, 284.

18. Berkovich, *Formirovanie,* pp. 116, 139.

19. S. N. Ikonnikov, *Organizatsiia i deiatel'nost' RKI v 1920–1925 gg.* (Moscow: Akademiia nauk SSSR, 1960), pp. 122–123; Kuibysheva, *Kuibyshev,* p. 219.

20. Il'enko and Shamsutdinov, *Nauchnaia organizatsiia truda dvadtsatykh godov,* pp. 276–277, 323–324, 405–406, 713; Kovalev, *Nauchnaia organizatsiia truda,* p. 189; *Tekhnika upravleniia,* no. 10, October 1926, p. 74. Due to Krupskaia's efforts, instruction in NOT was also introduced on an experimental basis in several secondary schools.

21. A. Z. Kamenskii, in *Kursy Krasnykh direktorov pri VSNKh SSSR: Uchebnyi plan i programmy* (Moscow: Izdatel'stvo kursov krasnykh direktorov, 1928), p. 5; *Voprosy istorii KPSS,* no. 10, 1976, p. 80; M. P. Shevchenko, "Deiatel'nost' kommunisticheskoi partii v osushchestvlenii podgotovki rukovodiashchikh kadrov dlia promyshlennosti (1926–1932 gg.)" (Dissertatsiia na soiskanie uchenoi stepeni kandidata istoricheskikh nauk, Moscow, MGU, 1967), pp. 125–132.

22. *Predpriiatie,* no. 7, July 1926, p. 75; see also no. 7, July 1927, p. 16; and *Kursy Krasnykh Direktorov,* p. 10.

23. *Predpriiatie,* no. 7, July 1926, p. 76. See also Shevchenko, "Deiatel'-nost'," pp. 128–129. Only in June 1928, when Kuibyshev decreed that enterprise directors be given leave from their jobs in order to study, was this problem partially overcome.

24. See Sheila Fitzpatrick, *Education and Social Mobility in the Soviet Union, 1921–1934* (Cambridge: Cambridge University Press, 1979), pp. 146, 181.

25. Shevchenko, "Deiatel'nost'," pp. 163–164; E. H. Carr and R. W. Davies, *Foundations of a Planned Economy, 1926–1929,* vol. 1, pt. 2 (London: Macmillan, 1969), pp. 593–594; V. I. Lenin, *O rabote s kadrami* (Moscow: Politizdat, 1979), pp. 359–360; *Predpriiatie,* no. 4, April 1927, pp. 80–81; *Voprosy istorii,* no. 10, 1976, p. 81; I. Dubinskii-Mukhadze, *Kuibyshev* (Moscow: Molodaia gvardiia, 1971), pp. 246–247.

26. *Za promyshlennye kadry,* no. 6, June 1931, p. 19; Berkovich, *Formirovanie,* p. 140; M. P. Kim, ed., *Sovetskaia intelligentsiia (Istoriia formirovaniia i rosta, 1917–1965 gg.)* (Moscow: Mysl', 1968), pp. 202–203.

27. *Tekhnika upravleniia,* no. 5, May 1925, p. 72. For similar courses offered by Orgstroi, a rationalization unit affiliated with the NKRKI, see Kovalev, *Nauchnaia organizatsiia truda,* p. 294; *Tekhnika upravleniia,* no. 8, August 1926, p. 77; no. 11, November 1926, pp. 74–75; no. 3, March 1927, pp. 88–89.

28. Personal Archive of A. K. Gastev, in possession of his son Yu. A. Gastev, typescript, "TsIT i ego rabota," vol. 8, p. 191, New York. See also A. K. Gastev, *Trudovye ustanovki* (Moscow: Ekonomika, 1973), pp. 225–227; *Organizatsiia truda,* no. 11, 1926, pp. 55–56; *Vestnik truda,* no. 3, 1926, pp. 78–79.

29. *Vestnik truda,* no. 3, 1926, p. 78; A. K. Gastev, *Kak nado rabotat'* (Moscow: Ekonomika, 1966), pp. 140, 167, 192–193, 196–197. For more on TsIT's training methods, see *TsIT i ego metody NOT* (Moscow: Ekonomika, 1970), pp. 60–78.

30. Il'enko and Shamsutdinov, *Nauchnaia organizatsiia truda dvadtsatykh godov*, pp. 720–721; *Vestnik truda*, no. 11, 1927, pp. 94–96.

31. *Predpriiatie*, no. 4, April 1926, p. 91; F. E. Dzerzhinskii, *Izbrannye proizvedeniia*, vol. 2 (Moscow: Politizdat, 1967), pp. 248–249.

32. *Vestnik truda*, no. 12, 1926, pp. 54–56. See also Il'enko and Shamsutdinov, *Nauchnaia organizatsiia truda dvadtsatykh godov*, p. 721; O. A. Pozdniakov, *Lenin o problemakh nauchnoi organizatsii truda i upravleniia* (Leningrad: Lenizdat, 1969), p. 52; *TsIT i ego metody NOT*, p. 29; Kovalev, *Nauchnaia organizatsiia truda*, pp. 151–152; *Pravda*, March 17, 1926, p. 5.

33. *Vestnik truda*, no. 12, 1926, p. 56; no. 10, 1926, p. 46.

34. *Pravda*, July 22, 1926; October 28, 1926; June 15, 1926; *Predpriiatie*, no. 1, January 1927, pp. 14–17; *Vestnik truda*, no. 2, 1927, pp. 68–79. On Gastev's quarrel with the educational ideas of Lunacharskii and Krupskaia as far back as 1924, see Gastev, *Trudovye ustanovki*, pp. 43–47.

35. *Vestnik truda*, no. 10, 1926, p. 56; see also no. 12, 1926, pp. 52–59; nos. 6–7, 1927, pp. 135–146. There was considerable overlap between TsIT's ideological enemies from the debates of the early 1920s and TsIT's opponents on the issue of FZU reform. See *Vestnik truda*, no. 8, 1927, p. 152, in which Shpil'rein made a direct connection between TsIT's "deviations" in the two controversies.

36. *Komsomol'skaia pravda*, April 30, 1929, p. 2.

37. Kuibysheva, *Kuibyshev*, p. 228.

38. Anthony Downs, *Inside Bureaucracy* (Boston: Little, Brown, 1967), pp. 148–153.

39. Morozov, *Organy TsKK-NKRKI*, pp. 20–22, 39–40; Rozmirovich, *NOT, RKI, i partiia*, pp. 32–35.

40. See Stephen F. Cohen, *Bukharin and the Bolshevik Revolution: A Political Biography, 1888–1938* (New York: Random House, 1975), pp. 22–24. During these years Rozmirovich clashed with Lenin three times over party policy. Not only did she participate in the so-called Baugy group with Bukharin and Krylenko, but she also attempted on several occasions to warn Lenin about the activities of Roman Malinovskii, head of the Bolshevik Duma delegation, whom she correctly suspected of being a police spy. Finally, she dissented from Stalin's and Lenin's pronouncements on nationalities policy on the eve of the war. See also Robert C. Tucker, *Stalin as Revolutionary, 1879–1929* (New York: W. W. Norton, 1973), p. 156.

41. *Pravda*, February 20, 1924, p. 2. See also *Pravda*, February 24, 1924, p. 4; Rozmirovich, *NOT, RKI, i partiia*, pp. 194–243. It is interesting to note that while both Gastev and Vitke spoke of developing a "science of social engineering," Rozmirovich condemned the Fayolist position but lauded the "progressiveness" of Gastev's idea. Rozmirovich saw a challenge to Marxism in the Fayolists' glorification of administrative leadership, but Gastev's attempts to mold man to machine, she believed, were in full accord with Marxist thought.

42. Rozmirovich, quoted in Kruk, *Razvitie teorii*, p. 122; *Tekhnika upravleniia*, no. 1, January 1925, pp. 5–11. Gastev even corresponded with

Ford in 1928. See Gastev, *Kak nado,* pp. 310–319; *Organizatsiia truda,* no. 8, 1927, pp. 51–59. The anti-Ford books published during these years included: O. A. Yermanskii, *Legenda o Forde* (Moscow: GIZ, 1926); N. Rozenblit, *Fordizm* (Moscow: Ekonomicheskaia zhizn', 1925); and A. Fridrikh, *Genri Ford* (Moscow: Moskovskii rabochii, 1925). Works which saw Ford's method as a worthy innovation included: I. O. Rabchinskii, *Printsipy Forda* (Moscow: Gostekhizdat, 1925); Ia. Val'kher, *Ford ili Marks* (Moscow: Profintern, 1925); and S. Strel'bitskii, *Fordizm i ego budushchee* (Kharkov: Ukrainskii rabochii, 1926). By 1927 Ford's memoirs had been translated and republished in eight editions.

43. Morozov, *Organy TsKK-NKRKI,* p. 80; Ikonnikov, *Organizatsiia i deiatel'nost',* pp. 135–136.

44. *Tekhnika upravleniia,* no. 11, November 1925, pp. 3–11; no. 1, January 1926, pp. 107–108; no. 12, December 1926, pp. 63–65; Morozov, *Organy TsKK-NKRKI,* pp. 22–23; Kovalev, *Nauchnaia organizatsiia truda,* pp. 293–294.

45. O. V. Kozlova, O. A. Deineko, A. I. Trosheva, *Sotsializm i upravlenie proizvodstvom* (Moscow: Ekonomika, 1969), p. 76; *Tekhnika upravleniia,* no. 12, December 1925, pp. 3–7; no. 3, February 10, 1928, pp. 57–58. The orgburo was patterned on similar units in German government and private industry at the time.

46. Morozov, *Organy TsKK-NKRKI,* pp. 61–62; *Tekhnika upravleniia,* no. 10, May 25, 1929, pp. 281–283. The weekly meetings drew an attendance of approximately 2300 people in 1928. *Tekhnika upravleniia,* no. 3, March 1930, p. 117.

47. Kovalev, *Nauchnaia organizatsiia truda,* p. 191; Morozov, *Organy TsKK-NKRKI,* pp. 54–56.

48. Il'enko and Shamsutdinov, *Nauchnaia organizatsiia truda dvadtsatykh godov,* p. 445.

49. Kovalev, *Nauchnaia organizatsiia truda,* pp. 174–184; Morozov, *Organy TsKK-NKRKI,* pp. 30–32, 52. For a description of a similar alliance between plant directors and local party officials against rationalization, see A. F. Khavin, *U rulia industrii* (Moscow: Politizdat, 1968), p. 147.

50. *Tekhnika upravleniia,* no. 4, April 1925, p. 11; no. 3, February 10, 1928, pp. 63–64.

51. *Torgovo-promyshlennaia gazeta,* October 28, 1928, p. 5; *Tekhnika upravleniia,* no. 3, February 10, 1928, pp. 63–64, 78. See also *Tekhnika upravleniia,* nos. 8–9, August-September 1927, p. 89; Burdianskii, *Osnovy ratsionalizatsii,* pp. 354–355; Kovalev, *Nauchnaia organizatsiia truda,* pp. 310, 321. In one case in the Ukraine, an orgburo was attached to "the secret section" of a trust (a secret police unit) in order to watch over its operations. *Tekhnika upravleniia,* nos. 19–20, October 10–25, 1928, p. 537.

52. *Tekhnika upravleniia,* nos. 8–9, August-September, 1927, pp. 90–91; nos. 19–20, October 10–25, 1928, p. 537. See also Kovalev, *Nauchnaia organizatsiia truda,* p. 310; Burdianskii, *Osnovy ratsionalizatsii,* p. 355.

53. *Torgovo-promyshlennaia gazeta,* July 4, 1928, p. 3; July 12, 1928, p. 3.

54. *Tekhnika upravleniia,* no. 18, September 25, 1928, p. 494. See also Kovalev, *Nauchnaia organizatsiia truda,* pp. 324–330.
55. *Tekhnika upravleniia,* nos. 19–20, October 10–25, 1928, p. 536.
56. Ikonnikov, *Organizatsiia i deiatel'nost',* pp. 90–91; Kuibysheva, *Kuibyshev,* p. 212.
57. Kovalev, *Nauchnaia organizatsiia truda,* pp. 307, 314; Ordzhonikidze, in A. Gol'tsman, ed., *Na bor'bu s biurokratizmom* (Moscow: NKRKI, 1927), p. 4.
58. Kovalev, *Nauchnaia organizatsiia truda,* pp. 314–318.
59. F. V. Samokhvalov, *Sovety narodnogo khoziaistva v 1917–1932 gg.* (Moscow: Nauka, 1964), pp. 208–216; Alec Nove, *An Economic History of the U.S.S.R.* (Harmondsworth, Eng.: Penguin, 1969), p. 212; Ikonnikov, *Organizatsiia i deiatel'nost',* pp. 203–204.
60. For some success stories, see Morozov, *Organy TsKK-NKRKI,* pp. 66–69.
61. Quoted in Khavin, *U rulia industrii,* p. 14.
62. Ordzhonikidze, in Gol'tsman, *Na bor'bu s biurokratizmom,* pp. 9, 13.
63. Morozov, *Organy TsKK-NKRKI,* p. 77.
64. Il'enko and Shamsutdinov, *Nauchnaia organizatsiia truda dvadtsatykh godov,* pp. 469–470; Kovalev, *Nauchnaia organizatsiia truda,* p. 307.
65. Morozov, *Organy TsKK-NKRKI,* pp. 84–85. See also Ikonnikov, *Organizatsiia i deiatel'nost',* pp. 93–94; Kuibysheva, *Kuibyshev,* p. 230.
66. Kuibysheva, *Kuibyshev,* pp. 231–232.
67. See *Tekhnika upravleniia,* nos. 8–9, August-September 1927, pp. 87–95; no. 3, February 10, 1928, pp. 78–79; nos. 13–14, July 10–25, 1928, pp. 339–341; no. 2, January 25, 1928, pp. 45–46. One indication of the decline of interest in rationalization was the number of regular participants in the ITU's weekly seminars, which dropped by nearly one-half in 1929. *Tekhnika upravleniia,* no. 3, March 1930, p. 117. Kruk also notes a decline of interest in rationalization in 1928. Kruk, *Razvitie teorii,* p. 138.
68. *Tekhnika upravleniia,* no. 2, February 1925, p. 78.
69. Kerzhentsev, *Printsipy organizatsii,* p. 288. See also *Voprosy Istorii KPSS,* no. 8, 1965, p. 10; Il'enko and Shamsutdinov, *Nauchnaia organizatsiia truda dvadtsatykh godov,* pp. 9–10, 407.
70. *Pravda,* June 2, 1922, p. 1; February 21, 1923, p. 3; June 27, 1923, p. 4; *Tekhnika upravleniia,* no. 5, May 1927, p. 79; Kozlova, *Sotsializm i upravlenie proizvodstvom,* p. 76; Berkovich, *Formirovanie,* p. 97; Kovalev, *Nauchnaia organizatsiia truda,* pp. 45, 49; Il'enko and Shamsutdinov, *Nauchnaia organizatsiia truda dvadtsatykh godov,* pp. 494, 510–511. In 1923 Lenin noted the existence of three major centers of NOT research in the country: TsIT, the NKRKI, and the military. O. A. Pozdniakov, *Lenin o problemakh nauchnoi organizatsii truda i upravleniia* (Leningrad: Lenizdat, 1969), p. 74. On the varied work carried out by the NKRKI in the military during these years, see *Tekhnika upravleniia,* no. 3, March 1926, pp. 91–92; no. 5, May 1927, pp. 63–65; nos. 11–12, June 10–25, 1928, pp. 294–296.
71. Morozov, *Organy TsKK-NKRKI,* p. 52. For a map of the locations where TsIT instructors were stationed in 1926, see Gastev, *Trudovye ustanovki,*

p. 226. On the NOT activities of the NKRKI in the provinces, see Kovalev, *Nauchnaia organizatsiia truda,* pp. 55–96.

72. For examples, see *Pravda,* October 22, 1924, p. 7; December 20, 1924, p. 7; March 14, 1925, p. 7; March 26, 1925, p. 6; April 25, 1924, p. 7; *Predpriiatie,* no. 4, April 1928, pp. 83–84.

73. *Vestnik truda,* no. 7, 1926, p. 123; *Tekhnika upravleniia,* no. 3, February 10, 1928, p. 60; nos. 11–12, June 10–25, 1929, p. 331.

74. *Tekhnika upravleniia,* no. 12, December 1925, pp. 23–32.

75. Dzerzhinskii, *Izbrannye proizvedeniia,* 2:61–62, 379. See also 2:31, 55, 187–188.

76. Morozov, *Organy TsKK-NKRKI,* p. 85; Gol'tsman, *Na bor'bu s biurokratizmom,* pp. 3, 12.

77. Dzerzhinskii, *Izbrannye proizvedeniia,* 2:114.

78. See Nove, *An Economic History of the U.S.S.R.,* pp. 96–102, 136–144; Gol'tsman, *Na bor'bu s biurokratizmom,* p. 12.

79. Kuibysheva, *Kuibyshev,* p. 208; Morozov, *Organy TsKK-NKRKI,* pp. 54–56.

80. *Tekhnika upravleniia,* no. 18, September 25, 1928, p. 494.

81. *Predpriiatie,* no. 2, February 1926, pp. 81–82; *Tekhnika upravleniia,* no. 3, February 10, 1928, p. 78; *Torgovo-promyshlennaia gazeta,* July 12, 1928, p. 3.

82. Kovalev, *Nauchnaia organizatsiia truda,* p. 66; see also pp. 70, 250; and Il'enko and Shamsutdinov, *Nauchnaia organizatsiia truda dvadtsatykh godov,* pp. 409, 417–419; *Tekhnika upravleniia,* nos. 23–24, December 10–25, 1928, p. 650.

83. *Trud,* February 16, 1929, p. 2.

84. Victor Kravchenko, *I Chose Freedom* (New York: Charles Scribner's Sons, 1946), p. 53.

85. Gastev, *Trudovye ustanovki,* pp. 216–218.

86. *Pravda,* December 10, 1924, p. 7; see also June 27, 1924, p. 7; and *Tekhnika upravleniia,* no. 11, November 1926, p. 5.

87. *Trud,* February 16, 1929, p. 2; February 29, 1929, p. 2; Burdianskii, *Osnovy ratsionalizatsii,* p. 334.

88. *Torgovo-promyshlennaia gazeta,* July 12, 1929, p. 3; *Tekhnika upravleniia,* no. 1, January 1930, p. 33.

89. Kuibysheva, *Kuibyshev,* p. 275.

90. Ordzhonikidze, in Gol'tsman, *Na bor'bu s biurokratizmom,* p. 6.

91. Morozov, *Organy TsKK-NKRKI,* p. 86.

3. Stalinism as Antibureaucracy

1. I. V. Stalin, *Sochineniia,* vol. 12 (Moscow: Gospolitizdat, 1949), p. 118.

2. Peter M. Blau, *The Dynamics of Bureaucracy* (Chicago: University of Chicago Press, 1955), p. 215.

3. Moshe Lewin, *The Making of the Soviet System: Essays in the Social History of Interwar Russia* (New York: Pantheon Books, 1985), p. 45.

4. Victor A. Thompson, *Modern Organization* (New York: Alfred A. Knopf, 1961), pp. 170, 173, 176.

5. Six of those condemned to death had their sentences commuted to life imprisonment. See N. V. Krylenko, *Ekonomicheskaia kontr-revoliutsiia v Donbasse* (Moscow: Iuridicheskoe Izdatel'stvo, 1928); Kendall E. Bailes, *Technology and Society under Lenin and Stalin* (Princeton, N.J.: Princeton University Press, 1978), pp. 69–94; Aleksandr Solzhenitsyn, *The Gulag Archipelago*, vols. 1–2 (New York: Harper and Row, 1973), pp. 373–374; D. L. Golinkov, *Krushenie antisovetskogo podpol'ia v SSSR*, vol. 2 (Moscow: Politizdat, 1978), pp. 295–305.

6. *Resheniia partii i pravitel'stva po khoziaistvennym voprosam (1917–1967 gg.)*, vol. 1 (Moscow: Politizdat, 1967), pp. 709, 744–745.

7. Robert C. Tucker, "Stalinism as Revolution from Above," in Robert C. Tucker, ed., *Stalinism: Essays in Historical Interpretation* (New York: W. W. Norton, 1977), pp. 77–108.

8. Bailes, *Technology and Society*, p. 70; Jeremy R. Azrael, *Managerial Power and Soviet Politics* (Cambridge, Mass.: Harvard University Press, 1966), p. 217.

9. *Tekhnika upravleniia*, nos. 19–20, October 10–25, 1928, p. 537; no. 1, January 1930, p. 36.

10. *Pravda*, September 30, 1928, p. 2.

11. *Trud*, February 16, 1929, p. 2.

12. I. Trifonov, *Ocherki istorii klassovoi bor'by v SSSR v gody NEPa (1921–1937)* (Moscow: Politizdat, 1960), p. 153.

13. Solzhenitsyn, *The Gulag Archipelago*, vols. 1–2, pp. 44–45, 374–375; Trifonov, *Ocherki istorii klassovoi bor'by*, pp. 159–162. For more on von Meck's life, see Galina von Meck, *As I Remember Them* (London: Dennis Dobson, 1973). Von Meck participated in the First NOT Conference, where he is alleged to have said: "If we were anywhere in Germany or America, I would suggest that we proclaim a 'hurrah' for Taylor and his followers." I. M. Burdianskii, *Osnovy ratsionalizatsii proizvodstva*, 2nd ed. (Moscow: Moskovskii rabochii, 1931), p. 364.

14. N. S. Il'enko and K. Shamsutdinov, eds., *Nauchnaia organizatsiia truda dvadtsatykh godov: Sbornik dokumentov i materialov* (Kazan: VNII okhrany truda, 1965), p. 396; *Pravda*, February 12, 1930, p. 3; February 13, 1930, p. 4. Vysochanskii also participated in the work of the Moscow Club for Red Directors, acting as a consultant on rationalization. See *Predpriiatie*, no. 1, January 1929, p. 80.

15. For more on this case, see Bailes, *Technology and Society*, pp. 95–121; Solzhenitsyn, *The Gulag Archipelago*, vols. 1–2, pp. 376–399; Roy A. Medvedev, *Let History Judge* (New York: Random House, 1971), pp. 114–115; *Wreckers on Trial: A Record of the Trial of the Industrial Party* (New York: Workers' Library, 1931).

16. N. F. Charnovskii, *Organizatsiia promyshlennykh predpriiatii po obrabotke metallov* (Moscow: Tipografiia Russkogo Tovarishchestva, 1911); N. F. Charnovskii, *Osnovnye motivy v sovremennoi postanovke massovogo proizvodstva* (Moscow: TsIT, 1921); N. F. Charnovskii, *Tekhnoekonomicheskie printsipy v metallopromyshlennosti* (Moscow: Orgametall, 1927). See also *Vestnik Kommunisticheskoi Akademii*, nos. 8–9,

August-September 1931, pp. 10–11. Charnovskii always considered himself closer in thinking to Ford than to Taylor.

17. G. K. Ordzhonikidze, *Stat'i i rechi*, vol. 2 (Moscow: Gospolitizdat, 1957), p. 233.
18. V. V. Kuibyshev, *Izbrannye proizvedeniia* (Moscow: Gospolitizdat, 1958), pp. 140, 161. For more on the views of Kuibyshev and Ordzhonikidze toward the Shakhty affair, see Bailes, *Technology and Society*, pp. 72–82.
19. Stalin, *Sochineniia*, 12:14.
20. *Izvestiia*, August 3, 1930, p. 2; February 14, 1930, p. 2; *Pravda*, February 12, 1930, p. 9.
21. *Izvestiia*, February 13, 1930, p. 4.
22. *Za industrializatsiiu*, November 3, 1930, p. 2. See also *Bol'shevik*, no. 2, 1931, pp. 73–81, where bourgeois specialists were accused of engaging in wrecking activities in their works on rationalization technology, the rationalization of railroad management, and accounting procedures.
23. *Vestnik truda*, no. 1, 1926, pp. 53–63; no. 2, 1926, pp. 59–72; no. 6, 1926, pp. 78–85; no. 9, 1926, p. 156.
24. O. A. Yermanskii, *Teoriia i praktiki ratsionalizatsii* (Moscow: Gosizdat, 1928). See also *Planovoe khoziaistvo*, no. 2, 1929, pp. 197–229.
25. *Problemy ekonomiki*, no. 1, 1929, pp. 164–167; *Pravda*, October 29, 1929, p. 5; *Planovoe khoziaistvo*, no. 11, 1929, pp. 152–166; D. M. Kruk, *Razvitie teorii i praktiki upravleniia proizvodstvom v SSSR* (Moscow: Minvuz SSSR, 1974), pp. 100–101.
26. *Vestnik Kommunisticheskoi Akademii*, no. 39, 1930, p. 193; see also no. 29, 1930, pp. 84–90; and David Joravsky, *Soviet Marxism and Natural Science, 1917–1932* (London: Routledge and Kegan Paul, 1961); George Enteen, "Marxist Historians during the Cultural Revolution: A Case Study of Professional In-Fighting," in Sheila Fitzpatrick, ed., *Cultural Revolution in Russia, 1928–1931* (Bloomington, Ind.: Indiana University Press, 1978), pp. 154–168.
27. *Protsess kontrrevoliutsionnoi organizatsii Men'shevikov* (Moscow: Sovetskoe Zakonodatel'stvo, 1931).
28. Ibid., p. 171.
29. O. A. Yermanskii, *Teoriia i praktika ratsionalizatsii*, 2nd ed. (Moscow: Gosizdat, 1931), pp. 425, 438–440. Gastev and associates were charged with engaging in "an attempt at self-defense from my criticism, which (for example, in the field of the problem of chronometric norming of labor) is perceived . . . as a direct threat to their material existence." Burdianskii, Yermanskii charged, repeated the formulas of TsIT and "understands the 'productivity' of labor in a completely bourgeois way."
30. *Pravda*, June 6, 1931, p. 4. See also *Vestnik Kommunisticheskoi Akademii*, nos. 8–9, August-September 1931, pp. 15–16; Burdianskii, *Osnovy ratsionalizatsii*, pp. 222–226.
31. Bailes, *Technology and Society*, pp. 167–172.
32. *Pravda*, May 11, 1928, p. 6; *Spravochnik partiinogo rabotnika*, pt. 1, 7th ed. (Moscow: Gosizdat, 1930), p. 464; Sheila Fitzpatrick, "Cultural Rev-

olution as Class War,'' in Fitzpatrick, *Cultural Revolution in Russia,* pp. 8–40.

33. *Pravda,* June 7, 1928, p. 2; A. K. Gastev, *Trudovye ustanovki* (Moscow: Ekonomika, 1973), pp. 312, 342. Tomskii and Shmidt, like Kuibyshev, were frequent visitors at the Gastev home.

34. *Pravda,* May 8, 1928, p. 3; May 11, 1928, p. 6; May 15, 1928, p. 4; *Spravochnik partiinogo rabotnika,* pt. 1, p. 463.

35. A. V. Lunacharskii, *O narodnom obrazovanii* (Moscow: Akademiia pedagogicheskikh nauk RSFSR, 1958), pp. 404–408, 431; Sheila Fitzpatrick, ''Cultural Revolution as Class War,'' pp. 8–40.

36. A. V. Lunacharskii, *O vospitanii i obrazovanii* (Moscow: Pedagogika, 1976), pp. 272, 279. See also *Pravda,* June 2, 1928, p. 7; Lunacharskii, *O narodnom obrazovanii,* p. 450.

37. Gastev, *Trudovye ustanovki,* pp. 312–338.

38. Krupskaia, like Kerzhentsev, viewed NOT as a mass movement and part of ''production propaganda.'' She was among the first to publish in the Time League's journal *Vremia.* In April 1928 Lunacharskii suggested that the dissolution of the Time League had been a mistake. Lunacharskii, *O narodnom obrazovanii,* p. 413.

39. *Pravda,* June 7, 1928, p. 2; Il'enko and Shamsutdinov, *Nauchnaia organizatsiia truda dvadtsatykh godov,* p. 495.

40. Stalin, *Sochineniia,* 11:220.

41. Dogadov was later harassed at the Sixteenth Party Congress in July 1930 for his support of Tomskii. See *XVI S'ezd Vsesoiuznoi Kommunisticheskoi Partii (b): Stenograficheskii otchet* (Moscow: OGIZ, 1931), p. 276.

42. N. K. Krupskaia, *Pedagogicheskie sochineniia v desiati tomakh,* vol. 4 (Moscow: Izdatel'stvo Akademii pedagogicheskikh nauk, 1959), p. 182; *Spravochnik partiinogo rabotnika,* pt. 1, p. 510.

43. Il'enko and Shamsutdinov, *Nauchnaia organizatsiia truda dvadtsatykh godov,* pp. 509–510.

44. *Shestnadtsataia Konferentsiia VKP(b): Stenograficheskii otchet* (Moscow: Gospolitizdat, 1962), pp. 213, 264–265.

45. *Pravda,* June 9, 1929, p. 4. Even the trade union newspaper, *Trud,* joined in the attack on Gastev. Gastev's immediate protest, however, brought about a partial retraction. *Trud,* June 26, 1929, p. 1; Il'enko and Shamsutdinov, *Nauchnaia organizatsiia truda dvadtsatykh godov,* pp. 511–512.

46. *Bol'shevik,* no. 7, July 1929, p. 78.

47. L. Averbakh, *Spornye voprosy kul'turnoi revoliutsii* (Moscow: Moskovskii rabochii, 1929), pp. 108–109, 117, 110.

48. *KPSS v rezoliutsiiakh i resheniiakh s'ezdov, konferentsii, i plenumov TsK,* vol. 4 (Moscow: Politizdat, 1970), pp. 368–378.

49. *Komsomol'skaia pravda,* May 11, 1930, p. 4; May 16, 1930, p. 4; *TsIT i ego metody NOT* (Moscow: Ekonomika, 1970), p. 33; *Za industrializatsiiu,* April 5, 1930, p. 3; M. P. Evseev in V. S. Frelova, ed., *V. V. Kuibyshev: Vydaiushiisia proletarskii revoliutsioner i myslitel'* (Tomsk: Izdatel'stvo Tomskogo universiteta, 1963), p. 91.

50. Stalin, *Sochineniia,* 13:51–80. Nicholas Timasheff, who coined the term, dated the Great Retreat as beginning in 1934. Nicholas S. Timasheff, *The*

Great Retreat: The Growth and Decline of Communism in Russia (New York: E. P. Dutton, 1946).

51. *Trud,* January 27, 1931, p. 3; Il'enko and Shamsutdinov, *Nauchnaia organizatsiia truda dvadtsatykh godov,* pp. 535–536; Krupskaia, *Pedagogicheskie sochineniia,* 4:439.

52. *Za industrializatsiiu,* May 18, 1931, p. 3; *Partiinoe stroitel'stvo,* no. 23, 1931, pp. 63–64. See also Il'enko and Shamsutdinov, *Nauchnaia organizatsiia truda dvadtsatykh godov,* pp. 550–553; A. K. Gastev, *Kak nado rabotat'* (Moscow: Ekonomika, 1966), pp. 392–393; *Za industrializatsiiu,* April 19, 1931, p. 1.

53. *Resheniia partii i pravitel'stva,* 2:438–441.

54. *Vestnik Kommunisticheskoi Akademii,* nos. 8–9, August-September 1931, p. 17.

55. Stalin, *Sochineniia,* 11:131, 57–62.

56. *Shestnadtsataia konferentsiia VKP (b),* pp. 815–816. On the party's purge of the state bureaucracy, see *KPSS v rezoliutsiiakh i resheniiakh,* 4:226–229; Ordzhonikidze, *Stat'i i rechi,* 2:223. For an examination of Komsomol's role in the war against bureaucracy, see Sheila Fitzpatrick, "Cultural Revolution as Class War," pp. 23–27. More than 250,000 people had participated in such raids by May 1930.

57. *Spravochnik partiinogo rabotnika,* vol. 7, pt. 1, p. 584. See also L. F. Morozov, V. P. Portnov, *Organy TsKK-NKRKI v bor'be za sovershenstvovanie Sovetskogo gosudarstvennogo apparata (1923–1934 gg.)* (Moscow: Iuridicheskaia literatura, 1964), pp. 87–88; *Resheniia partii i pravitel'stva,* 2:8–14; *Shestnadtsataia konferentsiia VKP (b),* pp. 140, 231.

58. P. P. Kovalev, ed., *Nauchnaia organizatsiia truda, proizvodstva i upravleniia: Sbornik dokumentov i materialov, 1918–1930 gg.* (Moscow: Ekonomika, 1969), p. 316.

59. *Tekhnika upravleniia,* no. 6, June 1926, pp. 3–10; no. 5, May 1927, p. 86; nos. 15–16, August 10–25, 1929, pp. 415–421. For a subsequent critique of this line of thought, see *Organizatsiia upravleniia,* nos. 2–3, 1931, pp. 2–7.

60. *Pravda,* July 13, 1929, p. 3.

61. *Resheniia partii i pravitel'stva,* 2:136–142. For the draft proposals submitted by the NKRKI and VSNKh, see *Pravda,* July 13, 1929, p. 1; August 11, 1929, p. 1; *Torgovo-promyshlennaia gazeta,* September 12, 1929, p. 1.

62. *Resheniia partii i pravitel'stva,* 2:136–142; *Pravda,* August 13, 1929, pp. 5–6; Alec Nove, *An Economic History of the U.S.S.R.* (Harmondsworth, Eng.: Penguin, 1969), pp. 212–213; F. V. Samokhvalov, *Sovety narodnogo khoziaistva v 1917–1932 gg.* (Moscow: Nauka, 1964), p. 285; *Shestnadtsataia konferentsiia VKP (b),* pp. 477–478; *Torgovo-promyshlennaia gazeta,* September 12, 1929, p. 1; October 12, 1929, pp. 4–5.

63. Bailes, *Technology and Society,* pp. 107–110; *Wreckers on Trial,* pp. 11–12; *Torgovo-promyshlennaia gazeta,* October 15, 1929, p. 1; October 26, 1929, pp. 4–5. Charnovskii was a consultant to the Sector on Rationalization and Standardization of the Scientific-Technical Administration. He,

like most of the accused at the Industrial Party trial, was a member of the collegium of the Scientific-Technical Administration. For Bukharin's advocacy of rationalization efforts in the late twenties, see *Pravda,* January 20, 1929, pp. 2–3.

64. *Vestnik Kommunisticheskoi Akademii,* nos. 8–9, August-September 1931, pp. 8–26; Paul Maupin Cocks, "Politics of Party Control: The Historical and Institutional Role of the Party Control Organs in the CPSU" (Ph.D. diss., Harvard University, 1968), p. 161; Kruk, *Razvitie teorii,* pp. 123–125.

65. This problem was predicted before the reform was put into effect. See the objections raised in *Torgovo-promyshlennaia gazeta,* September 12, 1929, p. 4.

66. *Organizatsiia upravleniia,* no. 1, 1931, p. 5. See also Morozov, *Organy TsKK-NKRKI,* pp. 89–91; Samokhvalov, *Sovety narodnogo khoziaistva,* pp. 285–287; Nove, *An Economic History,* p. 213. For a scathing critique of similar reforms that Rozmirovich's institute introduced in the Commissariat of Railroads, see *Organizatsiia upravleniia,* nos. 2–3, 1931, pp. 4–6.

67. *XVI S'ezd Vsesoiuznoi Kommunisticheskoi Partii (b),* pp. 44, 317, 327, 728–729. Kuibyshev's biographers reveal that the VSNKh chairman was deeply troubled by Ordzhonikidze's attacks upon him at the Sixteenth Party Congress and lost an entire night of sleep pondering a response. G. V. Kuibysheva et al., *Valerian Vladimirovich Kuibyshev: Biografiia* (Moscow: Politizdat, 1966), pp. 299–302.

68. See *Pravda,* May 22, 1930, p. 6.

69. *XVI S'ezd Vsesoiuznoi Kommunisticheskoi Partii (b),* p. 312; Kovalev, *Nauchnaia organizatsiia truda,* p. 333.

70. Nove, *An Economic History,* pp. 213–214; Samokhvalov, *Sovety narodnogo khoziaistva,* pp. 290–291; *Resheniia partii i pravitel'stva,* 2:468–471.

71. Morozov, *Organy TsKK-NKRKI,* pp. 44–45.

72. Ordzhonikidze, *Stat'i i rechi,* 2:282.

73. *Organizatsiia upravleniia,* nos. 9–10, 1931, p. 57.

74. *Organizatsiia upravleniia,* no. 1, 1931, pp. 1–5; see also nos. 2–3, 1931, pp. 1–7; and *Izvestiia,* January 27, 1931, p. 3. Criticisms were also directed at the Ukrainian NKRKI's Institute for the Rationalization of Management and the Kazan Institute for NOT for sharing Rozmirovich's discredited conceptions.

75. *Bol'shevik,* no. 2, 1931, pp. 73–81.

76. *Organizatsiia upravleniia,* nos. 4–5, 1931, p. 2; see also nos. 7–8, 1931, pp. 1–21; no. 12, 1931, pp. 50–60.

77. *Vestnik Kommunisticheskoi Akademii,* nos. 8–9, August-September 1931, pp. 9, 12, 13, 18.

78. *Organizatsiia upravleniia,* no. 1, 1932, pp. 1–44 passim; Cocks, "Politics of Party Control," p. 162.

79. Morozov, *Organy TsKK-NKRKI,* pp. 49–50, 65–66; Burdianskii, *Osnovy ratsionalizatsii,* p. 370.

80. *Vestnik Kommunisticheskoi Akademii,* nos. 8–9, August-September 1931, pp. 14–15, 20.

81. Surveys in 1928 had found that less than 10 percent of rationalizers belonged to the party. By mid-1931 37 percent of Moscow rationalizers were party members. Another survey of rationalizers in sixteen Russian provinces found that almost a quarter were party members. In 1928 rationalizers with an elementary school education only constituted between 3 and 10 percent of the rationalization movement. By mid-1931 their number had grown to 30 percent. *Tekhnika upravleniia,* nos. 19–20, October 10–25, 1928, p. 537; no. 1, January 1930, p. 36; *Organizatsiia upravleniia,* nos. 9–10, 1931, pp. 52, 57–58.

82. Burdianskii, *Osnovy ratsionalizatsii,* p. 356.

83. Ordzhonikidze, *Stat'i i rechi,* 2:267.

84. *Predpriiatie,* no. 1, January 1930, pp. 36–37. For a similar account by another American engineer, see ibid., no. 4, February 1930, pp. 33–34.

85. *XVI S'ezd Vsesoiuznoi Kommunisticheskoi Partii (b),* pp. 496–499.

86. *Za industrializatsiiu,* May 7, 1930, p. 5. The account noted that managers suffered from serious administrative overload, despite the fact that they rarely permitted themselves rest or vacation days.

87. Ordzhonikidze, *Stat'i i rechi,* 2:285.

88. *Organizatsiia upravleniia,* nos. 9–10, 1931, pp. 52–56; nos. 4–5, 1931, p. 21.

89. Quoted in Lewin, *The Making of the Soviet System,* p. 239.

90. Stalin, *Sochineniia,* 13:75; Ordzhonikidze, *Stat'i i rechi,* 2:377.

91. *XVI S'ezd Vsesoiuznoi Kommunisticheskoi Partii (b),* p. 43.

92. For reviews of coercive industrial practices, see David Granick, *Management of the Industrial Firm: A Study in Soviet Economic Planning* (New York: Columbia University Press, 1954), pp. 189–202; Boris Souvarine, *Stalin: A Critical Survey of Bolshevism* (New York: Longmans, Green, 1939), pp. 525–526; Robert Conquest, *Industrial Workers in the USSR* (New York: Praeger, 1967), pp. 98–102; Solomon M. Schwarz, *Labor in the Soviet Union* (New York: Praeger, 1951), pp. 86–99.

93. M. P. Shevchenko, "Deiatel'nost' kommunisticheskoi partii v osushchestvlenii podgotovki rukovodiashchikh kadrov dlia promyshlennosti (1926–1932 gg.)" (Dissertatsiia na soiskanie uchenoi stepeni kandidata istoricheskikh nauk, Moscow, MGU, 1967), pp. 172–174; *Pravda,* May 26, 1930, p. 3; May 31, 1930, p. 4; June 3, 1930, p. 3.

94. Edward Crankshaw, ed., *Khrushchev Remembers* (New York: Bantam, 1971), p. 68.

95. Shevchenko, "Deiatel'nost' kommunisticheskoi partii," p. 175. See also *Za promyshlennye kadry,* no. 6, June 1931, p. 18.

96. F. N. Zauzolkov, *Kommunisticheskaia partiia—organizator sozdaniia nauchnoi i proizvodstvenno-tekhnicheskoi intelligentsii SSSR* (Moscow: Izdatel'stvo MGU, 1973), p. 82. Eleven were general, interbranch academies; twelve were branch academies.

97. Shevchenko, "Deiatel'nost' kommunisticheskoi partii," pp. 190, 194.

98. *Za promyshlennye kadry,* no. 9, May 1932, p. 22.

99. Lazar Pistrak, *The Grand Tactician: Khrushchev's Rise to Power* (New York: Praeger, 1961), pp. 57–58.
100. *Predpriiatie,* no. 6, June 1927, pp. 8–10; no. 12, December 1928, pp. 81–84; no. 5, May 1929, p. 95; no. 7, July 1929, pp. 90–92; P. Petrochenko and K. Kuznetsova, *Organizatsiia i normirovanie truda v promyshlennosti SSSR* (Moscow: Profizdat, 1971), pp. 60–61; Shevchenko, "Deiatel'nost' kommunisticheskoi partii," p. 134.
101. *Za industrializatsiiu,* May 17, 1931, p. 2; Shevchenko, "Deiatel'nost' kommunisticheskoi partii," pp. 155–156.
102. S. A. Fediukin, *Sovetskaia vlast' i burzhuaznye spetsialisty* (Moscow: Mysl', 1965), p. 243; Bailes, *Technology and Society,* pp. 216–243.
103. Yu. O. Liubovich, *Sotsialisticheskaia organizatsiia proizvodstva kak predmet prepodavaniia* (Moscow: Moskovskii inzhenerno-ekonomicheskii institut, 1938), pp. 8–10.

4. The Triumph of Violence

1. Alexander Dallin and George W. Breslauer, *Political Terror in Communist Systems* (Stanford: Stanford University Press, 1970), p. 48.
2. Quoted in Aleksandr I. Solzhenitsyn, *The Gulag Archipelago, 1918–1956,* vols. 1–2 (New York: Harper and Row, 1973), p. 381 (emphasis in the original).
3. Alvin W. Gouldner, *Patterns of Industrial Bureaucracy* (New York: Free Press, 1954), pp. 86–101.
4. E. A. Johns, *The Sociology of Organizational Change* (Oxford: Pergamon Press, 1973), pp. 134–135.
5. Yu. O. Liubovich, *Sotsialisticheskaia organizatsiia proizvodstva kak predmet prepodavaniia* (Moscow: Moskovskii inzhenerno-ekonomicheskii institut, 1938), pp. 77–78.
6. Barrington Moore, Jr., *Terror and Progress—USSR* (Cambridge, Mass.: Harvard University Press, 1966), p. 172.
7. *XVIII S'ezd Vsesoiuznoi Kommunisticheskoi Partii (b), 10–23 Marta 1939 g.: Stenograficheskii otchet* (Moscow: OGIZ, 1939), p. 257; Jeremy Azrael, *Managerial Power and Soviet Politics* (Cambridge, Mass.: Harvard University Press, 1966), p. 102.
8. Gastev was among those chosen to pay public tribute to his fallen protector. See *Izvestiia,* January 26, 1935, p. 4.
9. For a history of Soviet norm-setting, see Lewis H. Siegelbaum, "Soviet Norm Determination in Theory and Practice, 1917–1941," *Soviet Studies,* 36 (January 1984), 45–68.
10. *Za industrializatsiiu,* October 27, 1930, p. 2.
11. For a useful review of norm-setting practices in the late twenties, see P. Petrochenko and K. Kuznetsova, *Organizatsiia i normirovanie truda v promyshlennosti SSSR* (Moscow: Profizdat, 1971), pp. 79–109.
12. I. V. Stalin, *Sochineniia,* vol. 13 (Moscow: Gospolitizdat, 1949), pp. 56–57.
13. G. K. Ordzhonikidze, *Stat'i i rechi,* vol. 2 (Moscow: Gospolitizdat, 1957), p. 670.

14. *XVII Konferentsiia Vsesoiuznoi Kommunisticheskoi partii (b): Stenograficheskii otchet* (Moscow: OGIZ, 1932), pp. 104–105, 110–111.
15. A. K. Gastev, *Kak nado rabotat'* (Moscow: Ekonomika, 1966), p. 418.
16. See Siegelbaum, "Soviet Norm Determination," pp. 54–55.
17. *Pervoe vsesoiuznoe soveshchanie rabochikh i rabotnits Stakhanovtsev 14–17 noiabria 1935: Stenograficheskii otchet* (Moscow: Partizdat, 1935), p. 313.
18. Kravchenko accurately reflected the mood of managers toward the Stakhanovites: "What we needed most was smoother integration of the productive process. This seemed the worst possible moment for overloading either the men or the machines. Rhythmic teamwork, rather than spurts of record-breaking, was the key to steady output. More than fifteen hundred workers engaged on a common task, in which every operation meshed into the next, couldn't speed up arbitrarily without throwing the whole effort into chaotic imbalance." Victor Kravchenko, *I Chose Freedom* (New York: Charles Scribner's Sons, 1946), p. 187.
19. Ordzhonikidze, *Stat'i i rechi,* 2:673, 689.
20. *Pervoe vsesoiuznoe soveshchanie,* pp. 315, 201, 192, 375, 372. See also Siegelbaum, "Soviet Norm Determination," p. 61.
21. Ordzhonikidze, *Stat'i i rechi,* 2: 772.
22. *TsIT i ego metody NOT* (Moscow: Ekonomika, 1970), pp. 32–40, 95, 121; *Za industrializatsiiu,* April 19, 1931, p. 1; April 27, 1931, p. 2; *Partiinoe stroitel'stvo,* no. 23, 1931, pp. 63–64.
23. For newspaper accounts of the resistance to TsIT's functional scheme, see *Za industrializatsiiu,* May 19, 1931, p. 3; June 20, 1931, p. 3.
24. *XVII Konferentsiia Vsesoiuznoi Kommunisticheskoi Partii (b),* pp. 55, 66; *KPSS v rezoliutsiiakh i resheniiakh s'ezdov, konferentsii, i plenumov TsK,* vol. 5 (Moscow: Politizdat, 1970), p. 56. According to Kaganovich's later account, the order to liquidate work-place functionalism in light industry came directly from Stalin. *XVII S'ezd Vsesoiuznoi Kommunisticheskoi Partii (b), 26 ianvaria-10 fevralia 1934 g.: Stenograficheskii otchet* (Moscow: OGIZ, 1934), p. 537.
25. *XVII S'ezd Vsesoiuznoi Kommunisticheskoi Partii (b),* p. 532.
26. *Za industrializatsiiu,* April 19, 1931, p. 1; Gastev, *Kak nado,* pp. 392–394, 401–412. For evidence of Ordzhonikidze's support of TsIT, see *Za industrializatsiiu,* February 4, 1933, p. 2.
27. Gastev, *Kak nado,* p. 366.
28. Petrochenko and Kuznetsova, *Organizatsiia i normirovanie,* p. 175; *TsIT i ego metody,* p. 61.
29. Petrochenko and Kuznetsova, *Organizatsiia i normirovanie,* pp. 173–174.
30. *TsIT i ego metody,* p. 14.
31. *Organizatsiia upravleniia,* no. 2, March-April 1937, pp. 123–128. For excerpts from the book, see Gastev, *Kak nado,* pp. 316–347.
32. Petrochenko and Kuznetsova, *Organizatsiia i normirovanie,* p. 176; *TsIT i ego metody,* pp. 76–77; Roy Medvedev, *Let History Judge: The Origins and Consequences of Stalinism* (New York: Vintage, 1973), p. 225. For

the subsequent history of the Gastev family, see *Pamiat': Istoricheskii sbornik, Vypusk pervyi* (New York: Khronika, 1978), pp. 232–246.

33. A. V. Petrovskii, *Istoriia sovetskoi psikhologii: Formirovanie osnov psikhologicheskoi nauki* (Moscow: Prosveshchenie, 1967), p. 283. For the debates over psychophysiology at the end of the twenties, see Raymond A. Bauer, *The New Man in Soviet Psychology* (Cambridge, Mass.: Harvard University Press, 1959), pp. 67–102.

34. N. S. Il'enko and K. Shamsutdinov, eds., *Nauchnaia organizatsiia truda dvadtsatykh godov: Sbornik dokumentov i materialov* (Kazan: VNII okhrany truda, 1965), pp. 705–706.

35. Ibid., pp. 221–222.

36. N. K. Krupskaia, *Pedagogicheskie sochineniia v desiati tomakh*, vol. 4 (Moscow: Izdatel'stvo Akademii pedagogicheskikh nauk, 1959), pp. 156–157, 247–248, 355, 498–499. On the development of Soviet psychotechnics in the twenties, see Bauer, *The New Man;* Petrovskii, *Istoriia sovetskoi psikhologii,* pp. 262–286; I. N. Shpil'rein, in V. P. Volgin et al., eds., *Obshchestvennye nauki SSSR, 1917–1927* (Moscow: Rabotnik Prosveshcheniia, 1928), pp. 70–76.

37. *Vestnik Kommunisticheskoi Akademii,* nos. 37–38, 1930, pp. 167–170; no. 39, 1930, p. 190.

38. Ibid., no. 39, 1930, p. 188; Bauer, *The New Man,* p. 113; Petrovskii, *Istoriia sovetskoi psikhologii,* p. 122.

39. *Vestnik Kommunisticheskoi Akademii,* no. 7, July 1931, pp. 10–11; Petrovskii, *Istoriia sovetskoi psikhologii,* pp. 272–273.

40. Bauer, *The New Man,* p. 107.

41. Quoted in ibid., pp. 123–124; Krupskaia, *Pedagogicheskie sochineniia,* 4: 581. See also Petrovskii, *Istoriia sovetskoi psikhologii,* pp. 290–291.

42. Burdianskii's Kazan Institute for NOT was subjected to a thorough purge and was renamed the Kazan Institute for the Preservation of Labor, to emphasize the new direction of its research. Il'enko and Shamsutdinov, *Nauchnaia organizatsiia truda dvadtsatykh godov,* pp. 15–16, 686.

43. *Organizatsiia upravleniia,* no. 1, January-February 1935, pp. 12–30; no. 4, July-August 1937, pp. 3–13.

44. David Granick, *Management of the Industrial Firm in the USSR* (New York: Columbia University Press, 1954), pp. 110, 19 (emphasis in the original).

45. *Organizatsiia upravleniia,* no. 2, March-April, 1935, p. 5.

46. For a sampling of this enlightening literature, see *Organizatsiia upravleniia,* no. 4, July-August 1937, pp. 3–13; no. 1, January-February 1938, pp. 15–22, 70–80; no. 6, November-December 1937, pp. 19–50.

47. Ibid., no. 4, July-August 1937, p. 84; no. 1, January-February 1938, pp. 70–80.

48. Liubovich, *Sotsialisticheskaia organizatsiia proizvodstva kak predmet,* pp. 77–78.

49. O. A. Yermanskii, *Stakhanovskoe dvizhenie i Stakhanovskie metody* (Moscow: Gosudarstvennoe sotsial'no-ekonomicheskoe izdatel'stvo, 1940), p. 224. See also the muted critique of Yermanskii in Liubovich, *Sotsialisticheskaia organizatsiia proizvodstva kak predmet,* pp. 77–78.

Russian Taylorist I. M. Besprozvannyi survived the purge while working in teaching and research posts. He died in 1952.

50. Krupskaia, *Pedagogicheskie sochineniia,* 4:574.
51. *Za promyshlennye kadry,* no. 22, November 1935, p. 49.
52. *Organizatsiia upravleniia,* no. 1, January-February 1938, p. 71; B. Ya. Katsenbogen, *Organizatsiia proizvodstva v mashinostroenii: Uchebnik* (Moscow: ONTI, 1937).
53. Liubovich, *Sotsialisticheskaia organizatsiia proizvodstva kak predmet,* pp. 72–73, 76.
54. *Istoriia SSSR,* no. 4, 1961, p. 74.
55. *Voprosy istorii KPSS,* no. 10, 1976, p. 85; *Za promyshlennye kadry,* no. 8, June 1936, p. 20.
56. *Za promyshlennye kadry,* no. 8, June 1936, p. 20; no. 3, February 1936, p. 4.
57. Ordzhonikidze, *Stat'i i rechi,* 2:752.
58. *Za promyshlennye kadry,* no. 4, March 1936, p. 42; no. 13, September 1936, pp. 5–6.
59. M. Kim, *Kommunisticheskaia partiia—organizator kul'turnoi revoliutsii v SSSR* (Moscow: Gospolitizdat, 1955), pp. 336–337. IPKs for other professional groups, such as teachers and doctors, continued to operate throughout this period.
60. A. Liapin, in A. Savin, ed., *V pomoshch' ekonomicheskomu obrazovaniiu kadrov,* vol. 1 (Moscow: Moskovskii rabochii, 1941), p. 122. See also Sh. L. Rosenfel'd, *Organizatsiia upravleniia promyshlennost'iu SSSR* (Moscow: Gosplanizdat, 1950); A. F. Rumiantsev, *Organizatsiia upravleniia promyshlennost'iu SSSR* (Moscow: VPSh pri TsK KPSS, 1953).
61. Medvedev, *Let History Judge,* p. 482; I. Stalin, *Ekonomicheskie problemy sotsializma v SSSR* (Moscow: Politizdat, 1952), pp. 10–11, 150–151, 170–171.
62. P. D. Morozov, *Leninskie printsipy podbora, rasstanovki, i vospitaniia kadrov* (Moscow: Izdatel'stvo VPSh i AON, 1959), p. 46; A. D. Moshchevitin, *Podbor i vospitanie rukovodiashchikh kadrov* (Moscow: Moskovskii rabochii, 1962), p. 43.
63. I. V. Paramonov, *Uchit'sia upravliat': Mysl' i opyt starogo khoziaistvennika* (Moscow: Ekonomika, 1967), p. 163.
64. Granick, *Management of the Industrial Firm,* pp. 190–192; Gregory Bienstock, Solomon M. Schwarz, and Aaron Yugow, *Management in Russian Industry and Agriculture* (London: Oxford University Press, 1944), p. 11.
65. Gastev, *Kak nado,* pp. 421–422; David Granick, *The Red Executive: A Study of Organization Man in Russian Industry* (Garden City, N.Y.: Doubleday, 1961), p. 135.
66. *XVII S'ezd VKP (b),* p. 533.
67. Granick, *Management of the Industrial Firm,* pp. 191–192; Alec Nove, *An Economic History of the U.S.S.R.* (Harmondsworth, Eng.: Penguin, 1969), p. 261; *Resheniia partii i pravitel'stva po khoziaistvennym voprosam (1917–1967 gg.),* vol. 2 (Moscow: Politizdat, 1967), pp. 779–781.

For an excellent description of these laws and their application, see Solomon M. Schwarz, *Labor in the Soviet Union* (New York: Praeger, 1951), pp. 100–114, 298. Schwarz points out that the introduction of these measures was connected with the economic recession of the prewar years. On the fact that all these measures were looked upon by Stalin as a consistent package aimed at tightening industrial discipline, see the resolutions of the Eighteenth Party Conference held in February 1941, in *KPSS v rezoliutsiiakh,* 5:460–471.

68. The following discussion is drawn from three studies of managerial behavior during the period under examination: Bienstock, Schwarz, and Yugow, *Management in Russian Industry;* Granick, *Management of the Industrial Firm;* and Joseph S. Berliner, *Factory and Manager in the USSR* (Cambridge, Mass.: Harvard University Press, 1957).

69. Quoted in Azrael, *Managerial Power,* pp. 247–248.

70. Ibid., pp. 117–122.

71. For a list of TsIT survivors, see A. K. Gastev, *Trudovye ustanovki* (Moscow: Ekonomika, 1973), p. 6. For Bernshtein's critical position on the dogma of Pavlovian psychology in the 1940s and his cybernetic approach to physiology, see Loren R. Graham, *Science and Philosophy in the Soviet Union* (New York: Alfred A. Knopf, 1972), pp. 392–400.

5. The Rebirth of Managerialism

1. G. Maskimovich, *Besedy s Akademikom V. Glushkovym* (Moscow: Molodaia gvardiia, 1976), p. 56.

2. F. C. Pierson, *The Education of American Businessmen: A Study of University-College Programs in Business Administration* (New York: McGraw-Hill, 1959), pp. 8, 11; Sheldon Zalaznick, "The M.B.A.: The Man, the Myth, and the Method," *Fortune,* May 1968, p. 169; Nancy G. McNulty, *Training Managers: The International Guide* (New York: Harper and Row, 1969), p. 443; *The New York Times,* March 14, 1979, sect. D, p. 13; John E. Steele and Lewis B. Ward, "MBA's: Mobile, Well Educated, Well Paid," *Harvard Business Review,* 52 (January-February 1974), 100–101; *Careers and the MBA '78* (Boston: Harbus, 1978), p. 65.

3. Jan Kreiken, in Bernard Taylor and Gordon Lippitt, eds., *Management Development and Training Handbook* (New York: McGraw-Hill, 1975), pp. 13–14. From 1957 to 1959 only 3 percent of the graduates of Harvard Business School became management consultants. By the late 1960s that proportion had risen to 10 percent, and by the late 1970s to 23 percent. J. Sterling Livingston, "The Myth of the Well-Educated Manager," *Harvard Business Review,* 49 (January-February 1971), 86; *Careers and the MBA '78,* p. 38.

4. Harold Koontz, "The Management Theory Jungle," *Journal of the Academy of Management,* 4 (December 1961), 174–188.

5. *Postanovleniia Iul'skogo Plenuma TsK KPSS 1955 goda* (Moscow: Gospolitizdat, 1955), p. 7.

6. Ibid., pp. 15–18. See also *Sotsialisticheskii trud,* no. 11, 1957, p. 57.

7. Interview with Yuri Gastev, Harvard University Russian Research Cen-

ter, Cambridge, Massachusetts, May 22, 1984. In his efforts to rehabilitate his father, Gastev's son received support from a number of former TsIT personnel, including A. V. Smetanin, V. F. Kadobnov, L. A. Kanevskii, M. P. Zhuravlev, and S. M. Mikhailov.

8. *Sotsialisticheskii trud,* no. 7, 1957, p. 32; *TsIT i ego metody NOT* (Moscow: Ekonomika, 1970), p. 55.

9. *Sotsialisticheskii trud,* no. 3, 1957, p. 98; no. 7, 1957, pp. 18, 111–116; no. 8, 1959, pp. 97–104; no. 9, 1959, pp. 92–99; no. 2, 1960, pp. 93–97.

10. *XX s'ezd Kommunisticheskoi Partii Sovetskogo Soiuza, 14–25 Fevralia 1956 goda: Stenograficheskii otchet* (Moscow: Gospolitizdat, 1956), pp. 323–324.

11. See S. Florens, *Struktura promyshlennosti i upravlenie predpriiatiiami Britanii i SShA* (Moscow: Izd-vo inostrannoi literatury, 1958); *Voprosy proizvoditel'nosti v chernoi metallurgii SShA i Anglii: Otchet brigady angliiskikh spetsialistov o poezdke v SShA* (Moscow: Izd-vo inostrannoi literatury, 1958); *Uchet v upravlenii promyshlennymi predpriiatiiami SShA: Otchet brigady angliiskikh spetsialistov po voprosam ucheta i ochetnosti o poezdke v SShA* (Moscow: Izd-vo inostrannoi literatury, 1958). One of the employees of IMEMO at the time was Modest Rubinshtein, a member of the "communist fraction" in NOT in the 1920s and author of several works on Taylorism in the West. See Modest Rubinshtein, *Sovremennyi kapitalizm i organizatsiia truda,* 2nd ed. (Moscow: Moskovskii rabochii, 1923).

12. Loren R. Graham, in George Fischer, ed., *Science and Ideology in Soviet Society* (New York: Atherton Press, 1967), p. 93.

13. *XX s'ezd,* pp. 323–324; A. Birman, *Uchis' khoziaistvovat' (rasskazy ob ekonomike predpriiatiia)* (Moscow: Politizdat, 1959); M. A. Bishaev and M. M. Fedorovich, *Organizatsiia upravleniia promyshlennym proizvodstvom* (Moscow: Gosplanizdat, 1961); D. M. Kruk, *Razvitie teorii i praktiki upravleniia proizvodstvom v SSSR* (Moscow: Minvuz SSSR, 1974), p. 184. Numerous accounts of the development of mathematical economics in the Soviet Union have been published, including: Wassily Leontief, *Essays in Economics: Theories and Theorizing* (New York: Oxford University Press, 1966), pp. 223–236; Michael Ellman, *Planning Problems in the USSR: The Contribution of Mathematical Economics to their Solution, 1960–1971* (Cambridge: Cambridge University Press, 1973); Alfred Zauberman, *The Mathematical Revolution in Soviet Economics* (London: Oxford University Press, 1975); Aron Katsenelinboigen, *Soviet Economic Thought and Political Power in the USSR* (New York: Pergamon Press, 1980); James Clay Thompson and Richard F. Vidmer, *Administrative Science and Politics in the USSR and the United States* (South Hadley, Mass.: Bergin and Garvey, 1983), pp. 77–78.

14. Carl A. Linden, *Khrushchev and the Soviet Leadership, 1957–1964* (Baltimore: Johns Hopkins University Press, 1966), p. 135. See also Michel Tatu, *Power in the Kremlin: From Khrushchev to Kosygin* (New York: Viking Press, 1967), pp. 200–204.

15. G. Kh. Popov, *Problemy teorii upravleniia,* 2nd ed. (Moscow: Ekonomika, 1974), pp. 277–278.

16. D. M. Gvishiani, *Sotsiologiia biznesa: Kriticheskii ocherk amerikanskoi teorii menedzhmenta* (Moscow: Sotsial'no-Ekonomicheskaia Literatura, 1962).

17. *Kommunist*, no. 14, September 1962; *Pravda*, September 25, 1962, p. 7. On the significance of this draft in the founding of the NOT movement, see Chapter 1.

18. *Ekonomicheskaia gazeta*, no. 40, September 29, 1962, p. 7.

19. *Planovoe khoziaistvo*, no. 11, 1962, pp. 4–5.

20. *Pravda*, October 21, 1962, p. 3; October 24, 1962, p. 3. See also *Kommunist*, no. 16, November 1962, pp. 23–30; no. 17, November 1962, p. 66.

21. *Moskovskii literator*, November 5, 1962, quoted in N. S. Il'enko and K. Shamsutdinov, eds., *Nauchnaia organizatsiia truda dvadtsatykh godov: Sbornik dokumentov i materialov* (Kazan: VNII okhrany truda, 1965), pp. 21–22. Berg and the economists Nemchinov and Strumilin were identified by former TsIT personnel as having played instrumental roles in the rehabilitation of Gastev. Strumilin had been a member of TsIT's ruling council in the early twenties. According to Gastev's son, both Berg and Strumilin were interested in Gastev's rehabilitation only insofar as it furthered their own pretensions for power, whereas Nemchinov, one of the founders of the optimal planning school in the Soviet Union, had a more genuine interest. Berg, in particular, attempted to use Gastev's ghost to justify the dominance of cybernetics in the development of a new management science. Interview with Yuri Gastev, Harvard University Russian Research Center, Cambridge, Massachusetts, May 22, 1984.

22. N. S. Khrushchev, *Razvitie ekonomiki SSSR i partiinogo rukovodstva narodnym khoziaistvom* (Moscow: Izd-vo Pravdy, 1962), p. 33.

23. *Ekonomicheskaia gazeta*, no. 43, October 1963, pp. 7–8. The editors of the paper described Lisitsyn's article as "polemical," thereby hinting at opposition.

24. *Ekonomicheskaia gazeta*, no. 41, October 1963, p. 21.

25. P. Petrochenko and K. Kuznetsova, *Organizatsiia i normirovanie truda v promyshlennosti SSSR* (Moscow: Profizdat, 1971), pp. 280–281, 285–287. In both Sverdlovsk and Novosibirsk these projects were organized by Academician Prudenskii, then head of the Institute for the Economics and Organization of Industrial Production, who was known for his conservative economic views. Having been secretary of Sverdlovsk obkom during the war, Prudenskii enjoyed close ties with local party officials. The first secretary of Sverdlovsk obkom from 1962 to 1971, K. K. Nikolaev, had been a norm-setter in the early 1930s. The Sverdlovsk party organization played an important role in the revival of NOT throughout the sixties.

26. *Izvestiia*, May 19, 1963, p. 2; *Ekonomicheskaia gazeta*, no. 31, August 3, 1963, p. 21. Other projects that the council was supposed to coordinate included research on models of regional management, computer technology, centralization and decentralization, norm-setting, and the management of scientific research institutes. Gvishiani's deputy in the council

was none other than Yu. O. Liubovich, who had participated in the purging of Rozmirovich's institute and had been one of the hard-core Stalinists in the NOT movement in the 1930s. In the early sixties, Liubovich taught at the Ordzhonikidze Engineering-Economics Institute.

27. A. M. Birman, *Nekotorye problemy nauki o sotsialisticheskom khoziaist-vovanii* (Moscow: Izd-vo ekonomicheskoi literatury, 1963), pp. 10–11, 4. A synopsis of this book was published in *Planovoe khoziaistvo,* no. 3, March 1963, pp. 11–21.

28. D. M. Gvishiani, in V. N. Khramelashvili, ed., *Sorevnovanie dvukh sistem: problemy ekonomicheskoi nauki* (Moscow: Nauka, 1963), pp. 98, 91, 90.

29. *Metodologicheskie problemy nauki: Materialy zasedaniia prezidiuma Akademii Nauk SSSR* (Moscow: Nauka, 1964), pp. 40–41; *Sovetskoe gosudarstvo i pravo,* no. 9, 1964, p. 16.

30. Birman, *Nekotorye problemy,* pp. 10–11.

31. *Metodologicheskie problemy,* pp. 203–204.

32. *Kommunist,* no. 9, June 1963, p. 55.

33. *Sovetskoe gosudarstvo i pravo,* no. 6, 1964, p. 20; no. 9, 1964, pp. 15–27.

34. *Voprosy filosofii,* no. 10, 1963, pp. 154–157. For the claims of cyberneticians in regard to the field of management psychology, including a passing reference to Shpil'rein and his work, see *Voprosy filosofii,* no. 4, 1962, pp. 32–46.

35. *Sotsialisticheskii trud,* no. 1, 1964, pp. 12–15. This group included Academicians Strumilin, Prudenskii, Artobolevskii (a specialist in machine theory and automation), and A. Grigor'ev (head of the department of labor economics at the Moscow State Economic Institute). The State Committee for Labor and Wage Issues, which oversaw norm-determination research, found the Strumilin group's proposals in line with its own tastes. In the mid-fifties Prudenskii had been deputy chairman of the State Committee for Labor and Wage Issues. For his advocacy of NOT as an alternative to economic reform, see G. A. Prudenskii, *Vremia i trud* (Moscow: Mysl', 1964). For similar views, see *Kommunist,* no. 15, October 1964, pp. 39–46; *Sotsialisticheskii trud,* no. 3, 1964, pp. 11–18.

36. Birman, *Nekotorye problemy,* p. 12.

37. *Sovetskoe gosudarstvo i pravo,* no. 6, 1964, p. 20.

38. Ibid., no. 9, 1964, p. 16.

39. Ibid., no. 4, 1965, pp. 90–101.

40. *Planovoe khoziaistvo,* no. 1, January 1965, pp. 92–93.

41. John Dornberg, *Brezhnev: The Masks of Power* (New York: Basic Books, 1974), p. 193.

42. *Pravda,* December 10, 1964, p. 1.

43. *Resheniia partii i pravitel'stva po khoziaistvennym voprosam (1917–1967 gg.),* vol. 5 (Moscow: Politizdat, 1968), pp. 588–590.

44. *Planovoe khoziaistvo,* no. 4, April 1965, p. 8.

45. *Pravda,* May 17, 1965, p. 2; see also February 26, 1965, p. 1.

46. *Izvestiia,* May 21, 1965, p. 1.

47. *Sovetskoe gosudarstvo i pravo,* no. 2, 1965, pp. 85–91; no. 4, 1965, pp.

90–101; no. 9, 1965, pp. 3–11; *Voprosy filosofii*, no. 3, 1965, pp. 10–31; *Planovoe khoziaistvo*, no. 4, April 1965, pp. 39–48; *Sotsialisticheskii trud*, no. 7, 1965, pp. 51–58.

48. *Pravda*, June 23, 1965, p. 2; N. A. Tsagalov, ed., *Problemy sovershenstvovaniia planomernoi organizatsii i upravleniia sotsialisticheskim proizvodstvom* (Moscow: Ekonomika, 1969), pp. 36–37.

49. V. I. Tereshchenko, *Organizatsiia i upravlenie* (Moscow: Ekonomika, 1965). For an earlier article by Tereshchenko in which he contrasted Western business culture with that which he found on his return to the Soviet Union, see *Izvestiia*, March 29, 1964, p. 5.

50. *Literaturnaia gazeta*, June 22, 1965, p. 2.

51. *Sotsialisticheskii trud*, no. 3, 1964, pp. 11–18; Il'enko and Shamsutdinov, *Nauchnaia organizatsiia truda dvadtsatykh godov*, pp. 40–41, 677–679.

52. *Kommunist*, no. 12, August 1965, pp. 62–63; no. 17, November 1965, p. 6. Criticisms were also leveled at "a narrow cybernetic approach" and at alleged attempts to revive Bukharin's theory of "organized capitalism." For an argument by the reformist wing of the party against Afanas'ev's efforts to effect a compromise, see A. Rumiantsev, in *Kommunist*, no. 1, January 1966, pp. 42–52.

53. *Pravda*, September 28, 1965, p. 1; *Resheniia partii i pravitel'stvo*, 5:684.

54. *Kommunist*, no. 1, January 1966, pp. 42, 45, 51; *Ekonomicheskaia gazeta*, no. 41, October 1966, p. 23. See also Popov, *Problemy teorii upravleniia*, p. 248; *Pravda*, December 14, 1965, p. 2.

55. *XXIII s'ezd Kommunisticheskoi Partii Sovetskogo Soiuza: Stenograficheskii otchet*, vol. 2 (Moscow: Politizdat, 1966), p. 330.

56. N. V. Adfel'dt, in A. I. Berg, ed., *Organizatsiia i upravlenie (voprosy teorii i praktiki)* (Moscow: Nauka, 1968), p. 11.

57. D. M. Gvishiani and S. E. Kamenitser, eds., *Problemy nauchnoi organizatsii upravleniia sotsialisticheskoi promyshlennost'iu (po materialam Vsesoiuznoi nauchno-tekhnicheskoi konferentsii)* (Moscow: Ekonomika, 1968), pp. 614–615; Popov, *Problemy teorii upravleniia*, p. 79.

58. O. A. Deineko, *Metodologicheskie problemy nauki upravleniia proizvodstva* (Moscow: Nauka, 1970), p. 92; Yu. O. Liubovich, in D. M. Gvishiani, ed., *Materialy k vsesoiuznoi nauchno-tekhnicheskoi konferentsii "Problemy nauchnoi organizatsii upravleniia sotsialisticheskoi promyshlennost'iu,"* sect. 1 (Moscow: Ekonomika, 1966), pp. 18, 24–25.

59. *Ekonomicheskaia gazeta*, no. 24, June 1966, pp. 6–7.

60. *Resheniia partii i pravitel'stva*, 6:285, 286, 295; see also 6:587–589; and O. A. Pozdniakov, *Lenin o problemakh nauchnoi organizatsii truda i upravleniia* (Leningrad: Lenizdat, 1969), pp. 164–166; Kruk, *Razvitie teorii*, p. 193.

61. *Pravda*, December 2, 1968, p. 2.

62. *Voprosy ekonomiki*, no. 1, 1967, p. 9. See also F. Binshtok, *Nauka upravliat'* (Moscow: Moskovskii rabochii, 1967), pp. 19–21; Adfel'dt, in Berg, *Organizatsiia i upravlenie*, p. 11.

63. N. Baikov, in *Organizatsiia upravleniia* (Moscow: Ekonomika, 1971), pp. 162–163. As a result of the commission's efforts, the first Soviet management textbooks to be published in thirty years went to press at the

end of 1968. See *Nauchnye osnovy upravleniia proizvodstvom: Ucheb-noe posobie* (Moscow: Ekonomika, 1969); *Metody upravleniia sotsialis-ticheskim obshchestvennym proizvodstvom: Kurs lektsii* (Moscow: Izd-vo MGU, 1969).

64. *Pravda,* November 30, 1967, p. 3.
65. P. M. Kerzhentsev, *Printsipy organizatsii: Izbrannye proizvedeniia* (Moscow: Ekonomika, 1968), p. 16; D. M. Berkovich, *Formirovanie nauki upravleniia proizvodstvom: Kratkii istoricheskii ocherk* (Moscow: Nauka, 1973), p. 117. See also A. K. Gastev, *Kak nado rabotat'* (Moscow: Ekonomika, 1966), p. 13; O. V. Kozlova, O. A. Deineko, and A. I. Trosheva, *Sotsializm i upravleniia proizvodstvom* (Moscow: Ekonomika, 1969), pp. 61–62; *Sotsialisticheskii trud,* no. 4, April 1966, pp. 73–77.
66. Joseph S. Berliner, *The Innovation Decision in Soviet Industry* (Cambridge, Mass.: MIT Press, 1976), p. 520.
67. *Ekonomicheskaia gazeta,* no. 24, June 1966, pp. 6–7.
68. L. I. Brezhnev, *Voprosy upravleniia ekonomikoi razvitogo sotsialis-ticheskogo obshchestva: Rechi, doklady, vystupleniia* (Moscow: Politiz-dat, 1976), pp. 62, 73, 113, 209–211, 234–235. Kremlinologists interpreted these speeches as a "declaration of war on Kosygin and a bid for supreme power." Dornberg, *Brezhnev,* p. 244.
69. *KPSS v rezoliutsiiakh i resheniiakh s'ezdov, konferentsii, i plenumov TsK,* vol 10 (Moscow: Politizdat, 1972), pp. 98–100, 304–309.
70. *Kommunist,* no. 1, January 1970, p. 60.
71. *Materialy XXIV s'ezda KPSS* (Moscow: Politizdat, 1974), pp. 66, 65, 166, 167.
72. George W. Breslauer, *Khrushchev and Brezhnev as Leaders: Building Authority in Soviet Politics* (London: George Allen and Unwin, 1982), p. 179.
73. M. A. Suslov, *Izbrannoe: Rechi i stat'i* (Moscow: Politizdat, 1972), pp. 666–668 passim.
74. Popov, *Problemy teorii upravleniia,* p. 55.
75. Gvishiani and Kamenitser, *Problemy nauchnoi organizatsii upravleniia sotsialisticheskoi promyshlennost'iu,* pp. 11–12, 99–100.
76. Popov, *Problemy teorii upravleniia,* pp. 148–149, 158–161.
77. V. M. Glushkov, G. M. Dobrov, and V. I. Tereshchenko, *Besedy ob upravlenii* (Moscow: Nauka, 1974), p. 197.

6. *The Science of Victory*

1. Michael Schiff, in Peter F. Drucker, ed., *Preparing Tomorrow's Business Leaders Today* (Englewood Cliffs, N.J.: Prentice-Hall, 1969), p. 262.
2. *Tret'ia mezhvuzovskaia konferentsiia po teoreticheskim problemam upravleniia sotsialisticheskimi khoziaistvennymi organizatsiiami: Tezisy dokladov* (Tallin: Minvuz Estonskoi SSR, 1972), pp. 97–98. See also *EKO,* no. 5, 1977, p. 170; G. Kh. Popov, *Problemy teorii upravleniia,* 2nd ed. (Moscow: Ekonomika, 1974), p. 25.
3. See David Granick, *Managerial Comparisons of Four Developed Countries: France, Britain, United States, and Russia* (Cambridge, Mass.:

MIT Press, 1972); Eugene Emerson Jennings, *The Mobile Manager: A Study of the New Generation of Top Executives* (New York: McGraw-Hill, 1967).

4. *Ekonomicheskaia gazeta,* no. 43, October 27, 1965, pp. 4–5.

5. *XXIII s'ezd Kommunisticheskoi Partii Sovetskogo Soiuza: Stenograficheskii otchet,* vol. 2 (Moscow: Politizdat, 1966), p. 55.

6. *Ekonomicheskaia gazeta,* no. 41, October 1966, p. 28; see also no. 25, June 1966, pp. 20–21; and D. M. Gvishiani, ed., *Materialy k vsesoiuznoi nauchno-tekhnicheskoi konferentsii "Problemy nauchnoi organizatsii upravleniia sotsialisticheskoi promyshlennost'iu,"* sect. 1 (Moscow: Ekonomika, 1966), pp. 272–285.

7. *Ekonomicheskaia gazeta,* no. 34, August 1966, pp. 14–15.

8. Ibid., p. 3.

9. *Resheniia partii i pravitel'stva po khoziaistvennym voprosam,* vol. 6 (Moscow: Politizdat, 1968), pp. 404–408.

10. See *Planovoe khoziaistvo,* no. 7, July 1968, pp. 79–80; no. 5, May 1968, pp. 3–11; *Pravda,* January 19, 1968, p. 3; *Kommunist,* no. 8, May 1968, p. 70; *Novyi mir,* no. 8, August 1968, pp. 201–218.

11. *Pravda,* December 2, 1968, p. 2; March 13, 1970, p. 1. For other articles advocating management schools, see *Literaturnaia gazeta,* no. 11, March 1969, p. 10; *Ekonomicheskie nauki,* no. 3, 1969, pp. 38–43; *Kommunist,* no. 17, November 1969, p. 108; no. 1, January 1970, pp. 56–67; *Partiinaia zhizn',* no. 5, March 1970, pp. 15–16.

12. *Ekonomicheskaia gazeta,* no. 7, February 1971, p. 8; *Pravda,* February 2, 1971, p. 3. The trainees of IUNKh were supposed to include ministers, deputy ministers, members of the collegia of ministries, general directors of obed'ineniia, and directors of the largest enterprises in the country.

13. L. I. Brezhnev, *Voprosy upravleniia ekonomikoi razvitogo sotsialisticheskogo obshchestva: Rechi, doklady, vystupleniia* (Moscow: Politizdat, 1976), pp. 209–211; Foreign Broadcast Information Service, *Daily Report: Soviet Union,* 3 (February 2, 1971), C 1 (quotation).

14. *Materialy XXIV s'ezda KPSS* (Moscow: Politizdat, 1974), pp. 175, 101.

15. M. A. Suslov, *Izbrannoe: rechi i stat'i* (Moscow: Politizdat, 1972), p. 667.

16. L B. Baev, "Nekotorye voprosy sovershenstvovaniia sistemy podgotovki i povysheniia kvalifikatsii kadrov upravleniia: Na primere spetsial'noi podgotovki rukovoditelei promyshlennykh predpriiatii" (Dissertatsiia na soiskanie uchenoi stepeni kandidata ekonomicheskikh nauk, Moscow, Ordzhonikidze Engineering-Economics Institute, 1971), pp. 84–85.

17. *Sotsialisticheskii trud,* no. 10, October 1972, p. 88.

18. Brian Chapman, *The Profession of Government: The Public Service in Europe* (New York: Macmillan, 1959), pp. 75, 100, 114, 123.

19. *Vestnik vysshei shkoly,* no. 9, 1981, p. 52.

20. *Pravda,* December 19, 1975, p. 3; D. M. Gvishiani and S. E. Kamenitser, eds., *Problemy nauchnoi organizatsii upravleniia sotsialisticheskoi promyshlennost'iu (po materialam Vtoroi Vsesoiuznoi nauchno-tekhnicheskoi konferentsii)* (Moscow: Ekonomika, 1974), pp. 424–425.

21. *Ekonomicheskaia gazeta,* no. 52, December 1971, p. 11.

22. *Pravda,* March 22, 1978, p. 1.
23. *Literaturnaia gazeta,* no. 5, February 4, 1976, p. 12; "Otchet o rabote sistemy povysheniia kvalifikatsii rukovodiashchikh rabotnikov i spetsialistov narodnogo khoziaistva v IX piatiletke" (Report prepared for the Scientific-Methodological Office for Higher Education and the Upgrading of Qualifications of the USSR Ministry of Higher and Specialized Secondary Education, Moscow, 1976), pp. 13–14 (in possession of the author). See also "Analiz sistemy podgotovki rukovoditelei v SSSR" (Report prepared for the Scientific-Methodological Council for Problems of Upgrading the Qualifications of Executives and Specialists of the USSR Ministry of Higher and Specialized Secondary Education, Moscow, 1978), pp. 6, 51 (in possession of the author); M. K. Poltev, ed., *Sovershenstvovanie sistemy obucheniia rukovodiashchikh kadrov narodnogo khoziaistva* (Moscow: Izd-vo MGU, 1979), pp. 10–11; *EKO,* no. 5, 1977, p. 184; *Pravda,* December 19, 1975, p. 3.
24. Sidney Mailick, in Sidney Mailick, ed., *The Making of the Manager: A World View* (Garden City, N.Y.: Anchor Press, 1974), pp. 83–84, 89.
25. *Literaturnaia gazeta,* no. 49, December 3, 1976, p. 10.
26. *EKO,* no. 5, 1977, pp. 168, 184; no. 6, 1974, p. 34; *Literaturnaia gazeta,* no. 28, July 13, 1977, p. 11.
27. *Literaturnaia gazeta,* no. 28, July 13, 1977, p. 11 (emphasis in the original).
28. "Reshenie mezhvedomstvennogo soveta po povysheniiu kvalifikatsii rukovodiashchikh rabotnikov i spetsialistov narodnogo khoziaistva ot 12 Fev. 1980 g. 'O proekte plana komplektovaniia fakul'tetov po podgotovke organizatorov promyshlennogo proizvodstva na 1980–85 gg.' " (Government document, USSR Ministry of Higher and Specialized Secondary Education, Moscow—in possession of the author); *Pravda,* June 21, 1980, p. 2; February 5, 1981, p. 2; *Ekonomicheskaia gazeta,* no. 20, May 1983, p. 10. The Academy maintains affiliate programs in Minsk, Kiev, Tashkent, and Tbilisi.
29. *Literaturnaia gazeta,* December 3, 1976, p. 10; *Pravda,* February 2, 1971, p. 3. See also V. Yu. Ozira, *Soderzhanie i metody podgotovki kadrov upravleniia* (Moscow: Ekonomika, 1977), p. 57; *Uchebnye plany fakul'teta planirovaniia promyshlennogo proizvodstva* (Moscow: Minvuz RSFSR, 1979); Poltev, *Sovershenstvovanie sistemy obucheniia,* pp. 68–70.
30. *Literaturnaia gazeta,* no. 28, July 13, 1977, p. 11; A. Ia. Andrikson, in *Materialy nauchno-metodicheskoi konferentsii "Problemy sovershenstvovaniia organizatsii uchebnogo protsessa v usloviiakh instituta povysheniia kvalifikatsii"* (Riga: Latvian Interbranch IPK, 1975), p. 8; *Sovershenstvovanie metodov obucheniia na fakul'tetakh po podgotovke organizatorov promyshlennogo proizvodstva i stroitel'stva: Tezisy dokladov vsesoiuznoi nauchno-metodicheskoi konferentsii* (Alma-Ata: Kazakhskii politekhnicheskii institut, 1979), pp. 26–27.
31. *Pravda,* November 23, 1977, p. 3; interview with N. V. Igoshin, dean of the faculty of organizers of the Ordzhonikidze Institute of Management, Moscow, March 18, 1980.

32. E. V. Fedulova, in I. I. Sigov, ed., *Problemy povysheniia kachestva podgotovki i perepodgotovki spetsialistov* (Leningrad: Leningradskii inzhenerno-ekonomicheskii institut, 1975), p. 146.

33. "Otchet," p. 18; "Analiz," p. 52; *Literaturnaia gazeta,* no. 28, July 13, 1977, p. 11. See also V. N. Fedotov, *Problemy i metody podbora kadrov rukovoditelei proizvodstva* (Leningrad: Znanie RSFSR, 1971), p. 26; V. M. Glushkov, G. M. Dobrov, and V. I. Tereshchenko, *Besedy ob upravlenii* (Moscow: Nauka, 1974), p. 210. At the Plekhanov Institute of the National Economy, where I spent three months in the fall of 1979, I encountered several trainees who had been sent to the program to study in place of their superiors. Sheila Puffer, a Canadian business school student who also attended the Plekhanov Institute program, discovered that a number of the trainees were actually enterprise *tol'kachi* sent to train in place of managers. See Sheila M. Puffer, "Inside a Soviet Management Institute," *California Management Review,* 24 (Fall 1981), 90–96.

34. A. G. Kharchenko and A. S. Ushakov, in *Sovershenstvovanie metodov obucheniia,* pp. 25–26; *Pravda,* February 26, 1980, p. 3.

35. Yu. Ya. Liubashevskii, *Sotsial'naia psikhologiia dlia rukovoditelei* (Moscow: IUNKh, 1978), pp. 73–74; observations, Plekhanov Institute of the National Economy, Moscow, September 20, October 26, and December 6, 1979.

36. *Kommunist,* no. 6, April 1973, p. 33; *Novyi mir,* no. 7, 1972, p. 156; Fedoseev, quoted in William J. Conyngham, *The Modernization of Soviet Industrial Management: Socioeconomic Development and the Search for Viability* (Cambridge: Cambridge University Press, 1982), p. 39; V. Moev, *Brazdy upravleniia* (Moscow: Politizdat, 1977), pp. 103–104. Cases in which management scientists were censured and, at times, removed from their posts for excessive reliance on Western approaches did occur during these years. The classic example was that of Vitalii Ozira, a graduate of Harvard Business School and a vocal advocate of managerial professionalism, who was removed from his position as dean of the faculty of organizers at the Plekhanov Institute in the late seventies, apparently because of his outspoken views on management professionalism.

37. At the faculty of organizers of the Plekhanov Institute of the National Economy, political and ideological subjects make up 18 percent of the curriculum. See *Uchebnye plany fakul'teta.*

38. E. E. Vendrov, in Gvishiani, *Materialy k vsesoiuznoi nauchno-tekhnicheskoi konferentsii,* sect. 1, p. 125. See also Popov, *Problemy teorii upravleniia,* p. 79.

39. *Sotsialisticheskii trud,* no. 2, February 1977, p. 72. The first course in management psychology was taught in 1966 at the Ordzhonikidze Engineering-Economics Institute. Not until 1969, however, did a textbook suitable for training executives in the field appear. See E. E. Vendrov, *Psikhologicheskie problemy upravleniia* (Moscow: Ekonomika, 1969).

40. R. E. El'bur, *Vvedenie v psikhologiiu upravleniia: uchebnoe posobie* (Riga: Latvian Interbranch IPK, 1972), p. 4.

41. V. G. Shorin, rector of IUNKh, in his introduction to Liubashevskii, *Sotsial'naia psikhologiia dlia rukovoditelei*, pp. 6–7.

42. Ibid., p. 81.

43. Popov, *Problemy teorii upravleniia*, p. 95.

44. Mailick, *The Making of the Manager*, pp. 76, 78.

45. Popov, *Problemy teorii upravleniia*, p. 95; observations, Plekhanov Institute of the National Economy, Moscow, September 29, 1979.

46. V. G. Shorin, *Stil' raboty rukovoditelia* (Moscow: Znanie, 1972), p. 28; Liubashevskii, *Sotsial'naia psikhologiia dlia rukovoditelei*, p. 53.

47. Observations, Plekhanov Institute of the National Economy, Moscow, September 28, 1979.

48. Shorin, *Stil' raboty*, pp. 28–30; Liubashevskii, *Sotsial'naia psikhologiia dlia rukovoditelei*, p. 82.

49. Shorin, *Stil' raboty*, pp. 29–30; G. V. Viatkin, *Ovladevaia naukoi upravliat'* (Krasnodar: Knizhnoe izdatel'stvo, 1974), p. 60.

50. Liubashevskii, *Sotsial'naia psikhologiia dlia rukovoditelei*, pp. 38–39.

51. Shorin, *Stil' raboty*, pp. 22–23; observations, Plekhanov Institute of the National Economy, Moscow, October 16, 1979. For parallels with Russian political culture, see Hedrick Smith, *The Russians* (New York: Ballantine Books, 1976), pp. 333–336.

52. Shorin, *Stil' raboty*, pp. 22–23; V. G. Afanas'ev, ed., *Trud rukovoditelia: Uchebnoe posobie dlia rukovodiashchikh upravlencheskikh kadrov* (Moscow: Ekonomika, 1977), p. 250; observations, Plekhanov Institute of the National Economy, Moscow, October 16, 1979.

53. Afanas'ev, *Trud rukovoditelia*, p. 250; Shorin, *Stil' raboty*, p. 20; Liubashevskii, *Sotsial'naia psikhologiia dlia rukovoditelei*, pp. 84–85. See also O. V. Kozlova, *Teoriia upravleniia sotsialisticheskim proizvodstvom* (Moscow: Ekonomika, 1979), p. 242.

54. V. A. Protopopov and G. Kh. Popov, *Upravlenie sotsialisticheskim proizvodstvom: Uchebno-metodicheskoe posobie dlia seminarskikh prakticheskikh zaniatii* (Moscow: Moskovskii rabochii, 1974); G. Kh. Popov, *Iskusstvo upravleniia: Konkretnye situatsii* (Moscow: Ekonomika, 1977).

55. Popov, *Iskusstvo upravleniia*, pp. 7, 54.

56. I. V. Prokhorov and L. N. Sumarokov, *Banki upravlencheskikh situatsii i ikh ispolzovanie pri obuchenii* (Moscow: MTsNTI, 1977), p. 7.

57. Mailick, *The Making of the Manager*, p. 46.

58. *Sotsialisticheskii trud*, no. 2, February 1977, p. 139; Popov, *Iskusstvo upravleniia*, p. 207; observations, Plekhanov Institute of the National Economy, Moscow, November 14 and 16, 1979.

59. For more on the development of Soviet business games, see *Pravda*, September 8, 1972, p. 4; *Vestnik MGU: Seriia Ekonomika*, no. 2, 1975, pp. 79–86; *Ekonomika i matematicheskie metody*, no. 3, 1976, pp. 602–604; *EKO*, no. 2, 1975, pp. 149–158; no. 6, 1975, pp. 189–198; no. 3, 1979, pp. 139–148.

60. *EKO*, no. 6, 1978, p. 54; *Sovershenstvovanie metodov obucheniia*, p. 71; *Pervaia konferentsiia tsentrov sovershenstvovaniia rukovodiashchikh kadrov evropeiskikh stran-chlenov soveta ekonomicheskoi vzaimopomo-*

shchi, pt. 2 (Warsaw, 1971), p. 87; O. V. Kozlova, *Delovye igry i ikh rol' v povyshenii kvalifikatsii kadrov* (Moscow: Znanie, 1978), p. 8.

61. Robert C. Meier et al., *Simulation in Business and Economics* (Englewood Cliffs, N.J.: Prentice-Hall, 1969), p. 182.
62. *EKO,* no. 9, 1982, p. 75.
63. Meier et al., *Simulation in Business and Economics,* p. 187.
64. I. M. Syroezhin, *Ocherki teorii proizvodstvennykh organizatsii* (Moscow: Ekonomika, 1970), pp. 227–228. Western game designers have noted from their experience that "an ill-structured and inappropriate game may be worse than not using any game." Meier et al., *Simulation in Business and Economics,* p. 206.
65. *Pravda,* January 10, 1983, p. 2; D. M. Gvishiani and S. V. Emel'ianov, *Metod delovykh igr: Obzor* (Moscow: Mezhdunarodnyi tsentr nauchnoi i tekhnicheskoi informatsii, 1976), pp. 19–20.
66. I. M. Syroezhin, "Igrovye imitatsionnye modeli kak sredstvo obucheniia rukovoitelei i forma vyrabotki kollektivnykh reshenii" (Paper, Leningrad Finance-Economics Institute, Leningrad, 1976), p. 59 (in possession of the author); *Pravda,* January 10, 1983, p. 2.
67. William H. Whyte, *The Organization Man* (New York: Simon and Schuster, 1956), pp. 111–112 (emphasis in the original). See also R. A. Gordon and J. E. Howell, *Higher Education for Business* (New York: Columbia University Press, 1959); F. C. Pierson, *The Education of American Businessmen: A Study of University-College Programs in Business Administration* (New York: McGraw-Hill, 1959).
68. *Literaturnaia gazeta,* no. 51, December 17, 1975, p. 11.
69. *Istoriia SSSR,* no. 4, 1961, p. 64; Granick, *Managerial Comparisons,* p. 192; G. Kh. Popov, *Problemy teorii upravleniia,* 1st ed. (Moscow: Ekonomika, 1970), p. 192; *Literaturnaia gazeta,* no. 51, December 17, 1975, p. 11.
70. *Literaturnaia gazeta,* no. 4, January 28, 1976, p. 11; no. 31, August 4, 1976, p. 10; *Pravda,* April 14, 1982, p. 3. See also *Organizatsiia upravleniia* (Moscow: Ekonomika, 1972), p. 145.
71. G. V. Osipov, ed., *Industry and Labour in the USSR* (London: Tavistock Publications, 1966), p. 90; *Literaturnaia gazeta,* no. 4, January 28, 1976, p. 11.
72. See David Lane, *The End of Inequality? Stratification under State Socialism* (London: Penguin, 1971), p. 112; D. M. Kruk, *Razvitie teorii i praktiki upravleniia proizvodstvom v SSSR* (Moscow: Minvuz SSSR, 1974), p. 143; *Materialy XXIV s'ezda KPSS,* pp. 98–99.
73. *Literaturnaia gazeta,* no. 45, November 5, 1975, p. 11; see also no. 51, December 17, 1975, p. 11; and *Ekonomicheskaia gazeta,* no. 37, September 1972, p. 3; *Tret'ia mezhvuzovskaia konferentsiia,* p. 127; G. A. Iakshin, *Sputnik mastera: Spravochnoe posobie* (Gor'kii: Volgo-Viatskoe izd-vo, 1979), p. 4; *Organizatsiia upravleniia* (1972), p. 145.
74. G. Kh. Popov, *Otsenka rabotnikov upravleniia* (Moscow: Moskovskii rabochii, 1976), p. 31; A. I. Panov, in *Organizatsiia upravleniia* (1972), p. 145.
75. G. Kh. Popov, in Mailick, *The Making of the Manager,* p. 248; Gvishiani

and Kamenitser, *Problemy nauchnoi organizatsii,* p. 698; *Tret'ia mezhvuzovskaia konferentsiia,* p. 99.

76. *EKO,* no. 5, 1977, p. 168; "Otchet," p. 7. Yeliutin had been deputy director of the Stalin Industrial Academy in the 1930s.

77. *Literaturnaia gazeta,* no. 51, December 17, 1975, p. 11; no. 5, February 4, 1976, p. 12; see also no. 28, July 13, 1977, p. 11; and *Pravda,* September 20, 1975, p. 3; *Izvestiia,* July 28, 1976, p. 2; *Sotsialisticheskii trud,* no. 2, February 1977, pp. 72–75; *EKO,* no. 5, 1977, pp. 169–170; *Ekonomicheskaia gazeta,* no. 49, December 1976, p. 10.

78. *Literaturnaia gazeta,* no. 49, December 3, 1976, p. 10; *EKO,* no. 5, 1977, p. 171; no. 2, 1977, p. 101.

79. *Pravda,* September 20, 1975, p. 3; *XXV s'ezd KPSS: Stenograficheskii otchet,* vol. 2 (Moscow: Politizdat, 1976), pp. 77–78; *Sovetskaia Rossiia,* March 13, 1979, p. 2.

80. *Sotsialisticheskaia industriia,* October 27, 1976, p. 2.

81. *Pravda,* September 20, 1977, p. 1; *Vestnik vysshei shkoly,* no. 3, March 1978, p. 68; *Ekonomicheskaia gazeta,* no. 1, January 1978, p. 9; *Izvestiia,* November 22, 1977, p. 2.

82. Interview with N. N. Filimonova, dean of the Moscow Faculty of the IPK of Gossnab, Moscow, March 5, 1980.

83. *Ekonomicheskaia gazeta,* no. 41, October 1978, p. 3. Kirilenko described Brezhnev as the "initiator" of the program. Ibid., no. 26, June 1980, p. 5.

84. "Analiz," pp. 3–5; P. A. Papulov, "Aktual'nye problemy podgotovki kadrov upravleniia" (Paper delivered to the Economics Faculty of MGU, Moscow, January 1980—in possession of the author); I. B. Skorobogatov, *Formirovanie rezerva khoziaistvennykh kadrov* (Moscow: Znanie, 1979); Yu. A. Rozenbaum, *Podgotovka upravlencheskikh kadrov: Organizatsionno-pravovye voprosy* (Moscow: Nauka, 1981).

85. *Literaturnaia gazeta,* no. 29, July 21, 1976, p. 11; no. 5, February 4, 1976, p. 12. See also Skorobogatov, *Formirovanie rezerva,* p. 15; Mailick, *The Making of the Manager,* p. 253; *Sovershenstvovanie metodov obucheniia,* pp. 25–26.

86. *Literaturnaia gazeta,* no. 5, February 4, 1976, p. 12; see also no. 4, January 28, 1976, p. 11; no. 4, January 26, 1977, p. 10; and V. P. Kharlamova, "Sovershenstvovanie sistemy povysheniia kvalifikatsii rukovodiashchikh kadrov i ee vliianie na effektivnost' proizvodstva" (Dissertatsiia na soiskanie uchenoi stepeni kandidata ekonomicheskikh nauk, Ordzhonikidze Institute of Management, Moscow, 1978), vol. 2, app. 4, p. 8.

87. *Literaturnaia gazeta,* no. 5, February 4, 1976, p. 12.

88. Ibid. See also *Tret'ia mezhvuzovskaia konferentsiia,* pp. 125–126.

89. *Literaturnaia gazeta,* no. 29, July 21, 1976, p. 11; no. 45, November 5, 1975, p. 11.

90. Popov, *Problemy teorii upravleniia,* p. 196. See also *Literaturnaia gazeta,* no. 5, February 4, 1976, p. 12; *Tret'ia mezhvuzovskaia konferentsiia,* pp. 101–103.

91. *Ekonomicheskaia gazeta,* no. 43, October 1973, p. 22; *Literaturnaia gazeta,* July 13, 1977, p. 11. See also F. F. Aunapu, *Metody podbora i*

338 · Notes to Pages 217–221

podgotovki rukovoditelei proizvodstva (Moscow: Ekonomika, 1971), p. 45; *Tret'ia mezhvuzovskaia konferentsiia,* p. 101.

92. *Pravda,* February 21, 1977, p. 1; May 15, 1972, p. 2; *Sotsialisticheskii trud,* no. 2, February 1977, p. 73; Conyngham, *Modernization of Soviet Industrial Management,* p. 207; *Organizatsiia upravleniia* (1972), p. 147.

93. Peter M. Blau and Richard A. Schoenherr, *The Structure of Organizations* (New York: Basic Books, 1971), p. 120.

94. Kh. Kala, in *Tret'ia mezhvuzovskaia konferentsiia,* p. 101; Aunapu, *Metody podbora i podgotovki,* pp. 36, 25.

95. Popov, *Otsenka rabotnikov upravleniia,* p. 146; *Literaturnaia gazeta,* no. 42, October 20, 1976, p. 10. See also V. Yu. Ozira, *Soderzhanie i metody podgotovki kadrov upravleniia* (Moscow: Ekonomika, 1977), pp. 163–164; Aunapu, *Metody podbora i podgotovki,* pp. 36–37; I. S. Mangutov and L. I. Umanskii, *Organizator i organizatorskaia deiatel'nost'* (Leningrad: Izd-vo LGU, 1975), p. 192; *Literaturnaia gazeta,* no. 20, May 19, 1976, p. 13; A. A. Godunov and P. S. Yemshin, *Metodika otsenki delovykh i moral'no-politicheskikh kachestv rukovoditelei i spetsialistov sotsialisticheskogo proizvodstva* (Leningrad: Izd-vo LGU, 1971); L. I. Men'shikov, *Delovaia otsenka rabotnikov v sfere upravleniia* (Moscow: Ekonomika, 1974); L. I. Men'shikov, *Otsenka delovykh kachestv upravlencheskogo personala* (Moscow: Znanie, 1975); Vendrov, *Psikhologicheskie problemy upravleniia,* p. 130; G. A. Brianskii, *Podbor, rasstanovka i podgotovka rukovodiashchikh kadrov* (Moscow: Minvuz SSSR, 1974), p. 22; Gvishiani and Kamenitser, *Problemy nauchnoi organizatsii,* p. 400. There has been some Soviet interest in the standardized testing of the Educational Testing Service in Princeton, New Jersey.

96. Popov, *Otsenka rabotnikov upravleniia,* p. 172.

97. *Literaturnaia gazeta,* no. 8, February 23, 1977, p. 10 (emphasis in the original). See also *Izvestiia,* June 17, 1984, p. 2.

98. Brianskii, *Podbor, rasstanovka i podgotovka,* p. 22; V. G. Afanas'ev, *Upravlenie sotsialisticheskim proizvodstvom: Voprosy teorii i praktiki,* 2nd ed. (Moscow: Ekonomika, 1975), pp. 145–146. See also Popov, *Otsenka rabotnikov upravleniia,* p. 144. Not until the Gorbachev era, when management professionalizers gained renewed access to the halls of power, did efforts to professionalize management from above receive serious attention from the leadership. Certification for managerial employees was introduced into the July 1987 economic reforms. The results of certification, it was stipulated, should be used in determining promotions and demotions, salary increases, and bonuses. In addition, new laws were being prepared to regulate managerial careers, and efforts were made to upgrade managerial training. According to the July 1987 Law on Socialist Enterprise, "a high degree of professionalism and knowledge of the basics of management science and economic thought . . . are necessary for the contemporary executive." *Pravda,* July 1, 1987, p. 2.

7. The Irrational Rationalizers

1. *Sovetskaia Rossiia,* December 6, 1981, p. 2; *Ekonomicheskaia gazeta,* no. 37, September 28, 1965, p. 1.

2. *EKO,* no. 10, 1984, p. 170. Kruk cited a figure of 200 institutes working on management issues in 1974. D. M. Kruk, *Razvitie teorii i praktiki upravleniia proizvodstvom v SSSR* (Moscow: Minvuz SSSR, 1974), p. 194.

3. "Reshenie mezhvedomstvennogo soveta po povysheniiu kvalifikatsii rukovodiashchikh rabotnikov i spetsialistov narodnogo khoziaistva ot 12 Fev. 1980 g. 'O proekte plana komplektovaniia fakul'tetov po podgotovke organizatorov promyshlennogo proizvodstva i stroitel'stva i fakul'teta planirovaniia promyshlennogo proizvodstva na 1980–85 gg.' " (Government document, USSR Ministry of Higher and Specialized Secondary Education, Moscow—in possession of the author).

4. See Robert F. Miller, "The Scientific-Technical Revolution and the Soviet Administrative Debate," in Paul Cocks et al., eds., *The Dynamics of Soviet Politics* (Cambridge, Mass.: Harvard University Press, 1976), p. 152; Erik P. Hoffman, "Information Processing in the Party: Recent Theory and Experience," in Karl W. Ryavec, ed., *Soviet Society and the Communist Party* (Amherst: University of Massachusetts Press, 1978), pp. 77–83.

5. John B. Miner, *Studies in Management Education* (New York: Springer Publishing, 1965), p. 37; H. C. de Bettignies, in Bernard Taylor and Gordon Lippett, eds., *Management Development and Training Handbook* (New York: McGraw-Hill, 1975), p. 5. See also William H. Form and Arnold L. Form, "Unanticipated Results of a Foreman Training Program," *Personnel Journal,* 32 (November 1953), 207–212; A. J. M. Sykes, "The Effect of a Supervisory Training Course in Changing Supervisors' Perceptions and Expectations of the Role of Management," *Human Relations,* 15 (August 1962), 227–243; Reed M. Powell and John F. Stinson, "The Worth of Laboratory Training," *Business Horizons,* 14 (August 1971), 87–95.

6. Sidney Mailick, in Sidney Mailick, ed., *The Making of the Manager: A World View* (Garden City, N.Y.: Anchor Press, 1974), p. 16.

7. See D. M. Gvishiani and S. E. Kamenitser, eds., *Problemy nauchnoi organizatsii upravleniia sotsialisticheskoi promyshlennost'iu (po materialam Vtoroi Vsesoiuznoi nauchno-tekhnicheskoi konferentsii)* (Moscow: Ekonomika, 1974), p. 437; I. I. Sigov, ed., *Voprosy podgotovki i povysheniia kvalifikatsii rukoditelei i spetsialistov narodnogo khoziaistva: Mezhvuzovskii sbornik* (Leningrad: Minvuz RSFSR, 1977), p. 42; *Materialy nauchno-metodicheskoi konferentsii "Problemy sovershenstvovaniia organizatsii uchebnogo protsessa v usloviiakh instituta povysheniia kvalifikatsii"* (Riga: Latviiskii mezhotraslevoi IPK, 1975), pp. 10, 42.

8. Kh. Kala, *Sistema professional'no-dolzhnostnoi podgotovki khoziaistvennykh rukovoditelei v legkoi promyshlennosti Estonskoi SSR* (Tallin: Uchebnyi kombinat legkoi promyshlennosti Estonskoi SSR, 1973), p. 1; M. K. Poltev, ed., *Sovershenstvovanie sistemy obucheniia rukovodiashchikh kadrov narodnogo khoziaistva* (Moscow: Izd-vo MGU, 1979), p. 100; *EKO,* no. 6, 1974, p. 24.

9. I. V. Paramonov, *Uchit'sia upravliat': Mysl' i opyt starogo khoziaistvennika* (Moscow: Ekonomika, 1970), p. 166.

10. *EKO,* no. 2, 1977, p. 99.

11. *Novyi mir,* no. 7, 1972, p. 152.

12. Observations, Plekhanov Institute of the National Economy, Moscow, October 11, 1979; Sheila M. Puffer, "Inside a Soviet Management Institute," *California Management Review,* 24 (Fall 1981), 95–96.

13. V. Yu. Ozira, *Soderzhanie i metody podgotovki kadrov upravleniia* (Moscow: Ekonomika, 1977), p. 105; V. M. Glushkov, G. D. Dobrov, V. I. Tereshchenko, *Besedy ob upravlenii* (Moscow: Nauka, 1974), p. 212; A. M. Smolkin, *Aktivnye metody obucheniia pri ekonomicheskoi podgotovke rukovoditelei* (Moscow: Znanie, 1976), p. 10.

14. V. I. Tereshchenko, in *Besedy ob upravlenii,* p. 212.

15. At the faculty of organizers of the Ordzhonikidze Institute, I was told that the overwhelming majority of trainees received the grade of "excellent" on their course projects, that in the history of the faculty there had never been a poor course project written by a trainee, and that only 3 percent of trainees received as low a grade as "satisfactory." At one IPK I was told that it was practically impossible to give a trainee a grade of "D" for his work. "How would he explain such a thing to his boss and to his family?"

16. Jan Kreiken, in Taylor and Lippett, *Management Development and Training Handbook,* p. 16.

17. R. L. Kahn et al., "The Management of Organizational Stress," in John M. Thomas and Warren G. Bennis, eds., *The Management of Change and Conflict* (Harmondsworth, Eng.: Penguin, 1972), p. 445.

18. *EKO,* no. 6, 1978, p. 12.

19. Observations, Plekhanov Institute of the National Economy, Moscow, October 26 and November 16, 1979.

20. Observations, Plekhanov Institute of the National Economy, Moscow, October 11 and 16, 1979. Soviet offices are notorious for their lack of secretarial and support staff. One of the more flagrant examples of the misunderstanding of organizational processes by successive Soviet leaderships has been their failure to provide for the stable recruitment and training of secretaries.

21. Observations, Plekhanov Institute of the National Economy, Moscow, October 9, 1979; *Sotsialisticheskaia industriia,* March 1, 1983, p. 2; *Pravda,* March 17, 1983, p. 2.

22. V. Yu. Ozira, "Shchekinskii eksperiment: Khoziaistvennaia situatsiia" (Case-study exercise used at the Academy of the National Economy and the Plekhanov Institute of the National Economy, 1979), pp. 26, 33 (in possession of the author). On the Shchekino experiment, see Peter Rutland, "The Shchekino Method and the Struggle to Raise Labour Productivity in Soviet Industry," *Soviet Studies,* 36 (July 1984), 345–365; Henry Norr, "Shchekino: Another Look," *Soviet Studies,* 38 (April 1986), 141–169.

23. Observations, Plekhanov Institute of the National Economy, Moscow, November 14 and 16, 1979.

24. *Sovetskaia Rossiia,* December 6, 1981, p. 2; *Pravda,* March 17, 1983, p. 2; Anatolii Zlobin, *General'nyi direktor: Dokumental'naia povest' s tremia interv'iu* (Moscow: Sovetskaia Rossiia, 1978), p. 161.

25. Joseph S. Berliner, *The Innovation Decision in Soviet Industry* (Cambridge, Mass.: MIT Press, 1976), p. 520.

26. *Ekonomicheskaia gazeta,* no. 32, August 1968, p. 41; S. S. Novozhilov, *NOT—velenie zhizni* (Moscow: Znanie, 1971), pp. 141, 180–183; *Pravda,* June 21, 1973, p. 3.
27. *NOT na promyshlennom predpriiatii* (Sverdlovsk: Sredne-Ural'skoe Knizhnoe Izdatel'stvo, 1970), pp. 198–203; *Nauchnaia organizatsiia proizvodstva, truda i upravleniia* (Moscow: Moskovskii rabochii, 1974), pp. 166–169.
28. The highest payoffs came from measures aimed at improving norm-determination and labor payment. In 1969 only 8.4 percent of the NOT measures enacted fell into this category. Novozhilov, *NOT—velenie zhizni,* pp. 180–183; *Nauchnaia organizatsiia proizvodstva, truda i upravleniia,* pp. 23–24, 165, 423.
29. *Nauchnaia organizatsiia truda v promyshlennosti Ukrainskoi SSR* (Donetsk: Donbass, 1969), p. 99; Novozhilov, *NOT—velenie zhizni,* p. 149; *Nauchnaia organizatsiia proizvodstva, truda i upravleniia,* p. 423; *Pravda,* June 21, 1973, p. 3.
30. *Nauchnaia organizatsiia truda v promyshlennosti Ukrainskoi SSR,* p. 145; *Pravda,* April 17, 1973, p. 2. See also *Nauchnaia organizatsiia i normirovanie truda na predpriiatiiakh mestnoi promyshlennosti* (Odessa: Ukrniimestprom, 1974), p. 23; *Nauchnaia organizatsiia proizvodstva, truda i upravleniia,* pp. 146–147.
31. William J. Conyngham, *The Modernization of Soviet Industrial Management* (Cambridge: Cambridge University Press, 1982), p. 156.
32. *Nauchnaia organizatsiia proizvodstva, truda i upravleniia,* pp. 424, 434; *Pravda,* June 23, 1983, p. 2; March 9, 1984, p. 2.
33. *Sovetskaia Rossiia,* February 6, 1985, p. 3; *Voprosy ekonomiki,* no. 2, February 1979, pp. 125–126.
34. *EKO,* no. 12, 1984, p. 99.
35. *EKO,* no. 12, 1984, p. 100; no. 11, 1984, p. 62. See also *Pravda,* August 19, 1982, p. 2.
36. *Pravda,* September 20, 1975, p. 3; November 23, 1977, p. 3.
37. *EKO,* no. 11, 1984, p. 5; no. 7, July 1980, p. 49; no. 12, 1984, p. 116; no. 7, July 1980, p. 55; *Sovetskaia Rossiia,* February 6, 1985, p. 3.
38. *Literaturnaia gazeta,* December 24, 1966, p. 2; *EKO,* no. 6, 1978, pp. 4–5; *Pravda,* June 17, 1985, p. 2.
39. *EKO,* no. 12, 1984, p. 101; *Nauchnaia organizatsiia truda v promyshlennosti Ukrainskoi SSR,* pp. 112–113.
40. *EKO,* no. 11, 1984, p. 9; *Pravda,* December 5, 1982, p. 2.
41. *Pravda,* December 5, 1982, p. 2.
42. *Sovetskaia Rossiia,* February 6, 1985, p. 3; *Literaturnaia gazeta,* no. 45, November 10, 1982, p. 12.
43. *Pravda,* March 26, 1978, p. 2.
44. Zlobin, *General'nyi direktor,* pp. 97–98, 163.
45. *Sovetskaia Rossiia,* February 6, 1985, p. 3.
46. Gertrude E. Schroeder, "The Soviet Economy on a Treadmill of Reforms," in Joint Economic Committee of the U.S. Congress, *Soviet Economy in a Time of Change,* vol. 1 (Washington, D.C.: U.S. Government Printing Office, 1979), pp. 312–340.
47. *Pravda,* February 26, 1986, p. 2.

48. *Sovetskaia Rossiia,* December 6, 1981, p. 2.
49. *Resheniia partii i pravitel'stva po khoziaistvennym voprosam,* vol. 9 (Moscow: Politizdat, 1974), p. 239.
50. *Pravda,* April 29, 1985, p. 2; see also June 7, 1982, p. 2; and Conyngham, *Modernization of Soviet Industrial Management,* p. 158.
51. *Resheniia partii i pravitel'stva,* 7:484–487; 8:235–240.
52. *EKO,* no. 5, 1977, p. 132. See also *Pravda,* May 3, 1977, p. 2; *Ekonomicheskaia gazeta,* no. 17, April 1982, p. 1; *Resheniia partii i pravitel'stva,* 11:14–17.
53. Harold Seidman, *Politics, Position, and Power: The Dynamics of Federal Organization,* 2nd ed. (New York: Oxford University Press, 1976), p. 190.
54. On the origins of the reforms, see *Resheniia partii i pravitel'stva,* 8:126–133; 9:415–459; 11:65–113.
55. *Izvestiia,* May 13, 1984, p. 2; Conyngham, *Modernization of Soviet Industrial Management,* p. 226.
56. *Pravda,* May 8, 1981, p. 1.
57. *Izvestiia,* April 20, 1985, p. 1; *Pravda,* March 31, 1984, p. 2. See also *Pravda,* October 17, 1974, p. 2; March 29, 1984, p. 2; March 31, 1984, p. 2; *Izvestiia,* January 18, 1972, p. 2; January 14, 1982, p. 3; *Ekonomicheskaia gazeta,* no. 22, May 1976, p. 8.
58. Timothy Dunmore, "Local Party Organs in Industrial Administration: The Case of the Ob'edinenie Reform," *Soviet Studies,* 32 (April 1980), 195–217; Alice C. Gorlin, "Industrial Reorganization: The Associations," in Joint Economic Committee of the U.S. Congress, *Soviet Economy in a New Perspective* (Washington, D.C.: U.S. Government Printing Office, 1976), pp. 162–188.
59. *Pravda,* April 17, 1982, p. 2; *Izvestiia,* April 20, 1985, p. 1. See also *Pravda,* March 14, 1983, p. 2; May 11, 1983, p. 2; *Izvestiia,* August 21, 1981, p. 2.
60. *EKO,* no. 10, 1982, pp. 193–205.
61. See Conyngham, *Modernization of Soviet Industrial Management,* pp. 96–97; Paul Cocks, "The Policy Process and Bureaucratic Politics," in Cocks, ed., *Dynamics of Soviet Politics,* pp. 156–178; Paul Cocks, "Rethinking the Organizational Weapon: The Soviet System in a Systems Age," *World Politics,* 22 (January 1980), 228–257.
62. N. P. Fedorenko, *Nekotorye voprosy teorii i praktiki planirovaniia i upravleniia* (Moscow: Nauka, 1979), pp. 68–70; *Ekonomicheskaia gazeta,* no. 9, February 1981, p. 22.
63. *Problemy obshchei teorii sotsialisticheskogo gosudarstvennogo upravleniia* (Moscow: Nauka, 1981), p. 252.
64. *Pravda,* July 31, 1976, p. 2; see also May 30, 1981, p. 2; March 16, 1982, p. 2; May 5, 1983, p. 2.
65. *Pravda,* May 30, 1981, p. 2; March 16, 1982, p. 2; David S. Kamerling, "The Role of Territorial Production Complexes in Soviet Economic Policy," in Joint Economic Committee of the U.S. Congress, *Soviet Economy in the 1980's: Problems and Prospects,* pt. 1 (Washington, D.C.: U.S. Government Printing Office, 1982), pp. 242–266.

66. *EKO*, no. 1, 1982, p. 79.

67. Martin Cave, *Computers and Economic Planning: The Soviet Experience* (Cambridge: Cambridge University Press, 1980), p. 21.

68. Yu. P. Lapshin, *Razvitie avtomatizirovannykh sistem upravleniia v pro- myshlennosti* (Moscow: Ekonomika, 1977), pp. 14, 17, 95–96, 110; Cave, *Computers and Economic Planning*, pp. 21, 173; Martin Cave, "Com- puters in the Soviet Economy, 1963–83" (Paper delivered at conference on Computers in the Soviet Union, sponsored by MIT and the Harvard University Russian Research Center, Cambridge, Mass., November 1983), p. 8.

69. G. Maksimovich, *Besedy s Akademikom V. Glushkovym* (Moscow: Molodaia gvardiia, 1976), p. 66. See also V. Moev, *Brazdy upravleniia* (Moscow: Politizdat, 1977), pp. 23–24.

70. *Literaturnaia gazeta*, January 19, 1977, p. 11.

71. *Pravda*, March 2, 1977, p. 2; January 5, 1971, p. 2; October 9, 1972, p. 2. See also N. C. Davis and S. E. Goodman, "The Soviet Bloc's Unified System of Computers," *Computing Surveys*, 10 (June 1978), pp. 95–100.

72. *Pravda*, August 21, 1972, p. 2; see also October 9, 1972, p. 2; July 25, 1977, p. 2; May 12, 1980, p. 3; and *Izvestiia*, June 14, 1973, p. 3; *Nauch- naia organizatsiia proizvodstva, truda i upravleniia*, pp. 67–68.

73. *Pravda*, August 28, 1985, p. 1. See also *Ekonomicheskaia gazeta*, no. 31, July 1978, p. 15; no. 22, May 1978, p. 7; *Pravda*, May 12, 1980, p. 3.

74. *Pravda*, March 1, 1965, p. 2; February 10, 1973, p. 3.

75. *EKO*, no. 2, 1979, p. 50.

76. Moev, *Brazdy upravleniia*, p. 69; Lapshin, *Razvitie avtomatizirovannykh sistem*, pp. 31–32.

77. Maksimovich, *Besedy s Akademikom V. Glushkovym*, pp. 63, 79; *EKO*, no. 2, 1979, p. 42. See also Conyngham, *Modernization of Soviet Indus- trial Management*, p. 130.

78. *EKO*, no. 2, 1979, p. 52; *Literaturnaia gazeta*, no. 5, January 29, 1975, p. 10.

79. *Pravda*, April 18, 1977, p. 2.

80. *Pravda*, May 23, 1970, p. 2; see also September 8, 1971, p. 2; and *Izves- tiia*, February 19, 1971, p. 3.

81. *Trud*, May 12, 1983, p. 2.

82. Ibid. See also *Pravda*, July 2, 1983, p. 3; September 24, 1971, p. 3; Maksimovich, *Besedy s Akademikom V. Glushkovym*, p. 74; *EKO*, no. 2, 1979, pp. 33–48.

83. *EKO*, no. 6, 1974, pp. 87–96; *Pravda*, May 16, 1984, p. 1; May 16, 1984, p. 1; November 27, 1982, p. 2; Cave, "Computers in the Soviet Econ- omy, 1963–83," p. 9.

84. *Pravda*, May 12, 1980, p. 3.

85. *EKO*, no. 6, 1974, pp. 87–96.

86. Moev, *Brazdy upravleniia*, pp. 53–54.

87. *Planovoe khoziaistvo*, no. 7, 1973, pp. 55–58; no. 1, 1980, pp. 51–61.

88. Ibid., no. 1, 1980, p. 55. See also Cave, *Computers and Economic Plan- ning*, pp. 545–559.

89. Lapshin, *Razvitie avtomatizirovannykh sistem*, pp. 114, 151; Conyng-

ham, *Modernization of Soviet Industrial Management,* p. 123; Cave, *Computers and Economic Planning,* pp. 151, 163, 173–174.

90. *Literaturnaia gazeta,* no. 5, January 29, 1975, p. 10. See also Cave, "Computers in the Soviet Economy, 1963–83," p. 9.
91. *Pravda,* August 23, 1982, p. 2; *Planovoe khoziaistvo,* no. 4, 1983, p. 101.

8. Discipline and Reform

1. *Pravda,* February 26, 1986, p. 2.
2. Robert Leggett, "Soviet Investment Policy in the 11th Five-Year Plan," in Joint Economic Committee of the U.S. Congress, *Soviet Economy in the 1980s: Problems and Prospects,* pt. 1 (Washington, D.C.: U.S. Government Printing Office, 1983), pp. 139–140.
3. *Pravda,* May 20, 1987, p. 1.
4. *Samyi khudshii vnutrennyi vrag* (Moscow: Mysl', 1987); *Pravda,* January 28, 1987, p. 2; August 2, 1986, p. 1.
5. Alvin W. Gouldner, *Patterns of Industrial Bureaucracy* (New York: Free Press, 1954), p. 55.
6. L. I. Brezhnev, *Leninskim kursom,* vol. 7 (Moscow: Politizdat, 1979), pp. 536, 531.
7. Ibid., 8:210, 198, 211, 209, 207.
8. *Resheniia partii i pravitel'stva po khoziaistvennym voprosam,* vol. 13 (Moscow: Politizdat, 1981), pp. 197–224, 237–246.
9. Brezhnev, *Leninskim kursom,* 8:691 and 9:302–315.
10. In October 1980 the Minister of Tractor and Agricultural Machine-Building, I. F. Sinitsyn, was retired. Sinitsyn's ties with Kosygin, however, make it likely that his removal was more closely connected to the retirement of his patron than to the performance of his duties.
11. *EKO,* no. 9, September 1981, pp. 20–21. See also *Pravda,* August 5, 1981, p. 3; *Sotsialisticheskaia industriia,* October 4, 1981, p. 2.
12. *Pravda,* April 23, 1982, p. 1; April 27, 1982, p. 3; March 26, 1982, p. 1. Rekunkov revealed that a deputy minister of the fish industry had been executed for taking bribes—the first execution of a high official in two decades. See also *Pravda,* July 19, 1982, p. 2; August 7, 1982, p. 3; August 28, 1982, p. 3.
13. *Pravda,* November 23, 1982, pp. 1–2; December 28, 1983, p. 3.
14. *Vechernaia Moskva,* December 25, 1982, p. 1; *Komsomol'skaia pravda,* January 8, 1983, p. 2.
15. *Pravda,* November 23, 1982, pp. 1–2; see also December 28, 1982, p. 2; January 4, 1983, p. 2.
16. Ibid., February 28, 1986, p. 4.
17. Ibid., June 15, 1983, p. 1; June 16, 1983, p. 3.
18. Ibid., February 24, 1984, p. 1.
19. *Izvestiia,* August 22, 1985, pp. 1–2; *Voprosy ekonomiki,* no. 7, July 1987, p. 49. See also *Izvestiia,* May 13, 1984, p. 2; *Trud,* May 12, 1983, p. 2.
20. *Pravda,* April 29, 1985, p. 2. See also *Kommunist,* no. 3, February 1983, pp. 9–23; *Izvestiia,* April 24, 1985, p. 1.
21. Such was the case with the Minister of Ferrous Metallurgy, I. P.

Kazanets; the Minister for the Production of Chemical Fertilizers, A. G. Petrishchev; and the Minister of Industrial Production, A. M. Tokarev.

22. *Pravda,* April 11, 1984, pp. 1–2.

23. Gouldner, *Patterns of Industrial Bureaucracy;* Peter M. Blau, *The Dynamics of Bureaucracy* (Chicago: University of Chicago Press, 1963); James Q. Wilson, *Varieties of Police Behavior* (Cambridge, Mass.: Harvard University Press, 1968); Anthony Downs, *Inside Bureaucracy* (Boston: Little, Brown, 1967).

24. *Sotsiologicheskie issledovaniia,* no. 2, April-June 1983, pp. 121–126.

25. *Pravda,* January 9, 1983, p. 3.

26. Gouldner, *Patterns of Industrial Bureaucracy,* pp. 207–214; Charles A. O'Reilly III and Barton A. Weitz, "Managing Marginal Employees: The Use of Warnings and Dismissals," *Administrative Science Quarterly,* 25 (September 1980), 467–482.

27. *New York Times,* February 7, 1983, sect. A, p. 9; *Wall Street Journal,* July 22, 1983, pp. 1, 8.

28. *Pravda,* August 10, 1983, p. 1; see also August 7, 1983, p. 1.

29. Ibid., February 14, 1984, p. 2.

30. *Izvestiia,* April 24, 1985, p. 2; *Pravda,* April 10, 1985, p. 6. See also *Izvestiia,* June 27, 1985, p. 3; July 16, 1985, p. 3. For a case in which managers were prosecuted for poor-quality production, see *Sovetskaia Rossiia,* October 25, 1986, p. 2.

31. *Pravda,* February 26, 1986, p. 5.

32. Ibid., June 8, 1986, p. 3; June 26, 1987, p. 2.

33. One study conducted in a housing-construction combine showed that only 3.5 percent of the loss in work time over a period of four months was attributable to violations of labor discipline, while another study of the metalworking and machine-building industries indicated that absenteeism accounted for less than 2 percent of lost work time. Andreas Tenson, "Are Soviet Workers to Blame for Violations of Labor Discipline?" *Radio Free Europe–Radio Liberty Research Reports,* August 3, 1983, pp. 1–4; Philip Hanson, "Labor Discipline and Production Stoppages in Soviet Industry," *Radio Free Europe–Radio Liberty Research Reports,* May 18, 1983, pp. 1–4.

34. *Izvestiia,* February 21, 1984, p. 1.

35. *Pravda,* November 23, 1982, p. 1; *Kommunist,* no. 3, February 1983, p. 13.

36. *Kommunist,* no. 18, December 1982, pp. 48–59; *Voprosy ekonomiki,* no. 11, 1983, pp. 3–12; *EKO,* no. 11, 1985, pp. 3–31.

37. *Pravda,* November 23, 1982, pp. 1–2.

38. *Izvestiia,* August 18, 1983, p. 3.

39. *Pravda,* March 31, 1983, p. 2.

40. Ibid., July 1, 1983, pp. 2–3.

41. See "The Novosibirsk Report," *Survey,* 31 (November-December 1983), 25–42; *Kommunist,* no. 8, May 1983, pp. 94–99.

42. *Izvestiia,* August 18, 1983, p. 3; *Pravda,* February 14, 1984, p. 2; April 11, 1984, p. 1.

43. *Pravda,* November 23, 1983, p. 2; May 3, 1984, p. 2; June 20, 1984, p. 1;

June 26, 1984, p. 2; *Izvestiia,* March 9, 1984, p. 2; July 26, 1984, p. 2; July 7, 1984, p. 1.
44. *Izvestiia,* April 24, 1985, p. 1.
45. *Pravda,* June 12, 1985, pp. 1–2; June 26, 1987, p. 3.
46. Ibid., June 29, 1985, p. 2.
47. Ibid., February 27, 1986, p. 5.
48. Ibid., February 26, 1986, p. 5; September 20, 1986, p. 1; June 13, 1987, pp. 3, 1; Gorbachev, quoted in Elizabeth Teague, "Gorbachev Answers His Critics," *Radio Free Europe–Radio Liberty Reseach Reports,* July 15, 1987, p. 5.
49. *Pravda,* June 27, 1987, p. 2; see also July 1, 1987, pp. 1–4.
50. Ibid., June 17, 1986, p. 1; October 1, 1986, p. 1.
51. Ibid., December 2, 1986, p. 3.
52. Ibid., August 2, 1986, p. 1.
53. Ibid.; Gorbachev, quoted in Teague, "Gorbachev Answers His Critics," p. 3.
54. *Pravda,* June 13, 1987, p. 2.

Conclusion

1. Jerry F. Hough, *The Soviet Prefects: The Local Party Organs in Industrial Decision-Making* (Cambridge, Mass.: Harvard University Press, 1969), p. 292.
2. Peter M. Blau, *The Dynamics of Bureaucracy* (Chicago: University of Chicago Press, 1963), p. 250.
3. Anthony Downs, *Inside Bureaucracy* (Boston: Little, Brown, 1967); Harold Seidman, *Politics, Position, and Power: The Dynamics of Federal Organization* (New York: Oxford University Press, 1976); Francis E. Rourke, *Bureaucracy, Politics, and Public Policy* (Boston: Little, Brown, 1976); Hugh Heclo, *A Government of Strangers: Executive Politics in Washington* (Washington, D.C.: Brookings Institution, 1977).
4. James Q. Wilson, "The Bureaucracy Problem," *The Public Interest,* no. 6 (Winter 1967), p. 6.
5. Seweryn Bialer, *The Soviet Paradox: External Expansion, Internal Decline* (New York: Alfred A. Knopf, 1986), pp. 142–143.
6. *Pravda,* February 27, 1986, p. 2.
7. H. Gordon Skilling, "Group Conflict in Soviet Politics: Some Conclusions," in H. Gordon Skilling and Franklyn Griffiths, eds., *Interest Groups in Soviet Politics* (Princeton, N.J.: Princeton University Press, 1971), p. 403.
8. Richard Lowenthal, "The Ruling Party in a Mature Society," in Mark G. Field, ed., *Social Consequences of Modernization in Communist Societies* (Baltimore: Johns Hopkins University Press, 1976), p. 111.
9. Ferenc Fehér, Agnes Heller, and György Markus, *Dictatorship over Needs* (New York: St. Martin's Press, 1983), p. 63.
10. Maria Hirszowicz, *Coercion and Control in Communist Society: The Visible Hand in a Command Economy* (New York: St. Martin's Press, 1986), p. 30. For analyses of cycling behavior in China, see John Wilson

Lewis, "Leadership and Power in China," in John Wilson Lewis, ed., *Party Leadership and Revolutionary Power in China* (Cambridge: Cambridge University Press, 1970), p. 19; G. William Skinner and Edwin A. Winckler, "Compliance Succession in Rural Communist China: A Cyclical Theory," in Amitai Etzioni, ed., *Complex Organizations: A Sociological Reader,* 2nd ed. (New York: Holt, Rinehart and Winston, 1969), pp. 410–438.

11. Ota Šik, *The Communist Power System* (New York: Praeger, 1981), p. 82.

12. Marshall W. Meyer, *Change in Public Bureaucracies* (Cambridge: Cambridge University Press, 1979), p. 200.

13. *Radio Free Europe Research Report: Czechoslovak Press Survey,* June 9, 1967, p. 1.

14. David Granick, *Enterprise Guidance in Eastern Europe: A Comparison of Four Socialist Economies* (Princeton, N.J.: Princeton University Press, 1975), p. 456.

15. *Revista economică,* no. 28, 1974, p. 11; no. 1, 1975, p. 14 (translation by Margaret Hiebert Beissinger).

16. Leslie Holmes, *The Policy Process in Communist States: Politics and Industrial Administration* (Beverly Hills: Sage Publications, 1981), pp. 199–256.

17. Lenin, *Sochineniia,* vol. 44 (Moscow: Politizdat, 1970), p. 336.

18. Hans Peter Graf, "Reform of Enterprise Management: A Substitute for the Reform of the Economic Mechanism? The Case of the German Democratic Republic with Some Comparisons" (Paper delivered at the Second World Congress on Soviet and East European Studies, Garmisch-Partenkirchen, 1980).

19. Alfred D. Chandler, Jr., *The Visible Hand: The Managerial Revolution in American Business* (Cambridge, Mass.: Harvard University Press, 1977).

20. Włodzimierz Brus, *Socialist Ownership and Political Systems* (London: Routledge and Kegan Paul, 1975), p. 201.

21. Alexander Matejko, *Social Change and Stratification in Eastern Europe: An Interpretive Analysis of Poland and Her Neighbors* (New York: Praeger, 1974), p. 118.

22. Csaba Makó, "Effects of Quasi-Bureaucratic Control—Lack of Legitimacy of Initiative-Workers' Behavior in the Work Process" (Paper, Institute for Sociological Research of the Hungarian Academy of Sciences, Budapest, January 1983), p. 29 (in possession of the author). On much the same theme in Czechoslovakia and East Germany, see Ota Šik, *Czechoslovakia: The Bureaucratic Economy* (White Plains, N.Y.: International Arts and Sciences Press, 1972), p. 104; Graf, "Reform of Enterprise Management."

23. Eugen Loebl, *My Mind on Trial* (New York: Harcourt Brace Jovanovich, 1976), pp. 62, 144.

24. The accusations by Chinese workers during the initial phases of the Cultural Revolution that the piece-rate system fostered "tensions between young workers and veteran workers and maintenance workers" bear a striking resemblance to accusations against chronometric norm-

determination in the Soviet Union in the 1920s and 1930s. In 1966 and 1967 piece-rates were abolished in Chinese industry. See E. L. Wheelwright and Bruce McFarlane, *The Chinese Road to Socialism* (New York: Monthly Review Press, 1970), pp. 69–73; Stephen Andors, *China's Industrial Revolution: Politics, Planning, and Management, 1949 to the Present* (New York: Pantheon Books, 1977), pp. 125, 172–173, 218; Richard Lowenthal, "Development vs. Utopia in Communist Policy," in Chalmers Johnson, ed., *Change in Communist Systems* (Stanford, Calif.: Stanford University Press, 1970), pp. 33–116; David Lane, *The Socialist Industrial State: Towards a Political Sociology of State Socialism* (Boulder, Colo.: Westview Press, 1976), pp. 157–160; Peter Schran, "Economic Management," in John M. H. Lindbeck, ed., *China: Management of a Revolutionary Society* (Seattle: University of Washington Press, 1971), pp. 193–220. For accusations that Taylorism generated social tensions and disciplinary problems in Hungarian and Cuban industry, see Csaba Makó and Agnes Simonyi, "Can Taylorism Be Applied in Hungary?" (Paper, Institute for Sociological Research of the Hungarian Academy of Sciences, Budapest, 1985—in possession of the author); Carlos Franqui, *Family Portrait with Fidel* (New York: Vintage, 1984), p. 113.

25. János Kornai, *Overcentralization in Economic Administration: A Critical Analysis Based on Experience in Hungarian Light Industry* (London: Oxford University Press, 1959), pp. 210, 111–112, 115.

26. Branko Horvat, *The Political Economy of Socialism* (Armonk, N.Y.: M. E. Sharpe, 1982), p. 503. See also Bertram Silverman, ed., *Man and Socialism in Cuba: The Great Debate* (New York: Atheneum, 1973), pp. 3–28.

27. Friedrich A. Hayek, *The Road to Serfdom* (Chicago: University of Chicago Press, 1944), pp. 56–71.

28. *Pravda,* August 2, 1986, p. 2.

Index

Absenteeism, 14, 123, 153, 226, 264, 265, 267–268, 274, 297

Academy of Sciences: Scientific Council on Cybernetics, 165, 168; and revival of management science, 168, 170, 171, 177–178; research at, 180; Central Economic-Mathematical Institute, 181; Institute of Economics, 269

Academy of the National Economy, 191, 196, 198, 200, 201, 203, 204, 215

Acceleration (*uskorenie*), 263

Accounting methods, 40, 60, 74–76, 83, 84, 113, 114–115, 116, 118, 169, 253, 279

Adamiecki, Karol, 98

Adfel'dt, N., 167–168, 178

Adlerian psychology, 201

Administrative costs, 115–116, 183–184

Administrative reorganization, 76, 81–82, 102–103, 112–118, 184, 236, 241–246

Administrative strategy, 6–8, 15–16, 162–163, 183–184, 261–262, 286–287; defined, 4; radical, 8–9, 298; centralist, 9–10, 13–14, 19, 32, 86–87, 121, 162, 182–185; delegative, 9–11, 40, 162, 163, 182–185; disciplinary, 9–10, 14–15, 19, 29, 32–33, 45, 93–94, 111–112, 122–123, 128–131, 150, 152–153, 163, 176, 204, 263–264; managerial, 9–12, 15–16,

19, 33–34, 45–47, 111–112, 161–164, 176, 182–186; mobilizational, 9–10, 12, 19, 54–55, 111–112, 134–136, 163, 267–268; normative, 9–10, 12–13, 19, 54–55. *See also* Centralization; Coercion; Decentralization; Discipline; Management; Mobilization; Recentralization

Afanas'ev, V. G., 177

Aganbegian, A. G., 234, 237

Aircraft industry, 140–141

Aivaz strike, 21, 23, 26

Ake, Claude, 3

Alcoholism. *See* Drunkenness

Allilueva, N., 125

All-Russian Conference of Construction Workers, 30

All-Union Conference on Improving the State Apparatus, 117–118

All-Union Conference on Issues of Labor Force Training, 107

All-Union Congress on Psychotechnics and the Psychophysiology of Labor, 143

All-Union Industrial Academy (Stalin Industrial Academy). *See* Industrial academies

All-Union Institute for Experimental Medicine, 155

All-Union Scientific-Technical Confer-
ence. *See* First All-Union Scientific-
Technical Conference
Amosov, P. N., 75, 83
Andreev, A. A., 117, 147, 164
Andropov, Yu. V., 270, 273; attacks on
indiscipline, 265, 267, 268, 276, 277,
285; attacks on bureaucracy, 271, 285;
and economic reform, 276, 277, 278
Antibureaucratic movements, 93–94,
111–112, 263–264
Arendt, Hannah, 13
Arkhangel'skii, N. V., 78
Assembly line production, 26, 76, 144,
145, 256–257
Associations. *See* Ob'edineniia
Atzler, Edgar, 37–38
Austria, 291
Autocratic management style, 203–204
Automation, 11, 76, 161, 164, 246–247
Avanesov, V. A., 51
Avenarius, Richard, 25
Averbakh, L. L., 109
Azrael, Jeremy, 130

Baibakov, N. K., 277, 278
Bailes, Kendall, 114
Barth, Carl, 146
Bauman Higher Technical Institute, 148
Bazarov, V. A., 101–102
Bekhtirev, V. M., 37, 71, 141
Berg, A. I., 168, 172
Berliner, Joseph, 182, 231
Bernshtein, N. A., 155
Birman, A., 169–170, 171, 172
Black market, 227
Blat, 202
Blau, Peter, 10, 42, 285–286
Bogdanov, A. A., 24–25, 33, 56, 57, 151,
182
Bogomiakov, G. P., 220
Bogomolov, A., 190–191
Bogomolov, O. T., 284
Bolshevik-Maiak system, 173
Bolshevism, 15, 25, 46, 75, 127; and Sci-
entific Management, 5, 60; centralist
policy, 19–20, 32; industrial strategy,
19–20, 30; organizational strategy, 20;
administrative strategy, 33, 40, 48, 60;

and market activity, 40; economic pol-
icy, 173
Borodin, P. D., 231, 238–239
Branch training programs, 191, 193–195,
197–198, 213, 214
Brezhnev, L. I., 263, 272; and Scientific
Management, 183, 184–185, 186, 187,
190, 192, 211, 215, 221–222, 239–240,
262, 265; and discipline, 183, 262, 265–
266, 270, 271, 275; and indulgency pattern, 264–269; trust-in-cadres policy,
268–269
Brezhneva, G. L., 267
Bronia (reservation system), 105
Brus, Włodzimierz, 293
Bukharin, N. I., 75, 107, 129, 146; and
Taylorism, 29–30, 49; and rationalization efforts, 96, 102, 103, 114
Bulganin, N. A., 152
Burdianskii, I. M.: and Kazan Institute
for NOT, 42, 43, 44; and Gastev, 42–
44, 111, 118, 120; and Second NOT
Conference, 50–51; and rationalization
movement, 84, 101, 118–119; and Yermanskii, 101–102, 118, 120; and psychotechnics, 143, 144; arrest and death,
144
Bureaucracy, 13–14, 34, 128, 266, 286,
296; and accountability, 2, 267–269,
286; dysfunctions of, 3–4, 10, 11–12,
128, 266; rational-technical model of, 5,
93, 285; attacks on, 16, 46, 93, 111–119,
129, 262, 264, 267, 288, 289; and rationalization, 11–12, 60–61, 78, 86, 90, 128,
211–212, 293–294; and wrecking, 16,
128. *See also* Overbureaucratization
Bureaucratic discipline. *See* Discipline
Bureau of Budget, 112
Burlatskii, F. M., 199
Business games, 196, 204, 206–209, 291
Business schools: U.S., 68, 160–161, 169,
191, 210; Soviet, 190, 192, 193, 195,
198, 213–215

Capital-output ratios, 263
Career models, 215
Carnegie Corporation, 209
Case study method, 196, 204, 205–206,
229–230

Central Bureau for Standardization, 62–63

Central Committee of the Communist Party of the Soviet Union, 70; and worker training, 109; and industrial reform, 113, 116; and functional organization, 138–139; and psychotechnics, 142, 144; and management science movement, 179–180, 194, 269; administrative strategy, 183–184; Higher Party School, 222; and discipline campaigns, 265, 266; and production increases, 269; Economics Department, 276; and economic reform, 280–281

Central Control Commission. *See* TSKK (Central Control Commission)

Central Institute of Labor. *See* TsIT (Central Institute of Labor)

Central Institute of Labor of the Commissariat of Light Industry, 140

Centralization, 2, 10, 13–14, 86–87, 113, 121, 137, 162, 205; and Scientific Management, 11, 162, 182–185, 205–206, 241, 256; resistance to, 129, 153–154; excessive, 32, 129, 163–164, 256, 261, 296. *See also* Administrative strategy; Decentralization; Recentralization

Central planning, 86–87, 130, 132, 274, 275, 280, 281; and socialism, 1, 9; and overbureaucratization, 1–3, 6–15, 286–287; and discipline, 5–6, 8, 172, 223; and rationalization, 90, 169, 222–223, 236, 241, 250, 294–295. *See also* Economy

Central Research Institute for the Organization and Technology of Management, 169

Certification. *See* Personnel, certification

Chandler, Alfred, 293

Chapman, Brian, 193

Charnovskii, N. F., 98, 100, 111, 114, 118, 120, 128

Chernenko, K. U., 269, 270, 271, 273, 278

China, 295, 296

Chronometry, 20, 21, 79, 101, 135, 155, 169, 232; and norm-setting, 132–133, 134, 165, 295

Citroën, André, 26

Class: mobility, 106–107, 143, 144, 211–212, 216; warfare, 91, 107, 143

CMEA (Council for Mutual Economic Assistance), 291–292

Coercion, 4, 10, 15, 16, 94, 123, 150, 152, 153; as strategy against bureaucracy, 9, 29, 32, 127–128, 176, 203, 204, 265–266, 267–268, 296–297; vs. rationalization, 16, 128–129, 176; Stalin advocacy of, 29, 93–94, 122–123, 126, 150, 152, 153; Trotsky advocacy of, 33

Collectivization, 91, 123

Commission for the Scientific Organization of Management of the Ministry of Higher Education, 181, 191

Committee for Standardization, 63, 134

Communist Academy, 101, 143

Communist systems, 1–2, 5–6, 24; as bureaucratic society, 3–4, 286; rigidity and instability of, 3–4, 6, 263, 290; and markets, 4, 287, 289; discipline in, 5, 6, 7–8, 15, 222–223; and violence, 127–128, 294–296; cycling behavior in, 286–287, 289–290, 298; and pluralism, 288–289, 291. *See also* NOT (Scientific Organization of Labor), communist fraction in

Computer(s), 161, 169, 173, 191, 192, 247, 256–257, 269, 287; managerial applications of, 172, 180, 184, 196, 247–255, 256, 259; -simulated business games, 207; -aided personnel systems, 218–219; 220; network, 257–258, 297. *See also* Automation; OGAS (Statewide Automated System)

Construction industry, 228, 253, 265

Council of Ministers, 191, 246

Council of People's Commissars. *See* Sovnarkom

CPM (Critical Path Method), 253

Crises: of legitimacy, 4, 263; of effectiveness, 6–7, 263

Cuba, 296

Cultural revolution, 33, 54, 91, 103–111, 143, 264, 283, 295

Cybernetics, 155, 165, 258, 287; and Taylorism, 155, 168, 172; and management science, 168, 171–172, 177, 178, 179–183, 185, 186

Cycling behavior, 2, 7–8, 15–16, 239, 261–262, 286

Czechoslovakia, 183, 290, 291

Deborinites, 101
Decentralization, 9, 10–11, 40, 162, 163, 182–183, 184, 185, 247, 280–283, 290, 291; vs. discipline, 275–284. *See also* Economic reform
Decision-making techniques, 196, 227
Defense industry. *See* Military
Delegative strategy. *See* Administrative strategy; Decentralization
Democratic Centralists, 33–34
Denikin, A. I., 31
Discipline, 30, 266; bureaucratic, 5–6, 8, 13–14, 111, 290, 291; in communist systems, 6, 7–8, 15, 289; organizational, 7–8; strategies, 14–15, 19–20; and Scientific Management, 20; and norm determination, 28, 133; removal and arrest of workers and managers, 29, 45, 123, 152–154, 267–268, 297; debates over, 33; and Time League, 54–55; campaigns, 91, 94, 263–264, 265–266, 267–268, 269, 272–274, 297; problems with, 264–265, 266–267, 270–275; public attitudes toward, 266, 272; language of, 91, 122, 262–264, 265; decline in, 266–267; administrative, 270, 274; and markets, 275–276; vs. decentralization, 275–284. *See also* Coercion; Labor discipline; Labor, militarization of; Terror
Dispatcher systems, 145
Dogadov, A. I., 106, 107
Dolgikh, V. I., 215
Dominguez, Jorge, 4
Downs, Anthony, 2–3, 74, 286
Drunkenness, 14, 267–268, 274, 297; campaign against, 273–274
Dyman, V. A., 98, 100
Dzerzhinskii, F. E., 72, 82, 86, 174; as head of VSNKh, 63, 65, 68–69

East Germany, 292–293
Economic reform, 10–11, 162, 163–164, 166, 171, 173–178, 182–185, 190, 244, 247, 263–264, 275, 276–284, 290, 291
Economists, 165–166, 181, 269–270; and management science, 170–172, 175, 178, 185–186
Education: and rationalization, 66–74, 84, 103, 107; quotas, 105, 109; technical, 126; upward mobility, 216. *See also* Management training; *Vuzy* (higher educational institutions); Worker training
Engels, Friedrich, 5, 24, 147, 148
Engineers, 49, 62, 103, 113, 114; arrests of, 97–100; training of, 126, 148, 167–168, 210–211. *See also* Social engineering
England, 39, 47, 165
Enterprises: directors and managers, 235, 236, 238, 249, 257, 277, 278–279; personnel turnover in, 151–152; training programs at, 190; educational levels in, 210, 212. *See also* Rationalization, plant (industrial)
Esmanskii, P. M., 44, 50–51, 66
Estonian Ministry of Light Industry, 224, 235
Executive testing, 161, 210, 218–219
Expertise, 8, 174, 290. *See also* Specialists; Specialization

Factory rationalization. *See* Rationalization, plant (industrial)
Family circles, 154, 202
Fayolism, 56, 75–76, 119
Fedorenko, N. P., 244, 257, 258
Fedoseev, P. N., 150, 171, 199
First All-Russian Congress of Councils of the National Economy (*Sovnarkhozy*), 30, 31
First All-Union Conference on Rationalization, 63, 78
First All-Union Scientific-Technical Conference, 178–179, 182, 190
Five-Year Plans, 160, 282; First, 73, 95, 101, 104, 108, 112, 120–121, 126; Eighth, 232; Ninth, 248; Tenth, 241, 259; Eleventh, 244–245
FON (Special-Purpose Faculty), 148
Ford, Henry, 76, 98, 105, 106, 108, 165. *See also* Assembly line production
Ford Foundation, 209
France, 20, 26, 112, 244
Freudian psychology, 201
Frunze, M. V., 85
Functional organization system, 81–82, 112–118, 138–139, 161

FZU (factory-workshop schools), 72–73, 104–106, 108, 110

Gantt, Henry, 71, 161
Gantt chart, 67, 161, 253
Gastev, A. K., 181; and Taylorism, 21, 25–27, 30, 31, 32–33, 37; social engineering and automation philosophy, 26, 28, 31, 32, 38, 51, 52, 62, 104, 111, 119, 247, 287; and piece-rates, 27, 132; as director of TsIT, 31, 35, 38, 39, 41–43, 50, 58, 105, 117, 140, 152, 164; and cultural revolution, 33, 104, 106–107; and NOT movement, 38, 39, 40, 43, 55–58, 63–65, 168; and Burdianskii, 43, 111, 118, 120; criticism of and opposition to, 51–52, 54, 55, 58, 105–106, 108; and Time League, 53, 54, 61–62; and Kerzhentsev, 55–56; control of Scientific Management movement, 62; and SOVNOT, 62, 65; and industrial norms, 62–63; and Kuibyshev, 63–64, 65, 104–105, 108, 109, 131; and Ordzhonikidze, 65, 66, 110, 131, 139–140; rationalization efforts, 65, 88–89, 107, 138; educational policy and reforms, 71, 72–73, 104–105, 106, 110; and wrecking charges, 98, 111; and norm determination and Stakhanovism, 132, 134, 137–138, 139–140; and functional organization, 138, 139; arrest and death, 138, 140; rehabilitation of, 164–165, 168
Gastev, Yu. A., 164
Germany, 19, 153; and Scientific Management, 39, 47, 59, 77, 81–82, 112, 113, 125. *See also* East Germany
Gilbreth, Frank, 51, 55, 71
Glasnost' (openness policy), 283
Glavki (main administrations), 113–115, 117, 145, 243
Glavpolitput, 75
Glushkov, V. M., 160, 248, 254, 257, 258, 287
GOELRO, 244
Gol'tsman, A. Z., 25, 27; proposal for worker aristocracy, 32, 34, 51; and Trotsky, 32–33, 36; proposal for labor research institute, 35; and Second Conference on NOT, 56, 57; and industrial reform, 113

Gorbachev, M. S., 239, 261–262, 298; attacks on bureaucracy, 263, 264, 285; wage policy, 270; discipline campaign, 271, 273–274, 285; and economic reform, 279–281; *glasnost'* policy, 283–284
Gosplan, 50–51, 113, 169, 225, 279; funding of NOT institutes by, 44; and educational policy, 107–108; Research Institute for Planning and Norms, 181; and program management, 245, 246; computer system, 248–249, 257, 259
Gospriemka (quality-inspection service), 280
Goszakazy (state orders system), 281
Gouldner, Alvin, 14, 128, 264, 265
Government, unlimited, 8–9, 297–298
Granick, David, 145, 292
Great Purge, *See* Stalin, I. V., Great Purge
Great retreat, 109–110
Grossman, V. Ya., 118
GULAG, 222
Gushko, A. O. *See* Yermanskii, O. A.
Gvishiani, D. M., 166, 167, 169, 170, 172, 182–183; complex approach of, 179, 186; and business schools, 193

Harvard Business School, 169. *See also* Business schools, U.S.
Hawthorne experiments, 132
Hayek, Friedrich, 297
Higher Academy of Management, 191
Higher education. *See* Education; *Vuzy*
Hitler, Adolf, 149
Hoarding: of materials, 221, 254, 255; of labor, 229–230
Horvat, Branko, 296
Hough, Jerry, 285
Human relations theory, 161, 201–203
Hungary, 289, 293–294, 296
Huntington, Samuel, 4, 8

Il'ichev, L. F., 166, 168, 170, 171
IMEMO (Institute of the World Economy and International Relations), 165
Industrial academies, 70, 123–125, 149, 191
Industrial convergence model, 8, 286, 288
Industrialization, 90, 91, 101, 120–122

Industrial Party, 100; trials, 98, 99, 114, 118, 120, 128

Industrial psychology, 141

Industry: performance of, 19–20, 31–32, 92, 152, 159–160, 262–263; reorganization of, 82, 87, 112, 242–246

Initiative Commission for the Scientific Organization of Production, 35

Innovation, technological, 153, 229–230, 249–250, 257, 262–263, 274

Input-output tables, 258–259

Institute for Managerial Technology, 119

Institute for State and Law, 181

Institute for the Economics and Organization of Industrial Production (*Novosibirsk*), 169, 234, 237

Institute for the Experimental Study of Live Labor, 35

Institute for the Study of the Brain, 71

Institute of Labor, 164, 181

Institute of Philosophy, 171

Interagency Commissions, 83, 245–246

Interbranch training programs, 195–197, 200, 213, 214

IPK (Institutes for Upgrading Qualifications), 149–150, 191, 224; branch and interbranch, 193–197, 200, 213, 214

IPKKh (Institutes for Upgrading the Qualifications of Managers), 148–149, 177

ITU (Institute for Managerial Technology), 76, 112–113, 117–118, 119, 144, 145

Iuksviarav, R. Kh., 234, 235

IUNKh (Institute for the Management of the National Economy), 192, 195, 196, 219. *See also* Academy of the National Economy

Jurists and management science, 171, 172, 177, 179, 181, 185–186

Kaganovich, L. M., 97, 107, 123, 124, 130, 139, 140, 154; and Stakhanovism, 136–137; and TsIT, 140; and norm determination, 164, 165

Kaganovich, M. M., 115, 134

Kamenskii, A. Z., 70, 73, 124–125

Kantorovich, L. V., 236

Kaplun, S., 50, 52, 106

Kazakhstan, 222

Kazan Institute for NOT, 42–44, 67–68, 88, 142

Kerensky, A. F., 27

Kerzhentsev, P. M., 84, 101, 168, 181–182; and Time League, 53–55, 61–62, 108; and NOT, 55–57, 76

Khozrashchet (independent economic accounting), 40, 115, 279

Khrushchev, N. S., 124, 172, 173, 204; *sovnarkhoz* reforms, 150, 160, 163, 167; and administrative strategy, 163–164; and revival of management science, 163–174; division of party apparatus, 167, 171; Virgin Lands Program, 244

Kirov, S. M., 131

Kollegialnost' (collective decision-making), 34

Komsomol, 54, 130, 134; and worker training, 73, 103–104, 107–108; Eighth Congress, 105; attacks on Gastev, 105–106, 108, 109; and TsIT, 109, 110; Ninth Congress, 110; campaign against bureaucracy, 111

Konoplev, B. V., 214

Kornai, János, 296

Kosarev, A. V., 54, 108

Kosarev, V. M., 25

Kosygin, A. N.: management policy, 166, 169, 173, 174, 184, 185, 190; economic policy, 177, 182, 183, 184, 190, 276

Kozlova, O. V., 191, 235

Krasin, L. B., 48–49

Kravchenko, Victor, 88

Kronstadt revolt, 39–40

Krupskaia, N. K., 48, 73, 106, 107, 110, 147; and psychotechnics, 142, 144

Krzhizhanovskii, G. M., 44, 107, 108, 110

Kuibyshev, V. V., 48, 62, 66, 87, 121, 185–186; as head of NKRKI, 49, 50, 55, 56, 57–58, 63, 64, 74, 78, 81; and industrial norms, 63; and Gastev, 63–64, 65, 104, 109, 131; and Stalin, 63–64, 93, 103, 107, 130; rationalization efforts, 64–65, 66, 82, 83, 84, 90, 93, 115, 131; as head of VSNKh, 65, 90, 116; and wrecking charges, 99; educational policy, 103, 104–105, 108; as chairman of Gosplan, 110, 116–117; murder of, 131

Kulaks, 92, 111
Kultprop (Culture and Propaganda Department of the Central Committee), 104, 106
Kuprianov, S., 99

Labor: discipline, 28–29, 112, 122–123, 129, 152–153, 163, 264, 266–267; militarization of, 32, 33, 35, 36, 94; shortages of, 72, 104, 108, 154, 160, 262, 267, 274; physiology, 141–142, 161; scientific organization of, *see* NOT (Scientific Organization of Labor). *See also* Discipline; Personnel
Laboratory for Problems of Management. *See* MGU (Moscow State University)
Labor training. *See* Worker training
Leadership, concept of, 200–204
Left Opposition, 64, 65, 70
Lenin, V. I., 5, 24, 53, 119, 147, 148, 175, 248; and Scientific Management, 15, 22–24, 28–29, 37, 45–46, 48, 49, 50, 60, 150, 165, 166, 167, 188, 200, 218, 261; and Gastev, 25, 31, 38, 41, 52; industrial management strategy, 28, 31, 34; disciplinary strategy, 29, 30, 34, 296; health, 44–45, 46, 48; attacks on bureaucracy and red tape, 45, 48, 49, 292–293; and NKRKI, 47–48, 50, 74, 249; and Kerzhentsev, 53, 54; economic policy, 167, 173; electrification plan, 244
Levitov, N. D., 143
Lewin, Moshe, 93
Liberman debates, 170–171
Ligachev, E. K., 169, 280
Likhachev Automobile Works, 231, 238–239
Line Management System, 112
Lisitsyn, V. N., 169
Loebel, Eugen, 294, 295
Lowenthal, Richard, 289
Lunacharskii, A. V., 25, 109; educational policy, 73, 103–106

Mach, Ernst, 25
Main administrations. *See* Glavki (main administrations)
Management: techniques, 9, 67, 111, 161, 165, 182, 187, 188, 222, 236–237, 288, 292–293; theory, 47, 67, 145–146, 161, 172–173, 177, 199, 226, 294; experts, 71, 161, 221, 222–223, 231; mechanization of, 76–77, 246–247; consultants, 81, 161, 176, 203, 234–239, 242, 291; line, 112; technology, 116, 228, 229–230; psychology, 196, 199–203; and leadership, 200–201; autocratic style of, 203, 204; liberal style of, 203–204; distrust of, 295–296. *See also* Management science; Management training; Managerial research; Managers; Scientific Management
Management-information systems. *See* Computer(s)
Management schools. *See* Business schools
Management science, 11–12; and Scientific Management, 4–5, 161–162; during Stalin years, 146, 147–148, 150–151; revival in 1960s, 155, 161–162, 163–178, 180; in West, 161–162, 165, 244, 253; debates over, 163, 170–173, 176–178, 180, 182, 185–186, 187–188, 200–201; importation from West, 182, 187–188, 189, 199, 222, 261, 288, 294; and economic reform, 182–185; political controls over, 183, 184, 191, 199–207; and Brezhnev, 184, 221–222; theory and practice in, 207–209, 223, 226–231. *See also* Management training; Rationalization; Scientific Management
Management training, 151, 162, 168, 177, 180, 190, 221, 290; in 1920s and 1930s, 47, 49, 67–70, 123–126, 147–150, 151, 177; Western programs and methods, 67, 162, 168, 177, 180, 190, 221, 290; in *vuzy*, 68, 74, 126, 147–148, 190; curricula, 69, 70, 125, 193–194, 196, 205, 207, 214; attendance, 69, 149, 197–198, 226; background of trainees, 69, 125, 148–149; in post-Stalin years, 149–150, 151, 166, 167–170, 173–174, 177, 190–198, 212–215, 221; debates over, 174–175, 178, 191–195, 214; branch/interbranch, 191, 193–198, 200, 213, 214; effects of, 195, 206, 223–231. *See also* Business schools
Managerial professionalism. *See* Professionalism, managerial

Managerial research, 35, 166, 167, 170, 172, 180–181, 269–270; contacts abroad, 39, 47, 59–60, 77, 112–113, 118–119, 125, 139, 142–143, 165, 170, 176, 178, 187–188, 199, 244, 253; growth of, 40–44, 59, 76–77, 84–85, 169, 179–181, 221–222

Managers: and rationalization, 39, 63, 77–80, 88, 120–122, 153–155, 229–230, 232–239; and professionalism, 48, 68–71, 189, 198; backgrounds of, 67, 148, 210, 212, 216; controls over, 86–87, 121–122, 236; work schedules of, 121, 236; status of, 210, 211, 217, 293–294

March, James, 3

Markets, 3, 5, 221, 241, 281, 286, 287, 288, 293, 296, 297, 298; and communism, 4, 289, 291; reforms, 10–11; and centralization of economy, 87, 222; and production norms, 132; and business games, 207–208; and computerization, 258; introduction of, into Soviet economy, 279–280, 284

Marx, Karl, 22, 24, 147, 148

Marxism, 22, 23, 174, 270, 296; and Scientific Management, 5, 21–24, 38, 66–67, 102, 106–107, 119, 174, 188, 200, 201

Mathematical economics, 165–166, 173, 177, 181

Meck, Nicholas von, 97, 100

Medunov, S. F., 267

Medvedev, V. A., 194

Meierkhol'd, V. E., 54, 55

Mensheviks, 29–30, 37, 101, 102, 146

Metalworkers union, 23, 25–26, 27–28, 32, 72

MGU (Moscow State University), 175–176, 180; Laboratory for Problems of Management, 166–167, 180, 234, 237–238

Mikoian, A. I., 165

Militarization of labor. See Labor, militarization of

Military, applications of Scientific Management, 35, 74, 85, 97, 98, 115, 138, 140, 142, 155, 222

Ministries, 160, 163, 240, 241; control over executive recruitment, 189, 193–194, 197–198, 217–218; control over

management training, 189, 190–191, 194–195, 211, 213–214, 230, 245–246; and rationalization, 230, 236–237, 245–246; and computerization, 250–251, 257–258; authority over enterprises, 279, 281–282

Ministry of Chemical and Petroleum Machine-Building, 242

Ministry of Defense, 222

Ministry of Finance, 195, 256

Ministry of Higher and Specialized Secondary Education. See Minvuz

Ministry of Instrument-Making, Means of Automation, and Management-Systems. See Minpribor

Ministry of Internal Affairs, 222

Ministry of Light Industry, 224

Ministry of Railroads, 251

Ministry of the Chemical Industry, 230

Ministry of the Coal Industry, 243

Ministry of the Construction Materials Industry, 217–218, 224

Ministry of the Electronics Industry, 251

Ministry of the Radio Industry, 251, 252

Minpribor (Ministry of Instrument-Making, Means of Automation, and Management-Systems), 251, 252

Minvuz (Ministry of Higher and Specialized Secondary Education), 180, 181; executive training proposals, 190–191, 193, 197, 213, 214; Commission for the Scientific Organization of Management, 191; Scientific Methodological Office, 193, 195, 214; and management consulting programs, 235

Mitin, M. B., 143

Mobilization, 9–10, 12, 54–55, 111–112, 134–136, 163, 267–268

Molotov, V. M., 164

Monitoring bureaus, 2, 13–14, 74, 286

Moscow city party organization, 50, 52, 125, 190

Moscow Technical Institute, 98

Motivation of subordinates, 201–204, 227

Narkomfim (People's Commissariat of Finance), 41, 49

Narkompros (People's Commissariat of Enlightenment), 31, 103; and worker training, 68, 72, 73, 104–109; and psychotechnics, 144

Narkomtrud (People's Commissariat of Labor), 35, 42, 43, 50, 134, 142; Club of, 52; training and education policy, 72, 107–108

Narrow base, principle of, 51–52

Nemchinov, V. S., 258

NEP (New Economic Policy), 40, 41, 78, 86–87

Network planning methods, 253

NIAT (Scientific Institute for Technology and the Organization of Production of the Aircraft Industry), 141, 155

NKRKI (People's Commissariat of Worker and Peasant Inspections), 46, 47–48, 61, 119, 249, 258; reorganization of, 46–47, 47–50, 64–66, 74–77, 80, 84; Normalization Department, 47; and NOT, 47, 50, 55–57, 60, 61; and Lenin, 47–48, 50, 74, 249; and rationalization efforts, 60, 63, 64–66, 74, 75, 76–81, 82–86, 87–88, 112, 117, 119, 250; and SOVNOT, 62; research, 62, 81; training programs, 68; Administrative Technology Department, 74, 75–77, 81; Labor and Production Department, 74–75; and industrial reorganization, 81–82, 113, 116–117, 119

NKVD. *See* Secret police

Nomenklatura system, 76, 215, 217, 218, 282

Noncoercive control, 201

Normative net output, 228–229

Norm determination, 12–13, 19, 35, 62–63, 101, 139–140, 164, 181; bureaus, 27, 30–31, 36, 88, 132; opposition to, 30–31, 146; problems of, 132–134, 139–140, 240–241, 269, 270; and wrecking charges, 133; and Stakhanovite movement, 134–136, 137–138

NOT (Scientific Organization of Labor), 35, 52–53, 59, 118, 150, 167, 176, 178, 246, 270; First Conference on, 36, 37, 38, 39, 40–41, 44; and TsIT, 39, 42–43, 50–58; institutes of labor, 41, 43, 44, 50, 66, 145, 146; funding for, 44, 50; and NKRKI, 47, 60; communist fraction in, 50, 52, 53, 56, 100, 106, 119, 120, 143; research, 50, 59–60, 181; Sec-
ond Conference on, 50–51, 55–57, 58, 61, 68, 78, 100, 106, 176, 179, 185, 186; and Scientific Management abroad, 59–60; rationalization efforts, 60, 65, 84, 87, 120; training programs, 60, 68, 74, 126, 147; Third Conference on, 65, 112, 177; and military rationalization, 85; inefficiency and failure of, 85–86, 90, 120; and economy, 87, 168; and production levels, 89–90; and release of personnel, 232; administrative problems of, 232–234; and educational levels of employees, 233. *See also* Management science; Rationalization; Scientific Management; Taylorism; Time League (NOT League)

Novozhilov, S. S., 232–233, 258

Ob'edineniia (associations), 113–115, 205, 242–244, 292

Ochkin, V. I., 98–99, 114

Office for the Improvement of the State Apparatus, 49

Office for the Scientific Organization of Industrial Production, 125

Office technology, 76, 116, 161, 228, 247–250. *See also* Computers

OGAS (Statewide Automated System), 248–249, 257

OGPU. *See* Secret police

One-man management, 27–28, 34, 82

Operation Chronometer, 268

Operations research, 161, 253

Optimal planning, 244, 258

Ordzhonikidze, G. K. (Sergo), 271; as NKRKI chairman, 65–66, 81, 82–83, 117, 119; and Gastev, 65–66, 110, 131, 139–140; and rationalization efforts, 65–66, 86, 87, 90, 93, 99, 115–116, 117, 118, 121, 122, 131, 233; as VSNKh chairman, 109–110, 117, 119; suicide, 131, 140; and NOT, 131, 147; and norm determination and Stakhanovism, 134, 135–136, 137, 139; and Great Purge, 137; and TsIT, 139, 140

Ordzhonikidze Institute of Management (Engineering-Economics Institute), 147–148, 169, 191, 197, 235, 247

Organizational roles, 226–227, 229, 231

Organizational theory, 9, 74, 93, 128, 226–227, 264–265

Orgburos, 77, 78–80, 85

Orgstroi (State Bureau for Organizational Construction), 76–77, 85, 117

Osinskii, V. V., 29, 48

Overbureaucratization, 1–4, 6–9, 277, 283, 285, 287, 288, 293, 295, 297, 298

Pal'chinskii, P. I., 97, 98

Paperwork. *See* Red tape and paperwork

Paramonov, I. V., 151

Party apparatus: role in industry, 13–14, 163, 166, 205–206, 228, 230, 285; and rationalization, 61, 65–66, 78, 80, 84, 180, 222; division of, 167, 171; and executive selection, 214, 215, 219–220

Party Conferences: Sixteenth, 108, 111, 112, 115, 116; Seventeenth, 134, 138, 139

Party Congresses: Eighth, 31; Ninth, 33; Tenth, 39–40, 45; Eleventh, 45, 48; Twelfth, 48, 60; Fourteenth, 77, 83; Sixteenth, 99; Seventeenth, 152; Twentieth, 165; Twenty-Third, 178, 183, 190; Twenty-Fourth, 184, 192, 211; Twenty-Sixth, 266; Twenty-Seventh, 268, 273–274, 280, 287

Patronage, 217, 218

Pavlov, I. P., 141

Pavlov, V. Ya., 190

Peele, Vincent, 264

People's Commissariat for Aircraft Industry, 141

People's Commissariat for Defense Industry, 140

People's Commissariat for Heavy Industry, 131, 134, 139, 140, 144, 146

People's Commissariat of Enlightenment. *See* Narkompros (People's Commissariat of Enlightenment)

People's Commissariat of Finance. *See* Narkofim (People's Commissariat of Finance)

People's Commissariat of Labor. *See* Narkomtrud (People's Commissariat of Labor)

People's Commissariat of Railroads, 36, 72

People's Commissariat of State Control, 46

People's Commissariat of Worker and Peasant Inspections. *See* NKRKI (People's Commissariat of Worker and Peasant Inspections)

Personnel: selection and assignment, 47, 189, 198, 212, 215–216, 218–220; turnover, 122–123, 137, 138, 151–152, 271; certification, 217–218; assessment centers, 219; documentation, 219; policy, 268–269. *See also* Psychotechnics

PERT (Program Evaluation and Review Technique), 253

Petrakov, N. Ya., 258

Petrovskii, I. G., 166

Philosophers: and management science, 171, 177, 178, 185

Piatikov, G. L., 48, 131, 140

Piece-rate payment, 23–24, 26–27, 30–31, 36, 132, 133, 134; opposition to, 28–29, 30; progressive, 134

Plan indicators, 121, 153, 228–229, 230–231

Planning from the achieved level, 230

Platform of the Seventeen, 56

Platform on Worker Industrialism, 28

Plekhanov Institute of the National Economy, 198, 202, 203–204, 206, 225, 227, 228–230

Pluralism, 283, 288, 289, 296, 298

Poland, 290, 293

Police, 222, 267–268, 276. *See also* Secret police

Politburo, 107, 214, 280

Political culture, 201, 292–293

Political economists: and management science, 150, 170–171, 175–176, 178, 180–181

Political stability, 3–4, 6, 286, 298

Ponomarev, B. N., 277

Popov, G. Kh., 167, 237

Praktiki, 48–49, 148, 192, 212, 216, 219

Preobrazhenskii, E. A., 54

Prices, 5, 86–87, 281

Product classification codes, 255, 256

Production, 5, 146, 164, 200, 205–206, 279; norms, 26, 27, 30–31, 129, 132–136, 164; quality of, 26, 121–122, 123, 129, 153, 154, 155, 222, 241, 279, 280; declining levels of, 32, 35; and rationalization, 87–88, 121, 122; costs of, 121, 129, 153, 155, 222, 246; waste in, 121, 123, 160, 228, 246, 262–263; gymnastics, 142; innovations in, 237; automation of, 256–257, 287. *See also* Industry; Norm determination; Rationalization, plant (industrial)

Productivity, 22–23, 28, 86, 90, 112, 121, 122, 155, 180, 222, 229, 237, 240–241, 243. *See also* Rationalization

Professionalism, managerial, 9, 11, 12, 210, 212–220, 276, 290; opposition to, 48–49, 68–71, 189, 197–199, 215; and Stalin, 123–124, 125, 151, 154–155; and Brezhnev, 186, 188–190, 198–199; Western, 188, 209–210; ethos, 188–190

Profits, 86–87, 170–171, 188, 222; and business games, 208

Program-management methods, 237, 244–246

Proletkult movement, 32–33, 53, 106

Promvoensovet (Council for Military Industry), 35

Psychotechnical Society, 143, 144

Psychotechnics, 74, 85, 141, 142–144, 161, 218. *See also* Personnel

Purges, 111–112, 117–119, 127–153, 268–269

Quality, product. *See* Production, quality

Rabkrin. *See* NKRKI (People's Commissariat of Worker and Peasant Inspections)

Radus-Zenkovich, V. A., 56, 75

Railroad industry, 35, 75, 82, 100, 118, 123, 152, 265; and Taylorism, 36, 37, 97; dispatcher system, 145

Rakovskii, M. E., 251

Ratchet principle, 154, 230

Rationalization, 50, 64–65, 83, 86, 87, 96, 120, 230, 242; and bureaucracy, 11–12, 78, 86, 90, 128, 211–212, 293–294; and wrecking charges, 16, 40, 88–90, 92, 94–103, 115, 118–119, 128, 133, 136–137, 146, 292, 294–295; plant (industrial), 21, 63, 77, 79, 80, 87–89, 121, 122, 125, 261, 295; and military, 35, 74, 85, 98, 138, 140, 142; and industrialization, 60–61, 63, 87–90, 96–97, 99, 112; inefficacy

of, 60–61, 77–90, 92, 114–115, 223, 232–234, 239, 240–246, 250–260, 261–262, 269–270; and educational policy, 66–73; assumptions of, 74, 77, 87; falsification of data on, 86, 224, 242, 243, 254–255; incentives for, 87, 90, 153–155, 230–231, 233; and Stalin, 112, 115, 117–119, 120–122, 137; and Great Purge, 127–132, 141, 152, 155. *See also* Computers, Management science; Management training; Managerial research; Scientific Management

Rationalizers: as foreign element, 12, 87, 118–119, and managers, 39, 63, 87–89, 120–122, 133, 153–155, 233–234, 235–239; and political protection, 61–66, 117–119, 131; training for, 70–71, 98, 184, 235; backgrounds of, 71, 95–96, 120, 233; bureaucratic behavior of, 74, 83–84, 139, 225, 227–228, 231–234, 238–239, 241; and workers, 79–80, 89, 133, 138; and specialists, 79–80, 95–96, 120; isolation of, 79–80, 88–89, 121–122, 133, 233–234, 237–238; violence against, 80, 87–89, 97, 117–119, 133; working conditions of, 88, 121–122, 133, 233–234; status of, 88, 120–122, 133, 233, 234–235; and Right Opposition, 93, 96; and Great Purge, 127–132, 136–137, 141, 146, 147. *See also* Management consultants; Management experts

Recentralization, 86–87, 182–185, 247, 261, 290, 291

Recruitment practices, 11, 49, 70, 214, 294; control of, 189, 193–194, 197–198, 217–218; U.S., 209; and candidate quality, 210–211, 218–220

Red directors, 45, 102; vs. specialists, 31, 45, 46; and professionalization of management, 48, 49, 68–71; Clubs, 48, 56, 69, 78, 123, 125; educational levels and training of, 67, 68–71, 73, 149; and rationalization efforts, 78, 125, 155

Red tape and paperwork, 34, 45, 63, 112, 267; centralization as cause of, 32; and rationalization efforts, 75, 82–83, 90, 111–119, 121, 129, 228, 241, 253–254, 267, 280; and wrecking charges, 99; and computerization, 255–256

Reentry after training, 226–227
Regime of economy, 64–65, 79, 86, 112, 122, 265, 266
Rekunkov, A. M., 267, 272
Renault automobile plant, 20
Research. *See* Managerial research
Research Institute for Planning and Norms, 181
Reserve for promotion, 173, 195–196, 215
Restructuring (*perestroika*), 263–264
Right Opposition, 25, 93, 96, 98–99, 108, 111, 124, 125
Rigidity cycles, 2–3, 286
Role-playing exercises, 204
Romania, 292
Rourke, Francis, 11
Rozmirovich, E. F., 75, 98, 118, 131, 247, 287; and Gastev, 62, 76; and Bukharin, 75, 114; and NKRKI, 75–77, 79, 81, 82, 85, 144, 145; labor management policy, 76; and wrecking charges, 98, 114, 118; and administrative reform, 112–113, 114, 116, 139; criticism and removal of, 117–118, 119
Rubin, I. I., 101
Rudakov, M. P., 50
Rumiantsev, A. M., 177–178, 180–181
Russian Social Democratic Labor Party, 20, 21, 24, 25
Rykov, A. I., 25, 99, 103, 107
Ryzhkov, N. I., 276

Sabotage, 30, 33, 91, 94, 99, 123, 282, 294–295; witch hunts to uncover, 129; during Great Purge, 137. *See also* Wrecking
Schoenherr, Richard, 10
Scientific Council on Cybernetics, 165, 168
Scientific Management, 12, 20, 22, 24, 34, 44, 58, 85, 270, 288; defined, 4–5; and management science, 4–5, 161–162; and Marxism, 5, 21–24, 66–67, 174; and Bolshevism, 5, 60; and production, 11, 89, 132; and technocracy, 12, 15, 24–25, 32–33, 51, 55, 57–58, 61–66, 106, 109, 114, 131, 171, 177, 188–190, 198–199, 246–248, 287; foreign literature on, 39, 46, 47; state support of, 41; and NOT, 42–43; battle for control of

movement, 50–58, 102; Western, 51, 52, 57, 84, 160–162, 180, 288; and educational policy, 67–73, 104–105; research, 84; military applications of, 85; and engineering studies, 126; and wrecking activities, 141; Stalin attacks on, 144. *See also* Administrative strategy; Management science; Managerial research; NOT (Scientific Organization of Labor); Rationalization; Taylorism
Scientific-Research Institute for Management-Information Systems, 238
Second All-Russian Congress of Trade Unions, 30
Second All-Union Conference on the Scientific Organization of Labor, 57–58, 68, 78, 100, 106, 176, 182, 186
Second All-Union Scientific-Technical Conference on Problems of Improving the Management of Industrial Production, 186, 193, 200, 212–213
Secretarial personnel, 228
Secret police, 97–98, 102, 120, 123, 127, 131, 137, 147, 152, 154. *See also* Police
Segal, P. P., 105, 108
Sensitivity training, 204
Seventh Congress of Trade Unions, 86
Shakhty affair and trial, 70, 94–95, 97, 99, 111
Shatunovskii, Ia. M., 50, 101
Shchekino experiment, 229–230
Shchelokov, N. A., 267
Shcherbitskii, V. V., 198–199
Shmidt, O. Yu., 105, 106
Shmidt, V. V., 28, 29
Shock-worker (*udarniki*) movement, 63, 80, 134, 141
Shorin, V. G., 219
Show trials, 120, 131
Shpil'rein, I. N., 50, 53–54, 101, 142–144
Shvernik, N. M., 57, 108, 110, 164
Šik, Ota, 290
Simon, Herbert, 3
Slansky trial, 294
Social engineering, 12, 31–33, 38, 51–52, 71. *See also* Gastev, A. K., Social engineering and automation philosophy; Technocracy
Social-engineering machine, 51, 111, 155
Social psychology, 171, 200

Sociologists: and management science, 171, 172

Sovnarkhoz reform, 150, 160, 163, 167

Sovnarkom (Council of People's commissars), 31, 63, 73, 82, 83

SOVNOT (Council for the Scientific Organization of Labor), 49–50, 55, 60–62, 65, 68, 98, 104, 181; and Gastev, 62, 65; military center in, 85

Specialists: influence of, 8, 61, 287–288; from old regime, 31, 35, 36, 38, 91, 95, 125, 174; training of, 49, 70, 95, 180; vs. rationalization, 79, 99; attacks on, 91–103, 109. *See also* Expertise; Management experts; Management consultants; Rationalizers

Specialization, 2, 10, 138, 294

Special-purpose programs, 244–246

Spiral of coercion, 15, 128, 130, 272

Staff: cuts, 47, 79, 81–82, 83, 112, 229–230, 233–234, 242–243; growth of, 81–82, 90, 115, 160, 242

Stakhanov, A. G., 135

Stakhanovite movement, 129, 132, 134–136, 140, 146–147, 297; First All-Union Conference, 136, 137; and Kaganovich, 136–137; and Gastev, 137–138; and TsIT, 139; and NOT, 147, 149

Stalin, I. V., 5, 147, 148, 177, 210; discipline campaign, 15–16, 91, 93–94, 122–123, 129, 152–153, 285; attacks on bureaucracy and red tape, 16, 46, 92, 122–123, 127–132, 153, 155, 285; use of coercion, 29, 126, 129, 152; and NKRKI, 64, 65; Industrial Academy, 70, 123–125, 149; educational policy, 70, 103, 107, 191; recruitment policy, 70; industrial system and cultural revolution, 91, 93, 103–111, 119, 122, 126, 133–134, 159–160, 295; and rationalization, 115, 120, 122–123, 155; opposition to policies of, 123–124, 131; and Right Opposition, 125; Great Purge, 127–128, 130–141, 144, 146, 149, 152, 153–154, 295; administrative policy, 141; and Scientific Management, 144; and management science, 147–148, 150–151, 201; labor and management policy, 147–148, 150–151, 152–155, 270; and Stakhanovism, 149; and management

system, 150, 154–155, 218, 297; economic policy, 151, 153, 159, 168, 170, 263, 290; cult of personality, 204; and psychotechnics, 218

Stalinism, 154–155, 159; and bureaucracy, 91–93, 96, 109, 127–132

Standardization, 11, 62–63, 74, 114, 134, 164, 218, 269. *See also* Production, quality

State Committee for Coordination of Scientific Research, 169

State Committee for Labor and Wage Issues, 164–165, 180, 215–216, 233; Institute of Labor, 181

State Committee for Science and Technology, 192, 212–213, 257

State Committee for Standards, 62, 140, 241, 255

Statewide Automated System. *See* OGAS (Statewide Automated System)

Stepanov, V. P., 174, 175, 176

Stern, Wilhelm, 143

STO (Council for Labor and Defense), 42

Storming, 274

Strikes, 20, 21, 23, 26, 33, 128. *See also* Trade unions

SUIT (Secretariat of Institutions Studying Labor), 43, 44, 50, 51

Sukhanov, N. N., 101

Superministries, 245, 258

Supply of enterprise, 121, 122, 123, 154, 160, 237, 253, 254; disruptions, 278–279; control of, 281

Suslov, M. A., 150, 166, 185, 192

Sverdlov Communist University, 68

Sverdlovsk party organization, 56, 169, 180, 233

Syrtsov, S. I., 122

Systems analysis, 161, 186, 237, 242, 246

Table of Ranks, 217

Taganrog Institute for the Scientific Organization of Production, 44, 66

Tallin Polytechnical Institute, 234

Taylorism, 37, 69, 71, 146, 161; worker reaction to, 20–21, 22–23, 24, 26, 27, 28–29, 30, 38, 39–40; in West, 20–21, 51, 52, 161, 182, 232; and productivity, 22–23, 28; and Lenin, 22–24, 28–30, 31, 32; and technocracy, 24–25, 76; and

Taylorism, *continued*
production norms, 26, 27, 30–31, 132–136; and militarization of labor, 32, 33, 36, 98; research on, 34–35, 40–44; and railroad industry, 36, 37, 97; and TsIT, 56; and worker training, 67, 118–119; functional foremen systems, 89; and Stakhanovism, 135; and cybernetics, 155, 168, 172; revival of, 164, 165, 181; under Brezhnev, 231–234. *See also* Chronometry; Norm determination; NOT (Scientific Organization of Labor); Rationalization; Scientific Management; Management training
Technocracy, 9, 24–25, 32–33, 49, 50, 60–66, 106, 109, 114, 131, 171, 177, 189, 199, 288–289, 297; and utopianism, 287, 295, 296–297
Tereshchenko, V. I., 176
Territorial-production complexes, 244, 245–246
Terror, 15, 33, 123, 127–132, 141
Thompson, Victor, 93
Time and motion analysis, 27
Time League (NOT League), 53–55, 57, 61–62, 108, 268, 297
Tolchinskii, A. A., 143
Tol'kach (supply agent), 122, 145
Tomskii, M. P., 51–52, 65, 105, 106, 107, 108, 131
Torbek, G. G., 50, 143
Totalitarian model, 8, 286, 288
Trade unions, 25, 30, 52, 105, 108, 165, 297; metalworkers, 23, 25–26, 27–28, 32, 72; opposition to Taylorism, 27–30, 32–34, 52, 105; discipline in, 29, 33; Tsektran (railroad), 36; and NOT, 39, 43; and Time League, 61–62. *See also* Strikes; VTsSPS (All-Union Central Council of Trade Unions)
Troianovskii, A. A., 75
Trotsky, L. D., 40, 47, 48, 63, 75, 85, 93, 146; and militarization of labor, 32, 33, 35, 36, 94, 98; and Taylorism, 32–34, 36, 166
Trust-in-cadres, 268–269
Trusts, 40, 80, 82, 86–87, 113, 151
Tsagalov, N. A., 175
Tsektran (railroad union), 36

TsEMI (Central Economics-Mathematical Institute), 181, 257, 269
TsIK (Central Executive Committee of Soviets), 29, 81, 82
TsIO (Central Research Institute for the Organization of Production and Management of Industry), 144–146, 147
TsIT (Central Institute of Labor), 35, 155; and NOT, 39, 42–43, 50–58; funding for, 41–43; and NKRKI, 50; opposition to, 50–53, 56, 106; and social engineering, 51, 52, 111, 155; education and training programs, 57, 71–73, 85, 98, 104–105, 106, 107–108, 110, 140, 143; psychotechnical laboratory, 85; Komsomol investigation of, 109, 110; and functional organization, 138–139; and Stakhanovism, 139, 140; dissolution of, 140–141, 155; and psychotechnics, 143, 144; personnel turnover, 152; rehabilitation of, 164–165
TsKK (Central Control Commission), 47, 49, 84, 118. *See also* NKRKI (People's Commissariat of Worker and Peasant Inspections)
TsSU (Central Statistical Administration), 86
Tukhachevskii, M. N., 85

Uglanov, N. A., 108, 124, 125
Unions. *See* Trade unions
United States: labor productivity, 28; Scientific Management in, 39, 47, 59, 77, 112, 116; business schools, 68, 160–161, 169, 191, 210; rationalization in, 125; management science in, 160, 169, 170, 188, 189, 244; managerial techniques and policy, 165, 209–210, 219; Taylorism in, 182; business gaming in, 207–208; administrative policy, 241–242, 245; operations research in, 253
Universities, 191, 198, 213
Uskorenie (acceleration), 263
Ustanovka, 71–72
Utopianism, 287, 295, 296–297

Val (gross output indicator), 121, 153, 228–229, 231, 249, 251
Veinberg, G. D., 28, 29

Velichko, A. F., 97–98
Vitke, N., 76
Volkov, A. P., 164
Vorontsov, V. P., 21, 22
Voznesenskii, N. A., 150, 166
VSNKh (Supreme Council of the National Economy), 28, 86, 113, 117; Council for Military Industry, 35; control over trusts, 40, 86–87; red tape and mismanagement allegations against, 45, 63; educational programs, 68, 70, 73, 104, 106, 107–108, 109; rationalization efforts, 65, 90, 110, 112, 119; and TsIT, 110; and industrial reform, 113–116; Planning-Technical-Economic Administration, 113–114, 115, 117
VTsSPS (All-Union Central Council of Trade Unions), 29, 72; and TsIT, 35, 41, 43, 52, 107–108, 110; and Time League, 61; rationalization efforts, 80, 112; and Stalin, 107–108. *See also* Trade unions
Vuzy (higher educational institutions): and managerial instruction, 68, 126, 147–148, 166, 180, 190, 191, 193, 224; under Stalin, 109, 126; engineering training, 126, 147, 211; and management research, 181
Vyshinskii, A. Ya., 120

Wage-leveling (*uranilovka*), 14, 133–134, 240–241, 263, 276
Wages, 129, 278, 281; and productivity, 86; and norm determination, 240; employee bonuses, 257; incentives for, 276, 296. *See also* Piece-rate payment
War Communism, 261

War Industries Committee, 97
Waste. *See* Production, waste in
Weber, Max, 5–6, 93
Whyte, William, 210, 212
Worker aristocracy, 32, 34, 51–52, 105
Worker training, 102, 107; TsIT policy for, 57, 71–72, 143; and educational policy; 66–73, 106–107; controversy over, 71–73, 102, 104–110; at FZU schools, 72–73
Workers: and rationalization, 21, 27, 39–40, 79–80, 89, 138
Workers' Opposition, 39–40
Wrecking, 91, 123, 125; and rationalization, 16, 92, 94–103, 111, 115, 118–119, 123, 128, 136–137, 294–295; arrest of engineers and managers, 97–100, 101–102; and Great Purge, 129–130, 136–137; and Scientific Management, 141; and economic reform, 282; and central planning, 294. *See also* Sabotage

Yaroshenko, L. D., 150–151
Yaroslavskii, E. M., 84
Yeliutin, V. P., 213
Yel'tsin, B. N., 287
Yermanskii, O. A., 46, 147; opposition to Gastev and Taylorism, 37–39, 50, 52, 56, 100–102, 146; criticism of, 56, 100–102; and Burdianskii, 118, 120; and Stakhanovism, 146–147

Zamiatin, Eugene, 127
Zatonskii, V. P., 116
Zhdanov, A. A., 149
Zhimerin, D. G., 257
Zinoviev, G. E., 36, 49